The New Naturalist Library
A Survey of British Natural History

The Hebrides
A Natural History

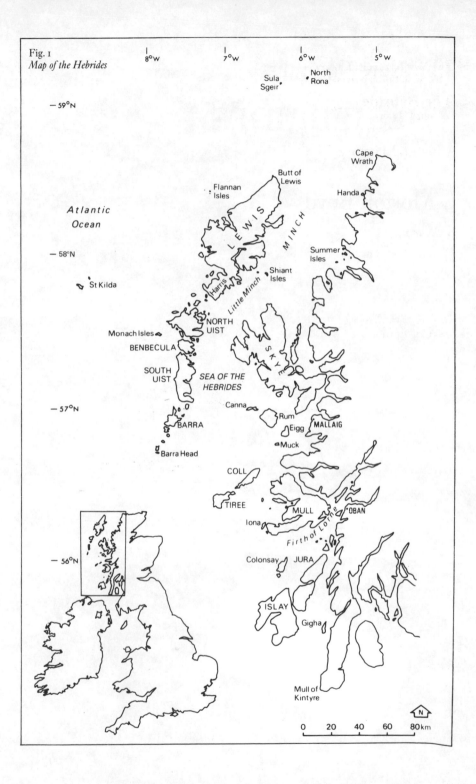

Fig. 1
Map of the Hebrides

8°W 7°W 6°W 5°W

Sula Sgeir
North Rona

— 59°N

Cape Wrath

Butt of Lewis
Flannan Isles
Handa

Atlantic Ocean

LEWIS
MINCH

— 58°N

Summer Isles

St Kilda

Harris

Shiant Isles

Little Minch

NORTH UIST
Monach Isles
SKYE
BENBECULA

SOUTH UIST
SEA OF THE HEBRIDES

— 57°N

Canna
MALLAIG
Rum
Eigg
BARRA
Muck

Barra Head

COLL

TIREE
MULL
OBAN
Iona
Firth of Lorne

— 56°N

Colonsay
JURA

ISLAY
Gigha

Mull of Kintyre

N

0   20   40   60   80km

The New Naturalist

THE HEBRIDES

A Natural History

J. Morton Boyd
and
Ian L. Boyd

Foreword by HRH Prince Philip,
Duke of Edinburgh

*With 21 colour photographs, and over
150 photographs in black and white*

COLLINS
Grafton Street, London

Editors

Sarah A. Corbet
Max Walters, ScD, VMH
Professor Richard West, ScD, FRS
David Streeter, FIBiol

Photographic Editor

Eric Hosking, OBE, Hon FRPS, FBIPP

TO WINIFRED
wife, mother and grandmother

The aim of this series is to interest the general reader in the
wildlife of Britain by recapturing the enquiring spirit of the old
naturalists. The Editors believe that the natural pride of the
British public in the native flora and fauna, to which must be
added concern for their conservation, is best fostered by maintaining a high standard of accuracy combined with clarity of
exposition in presenting the results of modern scientific
research.

William Collins Sons & Co. Ltd
London · Glasgow · Sydney · Auckland
Toronto · Johannesburg

First published 1990
© J. M. and I. L. Boyd, 1990

ISBN 0 00 2198 84/3 (hardback edition)
ISBN 0 00 2198 85/1 (limpback edition)

Typeset by Phoenix Photosetting, Chatham
Printed and bound in Great Britain by
Mackays of Chatham PLC, Chatham, Kent
© Textured background for limpback cover
'Marlmarque', G. F. Smith & Son

Contents

Part III: Islands and People

Foreword

It might be said that enthusiasm is the mother of creation. There is no doubt at all about the enthusiasm of the Boyd family for the Hebrides, and it shows in every line of this splendid book that they have created. Having sailed and cruised in Hebridean waters for many years and having acquired an interest in birds, I can quite understand the fascination of that very beautiful part of the world for those with a consuming passion for natural history.

If I had not already been involved in conservation through the World Wide Fund for Nature (WWF), I would have been converted by the changes I have witnessed in the Hebrides over the last twenty years. Plastic flotsam and oil pollution on most of the beaches, the decline in seabird populations and the intensity of commercial fishing reflect what is happening almost everywhere in the world.

I am sure that this book will become essential reading for all students of the Hebrides, and I believe that it will become a 'bench mark' for all those who are interested in the natural history of the islands in the future. It will provide an invaluable means of assessing any further degradation of the area, as well as making it possible to measure the success of any conservation efforts.

Editor's Preface

The Northern and Western Isles of Britain have long drawn the attention of naturalists by reason of their distinct landscapes and their exceptionally interesting communities of animals and plants. Added to this is the attraction of distant islands, with their own cultures and histories, and with climates subject to the severities of the North Atlantic ocean. The New Naturalist Series recognised this interest in the publication of Fraser Darling's *Natural History in the Highlands and Islands* in 1947, a book which received acclaim from the wide audience of those generally or especially interested in the wildlife of Britain. More recently, the series has published *The Natural History of Shetland* by R. J. Berry and J. L. Johnston (1980) and *The Natural History of Orkney* by R. J. Berry (1985), both continuing the tradition of a broad approach to natural history combined with an expert background of the fauna, flora, environments and history of the islands. An outstanding need in the series has been an account of The Hebrides; the islands lying to the west of the mainland of Scotland, north of the Mull of Kintyre, including the great islands of Mull and Skye and the 'Long Island', from the Butt of Lewis to Barra Head of the Outer Hebrides. The diversity of the landscapes in these islands is vast, from the mountainous and fresh scenery of Skye to the ancient lake-filled plateaus of North Uist and the coastal machairs, all with their characteristic fauna and flora. Few know these islands and their natural history better than the authors of this new volume in the series. J. Morton Boyd and Ian L. Boyd both have long experience of the Hebridean islands. Morton Boyd has been intimately concerned with natural history and conservation in the Hebrides since he joined the Nature Conservancy in Scotland in 1957, continuing with the Nature Conservancy Council until recently. Ian Boyd is an authority on sea mammals, especially the Atlantic grey seal, that symbol of marine life in the Hebrides. At a time when issues of wildlife and its future are rightly being more actively considered than ever, the Editors welcome this volume on an area of such diverse and intrinsic natural history interest.

Preface

A visit to Skye when I was six years of age made a deep impression in my mind—wild mountainous scenery, thatched houses, and seagulls over the stern of the paddle steamer *Fusileer* as she plied the narrow waters between Portree and Kyle of Lochalsh. Little did I know then what a large part the Hebrides were to play in my later life, nor how impressed Dr Samuel Johnson had also been by the same country some two centuries previously—

This (the passage to Raasay) now is the Atlantick. If I should tell at a tea-table in London, that I have crossed the Atlantick in an open boat, how they'd shudder, and what a fool they'd think me to expose myself to such danger... This (the Hebrides) is truly the patriarchal life: this is what we came to find.

It was not until 1948 that I returned to these islands, seeking a new outlook in life after my War Service. I found it in natural history, mountaineering, island exploration, and scholarship. The first three of these were nicely attuned to my natural instinct for an exciting and satisfying life. The last meant a great deal of hard work for me, but my enthusiasm was fired by two men of greater intellect than my own: they were my professor in zoology at Glasgow University, C. M. (later Sir Maurice) Yonge, leader of research on the Great Barrier Reef of Australia, and my mentor in nature conservation, F. (later Sir Frank) Fraser Darling, pioneer ecologist in the West Highlands and Islands. Each in his way had successfully combined the outward-bound and intellectual elements of life which I have espoused for as long as I can remember.

It could be said that this book has been forty years in the making. I would not have been convinced that I should attempt it had I not already collaborated with Fraser Darling in the revision of his *Natural History in the Highlands and Islands* (1947). That work, Number 6 in the New Naturalist Series, was highly popular among students, naturalists and lay readers with an appreciation of wild country, and an awareness of its effect upon people. However, it did receive criticism from academics, who saw the work as lacking in authority and accuracy. One eminent scientist wrote:

Clearly a book like this is exceptionally difficult to write, and most of us would not have the courage to attempt it . . . (however) . . . we might well have been worse off with the opposite extreme, a prosy compendium of incredible dullness, richly documented with footnotes.

I had used it as a student, and when I came to revise it I did so without destroying the flow of Fraser Darling's fine prose. Working from the inside, I could see the great advantages of having the book written by a single author, not just for the writing style, but also for the artistry of compilation behind a single comprehensive work containing the best fruits of many. The alternative is to compile a natural history with many experts contributing one or more chapters in a symposium-type volume, but that is a different type of book altogether from those produced by Fraser Darling (1947), Yonge (1949), Pearsall (1950), and others in the New Naturalist Series. Respectively, these authors were at once expert in one field, and naturalists of broad erudition and experience — interpreters of the broad spectrum, able to see and describe nature in the round.

This is the concluding work in a more extensive endeavour over the last ten years to describe the natural environment of the Hebrides, which in this book embraces all the islands lying off the western seaboard of Scotland, between the Mull of Kintyre and Cape Wrath. The islands of Lewis, Harris, North Uist, Benbecula, South Uist, and Barra and their outliers are the Outer Hebrides; all others, including Skye, the Small Isles (Canna, Rum, Eigg, and Muck), Mull, Tiree, Coll, Jura, Islay, Colonsay, Gigha and their satellites, are the Inner Hebrides. In 1977 and 1981, with the help of others, I organised two symposia on the Natural Environment of the Outer and Inner Hebrides respectively, in the Royal Society of Edinburgh. In doing so I made up my mind to follow the publication of the resultant symposia volumes with a more popular work which would reach a much wider public. These tomes (Boyd, 1979; Boyd and Bowes, 1983), and a major paper in the same series on the non-marine invertebrate fauna of the Outer Hebrides by A. R. Waterston (1981), were useful source works containing 67 papers by some 94 authors. The volume on the Outer Hebrides was followed by *Agriculture and Environment in the Outer Hebrides*, a report by Dr John Hambrey (1986) for the Nature Conservancy Council, which has also served as a ready source of information.

The writer of a natural history of such a diverse environment as the Hebrides is faced with a vast span in geological age, an enormous number of distinct forms of life, all of which are specially adapted to their living quarters, a wide range of temperate maritime habitats, and a group of human influences and impacts on the environment, rooted in Celtic and Norse cultures, strikingly different from those in mainland Britain. This great assembly is positively dynamic. It is not sufficient, therefore, to provide a 'snapshot' of nature today, but also to apply the dimension of history and unrelenting change. To encompass the work in a single volume was firstly a matter of eclecticism and presentation of part of the available knowledge; secondly, of consultation with experts over each chapter; and thirdly, the incorporation of these experts' comments.

The objective is a wholesome natural history. The chapters do not stand on their own, but are interdependent. They are not specialist essays written without regard to the total ecological purpose of the book or the readership to which it is directed. I am deeply aware that its shape and content are a matter of my personal choice—I found it difficult to decide what should be excluded, and there are many studies which deserve mention and which, in the hands of another compiler, would find a place. The fact that some works are restricted to a mention in the Bibliography does not necessarily reflect their importance in natural history.

I required a co-author to assist me in the review of the literature, primary drafting and editing of my text, the incorporation of expert comment, and the application to the work of the judgment and taste of a younger scientist. I did not require to look further than my second son, Ian Lamont Boyd. He made his first visit to the Hebrides in infancy, and came face to face with his study animal, the grey seal, for the first time on Gunna at the age of 19 months. Throughout his boyhood he was continuously on foot with me in the islands and later, like myself, had the benefit of a broadly-based degree in natural science from a Scottish university. He was awarded First Class Honours in zoology at Aberdeen, followed by a Doctorate at Cambridge with a thesis on the reproductive biology of the grey seal. Ian is now in charge of seal research in the British Antarctic Survey.

> Stark rocks stand in the sea:
> Curved islands against the sunset.
> Oh Hebrides! What are you telling me?
> I know wherein thy strength is set.
> In thy beauty which I oft-times see
> In ancient sea-girt, pillared rock beset,
> By thrift and auk and cuckoo-bee.

J. Morton Boyd
Balephuil
Isle of Tiree

Acknowledgements

Ian Boyd and I are greatly privileged that His Royal Highness the Duke of Edinburgh has written the Foreword to this book and so furthered the cause of science and conservation in the Hebrides. We wish to thank the following experts who kindly read and commented on one or more chapters of this book — an asterisk denotes more than one chapter. Miss S. S. Anderson, R. S. Bailey, M. E. Ball*, Prof. R. J. Berry*, Dr J. L. Campbell, R. N. Campbell*, Dr R. N. B. Campbell*, Dr T. H. Clutton-Brock, R. D. Cramond*, A. Currie*, Dr D. J. Ellett, Dr C. H. Emeleus*, Dr P. G. H. Evans, Dr R. J. Harding, Dr M. P. Harris, Dr G. Hudson, Dr J. Hunter*, Prof. P. A. Jewell, G. S. Johnstone, R. C. B. Johnstone, A. J. Kerr, J. Lindsay, Dr R. A. Lindsay, J. A. Love, Prof. A. D. McIntyre, H. McLean, Dr D. S. McLusky, Dr P. S. Maitland*, Dr J. Mason, Dr A. Mowle, S. Murray, Prof. T. A. Norton, Dr M. A. Ogilvie, Dr R. E. Randall, Prof. W. Ritchie, Miss M. G. Roy, A. H. A. Scott, Dr D. A. Stroud*, Dr D. J. Smith, Dr M. L. Tasker*, Miss V. M. Thom, Dr P. J. Tilbrook, A. R. Waterston, Dr C. D. Waterston, Dr R. C. Welch, and P. Wormell*.

Only four of these specialists felt strongly enough to state that they would have chosen to write on their subject differently from us, in style and order. We expected more to say so and worked hard to incorporate as much of the specialist advice as possible.

We thank the following who have provided valuable unpublished information and other special advice: A. Currie and Mrs C. Murray for revising their list of vascular plants; the Department of Biological Science, University of Stirling for a copy of *Mariculture Report* 1988; Professor P. A. Jewell for data on Soay sheep at St Kilda; the Nature Conservancy Council for a copy of *Agriculture & Environment in the Outer Hebrides*, and *Fish Farming and the Safeguard of The Natural Marine Environment in Scotland* and, together with the Seabird Group, data from the Seabird Colony Register; Dr M. A. Ogilvie and Dr D. A. Stroud for data on wintering geese; Miss M. G. Roy for helpfully abstracting for us climatic data from *Scotland's Climate* (Meteorological Office, 1989).

Advice on Gaelic literature and names of flora and fauna from the work of Dr Ellen Garvie, has been given by my eldest son Alan M. Boyd. The OS use the form *Rhum* for the name of that island. In this book we follow the advice of Professor D. S. Thomson who analyses the etymology of the name and states: 'Altogether it is clearly preferable to use *Rum* as the standard form in both Gaelic and English' (Boyd and Bowes, 1983).

We thank the authors of the two source volumes in the *Pro-*

ceedings of the Royal Society of Edinburgh (1979, 1983) and A. R. Waterston (1981) without whose joint effort the natural history of the Hebrides would remain scattered and inaccessible, and upon which this book greatly depends. We also thank the following for advice and practical help: K. J. Boyd, N. R. Boyd, R. D. Cramond, Miss A. Coupe, A. Currie, Mrs H. G. Forster, Sir Charles A. Fraser, R. Goodier, F. Hamilton, Mrs S. Hiscock, R. C. B. Johnstone, Prof. A. D. McIntyre, Dr D. S. McLusky, Dr D. H. Mills, Dr H. Prendergast, A. R. Waterston and others.

We also thank Miss Moira Munro who drew the diagrams, Mr J. K. Wilkie for photographic work and the following, who sent us photographs: Professor J. A. Allen, R. Balharry, M. E. Ball, British Geological Survey, Dr T. H. Clutton-Brock, D. MacCaskill, C. Maclean, Prof. T. Norton and M. A. Ogilvie. The Carnegie Trust for the Universities of Scotland very kindly gave a grant towards the cost of the colour plates, and the Highland and Islands Development Board gave a grant towards the cost of the black and white illustrations.

Over almost forty years, many naturalists who have not been directly involved in the writing of this book, have shared with J. M. B. their knowledge of the Hebrides. He has in mind particularly his colleagues in the Nature Conservancy (1957–73) and the Nature Conservancy Council (1973–85), especially J. C. (later The Viscount of) Arbuthnott, M. E. Ball, Dr J. Berry, C. Brown, R. N. Campbell, A. Currie, Dr W. J. Eggeling, Prof. D. Jenkins, Dr D. A. Ratcliffe, J. G. Roger and P. Wormell; the members of the Soay Sheep Research Team at St Kilda (1959–67), especially Prof. P. A. Jewell and Dr C. Milner; the Grey Seal Research Programme at North Rona and Harris (1959–69), especially R. Balharry, R. H. Dennis, J. MacGeoch and R. W. Vaughan; the Rum National Nature Reserve (1965–85), especially G. McNaughton, Dr T. H. Clutton-Brock and Miss F. E. Guinness; and the Sea Eagle Reintroduction Project (1975–85), especially R. H. Dennis, J. A. Love and H. Misund. We wish to take this opportunity of thanking them and saluting them for their knowledge of natural science and their contribution to the conservation of nature in the Hebrides.

The typescripts and proofs were corrected by our wives Mrs W. I. Boyd and Mrs S. M. E. Boyd, who also helped in many other ways. Proofs were also read by A. Currie and A. R. Waterston.

Prologue

When I was a little boy the Garden of Hesperides, Hy Brasil and the Hebrides were in,a curious way one in my mind. Two of these places are mythical; the Hebrides are real, but they reach into a legendary past and the limbo of my own mind and so, the Hebrides, however romantic they may have been in their beginnings in me, became a country which had to be trodden.

F. Fraser Darling

It is the purpose of this book to describe that reality of the Hebrides of which Fraser Darling was so conscious, and which has been experienced by many who have trodden the islands over the last few centuries. They were men and women of different philosophies and sciences, whose love of the islands and curiosity has taken them, with great energy and enthusiasm, into the remotest places. Many have left faithful accounts of their observations and experiences, though the literature can only be a minor part of the story. The remainder is held in notebooks, and in the memory of a community possessing a strong oral tradition. Every pair of eyes that has observed and every mind that has interpreted the passing scene, has been different. Naturalists have worked, alone and in groups, to produce a vast number of separate vignettes in a great natural history. Certainly, the Hebrides have been trodden!

The Soay Sound, St Kilda, looking from Hirta to Soay with Stac Biorach (73m) in the chasm (Photo J. M. Boyd)

Islands in Natural History

Islands cast a romantic spell upon people. They possess a mystique from which the pragmatist cannot escape, nor for which the scientist can find ready explanation. Nevertheless, this spell is real in island life, and engenders deep intellectual and physical responses in human beings. In the Hebrides themselves, it is an experience which many share, but which is deeply personal, and indicative of a singular, inner passion for the *ultima thule*. Charles Darwin knew it. According to Frank Sulloway (1984), Darwin raised the level of mystique of the Galapagos to that of 'enchanted islands' (which is the literal translation of *galapagos* from Spanish), in such unromantic works as biology textbooks and histories of science—so much so, that these islands have become 'the highly acclaimed symbol of one of the greatest revolutions in Western intellectual thought'. Twenty-four years were to elapse between Darwin's visit to the Galapagos in 1835, and the *Origin of Species* (1859). It is clear therefore, that his 'conversion' to the evolution theory did not occur in the heroic setting portrayed in the popular history of science. The idea of natural selection did not occur to Darwin until 1837, almost two years after he visited the Galapagos. However, the legend of a supreme, 'eureka-like' discovery by the great naturalist coming face to face with evolution in the primeval islands lives on, and has fired the imagination of generations of on-coming biologists.

The Hebrides do not occupy a grand plinth in scientific history as do the Galapagos, but, like all other archipelagos, they have their own endowment of nature and well-kept secrets to be discovered and enjoyed. The Galapagos are celebrated for their biology, but their geology (Simkin, 1984) is far less illustrious than that of the Hebrides. In studies of evolution and biogeography, the oceanic islands are unmatched by islands, like the Hebrides, that are strung along the continental edges. However, in studies of geology, ecology and animal behaviour, the continental edge is of the greatest interest. For example, the natural environment of the British Isles can be described as 'maritime', when compared with continental Europe. In greater detail, the western seaboard, including the Hebrides, when compared with the bulk of mainland Britain, is termed 'oceanic', because the communities of plants and animals there thrive in moist, mild conditions, or are greatly affected by the sea. It is this contrast of living conditions and life forms which has broadly attracted biologists to the Hebrides, while the geologists have been attracted to the Pre-cambrian and Tertiary rocks which are poorly represented in Britain south of the Great Glen. There are ample opportunities to observe how the structure of habitats changes from south-east to north-west, and also how each island has acquired its own rock base and complement of living things. Indeed, each island has its own unique and rich potential for the study of natural processes.

Island Races

Every island has a 'gene pool' and, between the islands and the mainland 'reservoir', there is a constant but usually small 'gene flow'. Each island is a unique assembly of species, which have been brought together by natural or man-assisted colonisation over long periods of time. Genetically, it is important to distinguish between 'relict' species which were present on the land before it became an island, and the colonisers which arrived after the land became an island. Small founder groups of either category possess fewer alleles of each gene than the large mainland populations from which they derive. When the founder group has grown and becomes established, the island species can have different frequencies of the different morphs than in the parent population. This is the theory anyway—in reality the situation is much more complex.

In the Hebrides, the islands became colonised from the south as the British Isles emerged from the retreating ice sheet. As time advanced more and more plants and animals arrived. Changes in sea level destroyed 'land bridges', thus isolating fragments of erstwhile mainland populations. The flora and fauna resulting from natural colonisation and physical isolation have been further complicated by man-assisted colonisation. Again in theory, many original colonisers of the north of Scotland may have been eliminated from the mainland by species which arrived later but did not reach the islands. The Hebrides, therefore, may possess relict life forms, such as the fossorial bee (*Colletes floralis*), the arctic charr (*Salvelinus alpinus*), and the plant *Koenigia islandica*. The Soay sheep (*Ovis aries*) of St Kilda is an outstanding example of a domesticated animal introduced by man to Britain in neolithic times, which became extinct as a breed (superseded by improved breeds of sheep) in all areas except the remotest and most inaccessible of islands, Soay at St Kilda.

The distribution of species in the Hebrides, therefore, begs many questions of when and how they came to be there. Analysis of pollen from peat and the beds of lochs have shown much of the time-scale and species of colonisation of the islands by vegetation; the affinities of most plant species to 'oceanic' and 'continental' biomes have been described; prob-

*St Kilda field-mouse
(Photo D.
MacCaskill)*

lems of taxonomy have arisen and identification of rare or key species has been questioned when voucher specimens and satisfactory records were lacking. However, the biogeography, taxonomy, and genetics of the Hebridean flora and fauna is still a wide-open field for research. This work is closely linked to the need for more information on the invertebrate fauna— and, with new techniques such as 'genetical fingerprinting' in the revision of existing information on the entire biota.

The flora and fauna of the Hebrides are rich in distinct island taxa: the St Kilda sub-species *hirtensis* and the Rum sub-species *hamiltoni* of the field mouse (*Apodemus sylvaticus*), (Delany, 1970); dark Hebridean forms of the dark green and the small pearl-bordered fritillaries (*Argynnis aglaia* and *A.selene*), the common blue (*Polyommatus icarus*), the grey mountain carpet (*Entephria caesiata*), the twin-spot carpet (*Perizoma didymata*), the mottled beauty (*Alcis repandata*), and the lesser yellow underwing (*Noctua comes*). Distinct forms of the bumble bee *Bombus jonellus* and the dragonfly *Sympetrum nigrecens* occur in the Hebrides. Amongst birds, the St Kilda wren (*Troglodytes t. hirtensis*) is distinct from that of the Hebrides (*T.t. hebridensis*), and in fact more closely resembles the Fair Isle wren (*T.t.fridariensis*), which in turn is distinct from the Shetland wren (*T.t.zetlandicus*). Starlings (*Sturnus vulgaris*) from Shetland and the Outer Hebrides are thought to be distinct from the race occupying the rest of Britain.

Professor R. J. Berry (1979, 1983) has examined the genetical and evolutionary significance of the Hebrides, where in his own words 'genes and geography meet'. He concludes:

The physical tides that have caressed and pounded the Western Isles have biological parallels: waves of animals and plants have beaten on the islands and formed their biological environment in the same way that the waves of rock, ice and water have determined their geographical limits. And just as the physical waves have laws which must be obeyed, so the interactions of drift, migration, and selection have forged the genetical constitution of the island races; and as the incoming tide cleans the sands and rocks over which it passes, but leaves unexplained features in secluded eddies, so the biological tides have left us with many genetical puzzles. The scientist believes as an article of faith that these eddies can be explained as knowledge accumulates, though some will remain as statistical anomalies of history.

Grand Relationships

We have used the example of genetical evolution and change to set the islands in the light of scientific discovery. We see the Hebrides not simply as the beautiful physical shapes they are, but as complete little worlds in themselves—each a unique repository of life. But there are also the rocks and the puzzles *they* hold. We try to interpret the genesis of the Hebrides from the Geological Record and find, in the great span of geological time, that part of the earth's surface which was destined to become the British Isles, moved northward across the surface of the globe from tropical to temperate latitudes. Having done so, and assumed its present geographical stance, the crustal plates parted and the British Isles were formed. This is a spellbinding story captured forever within the rocks of Ireland and Western Scotland, including the Hebrides. The disentanglement of the rocks on the north-west seaboard of Scotland, which plumb the depths of 3000 million years, is a wonderful achievement, and now part of classical geology of world-wide significance. The dynamic, three-dimensional perception of geological processes over such long periods of time, punctuated as they were by upheavals of the earth's crust

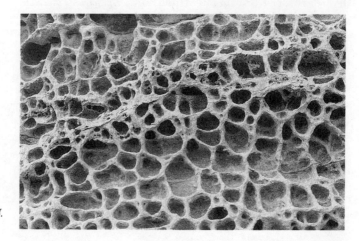

Looking like a living tissue, the Jurassic sandstone at Elgol, Skye has been eroded by the sea into this delicate, pale yellow, lacunary web (Photo J. M. Boyd)

such as the Grenville and Caledonian orogenies and the Moine Thrust, are so complex as almost to defeat lay presentation.

The coral islands of tropical seas display a biological process in which living corals extract lime from the sea water and build enormous reefs which, following changes in sea level, become raised islands or coastal platforms. In the Hebrides, there is at work a similar grand relationship between sea, land, and air, in which marine invertebrates and algae provide a vital link in the accretion of shell sand. Since the end of the last ice age, about 10,000 years ago, vast quantities of lime have been extracted from the sea-water by countless generations of shell-forming animals, whose remains have been ground in the surf and cast up by sea and wind upon the rocky shores. Spacious coastal platforms of dunes and machair (Hebridean maritime grass-land) have been formed in the southern Outer Hebrides, Tiree and Coll, enriching both the natural and human ecology of these islands (p. 386). The whole process is supported by untold numbers of animals and plants of many different kinds. A thimbleful of shell sand, spread and magnified, will reveal the fragmented shells of a host of humble creatures, each of which makes its tiny but vital contribution to the grand scheme.

Islands for Science

The Hebrides, therefore, have a potential for research in fundamental, natural processes, and none have been used more than Rum and St Kilda for this purpose. In the 1950s, both of these islands were recognised as outstanding for their unique flora and fauna. They have concise temperate/maritime eco-systems and classical geology, and are laboratories for long-term ecological research. Accordingly, they were made National Nature Reserves in 1957 and have been centres for research ever since.

Studies of the fundamental biology of large herbivores — the red deer on Rum and the Soay sheep on St Kilda — have been central research endeavours, which have provided an understanding not only of the animals themselves, but of the ecology of their whole island. The research on the red deer on Rum has been done in controlled conditions, which would be hard to obtain among wild deer on mainland deer forests. This has revealed the precise structure and dynamics of the deer population, and the behaviour of stags and hinds, through entire life-spans. At St Kilda, the mechanism of natural control of numbers of a free-ranging (unmanaged) population of Soay sheep has been studied over thirty years. These sheep have survived in their island home for probably over 1,000 years, and the mechanism of control of numbers seems to protect them and their habitat from degradation through overpopulation and inbreeding.

Twenty-two species of seabird breed in the Hebrides. St Kilda alone has fifteen species and possibly holds over a million seabirds in summer. The oceanic seabirds—petrels, auks, gannets and kittiwakes—have the mystical beauty of all truly wild creatures. They live most of their lives far upon the face of the wide ocean, and in summer they gather in their thousands

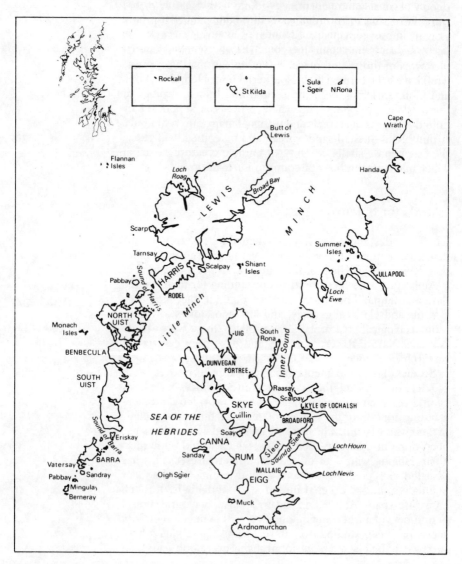

for a great carnival of nesting. The beauty and excitement of
the birds wheeling and darting in the splendour of sunlit cliff
and chasm brings awe and rapture to the dullest of hearts. For
those who brave the benighted tops of Rum or the cliff terraces
of the outliers there is a contrast equally as moving—the weird,
dark world of the night-flying petrels.

The study of the seabirds poses physical as well as intellectual problems. Simple routines of counting the birds and
interpreting the census data are difficult to achieve with any
degree of consistency between counts. Nonetheless, in the past
thirty years, marine ornithologists throughout the world have
greatly improved census methods of many species which
present different technical problems. For example, gannets
and fulmars nesting in the open require different techniques

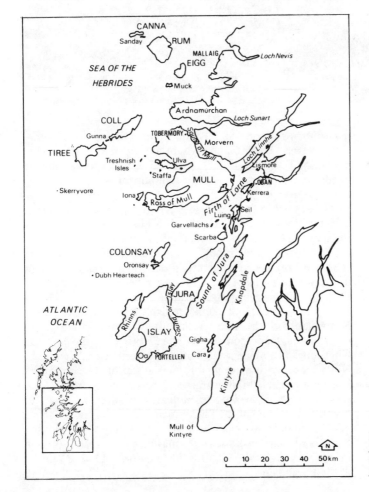

Figs. 2 a & b
Location maps of the
Outer and Inner
Hebrides

The south-east face of Sula Sgeir showing the northern limits of the gannetry in 1962 (Photo J. M. Boyd)

from burrowing puffins, and both are different from night-flying petrels. To detect changes in the size of the populations, a sustained census effort is required over decades, and this needs forward planning and the handing on of the techniques to successive workers.

The seabirds of the Hebrides are a major part of Britain's heritage of wildlife, requiring study for its own sake. However, the status of the seabird populations can also be an indicator of the health of their environment. Through the food chain which starts with the microscopic life in the sea and passes through invertebrates and fish, the seabirds can become the repository of pollutants such as polychlorinated biphenols (PCB's) and heavy metals. Such pollutants are likely to affect the breeding performance of the seabirds and the golden eagles and sea eagles which feed upon them in the Hebrides. In the case of a Chernobyl-like nuclear fall-out in the north-east Atlantic, St Kilda might prove an invaluable nuclear sensor. The great puf-fineries are rich in marine organic debris gathered from a wide area of ocean. They are grazed heavily by sheep which could become contaminated. The concentration of radio-active material in the individual seabird might be very small, but that in the bone marrow of the lambs may be much greater. Is it too imaginative to see the seabird-sheep islands as future sensors of the marine environment?

The Ecosystem of the Hebrides

PART I

Geology

CHAPTER I

> What happens to us
> Is irrelevant to the world's geology
> But what happens to the world's geology
> Is not irrelevant to us.
> We must reconcile ourselves to the stones,
> Not the stones to us.
>
> *Hugh MacDiarmid*

Natural history starts with the elements of fire, earth, air and water all of which long pre-date life on the face of the Earth. No clear understanding of the origins and nature of life can be obtained without knowledge of the rocks, weather and conditions of the seas and freshwaters. It is on the interface between these elements that all life has sprung and been maintained throughout aeons of time, and nowhere is this truth more explicit than in an archipelago. There, among the islands, the grand relationship between land, sea and sky is obvious and makes a deep appeal to the human mind. Islands are a source of inspiration and happiness; their beauty is enshrined in a multitude of native island cultures all over the world and appreciated by historian, artist and scientist alike. The Hebrides are no exception. In them it is possible to trace the connections between these base elements and the lives of the wild creatures and human beings that spring from them, and to see the islands as one large system with its own in-built stops and balances in terrain, weather and ocean. Let us start with the rocks.

The span of geological time represented in the rocks of the Hebrides is almost as great as anywhere in the world. Though we know that planet Earth is some 4,600 million years of age, in human terms, the Lewisian gneiss formed some 3,000 million years ago is as old as time itself, while on the beds of the sea and the deep lochs the rocks of the future are being formed from

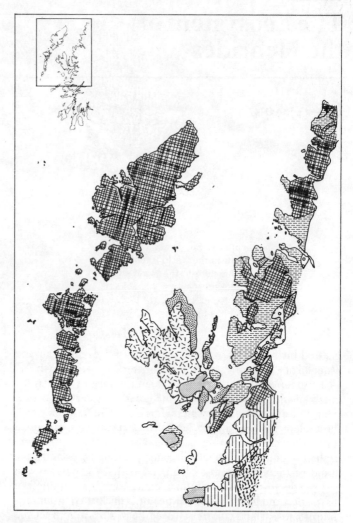

from the erosion products of by-gone glaciers, rivers and the
sea. The cycle of regeneration and decay of hard rock seems
timeless when compared with the timespan of human life.

In this vast interval of time, that part of the crust upon which
the Hebrides now stand underwent a gradual transposition
from tropical to temperate latitudes. Some ages of peace and
tranquility are marked by the depositions of the sedimentary
rocks: the Torridonian sandstone eroded from a range of
mountains and deposited in predominantly desert conditions,
1,000 to 800 million years ago; the sandstones, shales and limestones of Cambro-Ordovician/Dalradian age, 600 to 450 million years ago; and the limestones and mudstones of the

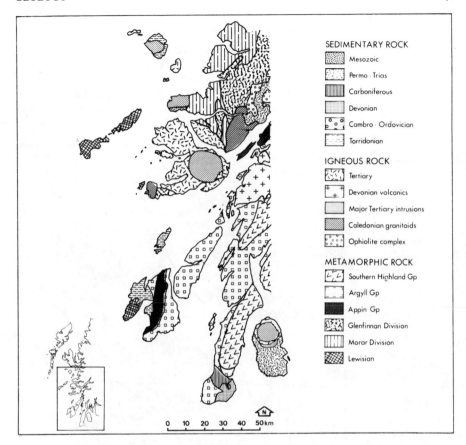

SEDIMENTARY ROCK

Mesozoic

Permo - Trias

Carboniferous

Devonian

Cambro - Ordovician

Torridonian

IGNEOUS ROCK

Tertiary

Devonian volcanics

Major Tertiary intrusions

Caledonian granitoids

Ophiolite complex

METAMORPHIC ROCK

Southern Highland Gp

Argyll Gp

Appin Gp

Glenfinnan Division

Morar Division

Lewisian

0   10   20   30   40   50km

Jurassic, deposited in shallow lacustrine or estuarine conditions *c.* 150 million years ago (called not after the island of Jura, but the Jura Mountains in France).

Between these periods of quiescence there were periods of profound crustal movement as blocks of continental crust fractured, jostled and were transported on plates of underlying crust, though the first of these hardly touches the Hebrides. During the Grenville mountain building about 1,000 million years ago, rocks which were probably the equivalent of the Torridonian strata far to the east of the present outcrops were compressed, deeply buried and heated in the crust, baked and altered to form the schists and metasandstones of the Moine Supergroup. These metamorphic rocks together with unaltered Torridian in turn formed a land surface on which were deposited limestones, shales and sandstones of Cambrian and early Ordovician age.

The second great upheaval was the Caledonian mountain

Fig. 3 *a* & *b* Geological maps of the Outer and Inner Hebrides (Smith and Fettes, 1979, Craig (ed) 1983)

building, 650 to 400 million years ago, when the rocks of the
mainland were again folded and altered to form the rocks of
mountains now occupying Scandinavia, Scotland and eastern
USA. Moine rocks were heated and altered again, while Cambrian strata became the schists of the Dalradian Supergroup.
Into the folded and refolded rocks, huge masses of molten
crust were emplaced as granite, now widespread in the
Highlands and represented in the Hebrides in the Ross of

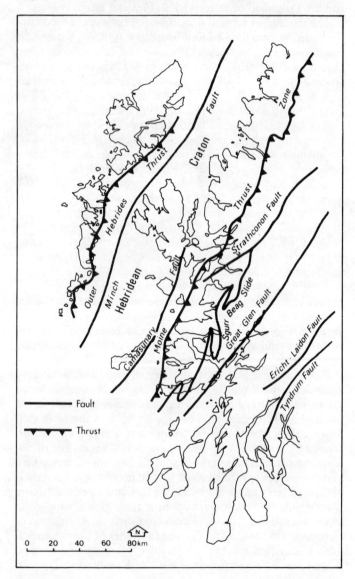

Fig. 4
*The main geological
faults of the Hebrides
and West Highlands
(Craig (ed) 1983)*

Mull. Along the western seaboard, however, rocks of the metamorphic mountains were thrust upwards and outwards in a dislocation of up to 80km. This is known as the Moine Thrust which runs on the land surface from Loch Eribol to the Point of Sleat in Skye. To the west of the Thrust, the Lewisian, Torridonian and Cambro-Ordovician rocks are in unmoved (and unaltered) sequence; to the east of the Thrust, within the Caledonian mountain belt, lie the Moines of Sleat and western Mull and the Dalradian of eastern Mull, Jura and Islay.

The mountains formed from this orogeny were subsequently eroded to form the Old Red Sandstone (ORS) c. 350 million years ago, a vast continental fluviatile and lacustrine deposit. Orkney is composed almost entirely of ORS but only small outcrops occur in the Hebrides—sediments in Kerrera and Seil, and lavas at Loch Don in Mull.

The third upheaval was the rift of the European and Greenland continental plates which created the British Isles, the continental shelf and the Hebrides, but not as we know them today. This rifting, which began 70 million years ago and still continues today, was accompanied by much volcanic activity, the thrusting up of masses of gabbro and granite, the outblasting of vast quantities of dust, ash and cinder and the outpouring of basalt lavas. These are the Tertiary volcanic complexes of Arran, Mull, Ardnamurchan, Rum Cuillin, Skye Cuillin and St Kilda, with associated plateau lavas in North Skye, Canna, Eigg, Muck, West Mull and Morven. They are related to other such centres in Ireland (Giant's Causeway), Faeroe Islands and Iceland, where the volcanic activity still continues. The islands as we know them today have been evolved through a northward drift of the crustal plate(s) of the planet from which the British Isles were formed, from a latitude of 30°S to the present latitude of 55°N. Throughout the drift, the palaeogeography was also continuously transformed by mountain building of the type described above, erosion, sedimentation, and volcanic activity. The genesis of the British Isles throughout geological time has been described simply by J.P.B. Lovell (1977).

Geological Framework

The solid geology is shown in Fig. 3 and Table 1.1. The Hebrides lie at the south-eastern margin of a crustal plate which included much of the material which forms Greenland and eastern Canada (Fig. 5). This plate broke and the parts drifted away from each other, 'floating' for tens of millions of years on the plastic sub-crust. The great trough between the parts now holds the Atlantic Ocean. This common basement between the Old and New Worlds contains some of the oldest rocks known to science, *c.* 3,000 million years old, from which younger rocks such as the Torridonian sandstone have been derived, and upon which the sandstones and other younger rocks are placed. In the Outer Hebrides, Tiree, Coll, Iona and Sleat in Skye the gneiss forms the present-day land surface— all the younger rocks have been removed by epochs of erosion. Elsewhere, the basement is covered by an array of younger rocks, or has been penetrated or pushed aside by great intrusions of magma and covered by extrusions of lava.

Era	Period	Age (m.y.)	Rocks	Islands
Pre-Cambian		+3000–600		
	Lewisian	+2800–1200	acid & basic gneisses, granites, limestones	N. Rona, Lewis, Harris, Uists, Barra, Coll, Tiree, Skye, Raasay, S. Rona, Iona, Islay
	Torridonian	1000–800	sandstones	Handa, Summer Isles, Raasay, Scalpay, Skye, Soay, Rum, Iona, Colonsay, Islay

Rocks east of the Moine Thrust affected by the Grenville Orogeny, *c.* 1000m.y.

	Moine Supergroup	1000–700	schists, granulites	Skye, Mull
Palaeozoic		600–230		
	Cambro-Ordovician	600–500	piperock, serp. grit, Durness limestone	Skye

Rocks east of the Moine Thrust affected by the Caledonian Orogeny, 500–400m.y.

	Dalradian Supergroup	+600–500	quartzites schists	Lismore, Kerrera, Seil, Garvellachs
			limestones, slates	Luing Scarba, Jura, Islay, Gigha
	Silurian	440–400	none	none
	Devonian	400–350	conglomerate	Kerrera, Seil
	Carboniferous	350–270	lava, sediments	Jura
	Permian	270–225	sandstones, conglomerate	Lewis, Raasay, Mull

Era	Period	Age (m.y.)	Rocks	Islands
Mesozoic		230–65		
	Triassic	225–180	sandstones, conglomerate	Lewis, Raasay, Skye, Rum, Mull
	Jurassic	180–135	sandstones, limestones	Shiants, Skye, Raasay, Eigg
	Cretaceous	135–70	sandstone	Skye, Mull, Eigg, Raasay, Scalpay, Soay
Cainozoic		70–0		
Tertiary		70–1		
	Eocene	70–40	basalts, granites, syenites, gabbros, dolerites, rhyolites	Shiants, Skye, Raasay, Rum, Eigg, Canna, Muck, Mull, Treshnish Is., Staffa, St Kilda, Oigh-sgeir
	Oligocene	40–45	erosion pdts	widespread
	Miocene	25–11	erosion pdts	widespread
	Pliocene	11–1	erosion pdts	widespread
Quaternary		1–Present		
	Pliestocene	0.6–0.013	erosion pdts	widespread
	Holocene	0.013–0	erosion pdts shell sand	widespread widespread

Table 1.1 The distribution and age in millions of years (m.y.) of the rocks of the Hebrides.

The major faults in northern Britain run from south-west to north-east (Fig. 4). The Southern Uplands Fault and the Highland Boundary Fault do not affect the Hebridean shelf; the Great Glen Fault (GGF), the Moine Thrust (MT), the Camasunary–Skerryvore Fault (C–SF) and the Outer Hebrides Thrust (OHT) all have an important bearing on the Hebrides. The GGF runs from Shetland to north Ireland, passes between Lismore and Kingairloch, through south-east Mull and just to the north of Colonsay; to the east there are the

Tertiary basalt pavement showing hexagonal jointing on Heisgeir (Oigh-sgeir) off Canna (Photo J. M. Boyd)

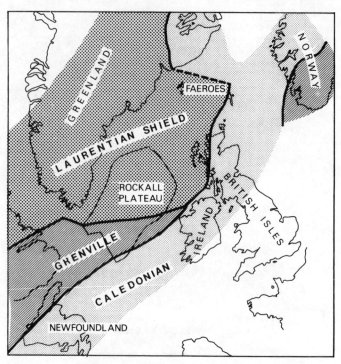

Fig. 5
*The tectonic provinces
of the North Atlantic
prior to continental
drift (Smith & Fettes,
1979)*

Caledonian granites with the Dalradian schists, slates and
quartzites; to the west there is the Moine Supergroup of
schists, bounded in the west by the Moine Thrust and interrupted in the south by the Tertiary complexes of Mull and
Ardnamurchan. The only terrestrial sections of the GGF in
the Hebrides are from Duart Bay to Loch Buie in Mull, which
is an area of great interest with faulted Liassic sediments folded
in Tertiary times around the Mull volcanic centre.

The MT runs from the west of Shetland, entering the Scottish mainland at Loch Eribol and traversing the north-west
Highlands roughly parallel to the coast, through Kylerhea and
the Sleat peninsula of Skye and possibly through the Sound of
Iona. To the west are the northern Inner Hebrides where the
gneiss basement is evident in Tiree, Coll and Iona and is interrupted in Skye, Small Isles and St Kilda by massive
emplacements of Tertiary lava, granite and gabbro. The Moine
and associated thrusts occur from Loch na Dal to the Point of
Sleat, and as far west as Broadford and Beinn an Dubhaich.
The MT may just clip Rum at Welshman's rock. To the east
there is gneiss; to the west there is Torridonian sandstone and
Durness limestone. Under the Sea of the Hebrides and the
Minches, there are trenches in the gneiss basement filled with

much younger sedimentary rocks. These have been derived from bygone mountains and are akin to the New Red Sandstones around Broad Bay in Lewis and to sedimentary strata of the wider shelf to the west of the Hebrides and around Orkney and Shetland, which may hold oil and gas. The C-SF, running from the Loch Scavaig in Skye through the Rum and Tiree Passages to the Skerryvore, is the western limit of a Mesozoic basin extending southward from Strathaird under Eigg and Muck to Mull.

Lastly, the OHT runs from the North Minch to beyond Barra Head along the east coast of the Outer Hebrides. It defines the main mountain chain of Barra and the Uists but northwards, in Lewis, it splits into a number of discontinuous planes before finally reaching the sea just north of Tolsta Head. To the east there are the sedimentary rocks in the submarine trench, while to the west is the Lewisian platform, interrupted in Harris and West Lewis by massive blocks of granite of Lewisian age.

Pre-Cambrian and Palaeozoic Rocks

These are mainly the Lewisian gneisses and granites, most of which were in existence 3,000 million years ago. In this vast span of time they have been changed. The granites, found mainly in Harris and west Lewis, are locally sheared and reduced to mylonite. South Harris is banded south-east to north-west with all the major rocks of the Lewisian series: gneiss, granite, gneiss veined with granite (all of acid character), metamorphic intermediate and basic igneous rocks, metasediments and anorthosite at Rodel. Metasediments are formed by the recrystalisation of sedimentary rocks, and occur at the north tip of Lewis, the south tip of Harris, and in the Uists and Benbecula. Substantial bands of mylonite (a slaty rock formed from crushed material along the OHT) occur in south-west Lewis and on the east coast of South Uist.

There were two distinct periods of metamorphic change, named after the districts of Sutherland where the original studies were done. The Scourian, 3,000 to 2,500 million years old, was followed by the Laxfordian, 2,500 to 1,400 million years old, and were separated by a period of crustal tension forming fissures into which a swarm of dykes were intruded. These are the Scourie Dykes which serve as distinct time-markers, separating Scourian from Laxfordian events. The Laxfordian period is marked by large-scale folding of the rocks. It concluded with the injection of the granites and pegmatites, 1,750 million years old, in Harris and Lewis, and the OHT, which

A quarry face in South Uist showing a section of Lewisian gneiss with characteristic banding of the minerals (Photo British Geological Survey)

was reactivated at the time of the Caledonian orogeny about 1,200 million years later, i.e. 400 million years ago (Smith and Fettes, 1979). None of the Torridonian, Moine, or Cambro-Ordovician rocks, which are well represented in the Inner Hebrides and the West Highland mainland, are present in the Outer Hebrides. The only sedimentary rocks are sandstones and conglomerates of Permian or Triassic age, 225 million years old, around Broad Bay in Lewis.

Among the Inner Hebrides the Pre-Cambrian rocks are widespread. The Lewisian complex occurs in Islay, Coll, Tiree, Skye, Raasay, and South Rona. Research on Rona has played a part in the elucidation of the Lewisian complex, and has revealed the oldest rocks in the British Isles — gneiss containing zircons older than 3,200 million years (Bowes *et al.*, 1976). As in the Outer Hebrides, there are metasediments among the predominant gneisses in Coll, Tiree, and Iona. These include garnet and graphite gneisses and marbles. Torridonian sandstones occur in Handa, Summer Isles, Raasay, Scalpay, Skye, Soay, Rum, Iona, Colonsay, and Islay. These sandstones and shales lie unconformably upon the Lewisian gneiss to the west of the Moine Thrust, have their greatest development in Wester Ross, and continue in a band some 150km long and 15km broad south-east from Skye, under the sea, to the west of Coll and Tiree. There are several different

groups of Torridonian characterised by their colour, grain-size and degree of deformation—'Sleat', Skye (3.5km thick), 'Torridon', Raasay (7km), 'Colonsay' (4km), 'Bowmore' Islay (4km), and 'Iona' (500m). Moine schists of similar age occur in Skye and Mull. Late Cambrian rocks, *c.* 550 million years old, are restricted to outcrops of pipe rock (quartzite with 'pipes' of worm burrows), serpulite grit and limestone in south-east Skye. Dalradian schists, which dominate the West Highland mainland south of the GGF, appear in the southern Hebrides. Quartzites, schists, limestones and slates occur in Islay, Gigha, Jura, Scarba, Garvellachs, Lismore, Luing and Seil. So far, no rocks of Silurian age have been found. Only small outcrops of Devonian (ORS) occur in Kerrera (130m thick) and Seil (5m) with contemporaneous lavas at Loch Don, Mull. The sole possible representatives of the Carboniferous period are lavas and sediments on Glas Eilein, Jura. Similarly, the only possible representative of the Permian period in the Inner Hebrides is a small pocket of boulder sediment on the Oa, Islay. New Red Sandstones in Skye, Raasay, Rum, and Mull are thought to be Triassic, but these continue under the sea and may include rocks of Permian age. Summary accounts of both the Pre-Cambrian and Palaeozoic rocks of the Hebrides are given in studies by Smith and Fettes (1979) and Anderton and Bowes (1983).

Torridonian sandstone eroded by the sea into freakish, dinosaur-like shapes on the north-west coast of Rum (Photo J. M. Boyd)

Mesozoic Rocks

The Triassic, Jurassic and Cretaceous periods are well represented in Raasay, Skye, Eigg and Mull with lesser outcrops in
Rum, Scalpay, Pabay, Soay and the Shiants, which, though
geographically part of the Outer Hebrides, are geologically
part of the Inner Hebrides (p. 36). These Mesozoic rocks are,
however, the exception rather than the rule in the Hebrides,
which, paradoxically, adds to their importance for two reasons:
firstly, they are a vital link in the geological history of the
islands, joining the distant Palaeozoic period and the much
more recent Tertiary era; secondly, they are predominantly
lime-rich rocks which have a marked effect on the ecology of
the islands in which they occur. The outcrops above sea-level
generally are set unconformably upon the Pre-Cambrian-
Paleozoic basement, and are overlain by the Tertiary volcanic
rocks. Under the North Minch and the Sea of the Hebrides,
these mesozoic rocks now fill deep basins, and are much more
extensive than on the islands, which may hold only thin fringe
outcrops on the margins of the submarine basins. Much of the
research data from these potential oil-bearing basins is unpublished. However, the labelling of the Stornoway Beds as
Permo-Triassic leads to the conclusion that these basins probably hold a New Red Sandstone series.

It is impossible to say whether or not the well-separated
Mesozoic rocks on the various islands are the surviving parts of
one continuous basin, or of separate basins, though the lateral
continuity of the Great Estuarine rocks from Muck in the south
through Eigg, Strathaird, and Raasay to Duntulm on the north

*Calcareous concretions
like cannon balls
exposed by marine
erosion of the Jurassic
sandstones at Bay of
Laig, Eigg (Photo
British Geological
Survey)*

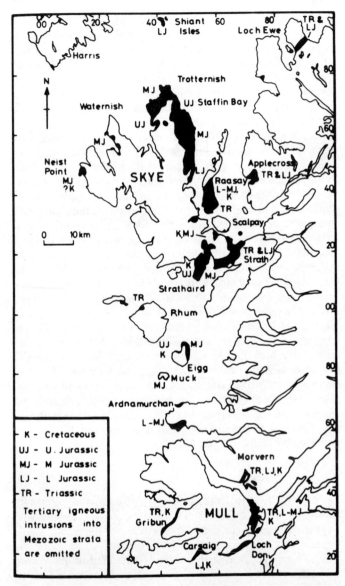

Fig. 6
Map showing the distribution of the Mesozoic rocks in the Hebrides (Hudson 1983)

point of Skye, is highly sustained. The most complete succession from the Triassic up through the Lower, Middle and Upper Jurassic to the Cretaceous occurs in Raasay and Trotternish (Fig. 6).

The Triassic rocks are mainly sandstone and conglomerates derived from riverine and lake-bed deposits—fossil soils indicate periodic inundations in a semi-arid climate. The Jurassic

rocks are by far the most extensive of the Mesozoic series above
sea level. They are mostly sandstones, shales and limestones in
that order of importance. However, the sandstones and shales
often contain carbonate concretions which are eroded out like
great cannonballs from the softer sandstone. The beds are
generally fossil-bearing allowing precise correlation between
strata at different sites using ammonites. The lower levels are
marine and fine-grained, the middle is riverine, estuarine and
deltaic in character, and the upper is again marine and fine-
grained. These are the finest fossil beds in the Hebrides, and
have attracted geologists since Hugh Miller so graphically
described his collecting foray in Eigg and Skye in *The Cruise of
the Betsey* (1858) (p. 321). Fossil sharks' teeth and the bones of
Pleisosauri and crocodiles have been found on Eigg; there are
specimens of these and other Hebridean fossils in the Royal
Museum of Scotland in Edinburgh. Lagoon beds were covered
with mussels (*Praemytilus*) and other indicator species include
brachiopods, oysters, and ostracods. Ammonites and belem-
nites abound in the shales and sandstones of Skye and Raasay.
The Mesozoic series is capped locally with thin beds of upper
Cretaceous sandstone in Skye, Raasay, Scaplay, Soay and
Eigg. These have a maximum thickness of 25m but are usually
less than 10m. They represent deposits in a shallow sea during
a short interlude of erosion between the end of the Jurassic and
the onset of the Tertiary volcanic epoch, when the Mesozoic
rocks were buried under several hundred metres of lava and
ash beds and cut by sills and dykes. A summary account of the
Mesozoic in the Hebrides has been given by Hudson (1983),
and the Jurassic and Cretaceous sediments in Scotland is
reviewed by Hallam (1983).

Tertiary Rocks

During the Eocene commencing 60–65 million years ago,
Europe and Greenland began moving apart. This crustal
movement created the wide rift now filled by the North Atlantic, and was accompanied by much volcanic activity along the
line of parting, from the south of England through Wales,
Ireland, western Scotland, the Faeroes, and Iceland to Greenland. The whole segment of the earth's crust is known as the
North Atlantic or Thulean Igneous Province, of which the
Hebridean Province, stretching from Ailsa Craig to St Kilda, is
a part. The main centres of volcanic activity were in Arran,
Mull, Ardnamurchan, Rum, Skye, St Kilda, and the submarine Blackstones Bank, all of which hold the magma chambers
of large volcanoes (p. 40). Most of these and other islands—
Treshnish, Staffa, Muck, Eigg, Canna and the Shiants—

The Sgurr of Eigg (387m) is a pile of Tertiary rocks. A layer of pitchstone on the summit ridge lies unconformably on basalt lavas (Photo British Geological Survey)

contain fragments of the laval flows and ash falls from these Eocene volcanoes. The sources of these outpourings are uncertain. One view is that they emanated from the above centres; another is that they issued from long fissures in the earth's crust above, and stretching away from, the centres, much as occurs in the 'shield' volcanoes of Iceland today. The country rocks of many islands are also intruded by dykes and sills. These trend south-east to north-west and consist of both basalt and its coarser-grained relative, dolerite (p. 40). C.H. Emeleus (1983) has reviewed the geology of the Tertiary in Scotland and C.H. Donaldson (1983) has provided a useful summary account of the Tertiary in the Hebrides.

There are two distinct types of igneous rocks—the fine-grained which have cooled quickly on or close to the earth's surface, and the coarse-grained which have cooled slowly at depth in the crust. Basalts, rhyolites and pitchstones are of the former; gabbros, dolerites and granites are of the latter. In the main centres, i.e. the magma chambers of the great volcanoes, granites and gabbros predominate. The granites are rich in silica and feldspar and are grey or pink; the gabbros are dark, rich in iron, magnesium and calcium and poor in silica. Of the fine-grained volcanic rocks, basalt is by far the most important. It is a dark, fine-to-medium-grained analogue of the gabbro. Basalt is the stuff of the plateau lavas of north Skye and west Mull, and the terraced tablelands and columnar scarps of Durinish (Macleod's Tables), Canna, Rum (Bloodstone), Eigg, Muck, Treshnish Isles, Staffa (Fingal's Cave), and The Burg (MacCulloch's Tree) in Mull. The Sgurr of Eigg is a layer of pitchstone overlying a conglomerate-filled valley in the basalt flows. The rock called Heisgeir off Canna has a hexagonal pitchstone pavement—a miniature Giant's Causeway (p. 31). Probably basalt of over a kilometre thick was extruded

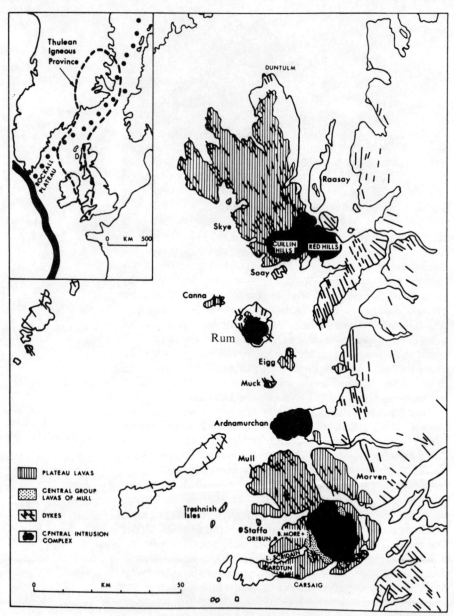

Fig. 7
Map showing the
Tertiary volcanic
centres and swarms of
dykes in the Hebrides
(Donaldson 1983)

over the crustal area now occupied by the Inner Hebrides.
Much of this has since been removed by erosion, but the
thickness of the existing basalt plateau reaches 1800m in
central Mull and 600m in Skye and the Small Isles. The maximum thickness of individual flows is about 30m with the

average about 8m, and the most extensive known flow stretches over 22km. An impression of the depth and extent of the Hebridean lava plateau in the late Tertiary (15 million years ago) can be obtained today in the Faeroe Islands, where a magnificent basalt plateau persists throughout most of the archipelago.

One of the salient features of the main Tertiary centres, particularly well-displayed in central Mull, is the formation of calderas caused by crustal ring fractures. Within these fractures—which were superimposed upon each other over millions of years—the solid rock sank, and the space was filled by upwelling magma. This has caused the fairly sharp juxtaposition of great masses of granite many cubic kilometres in extent with even greater masses of gabbro. The plane of fracture is a shatter zone in which fragments of the dark gabbro became embedded in the upwelling granite, or *vice-versa*, to create a breccia. This is well seen in the sheer cliff of Mullach Mor at St Kilda, where the eucrite (gabbro) to the west marches with the granophyre to the east, and is deeply veined by it. (A more detailed description of the magma-chambers of Rum and St Kilda is given in Chapters 15 and 16, respectively.)

The enormous explosive forces of these volcanoes resulted in the cracking and fissuring of the crust. The geological map shows Skye, Mull and Arran like the points of strike of bullets on a pane of glass, with the systems of cracks running roughly north-west to south-east. The cracks range from a hair's breath to over 30m thick and they have been filled with dark dolerite and basalt dykes (vertical) and sills (inclined). The swarms of Tertiary dykes from Skye, Mull and Arran traverse the crust from Lewis to Loch Linnhe, from Coll to Yorkshire and from Colonsay to Ayrshire respectively. The Inner Hebrides are riven with basalt and dolerite dykes which are usually 1–5m thick. These often become hard ridges among softer rocks like those in the Jurassic limestones on the shores and cliffs of Eigg, and trenches in harder rocks such as the gneiss on the shores of Tiree and Coll. The Camus Mor dyke on Muck is a striking example, which slices through the limestones and lavas and has a broad vertical exposure on the sea-cliff. Sills often occur in the bedding planes between lava-flows and sedimentary rocks and, like the lava, have columnar jointing. There are good examples of sill complexes to be seen in northern Skye and the Shiant Islands and, being composed of a hard coarse-grained dolerite, they often form a break of slope or escarpment edge in the basalt country. They play an important part in the composition of the landscapes of Raasay, Skye, and Mull.

The earthquakes which accompanied these episodes of

cracking and fissuring must have been enormous, certainly greater than any that happen in the world today. Another type of circular fissuring occurs as a result of great crustal explosions within the roots of the volcanoes, which split the existing igneous complex in a nest of conical cracks several kilometres in diameter at the present land surface. Sometimes they are several metres wide and are filled with basalts and dolerites— these are called cone-sheets. All the Tertiary centres possess them, and they are exceptionally well displayed on the Oiseval and Conachair cliffs at St Kilda and at Gribum in Mull.

Quaternary Features

In the last 18,000 years Scotland has endured a glaciation, and a period of emergence from the ice and the recovery of life. In the Devensian period between 18,000 and 11,000 years BP, the ice-age gradually declined leaving an arctic habitat with receding valley glaciers and seasonally exposed land and sea surfaces. The effect of the ice on the land was enormous, gouging and planing the uplands and depositing the detritus on an array of downstream surfaces ranging from large boulders to fine muds. About 13,000 BP, the summer temperatures must have been about 15°C, judging from the insect remains recovered from contemporary sediments, which, in Skye, also contain the pollen of birch, hazel, grasses, sedges, clubmosses, sorrel and others (Birks and Williams, 1983). By 12,000 BP, however, the insect evidence suggests a drop in summer temperature to 3°C, and there was a re-establishment of glaciation between 11,000 and 10,000 years BP. This is thought to have been caused by a sweep of polar water southward along the west coast, based on evidence of arctic Foraminifera and dinoflagellate remains in contemporary marine sediments off Colonsay. The main ice accumulation was in the West Highlands from Wester Ross to Loch Lomond and the episode is known as the Loch Lomond Readvance (LLR). It had a limited effect in the Hebrides, creating scree slopes on the mountains of Mull, Rum and Skye.

The disintegration of the ice sheets and the disappearance of the valley glaciers in the islands brought to light a great number of glacial and fluvio-glacial features; landslips, raised beaches, and accumulations of shell sand, dolomite, and peat. The end of the permafrost brought with it the collapse of many escarpments and cliffs and the shattering of rock-faces, resulting in a range of postglacial sheets of scree and stoneshoots, in which the islands abound and which are particularly well developed in the Cuillins of Skye. Landslips on a vast scale occurred at the Storr and Quirang in Skye, and below the northern ridge of Eigg. Fields of giant boulders were created—some as large as a house, with a cap of soil and vegetation, as in upper Guirdil in Rum. Solifluction terracettes and stone polygons related to the LLR are present on the summits of Mull and Rum.

The relationship of the wave-cut benches along the coasts and raised beaches to the glacial structures is not fully understood. The changes in sea level which accompanied the disappearance of the ice during the Quaternary period, resulted from two related factors—the melting of a great part of the polar ice caps which served to raise the sea level, and the isostatic raising of the land released from the superincumbent load of the ice sheet. The interplay of the two factors and the reworking of coastal and marine deposits by the sea at different levels is highly complex. The heights above present sea level of the raised beaches in the Hebrides are grouped around 8m and 30m, and on the west coast of Jura these two levels are well developed in the same system. Enormous drifts of even-sized quartzite pebbles are placed in steps above the waters of Loch Tarbert. J.B. Sissons (1983) has reviewed the Quaternary in Scotland and J.D. Peacock (1983) has given a useful summary account of it in the Inner Hebrides. Recent (Holocene) sediments and sedimentation, which include the dominant formations of shell sand and peat mentioned in later chapters of this book, are summarised by G.E. Farrow (1983).

The rocks of the Hebrides have therefore a dramatic story to tell. Those who have an eye for country can read the geology of the islands from their architecture, often at a great distance. The shape of the granite and quartzite hills is distinct from the gabbro, and both are distinct from the basalt. In Skye the granites of the Red Cuillin are cheek-by-jowl with the gabbros of the Black Cuillin; the former are smooth paps and the latter are a jumble of serrated peaks and ridges. The same is seen at St Kilda; viewed from North Uist on a clear day, the smooth granite cones of Conachair and Oiseval are flanked by the peaked gabbro of Dun, Mullach Bi and Boreray. The basalt islands, of which Canna, western Mull and northern Skye are typical, have stepped landscapes with beetling, horizontal scarps, terraces, tablelands, and galleried sea-cliffs several hundred metres high—the eroded basalt gives the Treshnish Isles the look of a fleet of dreadnoughts. The ecological effects of the country rocks is usually masked by wind-blown sand, a blanket of peat, or by agricultural improvement. However, the greenery of hill and wood in Raasay, Strath and Ord in Skye, Gribun and Loch Don in Mull, Lismore and around Ballygrant in Islay strongly suggests the presence of limestone.

CHAPTER 2

Climate and Hydrography

Climate

The weather puts demands enough upon coastal and rural communities in mainland Britain, but in the Hebrides the demands are much greater. Weather continuously prompts forethought of action, and in many fishing communities it still carries a sense of impending danger, damage and even tragedy. Island life is fashioned by the weather—the health and spirit of individuals and whole communities are all linked to it, just as are the intuitive and physiological responses of animals and plants.

The Weather System

The British Isles lie on a climatic frontier between moist oceanic air to the west and dry continental air to the east. These air masses differ in character and are in continuous interaction in a storm-belt which stretches for much of the time along the western seaboard of Ireland and Scotland to Scandinavia. This storm-belt has successions of depressions which course from mid-Atlantic to the Norwegian Sea. They are vigorous over the Hebridean shelf but, by the time they have reached the Norwegian coast, they have lost much of their strength.

In the Hebrides there can be periods when the islands are possessed by dry, calm continental air from the east which brings warmth in summer and frost in winter, instead of the usual wet and windy weather from the ocean. However, on the shorter time-scale there are the more rapid changes, which often occur in a matter of hours, particularly in the oceanic systems. Then fast-moving depressions bring active fronts sweeping across the Hebrides. These fronts are boundaries between warm and cold air, the warm rising over the cold at the warm front, and the cold undercutting the warm air at the cold front. Both are usually areas of cloud and rain. If a deep depression passes to the north, then high winds occur, at first southerly or south-westerly as the warm front approaches, then south-westerly in the warm sector, and eventually westerly or

north-westerly behind the cold front. Several hours of continuous and often heavy rain are usually followed by an easing in
the warm sector. The clearance at the cold front may be rapid
and accompanied by heavy rain, or it may be gradual with little
rain. Behind the cold front there may only be a few showers,
but at other times, particularly in autumn when the sea is still
warm, the showers are heavy and frequent. There is little
respite before the next frontal system moves in. On other occasions the depression may pass eastward through the Hebrides
giving easterly winds to the north of its track, and the more
usual sequence (above) to the south.

The view to the west is of a vast sky and seascape upon which
the weather forecast is often vividly written: squally troughs
may already be visible, with slanting shafts of rain which will
arrive in an hour or two's time; or there may be the prospect of
an afternoon or evening of unbroken sunshine. More subtly, in
a few hours a frontal depression may bring high winds and continuous rain over the horizon. The warm front is heralded by
cirrus cloud (mare's tails) grading westward to cirro- and alto-
stratus; the 'watery sun' in the alto-stratus casts a weird light
upon the sea and islands before the wind and the rain. Boats

An approaching warm front with a 'watery sun' shining a veil of cirro-stratus with bands of alto-stratus and strato-cumulus cloud over Ben Hynish and Traigh Bhaigh, Tiree (Photo J. M. Boyd)

run for shelter as the storm strikes, and livestock stand in the lee of stonedykes. Following the incessant rains of the warm front and the clearance of the cold front, the drenched islands emerge once more into bright sunshine.

The oceanic air may come from any latitude in the North Atlantic, but it is generally divided into southern or tropical Atlantic air from the Azores, and the northern or polar Atlantic air from Greenland and Iceland. Likewise, the continental air may come from central and Mediterranean Europe or from Scandinavia and Siberia. In the Hebrides the oceanic air dominates with long periods of changeable weather, particularly in autumn and early winter. When strong anticyclones develop over Scandinavia in winter, the cold easterlies on their southern flank may develop troughs which bring blizzards to the east of Britain, but these have usually lost their burden of snow over the mainland before they reach the Hebrides, which remain comparatively snow free.

Ecological Effects

The range in mean monthly temperature in the course of the year is about 9°C, but the growth of vegetation is slow because of the sluggish rise of temperature and slow drying-out of the soil—even in well-drained loams it is not usually possible to plough until early April. Crops grow slowly even in areas of high sunshine due to wind-blast, high rates of transpiration and low day-time temperatures. Moreover, the low islands have occasional summer droughts; a month's drought with bright windy weather in May and June will result in light crops of potatoes, grain and hay. Although the climate is generally mild, the combined effect of the elements makes it severe on plant growth, livestock and wild animals. Cattle and red deer lose heat rapidly in high winds and this is increased by driving rain, mist and snow. A wet, windy and cloudy summer can therefore retard the growth of pasture and increase the loss of body heat from animals on the hill. This means they will enter the winter in relatively poor condition and, in the case of stray sheep and red deer, may succumb in winter snow. Supplementary feeding of livestock against the energy deficit caused by normal Hebridean summer weather near sea level is similar to that prescribed at an altitude of 300m on the hills of Perthshire.

The loss of heat by the human body in days of strong winds and rain with temperatures around 10°C is enough to drive all but the fittest of people indoors. The draw-down in levels of physical energy and work-rate of those who work out of doors

is greater than one might expect by looking at the data. It is for this reason that the crofting way of life is regarded by the outsider as desultory and anachronistic, when it is a naturally reactive style of living related to a punishing and highly changeable climate.

Wind-blown shell sand has drifted over the ruins of the village on Mingulay, Barra Isles which lost its people earlier this century (Photo J. M. Boyd)

The two most obvious effects of weather are on tree-growth and blown-sand seen among the ruins of Mingulay. Wind, salt and water-logging reduce colonisation by trees in the Hebrides, although conditions vary from the exposed western rim of the Outer Hebrides and Tiree, to the more sheltered east-facing slopes of the Inner Hebrides. However, trees do grow in the more wind-blasted islands, naturally as at Allt Volagir on the lower western slopes of Beinn Mhor in South Uist, and as plantations at Northbay, Barra, but usually in defiles or sheltered hollows. The scrub woodlands on the islands of Loch Druidibeg, South Uist, show that willow, rowan, birch and juniper will grow in high wind exposures beyond the reach of salt spray, provided the ground is ungrazed and unburnt. On Rum, experimental plantations show what can be achieved by a variety of native species growing in the

A willow-birch-gorse thicket in a fenced plot on the west side of North Uist in the 1950s, typical of the natural wind-blasted woodland which would develop without grazing (Photo J. M. Boyd)

Hebrides in different exposures to prevailing winds and at different altitudes. It is clear from these and many other small scattered woods in the outer islands, that if man did not burn the ground and graze it with his sheep and deer, the Hebrides would possess a scrub forest today as in the past.

If it was not for shell sand drifting against the weather face of the islands and being carried by the wind several hundred metres inland, many fertile islands like Tiree and the western coastal plains of the Uists and Benbecula would be as barren as their rocky and peaty interiors. The scourge of the wind is softened a little by its burden of beneficent sand which buffers the acid of the peat, gives porosity to the soil, and supports agriculture.

In ecological terms, precipitation is considered together with the combined effects of evaporation and transpiration (evapo-transpiration) to provide an assessment of water-balance in soils, ground water and loch and stream systems. Physiological water-balance is also involved in the initiation and maintenance of growth in plants and animals. A potential water surplus leads to waterlogging and a large deficit to drought, and the point of balance between these extremes is seldom reached in the Hebrides—though they have, on average, a surplus of rainfall over evapo-transpiration every month—crofters therefore speak of 'wet' and 'dry' summers (June to August).

The latter occur when very little or no rain for several weeks is accompanied by sunshine and warm south-easterly winds, which rapidly draw moisture from the land. The water-table falls, shallow lochans and streams dry out and crops on sandy soils wilt for want of water. Occasionally, water deficits have occurred in February and March, when dry easterly winds have prevailed, usually with high evapo-transpiration and low rainfall. It is during these periods of drought that moorland fires occur and spread easily.

Humidity and Temperature

Evapo-transpiration potential relates to the relative humidity of the air, which is the ratio of the actual vapour pressure to the saturation vapour pressure at the same temperature, expressed as a percentage. This is important to plants and animals, as it affects physiological processes such as the opening of buds, seed capsules and sporangia, and the olfactory communication and stimulation of insects and mammals. The mean range of water-vapour pressure at 1.2m above ground in the Hebrides is 8 to 13 millibars which is similar to the rest of Britain. However, because of the low summer temperatures, the mean relative humidity in daytime in summer, when plants and animals are most affected, is 82%, compared with 67% at Edinburgh and 58% at London Airport (Heathrow). Anticyclones sometimes bring periods of very high relative humidity; in brilliant sunshine and calm conditions the islands become swathed in sea fog which curls over the lower slopes leaving the top bathed in sunshine. In such weather St Kilda lies shrouded in feathery mist, showing a sparkling array of sunlit humps and spires above. Sadly, it was at such times of poor visibility that the islands were so dangerous to low-flying aircraft during the Second World War; St Kilda alone had four airwrecks.

The North Atlantic Drift and the prevailing winds from the south-west dominate the weather picture and play a major role in determining the temperature regime—on Tiree we once found a whole coconut complete with green husk, presumably having come all the way from the Caribbean, and saw it as a symbol of the benign influence of the great ocean drift. The mean annual temperature at Tiree, 9.1°C, is only 1°C lower than southern England. The seasonal range is much less however: 8.5°C at Tiree compared with 11.6°C in Glasgow and 14°C in southern England. The maritime influences also reduce the diurnal range, which in July is only 5°C. The extremes of temperature recorded at various sites are: Stornoway 25.6–12.2°C; Tiree 26.1–7.0°C; Rum 27.9–9.5°C. To obtain these values for

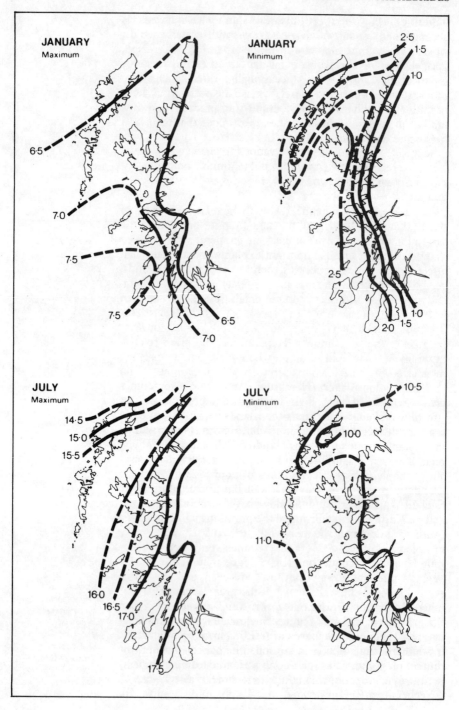

JANUARY
Maximum

JANUARY
Minimum

JULY
Maximum

JULY
Minimum

summer maxima, quiet unbroken sunshine with light south-
easterly winds over several days are required—conditions like
these have given a maximum at Benbecula of 27.2°C. These
figures cover the period of observation up to the present.
Winter minima occur on calm, clear nights with a fresh covering of snow. The oceanic character of the weather is most
accentuated in the low, small islands; the weather in the interiors of the high, larger islands has a wider range of temperatures caused by shelter, altitude and distance from the sea,
although we have very few observations to characterise these
areas. Average monthly maximum and minimum temperatures
from Tiree on the outer rim of the Hebrides and Perth in Scotland are shown in Table 2.1

| Station | Month | | | | | | | | | | | |
	Jan	Feb	Mar	Apr	May	Jun	Jul	Aug	Sep	Oct	Nov	Dec
Tiree Max	10.3	9.9	11.0	13.7	17.2	19.7	19.6	19.3	17.7	15.5	12.7	11.2
Min	−2.2	−2.8	−1.2	−0.2	2.2	5.2	7.3	7.0	5.2	3.2	0.1	−1.2
Perth Max	11.3	11.1	13.1	17.6	21.6	24.4	24.8	23.7	21.1	17.5	13.8	11.9
Min	−8.4	−8.0	−4.6	−2.5	0.3	3.7	5.2	4.0	1.6	−1.3	−5.2	−6.6

Table 2.1   The average monthly maximum and minimum temperatures from Tiree and
Perth over the period 1951–80 from *Scotland's Climate—Some Facts and Figures*
Meteorological Office (1989).

The growing season may be defined as the period in which
the soil temperature is above 6°C and in the Outer Hebrides it
lasts on average 245 days, similar to that near Stirling. It extends
from early April to early December. The intensity of the season
can be measured by the sum of day-°C, which, in Tiree
averages 1,505, a figure which is similar to those obtained for
lowland Scotland, but higher than for the Outer Hebrides.
The inner islands, therefore, have an advantage in temperature
over the outer islands, but this advantage is diminished by the
inner islands having a higher rainfall, except in Tiree, Coll,
Iona and Colonsay.

Soil Climate

The soil has a climate of its own which is related to, but
different from, the atmosphere. Moisture content, temperature and the physical stresses of freezing and thawing are all
important in the function of the soil. The effects of waterlogging on plant life, which cause the formation of blanket peat,
are to be seen everywhere in the interiors of the islands, but on
the other hand the effects of drought are often seen in dry

Fig. 8
*The mean daily
maximum and
minimum temperatures
(°C) for January
(above) and July
(below) 1951–1980,
from* Scotland's
Climate—Some
Facts and Figures,
Meteorological Office,
1989)

summers on sand dunes, bare hill slopes and hill-top gravels. Between the two, there are the semi-natural and cultivated loams in which the balance of the physical and biological features produces fresh machair, fields of sown grass, wheat and barley.

In summer the top 10 centimetres of soils near sea level are on average warmer by 3°C than the air above, whereas in winter they are 1°C colder. These figures are for bare ground such as a field ploughed and harrowed. Under tall grass cover, for instance, the temperature of the soil may be slightly cooler in summer and warmer in winter than the air immediately above. Therefore, the machair and stubble swards, which are generally closely grazed exposing the soil surface, will have temperatures close to those of the atmosphere, and subject to atmospheric fluctuations. Continuous cover of vegetation is therefore a great advantage. It not only reduces erosion but also extends the growing season in autumn—a point which seems to be missed in many crofting townships with extensive heavily-grazed dunes and machairs.

The difference of summer and winter soil temperatures is an important factor in the length and quality of the growing season. On the summits and ridges of high islands there are solifluction features caused by the incessant freezing and thawing of the land surface in winter. This 'frost heave' is seen well on Sgur nan Gillean, Rum, but nowhere in the Hebrides have we seen these features as well developed as on Hoy, Orkney and North Roe, Shetland.

An example of local variation is the comparison of temperatures recorded at two stations in Barra, Craigston and Skallary, over ten years in the 1930s and 40s. Craigston is on the exposed western side of the island about one mile from the sea; Skallary is on the sheltered eastern side about half a mile from the sea. Daytime temperatures at Craigston were above those at Skallary. The minimum temperatures at Craigston on clear nights fell slightly below Skallary, but the gain by day was greater. Overall, the daily temperature range at Craigston was greater than at Skallary and the growing season was longer. However, temperature is not the only factor to be taken into account. Rainfall at Skallary was affected by the hill of Heaval (367m), and it received much more rain and less sunshine than Craigston, but Craigston was windier. In the interval of days the climatic differences are small, but they are significant when considered together over the months from sowing to harvesting in the full span of pasture growth for grazing animals. They help to explain why the harvests generally begin earlier in the sunnier, drier and more exposed parts of the islands than elsewhere in the Hebrides.

Rainfall and Sunshine

In Britain the variation of rainfall with altitude is very variable, depending not only on the local topography but also on whether the major rain-bearing winds have already passed over hills or mountains where much of their moisture has been shed. As might be expected, the increase of rainfall with height is much greater on the west-facing slopes on the Inner Hebrides and the north-west Highlands than it is in the east, for example in the Cairngorms, and, on the annual basis, may reach about 450mm per 100m.

The maximum rainfall often occurs not at the top of a mountain, but just in the lee side of the summit. On small mountainous Rum comparisons can be made of the rainfall assiduously recorded over a number of years at seven sites. Near sea level on the windward west side of the island, the average annual rainfall is about 1,500mm (59 inches), on the north coast away from the highest mountains it is about 1,900mm (75 inches), while on the leeward side, still close to the mountains, it is about 2,500mm (98 inches) only 7km (4.5 miles) away from the driest part of the island.

Fig. 9
The average daily duration (hours) of bright sunshine in December and June 1951–80. In December, to the left of the line is 1+, to the right 1− from Scotland's Climate—Some Facts and Figures, *Meteorological Office, 1989)*

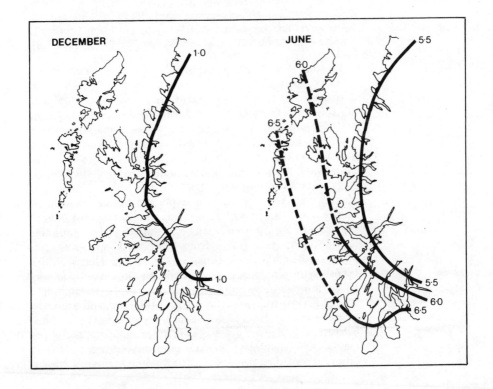

DECEMBER   JUNE

The meteorological records are mainly obtained from stations manned by persons in the line of duty such as at airports, lighthouses and nature reserves or by volunteer recorders. Together, the records give the climatic character of each station and of the whole Hebrides, but they do not show the detail of local variations, such as those provided by a network of stations on Rum, let alone the microclimates of soils, grasslands, heaths and woodlands which determine rates of growth and productivity of plant and animal populations. The monthly and annual average rainfall for Hebridean and mainland stations are compared in Table 2.2.

Station	Alt(m)	Jan	Feb	Mar	Apr	May	Jun	Jul	Aug	Sep	Oct	Nov	Dec	Year
Stornoway	15	115	77	80	66	62	67	72	74	103	126	129	125	1096
Benbecula	5	129	86	89	62	65	76	83	83	119	139	140	132	1203
Tiree*	9	120	71	77	60	56	66	79	83	123	125	123	123	1106
Skye*	27	182	116	129	93	91	104	113	118	170	204	203	210	1732
Mull (Aros)	37	210	116	142	97	96	109	120	133	199	208	203	220	1853
Islay#	21	139	85	92	70	67	74	93	93	128	139	149	149	1278
Perth	23	70	52	47	43	57	51	67	72	63	65	69	82	738
Edinburgh+	26	47	39	39	38	49	45	69	73	57	56	58	56	626

*Portree   #Eallabus   +Royal Botanic Gardens

Table 2.2   Monthly and annual averages of rainfall (mm) from six stations in the Hebrides and two on the Scottish mainland for comparison in the period 1951–80, taken from *Scotland's Climate—Some Facts and Figures*, Meteorological Office (1989).

Weather recording began at Stornoway Castle in 1856, continued at various sites around the town, and later moved to the Coastguard Station at Holm Point. An average annual rainfall of 1,266mm (49.6 inches) was published in *British Rainfall* from period 1881–1915. In 1942 the station was moved to the airport on the drier east side of the town, and from observations after 1942 a calculated average of 1,003mm (39.5 inches) for 1916–1950 was estimated. For the latest standard period (1941–70), the average was 1094mm (43.1 inches). This compares with 1,204mm (47.5 inches) in Tiree for the same period. Similar calculated averages for 1941–70 are: Tiree, 1,204mm (47.5 inches); Vatersay (Barra), 1,174mm (46.2 inches); Butt of Lewis, 1,100mm (43.3 inches); Back (10km from Stornoway), 1,100mm (43.3 inches). In such a windy climate as that of the Hebrides, the exposure of rain gauges is very important to ensure that rain falls in the gauge and is not blown over the top, so natural shelter or the construction of a turf wall is required, and exposure to sea spray must be avoided. Some of the apparent differences between sites may be due to problems of exposure, and there may also be significant differences in the averages between different recording periods. Taking this into account, it may be stated that the annual rainfall near sea level on the outer wester rim from Tiree to the Butt of Lewis is about 1,200mm, rising to about 1,400mm in Harris where the mountains are close to the sea. As has already been mentioned, large variations in sea level values of rainfall can occur due to the effects of local topography such as on Rum.

Thunderstorms are infrequent and of the 'one-clap' variety mostly in autumn and early winter, when rapidly-moving heavy showers come in from the west off a relatively warm sea. They can be accompanied by giant hailstones, such as fell in the Uig

A towering cumulo-nimbus over Benbecula with the church and manse caught in a shaft of bright sunshine, typical of a north-westerly airflow over the islands (Photo J. M. Boyd)

area of Skye in 1986. The thunderstorms, though short-lived, can be very violent, with cloud to earth discharges resulting in heathland fires. This is thought to be the source of charcoal layers in peat in north-west Scotland which antedate human occupation.

The temperate, oceanic climate has few days of falling snow, and this very rarely settles. It is unusual for the maximum temperatures near sea level to remain below freezing point for long, though long spells of freezing weather can occur on the high hills of Jura, Mull, Rum, Skye, South Uist and Harris. The weather stations near sea level at Stornoway and Tiree have recorded respective averages of 35 and 16 days of air frost annually. Similar averages of 10 and 4 days respectively of lying snow have been recorded. In exceptional winters, such as in 1946–47, the total at Stornoway rose to 31 days of lying snow with the snowfalls outlasting the midday thaw. At Kinloch Castle, Rum, the average for days of snowfall during 1948–80 was about 20 and that for Prabost, Skye 30. The averages for snow lying at these two stations were 10 and 24 days respectively. Comparative figures for Derry Lodge in the east Cairngorm for a similar period give an average of 85 days per year on both counts.

Because of their high latitude the Hebrides have some of the highest measurements of sunshine in a single day in Britain, daylength being much longer than further south. Sunshine measurements are made by using a glass ball as a lens to concentrate the sun's rays on a specially treated card, and measuring the length of the burn. The average monthly durations of sunshine in the period 1951–80 for Hebridean stations compared with the mainland are shown in Table 2.3. Because of the clarity of the air, the start and finish of the burn in the morning and the evening are often earlier and later, respectively, in the Hebrides than they would be where the atmosphere is less clear, as it is in most other parts of the United Kingdom.

Station	Alt(m)	Jan	Feb	Mar	Apr	May	Jun	Jul	Aug	Sep	Oct	Nov	Dec	Year*
Stornoway	15	1.2	2.5	3.6	5.2	6.0	5.9	4.2	4.4	3.6	2.5	1.5	0.8	1256
Benbecula	5	1.3	2.5	3.7	5.8	6.5	6.5	4.6	4.9	3.8	2.5	1.6	0.9	1361
Tiree	9	1.4	2.4	3.7	5.8	6.9	6.6	5.1	5.2	3.9	2.5	1.5	0.9	1400
Skye#	67	1.3	2.7	3.5	5.2	6.0	5.8	4.1	4.3	3.3	2.3	1.5	1.0	1243
Perth	23	1.4	2.3	3.2	5.1	5.7	6.0	5.5	4.3	3.7	2.7	1.8	1.1	1309
Edinburgh+	26	1.5	2.4	3.2	4.9	5.7	6.1	5.5	4.8	4.0	3.0	2.0	1.3	1351

*Average annual total (hours) of bright sunshine;   #Prabost;   +Royal Botanic Gardens

Table 2.3   The average duration of bright sunshine in hours for four stations in the Hebrides and two on the mainland, in the period 1951–80, taken from *Scotland's Climate—Some Facts and Figures*, Meteorological Office (1989).

Measurements of solar radiation on a horizontal surface have been made at Stornoway since 1983. These show maximum daily values which are as high as anywhere in the British Isles, despite the fact that the sun is at a lower elevation than further south.

Wind

The Hebrides are attractive to tourists who enjoy the challenge of changeable weather. Wind dominates everything. Yachtsmen can seldom make firm plans for more than six hours ahead; from their sheltered moorings on the mainland coast, they make cautious advances upon the Outer Hebrides and St Kilda with an ear to the weather forecast and an eye on a quick retreat to havens such as Castlebay, Canna and Tobermory, or the many safe little anchorages like Geometra, on the storm coast of Mull, and Loch Skipport, Rodel and Loch Shell on the leeward coast of the Outer Hebrides. St Kilda is an

A storm at St Kilda with the islands under a shroud of nimbo-stratus with continuous rain and a high wind from the south-west. The view is from Boreray (left) and Stac an Armin (right) looking to Stac Lee (centre) and Hirta (Photo J. M. Boyd)

ultima thule for many yachtsmen; its exposed position to heavy seas, which we describe more fully in Chapter 16, is a special challenge.

In the last decade wind surfing has become popular. The best conditions are obtained in spring and autumn when strong to gale-force winds are accompanied by high tides and huge breaking seas. Sand yachting has also been tried on spacious beaches like Traigh Mhor in Tiree, but has not become as widely popular as wind surfing. The 'hardy annual' visitor sees the weather as a game of chance — runs of warm sunny days are a 'jackpot'. For the occasional visitor, especially those who are accustomed to the well-wooded or well-paved mainland environments, the Hebrides can bring highly contrasting reactions. Those whose brief visit coincides with bad weather may never return, but those who have savoured the islands in their various moods of weather, tend to return again and again.

Both the wind and sea in the Hebrides have enormous power which at some time in the near future will be harnessed. Experiments with wave and wind generators are already in existence. Prototype wind generators in Orkney and 'wind farms' in other countries show the vast scale to which windmill development must be taken before it can contribute significantly to the national energy budget. However, wind generators on Fair Isle point the way to the local use of wind as an alternative to diesel engines in the Scottish islands. The Hebrides are one of the windiest places in Europe, so there is a great amount of wind energy waiting to be harnessed. This is shown in comparing the wind data of Tiree with that of Glasgow Airport on the west mainland (Table 2.4). The seas to the west of the outer rim of islands from Islay to the Butt of Lewis also possess enormous amounts of wave energy. With the progressive exhaustion of fossil fuels and the dangers which attend nuclear power generation, there are promising prospects for alternative technologies such as wind and wave power, and the Hebrides have great potential for such power. However, when it comes to be harnessed, the greatest care must be taken to safeguard the welfare and culture of the people, and to conserve the fragile environment of the islands.

Station	Jan	Feb	Mar	Apr	May	Jun	Jul	Aug	Sep	Oct	Nov	Dec	Year
Tiree	6.9	3.7	3.4	1.4	0.5	0.3	0.3	0.5	1.6	3.3	4.7	7.2	33.8
Glasgow Apt	1.2	0.4	0.4	0.2	0.1	0.2	0.0	0.0	0.2	0.2	0.4	1.0	4.3

Table 2.4 Monthly and annual average number of days with winds of gale force and over during the period 1951–80 at Tiree, compared with Glasgow Airport, taken from *Scotland's Climate—Some Facts and Figures*, Meteorological Office (1989).

Climate in the Past

Analysis of pollen from the beds of lochs and peat bogs shows a succession of climatic periods experienced by north-west Europe since the ice departed from Britain 10,000 years ago. The Hebrides were on the edge of the ice-sheet at the maximum of the Quaternary glaciation, but some islands like St Kilda may have been beyond the edge of the ice with small ice caps of their own. There is evidence from pollen in the soils which suggests that plants survived the ice-age in the Hebrides and some land was always free of ice in the arctic summer, possibly on nunataks, which are rocky islands protruding above the ice.

Through the ice-age and in the early phases of its retreat, the ecology would be arctic with stocks of plants and animals similar to parts of Greenland today. However, the change of the climate from arctic to temperate was not uniform. In the Boreal period, 10,000 to 7,000 years ago, immediately following arctic conditions (Preboreal), the weather was drier and warmer than today. The ice retreated and the conformation of the coastlines changed with changes in sea level; land animals, distributed widely by the ice-bridges, bergs and floes, became isolated in newly-created islands. There then followed two warm periods which took place between 7,000 and 3,000 years ago. These Atlantic and the Sub-Boreal periods were of about 1,000 years each with wet and dry conditions respectively. It was during the Atlantic period, about 6,500 years ago, that man first came to the Hebrides from the south, as a hunter-fisherman, and from thence to Orkney. During the wet Atlantic period, the birch-hazel woods of the new Boreal forest, which graded westward from the high forest on the mainland seaboard to low scrub on the islands, changed their character with an increase in the amount of alder and moss.

The terrain was probably well vegetated, reducing erosion on the lower ground, but chemical leaching of nutrients from the young soils probably stunted tree growth through nutrient deficiency. Added to this, there was waterlogging and growth of *Sphagnum* moss. Soil conditions must have ameliorated to some extent in the warm dry conditions of the Sub-Boreal, but a decline recurred in the cooler, wetter Sub-Atlantic which prevails today, and this natural decline in soil fertility has been accelerated by man's use of the land in the past 2,500 years.

There have been three minor fluctuations from the normal conditions of the Sub-Atlantic: between 1,000 and 1,200 AD the climate was on average 2°C warmer; the arrival of St Columba preceded this change and the weather was probably similar then to the present day; then came amelioration during the Viking occupation when, in both ecological and economic terms, the islands were more clement.

The effects of weather pervade the entire natural system on land and at sea. It affects the sea's surface and the penetration of light, heat and gaseous exchange at depth. Climate is all-embracing, having as great but different effects in the south on Gigha as on North Rona; on sheltered Lismore as on exposed St Kilda; on large Lewis as on small Colonsay; likewise on high Mull as on low Tiree. The great physical forces of atmosphere and sea on the North Atlantic seaboard are highly variable, but imposed upon this is local variation caused by the position and character of the individual islands each of which can be a little world unto itself.

Hydrography

We have described the mellowing effect of the sea on the climate in the Hebrides which means that snow rarely lies for more than a few hours except on the high mountains. The water masses around the Hebrides have about the lowest degree of annual variation in temperature of any area around the British Isles, a fact which owes much to the complex nature of the water masses which mix out to the west off the contintental slope. Subsurface waters of low salinity moving from the north-west into the eastern North Atlantic basin, plus deeper saline outflow from the Mediterranean, mean that the density gradient between surface and mid-depth waters is lower than normal. This has an important consequence because it means the slightly cooled surface waters in winter descend to greater depths, resulting in deep overturning of the water column, bringing warmer water to the surface. David Ellett of the Scottish Marine Biological Association has likened this to a large capacity storage heater. The idea that the Gulf Stream is implicated as a major factor in the warming of the British climate is now doubted by some, but there are still many reasons for considering that the heat energy contained within this northerly moving water mass is a significant proximate source of energy leading to climatic warming.

Some 3 to 6 million tons of water per second flow northward through the Rockall Channel to the west of the Outer Hebrides. This, the Atlantic Current, then breaks east towards Shetland. West of the southern Hebrides, it forms a large clockwise gyre. Another recently discovered current, the Slope Current, also moves north along the line of the continental slope off the Hebrides, bringing with it about one million tons of water per second. It sends fingers of dense, saline oceanic water into the Hebrides to mix with the fresher, less dense waters of the northward moving Coastal Current. This current is much affected by local tidal and climatic conditions, but it will deliver 40 to 100 thousand tons of water per second into the Sea of the Hebrides. It forms from the outflow of the Irish Sea which wends its way round Kintyre, the Mull of Oa and the Rhinns of Islay before debouching into the channels between the islands of the Hebrides. Much of the coastal current moves north, squeezing through the Little Minch and then The Minch. South of Skye, part of the Coastal Current breaks off to move clockwise along the east coast of the Uists and Barra, around Barra Head and then northward again along the west side of the Long Island.

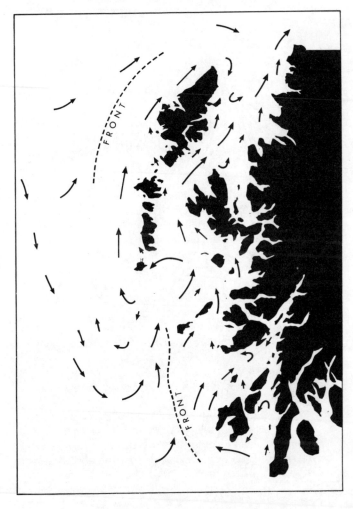

Fig. 10
Surface circulation in the sea to the west of Scotland in summer (from Ellett, 1979)

The oceanic water west of the Hebrides is a stratified water mass with a fairly constant gradient of salinity with depth. This is in contrast to the coastal water, which is mixed by tidal currents and the weather, and abuts onto the oceanic waters in places, such as west of Islay, to form fronts. The coastal waters also contain the run-off from rivers causing brackish conditions in the inner recesses of some lochs. The single largest source of freshwater is the Firth of Lorne through which drain much of the Glengarry, Lochaber, Lorne and Morvern catchments. The total run-off for the coast from Kintyre to Cape Wrath varies from 11–25 cubic km per year which is approximately 11–25 billion tonnes of water per year.

The influence of the coastal current and run-off on salinity

Fig. 11
Surface salinity of the sea, 0/00, 11–19 November 1977 (lower), and 2–12 February 1978 (upper) (from Ellett, 1983)

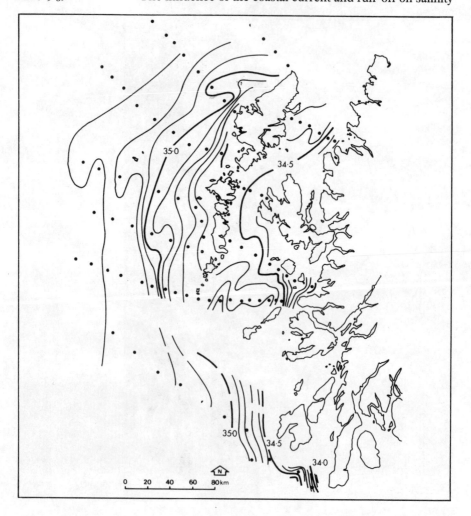

is well illustrated by the large salinity gradient on the western fringe of the Hebrides in summer, although in winter some of the deeper parts of the Hebridean seas are invaded by cold, dense tongues of oceanic water. The coastal current and run-off also cause a general lowering of summer surface temperature by about 2 to 3°C from an Atlantic maximum of 13°C. There is a similar pattern in winter when Atlantic waters stay at about 9°C while coastal waters dip to 6–7°C.

Allowing for tidal currents, the actual flow rate of the coastal current as it pushes through the Tiree passage between Coll and Mull can reach 18km per day in winter but is commonly 1–5km per day in summer. Further offshore, the slope current, at the rim of the Hebridean shelf, can run at 15–22km per day, but 2–9km per day may be more normal. The flow of these currents can be about half the surface flow rate near the bottom.

Radioactive caesium, released from Sellafield into the coastal current before it leaves the Irish Sea, has been a useful if dangerous marker to follow the progress of this water mass through the Hebrides. It has illustrated the sharp contrast between the unpolluted oceanic waters and the coastal waters, and has also helped to chart the velocity of the coastal current over long distances. An overall rate of flow from Islay to the Pentland Firth of 1.5km per day has been calculated.

The most immediate hydrographic feature of island archipelagoes is often their tidal races, and the inner sounds of the Hebrides often have considerable rips. At Corryvreckan,

The Gulf of Corryvreckan, the sound between Scarba (left) and Jura (right) which has whirlpools and overfalls in the tidal race (Photo J. M. Boyd)

between Scarba and Jura, there is an extreme example, while in the Lismore Passage overfalls give rough passage to yachts entering the Sound of Mull from the Firth of Lorne. The Corryvreckan rip arises from a one metre difference in sea level over 5km between the waters of the Sound of Jura and the Firth of Lorne. Currents of 8.5 knots are generated where the friction of the sea bed opposes the levelling flow of the water. In the main channels currents of 1–2 knots are normal, although they will reach 4 knots in the North Channel. Unusual tidal currents occur on the shelf at St Kilda which also affect the Sound of Harris. During summer neap tides, the stream running south-east flows all day, while in winter it flows all night, and vice-versa for the north-west flow.

Tidal amplitude in the Hebrides is not unusual by British standards. There is a point between Kintyre and Islay where the tides of the shelf, the North Channel and the Sound of Jura meet. Here, the tidal range is 0.5–1m. Around Skye and The Minch it is 1.6–4.5 metres at neaps and springs respectively, but there are no areas with extreme tidal ranges.

All this movement of water takes place over a varied submarine topography which plays an important part in mixing or separating the upper and deep waters. The glaciated landscape above sea level continues below with deep-graven rock basins such as the sea-lochs of Skye and Mull. Drowned fjords occur west of the Rhinns of Islay. There are also isolated trenches, many over 100m and some over 200m in depth in the Firth of Lorne, east of Barra Head and around the Small Isles, and the deepest at 316m off the north-east coast of Raasay. The water and communities of organisms in these deep waters are different from the mobile upper waters, and there is limited exchange between the two levels. The Raasay Deep, lying in the shelter of Skye, has been attractive to those who require deep water for construction of oil/gas production platforms and for naval research and tests.

Soils

Soils are formed from mixtures of minerals derived from rocks, and by microbial action on organic material in the presence of water and air. The soil type is dictated by the relative proportions of these components, particularly the types of minerals present, and the way in which they are organised from the soil surface to the base rock. Hebridean soils do not generally lend themselves to cultivation on a large scale; they are usually too wet, occasionally too dry, or are susceptible to being eroded by the wind. Even where there are extensive areas of cultivable land, the land surface is commonly uneven and rocky and so highly restrictive. Besides being the substrate of agriculture, the soils provide a range of habitats for plant and animal communities, foundations for houses and roads, and domestic fuel. Water for the tap is filtered through the soil, and water derived from peat accounts for the distinctive taste of the malt whisky of Islay, Jura and Skye.

Throughout the Hebrides there are signs, some recent and some ancient, that man has been at work with the soil. Soils are one of the few elements of the physical environment which man can actively modify for his own benefit, but in the Hebrides this is a continuous and arduous process. Through the centuries land has been progressively claimed from the hill or bog by drainage, to improve the grazing for livestock. Over many years, drains have become blocked, but some have recently been re-established in the Integrated Development Programme and the Agricultural Development Programme (pp. 338–9) in the Outer and Inner Hebrides respectively, which provided grant aid for agricultural improvement. *Feanagean* (spade cultivation in ridges sometimes called 'lazy beds') were dug on the thin wet soils, and long-derelict furrows are still seen corrugating the hillsides of Skye and Mull, Rum, Harris and the Barra Isles. Even the outlying islands of North Rona and St Kilda have their old lazy beds. Seaweed, always a plentiful commodity in the Hebrides, was applied to land as a fertiliser and this practice still continues. Sadly, it has been widely displaced by artificial fertilisers, with the consequent changes in the soil biomass affecting the ecology of the croftlands. Liming of the soils was rare, mainly because there is little

Feannagan *or 'lazy beds' in Glen Harris, Rum. The thin soil was raised in parallel ridges by spade-cultivation, fertilized with seaweed, and planted with oats, barley, potatoes and kale (Photo J. M. Boyd)*

limestone in the Hebrides, but since the last war calcareous shell sand has been added to the moorland soils by grant-assisted schemes in the Outer Hebrides (p. 336). This has the same effect as liming by improving rough grazing land and even increasing the area of tillage; it effectively adds a small amount of material of high carbonate content to another of low carbonate content to improve its agricultural potential, though a compound fertiliser is also added, together with a clover-grass seed mixture. Over the centuries, man has had a hand in the development of many of the Hebridean soils.

Soil development is slow and may involve a gradual movement of material transported from elsewhere by wind or water and then deposited over the existing soil or bedrock. Transient periods of occupation or cultivation by man can be distinguished as layers, or horizons, in this sequence of accumulation. This is especially obvious where subsequent chemical alteration or natural mixing of the soil components is slight, such as in the regosols (immature soils) which underlie the machair. Occupation horizons have been identified in the machair soils of Rosinish in Benbecula, Northton in Harris and Udal in North Uist. They are characterised by greater accumulation of dark organic material than in the intervening horizons. Horizons may also depict changes in the climate or vegetation (p. 51).

Hebridean soils have evolved within the last 10,000 years, and every soil has a parent material from which it has been derived to varying degrees. In some cases, the bedrock upon which a soil has developed may have contributed directly to the parent material, or it can influence the properties of the soil as it develops. However, most parent materials owe their origin to the deposition of the eroded fragments of the Tertiary and the pre-Tertiary rocks of western Scotland by glaciers and then by rivers and the sea.

The Soil Survey of Scotland recognised six different parent materials in the Hebrides, and each one of these has a range of soils developed within it depending on such factors as rainfall, topography, the nature of the bedrock and the level of biotic activity associated with them. These were: glacial till, morainic drift, outwash and raised beaches, colluvium, aeolian sand and montane frost-shattered detritus.

Glacial Till with Brown Forest Soils

The Quaternary ice sheet covered most of the Hebrides, and its great erosive power ground the underlying rock to powder. The resulting soils tend to be compact and lack surface boulders. This glacial till is found in many parts of the Outer Hebrides, where it is often positioned in the lee of hummocks in the bedrock of Lewisian gneiss, and therefore indicates the direction of movement of the ice sheet. Most of North Uist and Benbecula are covered with this kind of till, where it lies deepest on the northwest side of the rocky hummocks. Further south around Lochboisdale, the till lies on the west side and to the north of the small ice-cap of Harris and south Lewis, and is on the north of the hummocks. Further north on the line from Stornoway to Shawbost the hummocks fade out and a flat plain has developed where the till lies up to six metres deep over the gneiss. The flat topography and fine texture of this till restricts drainage, which leads to waterlogging. Peat, up to four metres deep in central Lewis, has accumulated on top and now forms a soggy featureless landscape. This till probably formed partly from plateau basalt rocks which could have overlain the gneiss in a thin layer, and which has now been completely removed by ice erosion. Such basalts are rich in many minerals required to form productive soils.

In the Inner Hebrides, the till deposits are sporadic and their composition reflects the rocks from which they were formed. On Skye the main sources of material were the plateau basalts and soft Jurassic shales. Other Mesozoic strata, much of which is now submerged below the sea, gave rise to tills on Islay, Colonsay, Tiree and the Ross of Mull. Where drainage is good, glacial till forms the basis for most of the productive cultivated land in the Inner Hebrides, the largest such area being on Islay. Tills derived from Jurassic rocks also provide productive croft

Brown calcareous soils at Torrin, Skye with a crop of potatoes and a rowan tree growing from the pile of stones cleared from the field. Blaven (913m) stands behind. (Photo J. M. Boyd)

land on Tiree and Coll, and at Glendale and Staffin on Skye, while tills from Mesozoic rocks give good grazing land on the Ross of Mull, north-west Islay and Colonsay.

Morainic Drift with Peat and Gleys

Morainic drift is formed from the rock debris of the retreating glaciers. It has a very wide range of particle sizes, from minute individual crystals to large boulders the size of a house which can be left perched on hilltops or bare hillsides. It forms the hummocky terrain on the floor of glens of the Inner Hebrides. In the Outer Hebrides it occurs around the shores of Loch Seaforth, west Loch Tarbert and along the western seaboard of North Lewis from Shawbost to North Dell. In the Uists and Barra it occurs at Balivanich, from West Gerinish to Daliburgh, and on the slopes of Heaval, Barra. Although these soils are normally fairly permeable to water, a hard impermeable consolidated horizon, thought to be a relict showing the upper extent of the permafrost until 10,000 years BP, often impedes drainage. This, and the high rainfall over much of the Inner Hebrides, has caused the development of peaty soils (gleys) on these moraines. Peats are formed typically in areas of high rainfall and poor drainage, and where the soil temperature is cool, thus preventing microbial action which would normally break down the organic material from dead plants. Such conditions are common throughout the Hebrides.

Outwash Fans and Raised Beaches

As the glaciers receded they released water which fed torrential rivers and streams. The land, free at last from its enormous burden of ice, began to flex imperceptibly upwards, causing a raising of the post-glacial shorelines to form present day raised beaches. The glacial torrents re-sorted many of the tills and moraines left by the retreating ice, transporting and re-depositing their loads of gravel, sand and silt. The rivers flowed fastest near their source and were able to carry most of the glacial debris, but as the gradient of their course declined, they lost their power to move large fragments. By this process, frag-ments were sorted according to their size. Coarse materials were dropped in outwash fans and most of the fine colloidal clays and sand ended up in the sea. Where steep gradients con-tinue all the way to the coast, as is often the case in the Inner Hebrides, boulders also ended up in the sea.

The debris deposited by this process is now often seen as terraced outwash plains of sand or gravel, the particles of which are rounded by impact against one another caused by the action of the water. Their extent is mostly limited to the low ground and river valleys and in some localities part of the deposit has been removed by the sea to form the pebbled and cobbled raised beaches found mainly in the Inner Hebrides. The value of the soils developed on these sands and gravels varies. At one extreme are stretches of unvegetated cobbles which may be piled to a depth of several metres on raised beaches which are

The calcareous sandy loam of the raised beach platform at Barrapol, Tiree being made ready for a crop of potatoes (Photo J. M. Boyd)

scenically magnificent but relatively lifeless. At the other extreme are the fine gravels and sands. These are highly permeable to water and, because of this and the wet climate, leached soils known as podzols have often developed on them. Humic acid, from decaying organic matter in the upper horizons, mixed with the downward draining water, causes leaching of minerals from the upper part of the profile, and a distinct white mineral-deficient horizon develops. However, the top horizons of most of these podzols have been mixed by tillage, causing the upper horizons to be obliterated. Such podzols form the nucleus of many crofting areas in the Inner Hebrides. Where the climate is most favourable, they form some of the best agricultural land in the Hebrides. Their value is limited by their local occurrence but, unlike soils in many other parent materials, they usually occur in relatively flat sheltered areas such as near the mouth of Glen Brittle on Skye. The most notable of these podzolic soils are on the shores of Lochs Gruinart and Indaal, Islay, and on much of the cultivated land on Tiree. (St Columba also chose a small patch of this soil on Iona on which to found his early mission.) One problem with these soils is that valuable nutrients can be quickly washed away. The close proximity of the Dalradian limestone on Islay has meant that limestone could be burnt and the resultant lime used to enrich the soils, and on Tiree, wind-blown shell sand has caused the same effect.

Colluvium and Shallow Drifts with Podzols

Areas of bare rock left after the retreat of the glaciers have subsequently been subjected to weathering by wind, rain and freeze-thaw conditions. The products of this form a soil parent material known as colluvium or shallow drift. The nature of the soil which develops from these drifts is highly dependent on the rock from which it forms. For example, basalts give loamy soils, quartzites stony acid soils and slates give silty soils. Colluvium occurs on slopes at most altitudes and this in itself may influence the evolution of the soil. Those at low altitudes can form rich loamy brown forest soils, but subalpine and alpine colluvial soils are formed at high altitudes. These are often podzols because of mineral leaching and are shallow and exposed to frost action for much of the year on the peaks of Mull, Skye and Rum. Peaty soils usually form at intermediate altitudes.

The landscape associated with soils developed in colluvium or shallow drift is variable, but the countryside is often rocky and undulating with small lochans in ice-gouged rock basins, peat flats and steep, occasionally terraced, slopes. The rocky nature of these soils means that they have little agricultural value and provide good or poor hill pasture. Apart from the high mountains, examples of colluvial soils are found on the Ross of Mull, eastern Jura and at Trotternish on Skye.

On the Dalradian limestones of Islay and the ultrabasic rocks of Rum, brown forest soils have developed in colluvium, but cultivation of these is usually restricted by the steep, rocky slopes. The extinct communities, at Dibidil, Harris and Papadil on Rum have left cultivation ridges, indicating that it was once feasible to cultivate these remote areas. Now, only red deer and feral goats exploit the lush herb-rich vegetation on these soils. Shallow drifts, derived from the Tertiary basalts, have also produced brown forest soils on Eigg, Muck and along many of the sheltered shorelines of Skye and Mull. They support some arable land on Skye and Mull, but steep slopes often restrict their use to pasture for livestock. They often also support mixed deciduous woodlands such as those at Loch Don, Loch na Keal, Loch Buie and near Craignure on Mull, on Skye, and Eigg and Jura. These are biologically rich soils and, even with high grazing pressures, they support a diverse flora and fauna of importance in nature conservation.

Aeolian Sand with Regosols

One of the most important soil-forming materials in the Hebrides is wind-blown, or aeolian, sand. Much of this sand is formed from the crushed remains of shells of marine molluscs and crustacea and is widespread in the Hebrides. The soils formed from this parent material are poorly evolved, differing little from the parent material itself. The landscape formed by these soils is machair, (the character and extent of which is discussed in Chapters 6 and 14), and the largest areas are on the western seaboard of the Outer Hebrides from Harris to Vatersay, with small pockets on other islands. These regosols are easily eroded by wind when the turf is broken and dune blowouts then form. Some of those nearer the coast are continually on the move, being cut by the wind and pushed inland. Heavy grazing by livestock, or rabbits on some islands, of the rich semi-natural grasslands of the machair, tends to encourage this instability. They are also dry soils, because the wind causes water removal by evaporation and water drains away easily to ditches and, via the water table, to the sea. Some trace nutrients such as cobalt, which are necessary for the health of grazing livestock, are lacking in the vegetation on these soils because the high pH does not favour their release to plant roots.

A section of untilled machair soil at The Reef, Tiree, showing the present-day sandy loam (top), a dark band of peaty soil from a past period of flooding (middle), and the base of shell sand (bottom) (Photo J. M. Boyd)

Despite their rudimentary form, machair soils are fertile and provide good quality grazings. In the Uists they are tilled and planted on a considerable scale. Elsewhere, cultivation is patchy and carries with it a risk of erosion.

Montane Detritus

Like aeolian sands, soils formed from frost-shattered detritus are poorly evolved. The screes of the Red Hills of Skye and the boulder fields just below the summits of Askival and Hallival on Rum are detritus formed from the freezing and thawing of water percolating through cracks in the rock. This gradually splits the rocks along lines of weakness, and the resulting debris tumbles downhill. Although this process is still continuing in the higher mountains of the Hebrides, many of the screes were formed during the later stages of the Quaternary glaciation. In the sub-arctic conditions of immediate post-glacial times, the cycle of freezing and thawing was particularly severe, especially on the peaks of Jura, Mull, Skye and Rum. The senescence of the glacial period was not a continuous process in western Scotland. The glaciers retreated, advanced a little and then retreated again. Like the cobbled raised beaches, the screes are usually unvegetated and the steepness of the slopes means that they are unstable and may move downhill. They are prone to erosion by rivers and eventually end up as components of outwash fans, thus contributing to the formation of other parent materials.

Human communities have relied on the soil as much as on the sea to produce food, and there was a time when the wealth of an island was based mainly upon the richness of its soils. Political turmoils like the collapse of the Lordship of the Isles or the transition from the clan to the feudal system of government associated with the landed lairds have, without doubt, revolved around the productivity of the land and the ability of the workers of that land to squeeze the goodness from its soil. It was probably no coincidence that the power base of the Lordship of the Isles was on the comparatively rich agricultural system of Islay which could compare favourably with those on the mainland and Ireland. We refer to the recent occupational history of the Hebrides in later chapters.

CHAPTER 4

Life in the Sea

Sir Maurice Yonge was an inspired marine biologist who enthralled his students by his lectures on 'The Seas'. He transferred his own sense of the infinite to young minds and described the enrivonment of the deep, the 'marine pasturage', with rare passion and enlightenment. He had an immense understanding of how so many forms and functions of life had evolved in one vast interconnected system, and as the course proceeded, so the sense of wonder grew of a world which, by its nature, is closed to human beings but which, by technology, has been partially revealed. What is unseen is imagined—the angler-fish (*Lophius piscatorius*) with its lights twinkling in the abyssal depths, the tiny shrimp (*Eurydice pulchra*) in the ever-lasting sandstorm of the breakers. The course of scientific exploration is driven on by that sense of awe engendered as the student comes face to face with the unknown, the fearsome, the bizarre and the beautiful.

Our knowledge of life in Hebridean waters comes mostly from fishermen and fishery research, though in the last ten years there has been a small but growing effort in the survey of the coastal seas for the purposes of nature conservation. The main communities of organisms are situated in the different parts of the hydrographic system; ocean depths, continental slope and shelf with sublittoral platforms in the shallow seas immediately around the islands. None are self-contained and all are connected by currents. Many species of fin-fish move from one to the other to feed or breed and others, such as copepods, arrow-worms, sea-gooseberries and the egg and larval stages of a diverse fauna, move passively in the plankton. The waters around the Hebrides possess a rich phytoplankton; this is the 'vegetation', which fixes gaseous carbon and nitrogen, and which is grazed by the zooplankton. The zooplankton are then eaten by other animals and thus the food-chain is begun. The large devour the small and so on up to the large carnivores—the large gadoid fish, seals, whales and seabirds. The glaring exception to the rule is the basking shark (*Cetorhinus maximus*). This is the second largest fish in the world and the largest in the Hebrides and yet its food consists only of plankton.

Fish

The communities of fin-fish are described as 'demersal' or bottom-living, and 'pelagic', which includes fish which live between the bottom and the surface. Both groups are well known because of their commercial value.

English	Scientific	Gaelic
Cod	*Gadus morhua*	trosg
Haddock	*Melanogrammus aeglefinus*	adag
Whiting	*Merlangius merlangus*	cuiteag
Spurdog	*Squalus acanthias*	gobag
Saithe	*Pollachius virens*	piocach
Hake	*Merluccius merluccius*	falmaire
Ling	*Molva molva*	langa
Skate	*Rajidae*	sgait
Angler-fish	*Lophius piscatorius*	carran
Plaice	*Pleuronectes platessa*	leabag-mhor
Lemon sole	*Microstomus kitt*	leabag-chearr
Megrim	*Lepidorhombus whiffiagonis*	—
Witch	*Glyptocephalus cynoglossus*	leabag-uisge
Dab	*Limanda limanda*	—
Sand-eel	*Ammodytidae*	siolag
Conger	*Conger conger*	as-chu
Halibut	*Hippoglossus hippoglossus*	leabag-leathann
Tusk	*Brosme brosme*	—
Turbot	*Scophthalmus maximus*	turbaid
Lythe	*Pollachius pollachius*	liubh

Table 4.1 Demersal species in the Hebrides which have commercial value

Most species have spawning grounds on the Hebridean shelf. The adult fish move back to deep water after spawning but the eggs and infant fish either remain in local nursery grounds where hydrographic conditions favour a settled life, or they drift north-east to waters around Orkney and Shetland and into the North Sea. Cod, whiting, saithe and plaice probably remain inshore for the first two years of life, often in sealochs and then, as recruits to the adult population, they move to the main feeding grounds further offshore. Surface trawling north and west of Orkney, at the outflow of coastal currents from the Hebrides, has netted sufficient numbers of young cod, haddock and whiting to suggest movement of these species from the Hebrides to the North Sea, while tagged cod, haddock and plaice from the North Sea have been caught on

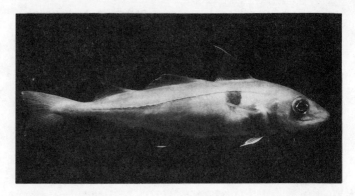

*Haddock (Photo
Crown Copyright)*

the Hebridean shelf, showing that there may be a passage of
adult fish from east to west. Spurdogs are viviparous and there
is evidence of a concentration of fish giving birth off north-west
Scotland in summer.

In the period 1953–67, Bennet Rae (*et al.*) made lists of rare
and exotic species of fish recorded in Scotland. Table 4.2
shows those found on the west coast.

English	Scientific	Gaelic
Blue shark	*Prionace glauca*	boc-glas
Six-gilled shark	*Hexanchus griseus*	—
Frilled shark	*Chlamydoselachus anguineus*	—
Long-finned bream	*Taractichthys longipinnis*	—
Black sea-bream	*Spondyliosoma cantharus*	—
Deal fish	*Trachipterus arcticus*	—
Boar fish	*Capros aper*	—
Sturgeon	*Acipenser sturio*	stirean
Pilchard	*Sardina pilchardus*	geilmhin
Ray's bream	*Brama brama*	—
Red mullet	*Mullus surmuletus*	—
Snipe fish	*Macroramphosus scolopax*	—
Black scabbard-fish	*Aphanopus carbo*	—
Red band fish	*Cepola rubescens*	—
Sunfish	*Mola mola*	—
Electric ray	*Torpedo nobiliana*	craimb-iasg
Pilot fish	*Naucrates ductor*	—
Opah or Moonfish	*Lampris guttatus*	—
Angel-fish	*Squatina squatina*	sgait-mhanaich
Eagle-ray	*Myliobatis aquila*	—
Bogue	*Boops boops*	—
Stone-bass	*Polyprion americanus*	—

Pearl-fish	*Echiodon drummondi*	—
Black fish	*Centrolophus niger*	—
Blue-mouth	*Helicolenus dactylopterus*	—
Tunny	*Thunnus thynnus*	—

Table 4.2   Rare and exotic fish recorded on the West Coast of Scotland

Pelagic fish feed in the surface- and mid-waters. They occur in shoals, feeding on plankton and the young pelagic stages of other fish.

English	Scientific	Gaelic
Herring	*Clupea harengus*	sgadan
Mackerel	*Scomber scombrus*	rionnach
Sprat	*Sprattus sprattus*	—

Table 4.3   The main species of pelagic fish in the Hebrides

The main food of the herring are tiny copepods, including *Calanus finmarchicus*, a key species of the zooplankton upon which depend pelagic fish and possibly the infant stages of some demersal fish. Copepods, in turn, feed on even tinier diatoms and dinoflagellates in nutrient-rich waters flowing northward along the continental shelf.

The plankton have a diurnal rhythm within the photic zone, where sunlight penetrates. During the day, the main biomass

Herring (Photo Crown Copyright)

may be 10m below the surface but, at night, it is much nearer
the surface. At night, therefore, plankton feeders are also near
the surface and within reach of many types of net operated on
the surface. In the Hebrides herring were traditionally fished
with drift nets by small boats, but now, when fishing is allowed,
the pelagic fish are caught by mid-water pair trawlers and
purse-seiners.

Surveys of herring larvae in the plankton show that herring
spawn from late August to early October. The spawning
grounds are mainly within 20–30 miles of the coast, eggs are
demersal, and the herring is rather unusual in that it deposits
its eggs on a carpet of gravel. This localises the spawning
grounds and, because of the large numbers of gravid adults
which congregate in these restricted areas, this has meant that
the herring has been easy to over-exploit. Spawning areas are
smaller in the Hebrides than in the northern North Sea and
occur east of the hydrographic fronts on a line which follows
the western shore of the Outer Hebrides, but east of St. Kilda.
There are also spawning grounds close inshore to the west and
north of Tiree. After hatching, the larvae become pelagic and
disperse slowly until they enter the frontal zone when they are
transported north with the currents. This takes them both into
the sea lochs of the Minch and Skye and into the North Sea.
Here they mature for about two years and they then migrate
back to their natal spawning grounds to be recruited as adults.

Mackerel have a wider diet than herring and can be caught
by lures on short-lines in summer from the inner sounds and
sea-lochs to St Kilda. They also occur on the surface, making

*Mackerel (Photo
Crown Copyright)*

the sea boil with a ripping sound as the shoal breaks the surface and changes direction in the same instant. They feed on macro-plankton and small fish, and there appear to be two stocks which move to and from their spawning grounds in the North Sea and south-west of Ireland respectively. The western stock seems to predominate in the Hebrides and probably constituted most of the catch in the prolific Minch fishery.

There is little known about the distribution of the sprat on the Hebridean shelf. It occurs inshore in winter in the sea-lochs of the mainland and in the Minch and disperses offshore to spawn and feed in spring and summer, small numbers having been recorded off St Kilda and Skerryvore. Surveys of eggs and larvae have shown that large numbers of sprat spawn occur in June in the north Minch and north of the Butt of Lewis. The Norway pout (*Trisopterus esmarkii*) also occurs in the north Minch and on the shelf to the west of the Hebrides in water 100–200m deep. Unlike the sprat, the Norway pout is not found in the inner sounds and sea-lochs; it is a bottom-living fish which inhabits relatively deep areas with a mud substrate. Research ships have recorded stocks similar in density to those in the north North Sea. In the Minch, main concentrations occur between Tiumpan Head, Lewis and the Clash Deeps off Sutherland. Sand eels (mainly *Ammodytes marinus*) shoal on the shelf from the inner sounds to waters around St Kilda. Until recently, this species, which is important feed-stock for predatory fish and sea birds, has been disregarded by the fishing industry, but it is now recognised as a profitable source of oil and meal.

Benthos

The rocky bed of the Hebridean shelf is masked by sediments deposited by past glaciers and past and present rivers flowing westward from the mainland plateau. It is sorted by sea-currents and the activity of benthic animals and man. In the most sheltered areas there are muds, and in the most exposed, bare rock and pebbles; in between there are grades of muddy sand, coarse sand, shell- and 'coral' sand and gravel.

Mud-dwellers like the Norway lobster *Nephrops* and the red-band fish *Cepola rubescens* live in burrows, as do the sea-pens *Virgularia mirabilis* and *Pennatula phosphorea*. Off the east coast of Rum, mud is present at a depth of 20m and this contains the large sea-pen *Funiculina quadrangularis* and the cup coral *Caryophyllia smithii*. The characteristic community of the muds and sandy muds at over 100m contains many bivalves, including the smooth artemis *Dosinia lupinus*, the small razor

Phaxas pellucidus, the basket-shell *Corbula gibba*, the striped venus *Venus striatula*, trough-shell *Spisula elliptica*, *Nucula* spp. and *Abra* spp., plus echinoderms including the heart urchin *Echinocardium cordatum* and the brittle stars *Amphiura* spp. Worms which are present include the proboscis worm *Phascolion strombi*, peacock worms *Sabella pavonina* and *Owenia fusiformis* and the crustaceans *Nephrops* and *Calorcaris macandreae*.

The sand-dwelling community is characterised by bivalves; the razor shell *Ensis arcuatus*, trough shells *Spisula elliptica* and *Abra prismatica* the heart urchin, the worm *Lanice conchilega* and sand-eels *Ammodytes* spp. Bivalves are also found in the gravels, such as the oval and banded venuses, the dog-cockle *Glycymeris glycymeris*, the banded carpet-shell *Venerupis rhomboides*, the rib-saddled oysters *Monia patelliformis* and *M. squama*, the small scallop *Chlamys distorta* and the horse mussel *Modiolus modiolus*. Gastropod snails include, *Colus glacilis*, the cowrie *Trivia monacha*, the grey top shell *Gibbula cineraria*, the whelk or buckie *Buccinum undatum* and *Calliostoma zizyphinum*, plus the sea urchins *Echinus esculentus* and *Psammechinus miliaris*, the starfish *Asterias rubens* and the brittle stars *Ophiothrix fragilis* and *Ophiopholis aculeata*. Crustaceans include barnacles *Balanus* sp. and *Verruca stroemia*, Cup coral, brachiopods, bryozoans and hydrozoans, and the encrusting algae *Phymatolithon calcareum*, *Lithothamnion glaciale* and *L. sonderi* are also present in the gravels.

Among extensive beds of pebbles and boulders off the west and north coasts of Tiree, the community is dominated with *Lithothamnion*, barnacles *B. crenatus*, the sponge *Mycale rotalis*, the colonial squirt *Botrylloides leachi*, vast beds of brittle stars *Ophiocomina nigra* and *Ophiothrix fragilis*, the sea cucumber *Neopentadactyla mixta*, and the banded carpet shell.

The solid rock habitats are well represented in the exposed islands, with near-vertical walls and extensive shelving. Many of these surfaces are swept clear of rock debris and form the walls, floors and ceilings of submarine caves and tunnels, all encrusted with marine growth. This is a world which is shut to all but the most daring of divers in settled weather.

In 1988, Susan Hiscock dived under the plummeting cliffs of St Kilda and found them descending below as above the sea 'with vertical drop-offs to 40m and beyond, huge arches and sheer-sided tunnels'. She found the water exceptionally clear with very good light penetration. Sloping terraces held luxuriant forests of *Laminaria*, and vertical walls were festooned with sea anemones, sea firs (hydroids), sea mats (bryozoans), and sponges. The white anemone *Sagartia* spp., the dahlia anemone *Tealia felina* and the tiny jewel anemone *Corynactis viridis*

were abundant, the latter being the most beautiful, with a brilliant fluorescence. In deeper water, the white trumpet anemone
Parazoanthus anguicomis hung in clusters from overhangs with
its rosettes of tentacles in full display to catch passing plankton.
The mosaics of anemones had patches composed of animals of
identical colouring, representing clones which had developed
from off-buds from a single coloniser. Small pink and purple
sea slugs and small bright red scorpion fish were also caught in
the beam of the diver's torch, which illuminated an underwater
wonderland remote from man.

*Queen scallop
(Chlamys
opercularis) with a
commensal sponge
(Suberites sp.),
starfish (Henricia
sp.), and brittle stars
(Ophiocomina nigra)
(Photo Crown
Copyright)*

    The meeting of the oceanic and coastal waters in the
Hebrides brings together two different biotas. The Hebridean
biota contains southern, or Lusitanian, species in a predominantly Boreal or Atlantic system. Many marine species are at
their northern limits, such as the sponge *Ciocalyta penicillusthe*,
anemone *Aureliania heterocerathe*, paper piddock *Pholadidea
loscombiana*, the cotton spinner *Holothuria forskali*, the bryozoan *Pentapora folicea* and the algae *Bictyopteris membranacae*
plus four others. On the other hand, northern species such as
the anemone *Protanthea simplex* and the soft coral *Swiftia pall-
ida* are at their southern limits. There are rarities to the British
biota such as the anemone *Arachnanthus sarsi* and the alga
Erythrodermis allenii. The large sea urchin *Echinus* is abundant
in the Hebrides and feeds on sessile organisms, locally reduc-

ing the diversity of the sea-bed communities. A comprehensive survey and classification of the varied habitats of the marine benthos of the British Isles is required as an essential prerequisite of nature conservation in British waters. This is already under way, but needs much more research.

Commercial species occupy a wide range of sea-bed habitats: the Norway lobster *Nephrops*, which forms the basis of the popular dish 'scampi', lives in mud; scallops live on sandy gravel; lobsters and edible crabs on the rocky sea bed. *Nephrops* is a burrow-living predator found in fine, sticky mud in the Minch and well into sea-lochs, around Skye and the Small Isles, Mull, Colonsay and the east coast of Islay. Scallops are filter-feeders often lying recessed in the sand, opening the upper valve to feed and breathe, or sometimes swimming freely by clapping of the valves. They occur in depths to 50m. Lobsters and edible crabs are powerful predators, mostly on hermit crabs *Eupagurus* and molluscs. The edible crab is more widely distributed than the lobster. It excavates sandy pits to a depth of 20cm in search of tellins *Tellina* spp. and razor-shells. Lobsters and crabs are caught in depths down to 60m throughout the rock-sand transitions of sea bed, and they thrive in the fringes of the kelp forest. The spiny lobster *Palinurus elephas*, which is at the northern limits of its range in the Hebrides, feeds on echinoderms and molluscs and is present in small

Norway lobster inhabits burrows in seabed mud (Photo Crown Copyright)

numbers to depths of 20m on inshore reefs, often interspersed with steep rock faces and swept by strong tidal currents, off Skye, Raasay, Mull and in the Firth of Lorne.

Squid *Loligo forbesi* migrate inshore in late summer and early autumn preparatory to spawning from December to March. They are taken incidentally in trawls and seine nets and when abundant they are fished directly by trawl and jig and most of the catches are exported to the Mediterranean. Another squid, *Todarodes sagittatus*, is sometimes abundant and taken in trawls. The octopus *Eledone cirrhosa* is taken in lobster creels and *Nephrops* trawls. The shrimp *Dichelopandus bonnieri* is also taken in *Nephrops* trawls and the squat lobster is taken in *Nephrops* creels; the latter lives in sandy muds and gravels close to the mud beds of *Nephrops*.

In 1953 about 100 tonnes were landed in the Inner Hebrides, mostly as incidental 'take' in white fish trawling and seining, whereas in 1979 about 6,800 tonnes, with a market value of £9 million, were landed in the same area as the result of direct fishing. This was 53% of the Scottish shellfish landings of *Nephrops* for that year. Scallops are fished now as much by skin-divers as by dredges. In 1972 a peak was reached when, at Stornoway, 141 tonnes fetched £33,000, while in 1976 the peak was 2,561 tonnes from Inner Hebridean grounds. Stocks of clams in the Hebrides are small compared with other parts of Scotland. In 1980, for example, of the market value of just over £1.1 million, only £15,000 (1.5%) accrued to the Inner Hebrides, with little more from the Outer Isles. Unfortunately, fishing for shellfish can have a severe impact on the sea bed because of the methods used; frequent trawling and dredging of fine muds scarifies and denudes the bottom of the sea.

Plankton

We have spoken of the fish and plankton and the interconnected web of life which knits them into one whole creation. A silk drogue drawn through the surface waters of the Minch at midnight in summer will produce a wonderful display of winking lights. Under the microscope, the washings from the drogue are alive with a diversity of shapes; diatoms, medusae, shrimps, flagellates, eggs, arrow-worms, bizarre larvae of crabs and sea cucumbers. Among them is a copepod, *Calanus finmarchicus*, which is extremely abundant and is the food of the herring, the basking shark and other gill-feeding fish. *Calanus* itself is an efficient feeder with a filter mechanism which retains organisms for ingestion ranging in size from 20–30 microns. Almost all diatoms, flagellates and other single-celled green creatures can be utilised. *Calanus* occupies a crucial position in the food chain, channelling much of the fixed energy of the sun to a diverse range of other animals.

Marine Mammals

Records of whales in British waters have been reviewed by Peter Evans from strandings and sightings. Waters around the Hebrides are thought to be under-represented due to lower coverage of reporting than elsewhere. Nonetheless, 20 species of whale have been recorded from the shelf between Connemara and Cape Wrath, including the North Channel and Hebridean waters (Table 4.4).

English	Scientific	Gaelic
Minke whale	*Balaenoptera acutorostrata*	muc-mhara-mhionc
Fin whale	*B. physalus*	muc-an-sgadain
Sei whale	*B. borealis*	muc-mhara-sei
Blue whale	*B. musculus*	muc-mhara-mhor
Humpback whale	*Megaptera novaeangliae*	—
Right whale	*Balaena glacialis*	—
Sperm whale	*Physeter macrorhinchus*	muc-mhara-sputach
Bottle-nosed whale	*Hyperoodon ampullatus*	—
Cuvier's whale	*Ziphius cavirostris*	—
Sowerby's whale	*Mesoplodon bidens*	—
White whale	*Delphinapterus leucas*	—
Porpoise	*Phocoena phocoena*	peileag
Common dolphin	*Delphinus delphis*	deilf
Bottle-nosed dolphin	*Tursiops truncatus*	muc-bhiorach
White-sided dolphin	*Lagenorhynchus acutus*	*
White-beaked dolphin	*L. albirostris*	deilf-gheal-ghobach
Killer whale	*Orcinus orca*	mada-chuain
False killer whale	*Pseudorca crassidens*	—
Pilot whale	*Globicephala melaena*	+
Risso's dolphin	*Grampus griseus*	deilf-Risso

* deilf-chliathaich-ghil   + muc-mhara-chinn-mhoir   — no Gaelic name

Table 4.4   Whale species recorded from the shelf between Connemara and Cape Wrath.

The porpoise and the white-beaked dolphin appear to be the most common cetaceans in the Hebrides followed by white-sided and Risso's dolphins; minke whales, killer whales, pilot whales and bottle-nosed dolphins are less common but regular in summer. Bottle-nosed whales and common dolphins are uncommon and mainly found offshore, while all others on the list are only rarely seen. Most species occur between April and October. Occurrences of large whales such as the blue, fin and bottle-nose are related to the annual latitudinal migrations, whereas others such as the porpoise, killer whale and the dolphin are resident in narrower latitudinal limits although they can move great distances in search of prey. The large whales breed in low latitudes and probably follow the progressive growth of plankton and shoals of plankton-feeding fish, northward along the continental edge in spring and early summer. The smaller whales, including the pilot whale, killer whale, white-beaked whale and Risso's dolphin, move inshore in summer and autumn, probably following inshore feeding movements of fin-fish and squid.

The porpoise is much more common in the Hebrides from August to October than in other months, and more so on the west coasts of Britain than in the North and Irish Seas and English Channel. This may be due in part to pollution and disturbance by shipping, since chlorinated hydrocarbon residues, similar to those found in fish, seabirds, seals and marine sediment, are found in the fat of porpoises from the North Sea. Hebridean waters are comparatively low in such pollutants, and numbers of porpoises are high. They feed on pelagic fish of less than 25cm in length, mainly herring and whiting, but they also take a variety of other species including mackerel, cod and hake. Salmon are too large a prey for porpoise and records of them taking salmon are probably cases where the identity has been mistaken for the bottle-nosed dolphin with which the porpoise sometimes associates. It also associates with minke and fin whales while feeding on shoals of sprats and sand-eels. Schools of about 10 porpoises are usual but over 100 are occasionally seen together; Fraser Darling saw 'two or three hundred' in the Badentarbat Sound, Summer Isles in 1939 and 150 were seen off Harris in October 1973. Porpoises are born in June; one baby porpoise was found in Loch Hourn in June 1975.

The killer whale is easily identified by its prominent dorsal fin and pale markings behind the eyes, dorsal fin and hind flanks. Killer whales are most surely and frequently identified than most other species of whales although they are sometimes confused with Risso's dolphin because of its large dorsal fin, though the latter may be distinguished by its grey, speckled body. A school of killer whales is an awesome sight; like sharks they have a bad name from their aggressive carnivorous habit of chasing and savaging their prey, particularly other smaller whales and seals. One observer, P. Taylor (Evans, 1980) described a kill by a school of one male, two females and a juvenile:

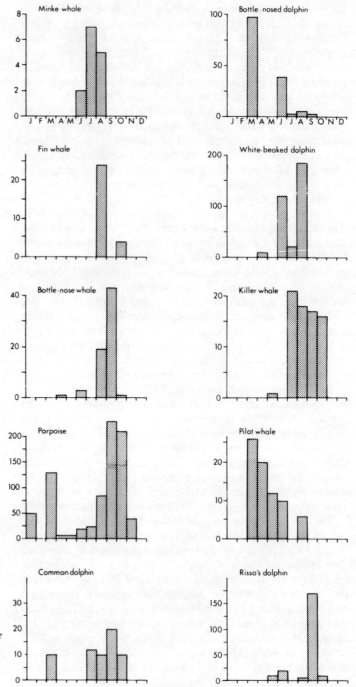

Fig. 12
The seasonal occurrence
of the main species of
cetaceans in Hebridean
seas (adapted from
Evans, 1980)

the herds followed close to the cliffs occasionally making high-pitched squeaks, and then suddenly united and dashed for a seal which was making for the rocks. On capture, the male took it in his jaws and carried it out to deeper waters where the others appeared to queue up and play with the seal before dividing it up.

Currie (1988) reported a pod of six or seven killer whales feeding on seals at the Flannan Isles. The behaviour of killer whales in the wild does not seem to fit the same species that provides such a show of gentleness and affection to its fellow creatures when tamed in a dolphinarium!

Little is known about the breeding of killer whales. They may be polygamous but with stable matriachal social groups. Schools of about 5–10 adult females plus immatures of both sexes with one adult male are often seen—excess young males form bachelor groups. More males become stranded than females. Killer whales disappear from the Hebrides in October and reappear in May; it is thought that they move into distant offshore waters to mate and give birth. Recent research on killer whales off the Pacific coast of Canada has shown that they live in stable family groups of closely related individuals with a high degree of fidelity to a particular home range.

Killer whales have been seen with white-beaked dolphins and diving gannets among herring shoals. They eat porpoises, dolphins, seals, seabirds, large squid, salmon, cod, sand-eels and halibut. Little is known about the false killer whales in the Hebrides, but a herd of six small whales off north-west Scotland in November 1976 resembled this species, and at least one school of false killers has been identified west of the Outer Hebrides in recent years.

The white-beaked dolphin is most frequently seen in the Hebrides in June to September. Herring, mackerel and haddock are reported as important prey and in August large numbers of white-beaked dolphins are seen off the coast of Sutherland, keeping company with Risso's dolphins and gannets. Like other dolphins, small family groups unite to form large ephemeral schools when migrating or when gathered round a prolific source of food. The breeding season is probably between July and September and coincides with the spawning of herring off north Scotland.

Risso's dolphin is relatively frequently recorded, possibly because it occurs inshore in summer and is more easily identified by its grey body and high recurved dorsal fin. In September 1971, a herd of 100–200 was seen off the Outer Hebrides. Because of their ease of identification, some behaviour patterns which are common to many species of whale are attributed solely to Risso's dolphin: 'bottling' like seals, repeated breaching, head-slapping, tail-slapping of the sea's surface and swimming in unison with touching flippers. They probably breed between April and July in deep waters to the south-west and west of Britain, moving into waters around the Hebrides, Orkney and Shetland from June or July to November.

The pilot whale appears in the Hebrides from March to September, but in smaller numbers than in Orkney and Shetland between September and November. This is the species that is hunted so inhumanely on the Faeroe islands. Pilot whales feed mostly on large squid, but cod, turbot and horse-mackerel (*Trachurus trachurus*) have also been recorded. They are often associated with bottle-nosed dolphins and have been seen with large flocks of Manx shearwaters and gannets. It is thought that pilot whales breed in deep waters north of Britain mainly in early spring though births probably occur during most months. In March 1976 a herd of 25 recorded off Lewis included very small calves. There is a correlation between catches of herring and occurrences of pilot whales which suggests that pilot whale numbers in the Hebrides are either directly or indirectly linked to pelagic fish numbers. Common dolphins, white-sided dolphins and bottle-nosed dolphins all feed on squid and a selection of fin-fish including herring, mackerel and salmon. Whitebeaked dolphins also take haddock, plaice and dab while bottle-nosed dolphins feed mainly inshore and in estuaries taking mullet and occasionally 'rounding-up' salmon.

D'Arcy Thompson, whose papers on Scottish whaling 1908–27 are a key to our understanding of the status of cetaceans in Scottish waters this century, recorded small numbers of sperm whales off western Ireland and the Outer Hebrides. Strandings have been from June to August and all have been males; female sperm whales do not migrate as far north as males and are therefore not found in the Hebrides. A juvenile was stranded in the Outer Hebrides in June 1955 and a large bull at Gortantaoid, Islay in summer 1985. Sperm whales probably move northwards in deep water off the edge of the Hebridean shelf in quest of their staple food, squid.

Turning to the baleen whales, the minke, or lesser rorqual, is more common in the Hebrides, Orkney and Shetland, than elsewhere in British waters. It is sometimes seen amongst shoals of sand-eels in company with porpoises and auks. The minke will also take young herring, mackerel and cod, and probably follows spawning concentrations of these species. The fin whale, or common rorqual, occurs in the Hebrides in late summer and autumn, moving along the continental shelf edge. Following the whaling of the 19th and early 20th centuries, this species, amongst others, went into a decline from which it has not yet recovered. In 1974, the population of the North Atlantic was possibly less than 5000. The fin whale feeds on euphausid shrimps and copepods but also forages in deep waters off the Outer Hebrides for herring spawn in September and October. Like minkes, fin whales are usually sighted singly or in pairs. No young fin whales have been seen in British waters and probably the young remain in lower latitudes.

The largest living animal in the world, the blue whale, grows to a length of 30m and weighs up to 150 tonnes. It used to be common, but has become increasingly rare, and is now protected in the North Atlantic, where, until 1955, hunting continued by Norwegian, Faeroese and Icelandic whalers. British hunting ceased in 1928, but earlier, small numbers were landed each year at the Bunaveneadar station, Harris. Two years of whaling in 1950–51 (Maxwell, 1955) yielded six blue whales. In 1974, the population in the North Atlantic was probably less than 2000, with less than 500 in the north-east Atlantic. The huge blue whale feeds mainly on the microscopic euphausids and probably follows the flushes of these and other plankton on the upwelling waters on the continental slope.

The humpback whale is another species that declined because of whaling and, like all other whales, it is now completely protected. Small numbers were landed in Harris but none after 1920 and, though the North Atlantic population may be less than 2000, there are signs of recovery, on the American coast at least. It feeds on plankton swarms, small squid, and young of herring and mackerel. Between 1904–14, 91 Biscayan or right whales were caught just inside the shelf and landed in Harris, but only three were caught after 1918. Even though this species has been totally protected since 1946, there are still no signs of recovery, and the North Atlantic population was assessed in 1974 as 'low hundreds'. Spending the winter in the Bay of Biscay, the right whales, in a similar way to fin and blue whales, probably move northwards and perhaps remain in the Hebrides through the summer. A white whale was seen off Soay, Skye in 1950.

Peter Evans (1982) has also looked into the associations of whales and seabirds. The sea going naturalist in the Hebrides might detect the presence of whales by observing the behaviour of seabirds feeding on similar prey to that of whales, or scraps of whale food or on whale faeces. Cormorants and shags have not so far been recorded in attendance with whales, but being mainly inshore species this is perhaps not surprising. Among the whales the most common seabird associates are minke and pilot whales, common dolphins and porpoises, and among the birds, gannets and kittiwakes. Though whales may be guided to prey by birds, the birds would seem to gain more by following whales which may drive prey species near to the surface and within striking depth of diving birds. During sea passages to the Outer Hebrides, particularly in late summer when gannets are feeding young, a sea-watch of gannets may bring the unexpected sighting of a pod of minke whales or common dolphins.

The Hebrides hold populations of grey seals (*Halichoerus grypus*) and common or harbour seals (*Phoca vitulina*). These are of outstanding interest and are described in Chapter 12. The otter (*Lutra lutra*) is mainly a marine species in the Hebrides, and is described in Chapter 5.

Turtles

The loggerhead (*Caretta caretta*) and leatherback (*Dermochelys coriacea*) appear occasionally. Loggerheads have been reported from Vallay (North Uist) and Dunvegan (Skye), and a leatherback was reported from Tiree in 1985. Kemp's loggerhead turtle *Lepidochelys kempi* was found at Kinlochbervie, Sutherland.

The Sea Shore

The sea shore is the meeting place of sea and land. It is for that reason the most fascinating and the most complex of all the environments of life.

C.M. Yonge

The Vivid Frontier

The realms of sea and land are worlds apart, governed by an entirely different set of physical principles and having their own separate relationships with the atmosphere. However, they are interdependent and face each other across a worldwide frontier of which the shores of the Hebrides form a small but nonetheless wonderful part.

The rocky coast of North Rona exposed to the full force of the Atlantic holds surf-adapted communities, including the grey seal in autumn (Photo J. M. Boyd)

Set in a tempestuous climate and exposed to the full force of the Atlantic's temperate waters, the islands present a front ranging from the high, west-facing, vertical, rocky ramparts of St Kilda to the low, east-facing, silty flats of Loch Spelve in Mull, with all manner of variation and permutation in between: from exposed to sheltered shores, rocky to sandy, and sunlit stretches to sunless recesses of sea caves.

To add to this variety, the habitat is covered by the sea and exposed to the air twice each day. The highest and lowest parts of the shore are covered and exposed by the sea respectively at spring tides once a month—the very highest and lowest perhaps twice a year, at the exceptionally high vernal and autumnal spring tides. Above the full flood of the tide, there is a spray zone which fades further from the sea; conversely, immediately below the full ebb there is a zone of turbulence which fades as the water deepens. The zonation of upper, middle and lower shore is arbitrary and not observed by shore-dwellers, but it serves nonetheless as a useful frame of reference in describing the limits of settlement of species and communities. (The interactions of land and sea which fashion the shore are described by Yonge in Chapter 5 of *The Sea Shore* in this series and is summarised in Fig. 13, taken from that work.)

Fig. 13
Shore levels in relation to tidal changes. In the labelling A = average, E = extreme, H = high, L = low, M = middle, N = neap, S = spring, T = tide, W = water (from Yonge, 1949)

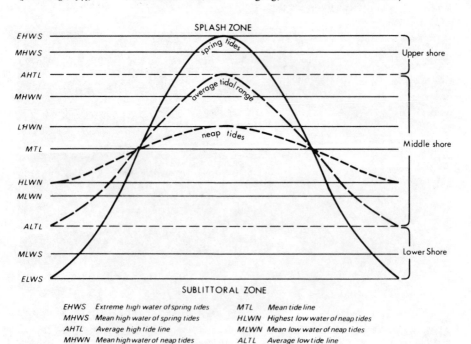

EHWS	Extreme high water of spring tides
MHWS	Mean high water of spring tides
AHTL	Average high tide line
MHWN	Mean high water of neap tides
LHWN	Lowest high water of neap tides
MTL	Mean tide line
HLWN	Highest low water of neap tides
MLWN	Mean low water of neap tides
ALTL	Average low tide line
MLWS	Mean low water of spring tides
ELWS	Extreme low water of spring tides

The character of Hebridean shores is dominated by the stark contrast between the hardness, darkness and angularity of the rocky shores and the smoothness, lightness and elegant curvature of the sandy beaches and wide expanses of tidal flat. An aerial view of South Uist shows this contrast well; the west coast is of the latter and the east coast of the former type, with an entirely different shoreline.

Boulder, pebble and shingle beaches abound in the Hebrides with sometimes banks of all three present on the same shore. The surf has enormous power—at full-strength with a force of over 20 tonnes per m^2, the sea can move large rocks. However, normal surf, with five breakers a minute, will soon reduce the pebbles to shingle and the shingle to sand. A break-point is ultimately reached when the particles become so small that, when wet, each grain has an aqueous coat maintained by capillary action, causing them to slide across one another. Thus the energy of the sea is eventually dissipated upon sandy beaches with little or no physical change to the beach sand and the islands have a beautiful shield from the fury of the Atlantic.

The thrust of the surf up the beach has the effect of building storm-beaches, sometimes of massive boulders like the one at Village Bay, Hirta, but more usually with a bank of large pebbles, which in many of the Inner Hebrides lie about 10m below the post-glacial raised beach. The backwash has the function of shifting and sorting the pebbles into uniform bands, the smallest being carried furthest. With sand of uniform grain-size, the minerals of low specific gravity travel furthest. Thus in the pale shell-sands of Tiree, the heavy dark minerals are left behind (the same principle is involved in panning for gold) and in the dark basalt sands of Mull, the light shelly material travels furthest. In sunshine this dark streaming sand is like polished lignite. Pebbles of a kilogram or more on the floor of the off-shore Laminarian forest, are floated up from the sea bed by the massive growth of weed attached to them, and cast ashore. In time offshore banks of loose small pebbles are transported in this way to the upper shore by storms.

Each year vast quantities of beach material are moved by surf and tide. In summer, sand moves from the shallow offshore shelf onto the beach only to be sucked back into the sea by autumn and winter storms and tides. The sandy beach at Village Bay, St Kilda almost disappears in winter, and over many years we have seen the huge oscillations of sand on Traigh Bhi where we live on Tiree. Strong cross-currents carry material along the beaches in one season and return them in another. Onshore winds, with many hundreds of miles of a 'fetch' across the ocean, pile tides high on the islands; conversely—and with less effect—offshore winds tend to diminish the tide and swell of the ocean and take long veils of spindrift from the top of the breakers.

Each tidal pool is a microcosm with an ecology of its own—not simply a detached particle of the vast ocean. For example, the changes in temperature, salinity, oxygen and carbon dioxide content are much greater than in the open sea, and competition for space and resources between the inmates is also far greater than on the sea bed. The higher on the shore the pool is situated, the greater are the environmental changes in it between tides; exposure to sunshine and shadow affect photosynthesis; wind and shelter affect aeration of the water.

In the Hebrides the tidal pool may lie in the rounded surf-smoothed, sculpture of pink and blue-grey Lewisian gneiss; in rough, brick-red sandstone; among the broken, dark purple pillars of Tertiary basalt and slabs of pink granite; or in the splintered shelves of pale yellow limestone. The shores of Skye possess all these rocky substrates and these, combined with a 360° front to sea, make that island particularly attractive to the naturalist.

In this world of variety, the flora and fauna have adapted to meet the needs of life, each to its own niche with its own formula for survival. Almost all the invertebrate groups have found a place on the shore. There are shore fish, vast numbers

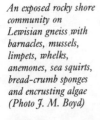

An exposed rocky shore community on Lewisian gneiss with barnacles, mussels, limpets, whelks, anemones, sea squirts, bread-crumb sponges and encrusting algae (Photo J. M. Boyd)

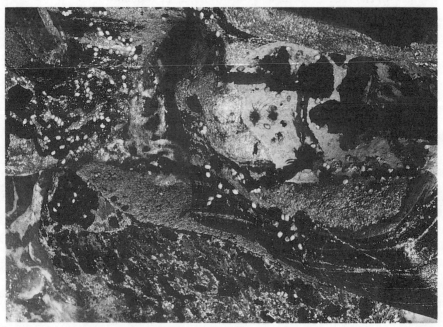

of seabirds and waders feed on the rich pickings of the tideway, and Hebridean shores also have seals and otters. The seaweeds have different sensitivities to turbulence, exposure to air and changes in salinity, and this results in a distinct banding of the shore by different communities of weed, each well settled within the strict limits of its own tolerance to surf, wind and freshwater.

Therefore, the shore is both a fine training ground for the life-scientist and a joy to the naturalist. However, apart from birds and insects, few naturalists have a knowledge of even the most common animals and plants of the shore: molluscs, crustaceans, worms, starfish and sea urchins, sponges, sea squirts, hydroids, medusae and algae, and very few organisms have popular names. Accordingly, we shall select from the assortment of shore communities in the Hebrides, those which are readily recognisable and which possess well known species.

At low tide, the rocky inlets on the east coast of Benbecula show at a glance the pronounced zonation of the seaweeds, characteristic of sheltered shores of the Hebrides. The bevelled sides of the creeks are like a garment woven in various bands of brown and yellow and the shallow, sea-filled lagoons are a mass of tangle moving to the rhythm of the gentle swell. An expression of the same in an entirely different setting is found in the sea caves of St Kilda, exposed to the full force of the Atlantic: the walls are near vertical and their surfaces resemble plasterwork in vivid bands of blue-green, emerald and pink algae above a sea made turquoise by the droppings of countless seabirds. While we attempt to describe the zonation of the shore, therefore, we must stress that no two shores are alike.

Upper Shore

The upper shore is the area above average high tide. In the Hebrides the rocky upper shores are dominated by the channelled wrack *Pelvetia canaliculata*, the flat wrack *Fucus spiralis* and the barnacle *Chthamalus stellatus*. A more detailed examination, however, will reveal the two small periwinkles *Melaraphe (Littorina) neritoides* and *Littorina rudis*. The former reaches well above the highest tide into the spray zone, which is also marked by the grey (*Lecanora* spp.), orange (*Ramalina* spp.) and black lichens (*Placodium* spp. and *Verrucaria maura*) in descending order. The thick top-shell (*Gibbula lineatus*), a true middle-shore snail, just reaches the upper shore. All the upper shore seaweeds (except *P. canaliculata*) and periwinkles (except *M. neritoides*) are found in the middle shore, but none of the

The mixed sandy and rocky shore typical of the shell-sand islands (in this case Tiree), with seaweed beds and rock-pools cheek-by-jowl with sand and pebble beds (Photo J. M. Boyd)

middle or lower shore species mentioned below, appear in the upper shore.

In the uppermost limits of the rocky shore there are often deposits of weed and other jetsam which harbour large populations of the sand-hoppers (amphipods) *Orchestia gammarella* and *Talitrus saltator*. The former was found in North Uist and Barra over 100m from the sea and from west to east coast in South Uist through Loch Bee. The same banks of rotting weed are habitat for swarms of the fly *Clunio marinus*, the bristle-tail *Petrobius maritimus* under pebbles and jetsam, and the seaslater *Ligia oceanica*, which is also abundant under jetsam and in rocky niches in the upper shore. These are all common to the upper sandy and muddy shore as well, and, together with the periwinkle (*M. neritoides*), are more land than sea creatures.

Where there is heavy sedimentation of the shore in sheltered tidal and estuarine flats, there are saltmarshes. These may be narrow strips of salting between shore and land, but are usually flats of closely grazed sheep pasture flooded by the sea at the highest tides. They have erosion features such as pans and creeks, and possess a salt-tolerant flora. The swards are dominated by the saltmarsh grass (*Puccinellia maritima*), thrift

(*Armeria maritima*), sea plantain (*Plantago maritima*), and red
fescue grass (*Festuca rubra*). Usually grazing is too heavy to
allow the full flowering of the saltmarshes in the Hebrides, but
occasionally, when sheep are taken from the machair to the hill
land after the lambing in June, the saltings become pink with
thrift and greatly enhance the beauty of the coast. In exposed
places, scurvy grass (*Cochlearia* spp.) and the sea milkwort
(*Glaux maritima*) are common, and in the sheltered places the
sea aster (*Aster tripolium*) and the glasswort (*Salicornia euro-
paea*) are also common. The sea milkwort, the rush (*Juncus ger-
ardi*), the early marsh orchid (*Dactylorhiza incarnata*) and the
mare's tail (*Hippurus vulgaris*) are found on the transitions to
freshwater habitats.

Though the structure and diversity of saltmarshes would
appear simple compared with other habitats, on closer examination this is not so. The marshes are a mosaic of plant and
animal communities, representing transitions from brackish to
freshwaters, from sheltered to exposed sites, and with pioneer
and long-established swards (Ratcliffe, 1977; Doody, 1986).

*Scurvy-grass on
Dun, St Kilda (Photo
J. M. Boyd)*

Hebridean saltmarshes are generally poor in species, and the frequency of the dominant species can be influenced by grazing; heavy grazing tends to increase the incidence of thrift and plantain, whereas light grazing does the same for red fescue. Nowhere is this more obvious than on the sea-sprayed grasslands of Hirta and Dun, which have saltmarshes on cliff-top slopes. On opposite sides of a sea-filled chasm, Dun, without sheep, has luxuriant fescues, while Hirta, with many sheep, has smooth slopes of thrift and sea plantain.

Saltmarsh habitats are widely distributed in both the Inner and Outer Hebrides. Loch Indaal and Loch Gruinart in Islay, Baleshare and Kirkibost in North Uist, Northton Bay and Luskentyre in Harris, Tong and Gress in Lewis being amongst the most important, but there are many others which provide breeding sites for the oystercatcher, ringed plover, lapwing, dunlin and redshank. In winter, the Hebridean saltings attract large numbers of other waders, and wildfowl (see Chapter 13).

Middle Shore

This is the area between the average high and average low tides, and on gently sloping, moderately exposed shores contains a welter of marine life. The physical surface open to the settlement of living creatures is enormous; the untold hectares of boulders and pebbles as well as the solid bedrock, the capillary surfaces of sands and muds which hold the microscopic interstitial flora and fauna. Also the external surfaces of the animals and plants themselves provide suitable settlement for many smaller creatures and their internal lumen, acting as a home for diverse, highly specialised parasites.

With such a great choice of surfaces and conditions, competition for living-space might logically be light; yet the exact opposite is the case. Each niche is colonised only by those creatures which have become perfectly adapted to maintain themselves within the specialised conditions of the niche to which they are fitted. Life in rock pools, under stones, on and under weed, on firm or loose rock, in sand and mud, and on the backs of animals is a continuous fight for living space. The entire middle shore is clad with life; the only space for new life is in place of the dead and departed.

Species of the upper shore, mentioned above, extend into the middle shore but are not dominant. Channel and flat wracks are replaced by the bladder wrack (*Fucus vesiculosus*) and the saw wrack (*F. serratus*); the former is recognisable by its 'blistered' and the latter by its 'toothed' fronds, often bearing the small white tubes of the worm *Spirorbis*. The bladder wrack

*Beds of wrack showing
the main species of*
Fucus *and*
Ascophyllum *typical
of the middle shore on
sheltered rocky shores
(Photo J. M. Boyd)*

floats upward and is spread on the sea's surface, whereas the
saw wrack is short and is totally immersed; both have great
flexibility and inhabit the exposed rocky coast or areas of strong
tidal current, in which the more delicate knotted wrack (*Ascophyllum nodosum*) cannot thrive (Norton, 1986). The latter
grows vigorously off sheltered shore, occupies great areas of
the middle shore and forms a dense olive-green mat which is
floated upwards in the rising tide by its large bladders. It is
these extensive areas of dense wrack which have been the harvest fields for alginates. The saw wrack is more sensitive to des-
iccation than the others and reaches well into the lower shore
(Schonbeck and Norton, 1978). Another species *Fucus ceranoides* which grows in brackish water along the rocky and shingle margins of estuaries is often in company with a specialised
form of the knotted wrack (*A.n.f. mackaii*) and fresh green
Enteromorpha spp. Other seaweeds are very sensitive to
changes in salinity.

Branched threads (*Cladophora* and *Bryopsis* spp.) grow in
dark green tufts underneath the mats of knotted wrack, the
appearance of which is often greatly changed by luxuriant fes-
toons of the deep red filamentous alga *Polysiphonia lanosa*. The

emerald green sea-lettuce (*Ulva lactuca*) brightens the middle and lower shore, provides food for herbivorous molluscs, is a photosynthesiser of tidal pools and an inhabitant of estuaries. The Hebrides are a meeting ground for northern and southern species of algae. For example the subarctic *Fucus distichus* is found at its southern limit in Lewis and St Kilda; the distinctive southern species *Cystoeeira tamariscifolia* reaches Barra.

There is a fine array of molluscs each beautifully adapted for life on the middle shore. The design of the common limpet (*Patella vulgata*) with its flat, obtuse, conical shell, its massive foot which almost subtends the entire body; its radula or tongue resembling a microscopic band-saw with which it rasps microalgae and tiny sporelings of seaweed from the rock surface, is suited for survival on smooth, exposed rocks. Somewhat different in design and accordingly in distribution are the flat periwinkles (*Littorina littoralis* and *L. mariae*) and the edible periwinkle (*L. littorea*). The former are confined largely to the zone of bladder and knotted wracks upon which the snail feeds. *L. littoralis* is dominant among *Ascophyllum* and *L. mariae* among *F. serratus*. The latter is the most widespread of all the periwinkles on Hebridean shores, ranging from high-water neaps to low-water springs. Living on bare rock surfaces, often in company with limpets and mussels (*Mytilus edulis*) and feeding on algae, it is the only periwinkle to be found below low-water of spring tides.

Zonation of the shore is perhaps more firmly defined by the sessile rather than the mobile animals, particularly the two species of barnacle *Semibalanus balanoides* and *Chthamalus stellatus*. The settlement of these on the shore follows a free-swimming larval life in the sea. They are members of different faunas which meet on the west coasts of Britain; *Semibalanus* is a northern species the spat of which settles on the shore in early summer while the latter settles in autumn and winter; *Semibalanus* occupies the middle and lower shore while *Chthamalus* is on the middle and upper shore. There is an area of overlap but, in the Hebrides, the barnacles on the low shore are likely to be the former and on the high shore, the latter. *Chthamalus* withstands exposure to surf better than *Semibalanus*—on the most sheltered shores it appears in a narrow band about mean high water neaps, always above *Semibalanus*. On exposed faces at St Kilda, *Chthamalus*, of which there may be two species, *stellatus* and *montagui* (Southward, 1976), occurs in the full range of tide and spray zone. *Balanus crenatus*, on the other hand, is sensitive to exposure to air, and is restricted to the lower shore on stones, shells and flotsam. An example of the distribution of barnacles and seaweeds on Goat Island, Jura (Fig. 14) indicates clearly the different sensitivities to wave exposure possessed by the

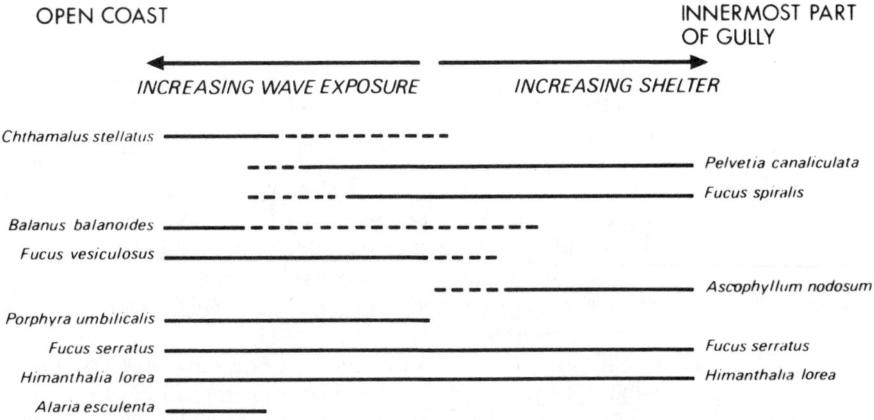

OPEN COAST   INNERMOST PART
                                                             OF GULLY

◄────────────────────────── ──────────────────────────►
      INCREASING WAVE EXPOSURE   *INCREASING SHELTER*

Chthamalus stellatus ─────────── ─ ─ ─ ─ ─ ─ ─ ─ ─ ─
                            ─ ─ ─ ───────────────────────────────────── *Pelvetia canaliculata*
                            ─ ─ ─ ─ ─ ─ ─────────────────────────────── *Fucus spiralis*
Balanus balanoides ─────────── ─ ─ ─ ─ ─ ─ ─ ─ ─ ─ ─ ─ ─ ─
  Fucus vesiculosus ─────────────────────────── ─ ─ ─ ─
                            ─ ─ ─ ─ ───────────────────────────────── *Ascophyllum nodosum*
Porphyra umbilicalis ───────────────────────────
    Fucus serratus ── *Fucus serratus*
  Himanthalia lorea ── *Himanthalia lorea*
    Alaria esculenta ───────────

barnacles and seaweeds which give the Hebridean shores their conspicuous zonation.

The top-shells (*Gibbula cineraria* and *G. umbilicalis*) abound on the middle and lower shore, the latter mainly below low-water neaps. A southern species (*G. magus*) was found on the shore at and west of Kyleakin. The painted top-shell (*Callio-stoma zizyphinum*) with its red, ribbed and mottled cone, is a common yet always admirable find. The dogwhelk (*Nucella lapillus*) is usually off-white, but possesses a wonderful range of colours and is occasionally vividly striped. It feeds on barnacles and occurs in large numbers usually with mussels and periwinkles with which it does not compete for food. Whelks gather in the crevices of barnacle-covered, surf-swept rocks, where they lay clusters of up-ended white egg capsules.

Turning to the sandy and muddy shores, we have an entirely different habitat to the rocky shore. Instead of possessing an ability to hold tight against being swept away and battered in the surf and to sustain considerable changes in temperature, aeration, sunlight and salinity, the fauna (there is little flora) escapes by burrowing to depths of 20cms or more where the habitat is in a fairly steady state between tides. The most exposed beaches of the Hebrides are nonetheless very austere, holding sparse communities of a few highly adapted crustacea, mollusca and worms. For example, at west-facing Traigh na Cleavag at Northton, Harris, using a method of coring to a depth of 10cms, Angus (1979) found only 'a few lugworms (*Arenicola marina*) well below sampling depth and a few sandhoppers (*Talitrus saltator*)'. However, where the strand is more sheltered on the other side of the isthmus at Scarasta, he found seven species, and where it is yet more sheltered at Seilebost and Luskentyre, at least twenty. The exposed beaches usually

Fig. 14
Distribution of species of animals and plants with relation to varying degrees of wave exposure in Jura (after Kitching, Trans. Roy. Soc. Edinb., *LVIII, 368)*

hold small numbers of amphipods (*Bathyporeia* sp., *Pontocrates norvegicus* and *T. saltator*), the isopod (*Eurydice pulchra*), a few worms (*Nephthys* sp. and *Nerine cirratulus*) and sand-eels—no molluscs. Moderately exposed beaches (eg Traigh na Berie, Lewis) have as dominants these worms and bivalves (*Tellina tenuis* and *Donax vittatus*). The sheltered beaches (eg Traigh Mhor, Barra) have the bivalves (*Cerastoderma edule* and *Macoma balthica*), the worms (*A. marina* and *Nereis diversicolor*), the urchin (*Echinocardium cordatum*) and on more muddy and brackish shores, the sandhopper (*Corophium volutator*), shrimp (*Crangon vulgaris*), the snail (*Hydrobia ulvae*) and the crab (*Carcinus maenas*).

Life in sheltered sandy mud and fine mud requires somewhat different adaptations to those that must be made in sand. Apart from withstanding the changes in salinity in estuarine sediments, the fauna have the problems of feeding and respiring in a clogged environment. The cockle and tellins which are abundant in the clean sand are scarce in muddy sand and absent from mud. The thin tellin (*T. tenuis*) is sand-dwelling, while the Baltic tellin (*M. baltica*) thrives in muddy sand.

However, the fine mud has a dense but simple community of the mud-feeding bivalve (*Scrobicularia plana*), the tiny snail (*H. ulva*), the burrow-dwelling amphipod (*C. volutator*) and the rag-worm (*N. diversicolor*), all of which feed on organic detritus. The muddy shore is a comparatively rare environment in the Hebrides, occurring in or near the sheltered estuaries of slow-flowing streams from cultivated land, such as at Bridgend and Gruinart in Islay, at Laxadale in Lewis, or in that ramifying system of tidal embayments and channels north of Lochmaddy, North Uist. In the latter, Edith Nicol found that the salinity varied from 30 to three parts per thousand, and the pH, 5.4–7.8–9.9, from the sea to the brackish-waters respectively. In this range there were 59 marine, 25 brackish, 24 freshwater and five euryhaline species, like sea trout which are at home in both sea and freshwaters.

Eel grass (*Zostera* spp.), the only truly marine, flowering plant, and *Enteromorpha* spp. form green mats on the expanses of mud and sand. The eel grass was greatly reduced by disease in the first half of this century but has since recovered and now abounds in favourable habitats such as the Vallay Strand in North Uist and Loch Gruinart in Islay. *Z. angustifolia* occurs on estuary mud in the middle and lower shore and merges with *Z. marina* which is below low watermark but reaches onto the lower shore. These greens are pasture of the fauna of the sandy-mud, of wigeon (*Anas penelope*) and brent geese (*Branta bernicla*) and form eye-catching, flowing shapes upon the spacious tidal flats.

Lower Shore

Below mean low tide, most of the inhabitants of the middle and upper shore have either disappeared or are greatly reduced in numbers. Among the seaweeds *F. serratus* still persists and is accompanied by dulse (*Rhodymenia palmata*), *Laurencia* spp., *Gigartina stellata*, carragheen (*Chondrus crispus*), tangle (*Laminaria digitata*) and thong-weed (*Himanthalia elongata*). These can sustain heavy wave action, but in the most exposed faces *Alaria esculenta* is dominant. Bootlace (*Chorda filum*) is almost always attached to shells and pebbles and is easily washed ashore. Limpets, barnacles, periwinkles and top-shells of the middle shore reach well into the lower rocky shore, and are joined by the grey top-shell *G. cineraria* and cowries (*Trivia arctica* and *T. monacha*). The large dog-whelk *Buccinum undatum*, whose empty shells and chitinous egg-shell clusters are common on the shore, lives in the sub-littoral and ventures on to the lower shore when young at spring tides. Similarly, the common lobster (*Homarus vulgaris*) and the squat lobsters (*Galathea* sp.) inhabit the flooded cavities under rocks on the lower shore and present a fierce front to the intruder.

In a survey of polychaete worms, J.D. George (1979) recorded 107 species above and below low-tide; 20 confined

The shore at the estuary of the Ord River, Skye, showing the local brackish-water habitats at the river mouth and the marine seaweed beds beyond (Photo J. M. Boyd)

to the littoral zone; 59 confined to the sub-littoral and 28 occupying both zones. Syllidae were dominant with 17 species, notably *Typosyllis armillaris* and *Eusyllis lamelligera* in the holdfasts of laminarians, and *Brania pusilla* in *Corallina*; 12 were Serpulidae, notably *Pomatoceros triqueter* on stones, *Laeospira borealis* on seaweeds and *L. rupestris* amongst *Lithothamnion* and *Corallina*; 11 were Spionidae, notably *Polydora caeca* on *Corallina* and *Pecten* shells; and eight were Sabellidae, notably *Potamilla torelli* in *Corallina* and holdfasts.

The silted, lower shores also have high densities of bivalves, the occurrence of which relates to the salinity and the proportions of sand and mud. The razor-shells *Ensis* sp., the venuses (*Venus* sp.), the wedge-shell (*Donax vittatus*) and the thin tellin, inhabit clean sand, while the gapers (*Mya* sp.) and the Baltic tellin are in sandy-mud.

Distributed in the shore habitats there are many species of fish adapted to the changeable conditions of the rocky, weedy recesses and the shifting sands of shore and estuary. The tidal pool is a study of still life until, moved by shadow, small fish dart hither and thither between hidey-holes in rock and weed. These are likely to be one of the following:

English	Scientific	Gaelic
black goby	*Gobius niger*	—
spotted goby	*G. ruthensparri*	—
common goby	*G. minutus*	buidhleis
butterfish	*Centronotus gunnellus*	clomhag-chaothaich
3-spined stickleback	*Gasterosteus aculeatus*	biorag-lodain

The last fish has a wide range of salt tolerance and is as happy in a tidal pool as in a freshwater stream. At Loch Bee, which spans South Uist from the sand-silted Atlantic shore to the rocky shores of the Little Minch, the three-spined stickleback is found throughout the salinity range while the ten-spined (*Pungitius pungitius*) and the fifteen-spined sticklebacks (*Spinachia vulgaris*) have a more restricted distribution. Flounder (*Platichthys flesus*), sand smelt (*Atherina presbyter*), eel (*Anguilla anguilla*) (easgann), common goby, trout and pollack also occurred. In the large tidal pools of the lower shore and in the rocky sub-littoral, colourful ballan wrasse (*Labrus bergylta*), lumpsuckers (*Cyclopterus lumpus*) and sinister congers are seldom seen except when landed by a foraging otter or heron. Sheets of tidal water on sandy flats contain the young of sand-eel, plaice, dab and flounder.

Shore Birds and Otters

If the detailed biology of the sea-shore is enjoyed only by a few naturalists, the birds of the shore are a delight to all ornithologists. For to them, the Hebrides, positioned on the edge of Europe and facing the great ocean, has the best of both worlds. Many visitors from central Europe, who live far from the sea, are astonished at the variety and numerical scale of the avifauna of the Scottish coasts. All species are to some extent connected with the sea-shore; some, like the oystercatcher (*Haematopus ostralegus*), ringed plover (*Charadrius hiaticula*), herring gull (*Larus argentatus*) and common gull (*L. canus*), feed, roost and breed on the shore; others, like the cliff-nesting oceanic species, have little contact with the shore *per se* but have a manurial effect on the cliff-base. Between these two extremes there are other species which occupy the shore at some time in their annual life-cycle. In the Hebrides, there are some 37 species which nest on the shore above mean high spring-tide within the spray-zone, and some 82 species which regularly occupy Hebridean shores at some time of the year.

In summer the sound of the breakers is mixed with the piercing calls of oystercatchers, the piping of ringed plovers, the screech of Arctic terns (*Sterna macrura*) (and more rarely of little terns (*S. albifrons*)), and the cries of gulls, all anxious for the safety of eggs or young among pebbles, small jetsam and cushions of thrift. To find the nests with their dappled eggs matching perfectly their stony cup is always a thrill, and to spot the fluffy hatchlings crouching in a shady nook, pretending to be just another pebble, is sheer delight. The tiny, sharp, 'tseep-tseep' of the rock pipit (*Anthus spinoletta*) and the shrill but delicate 'tschizzik' of the pied wagtail (*Motacilla alba*) contrast with the harangue of oystercatchers, as they flit back and forth from shore to nesting-sites in the rocks above, often raising two broods under an overhang of thrift or marram grass. Eider ducks (*Somateria mollissima*), red-breasted mergansers (*Mergus serrator*), shelduck (*Tadorna tadorna*) and mallard (*Anas platyrhynchos*) with ducklings, dive and dabble in sheltered weedy inlets. Dunlin (*Calidris alpina*) and redshank (*Tringa totanus*) breed inland and feed on the shore at low tide; in the Uists there are an average of 15 pairs per km^2 of both species on wet machair with over 40 pairs in the densest areas. Small numbers of turnstones (*Arenaria interpres*) and sanderling (*Calidris alba*) which breed in the high arctic, spend the summer on Hebridean shores. Herons (*Ardea cinerea*) nest mostly in trees and occasionally on the ground, but feed on the intertidal, stalking prey in the shallow weedy inlets of the sheltered shores of all the islands.

The shores, particularly of the Uists, attract large numbers of migrant and wintering wildfowl: shelduck, wigeon (*Anas penelope*), teal (*A. crecca*), mallard, pintail (*A. acuta*), shoveler (*A. clypeata*), tufted duck (*Aythya fuligula*), scaup (*A. marila*)—especially in Islay—eider, red-breasted merganser and waders: the oystercatcher, ringed plover, golden plover (*Pluvialis apricaria*), lapwing (*Vanellus vanellus*), sanderling, purple sandpiper (*Calidris maritima*), dunlin, bar-tailed godwit (*Limosa lapponica*), curlew (*Numenius arquata*), redshank, turnstone, and greenshank (*Tringa nebularia*).

To these can be added many rarer species which make the shores of the Hebrides an enchanting place in the bright sharp winter days. Unfortunately the richest areas are shot-over by wildfowlers and the birds take flight at the slightest disturbance except, that is, for the purple sandpipers, which we have had walking between our feet.

The sight of an otter (*Lutra lutra*) on the shore is always exciting; their sleek glistening bodies and elegance of movement in and out of the sea epitomise the beauty of wildlife and the spirit of wilderness. On Hebridean shores the signs of otters are common, and they are often seen. Now fully protected, they are, as Gavin Maxwell described in *Ring of Bright Water*, very confident in their undisturbed habitat on the sea shore, diving and foraging among the weed and often surfacing with and landing a lumpsucker, wrasse, pollack, butterfish or scorpion fish (*Myoxocephalus scorpius*). They are often drowned in eel fyke nets and lobster creels, entering the creels, it is thought, to take pollack, codling and congers which are already trapped. In eighteen months during 1975–76, Jane Twelves recorded the deaths of 20 otters (17 females and three males) in eel fyke nets in South Uist and Benbecula. The damage to local stocks must have been great—one netsman accounted for 13 out of the 20! In 1984, after an eight-year cessation, eel-netting recommenced in the Uists, hopefully with safeguards to the legally-protected otter.

The otter has declined in numbers during the last 30 years in England and lowland Scotland, but it is still numerous in the Highlands and Islands and particularly so in the Hebrides and Shetland. In the 1977–79 survey of otters in Scotland, the highest numbers were recorded from Islay, Colonsay and Oronsay; the largest holts which we have seen were on Eilein Ghaoideamal off Oronsay, Am Fraoch Eilean in the Sound of Islay and at Kylerhea in Skye, where the Forestry Commission has built a hide from which the otters can regularly be seen. The survey showed that the otter is mainly a marine species in the Hebrides, though its spraint and runs are widespread throughout the islands. In the Outer Hebrides 227 sites were examined and 221 (97%) showed signs of otters. During the survey, 20 otters were seen by chance in daylight and only two of these were inland; 18 were in the marine habitat and 12 were seen in the Hebrides. The east coast of the Outer Hebrides—uninhabited, sheltered, indented, rocky and weedy—is ideal otter habitat which is now attractive to fish-farmers. A code of practice is required for the management of fish-farms and otters and other protected species of wildlife, and this is now in hand (see p. 366). The fishing otter is often accompanied at a safe distance by a herring gull keen to take scraps of food, and in Norway the presence of otters is often shown by a hovering sea-eagle, ready to swoop and dispose of any fish the otter might land. The same may now happen in the Hebrides with the recently reintroduced sea-eagles (see pp. 287–90).

Of all the habitats possessed by the Hebrides, the sea-shore is by far the richest in life and the most interesting to the naturalist. It is also an inspiration to artist and poet alike, and an unending source of wonder to both old and young. To us the pellucid 'crab' pools in the surf-polished gneiss in front of our house are tiny cells, brimming over with life and cupped in the oldest rock in the world but to children, they are sheer magic!

CHAPTER **6** **Sand Dunes and Machair**

Windblown Sands

In the Hebrides, there are sands of pure quartz such as the Singing Sands of Camus Sgiotaig on Eigg, coral sands at Claigan near Dunvegan on Skye, basalt sands at Carsaig in Mull, heterogeneous mineral sands in many islands, but most of all, there are shell sands formed from the ground-up remains of marine invertebrates and algae. Large geographical structures owe their existence to these sands of organic origin; the large sweeping beaches of the Outer Hebrides, backed by high, extensive systems of dunes and slacks which lead inland to a smooth, flat sea-meadow or machair. The Hebridean machair has no exact equivalent anywhere else. It is similar to links but is richer in calcium carbonate—about 20% on links compared with 80% on machair. This has a concomitant effect on the flora and fauna it supports and, if anything, makes it a richer habitat.

Dry sand begins to move when the wind is travelling at about 16km/10mph or more. Dry, windy weather moves sand on beaches and 'mobile' dunes, while on-shore winds move it inland to become locked up in the terrestrial system. Off-shore winds return the sand to the sea only to be recycled to the beach by tide and wave-action. In the wet, windy weather most prevalent in the Hebrides, rain wets the sand and the hydrogen bonding of water in the thin, wet crust binds the grains and prevents sand-blow.

Behind the beach the land is upswept, usually to an undulating vegetated landscape but, in sheltered places on lee shores, it gives way to a relatively level, green platform. The frontage of slope and scarp varies greatly between and within systems according to their rocky settings, angle to the prevailing winds, and history of coastal and sea level changes. Islands like Oronsay, Tiree, the Monach Isles and Vallay which are encircled by sand have sandy landscapes of great variety. The storm coasts have ramparts of sand raised 10m with extensive, upwind systems of dunes, while those on lee shores have scarpes of 2m with little or no formation of dunes. The contrasts of windward and leeward shores are succinctly seen in

the sandy isthmuses of Eoligarry and Vatersay, Barra and Vaul, Tiree, and Toe Head, Harris. The Eoligarry is a particularly important site to which we will return.

The Luskentyre Banks, Harris, possibly the highest shore dunes in the Hebrides (Photo J. M. Boyd)

In Chapter 5 we explained the transformation of the Hebrides by blown sand on a front from Luskentyre, Harris to Laggan, Islay with a major lee coast system at Broad Bay, Lewis associated with the local formations of New Red Sandstone. Every system is different, but all are created by the same set of physical and biological forces and man's use of the land. The sand forms a platform, often on top of raised beaches, fluvio-glacial deposits or glacial till, and stretches landward until it strikes bare country rock or blanket peat. In the Uists and Benbecula, the sandy platform sometimes lies upon peat; at Borve in Benbecula, the peat is found below low-water mark. It was apparently placed at that level by a rise in sea level some 5,800 years ago, due to the melting of the ice-sheet.

To understand the dune landscape, the mind's eye traverses the millenia since the islands were rid of the ice, and sees a

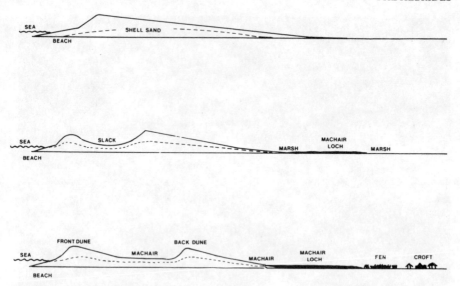

Fig. 15
Three stages in the development of the dune-machair system of the Hebrides showing the accretion of sand and the shaping of the present-day landform. (simplified from Ritchie, 1979)

build-up of high ridges of thinly-vegetated sand above the shore. These ridges were roughly shaped by the wind into wedges of sand possessing a steep seaward scarp, a crest and a long landward slope. However, the simultaneous processes of sand movement, plant colonisation and human settlement have caused large-scale changes in the wedge-shaped profile. The up-sweep of the wind on the scarp above the shore causes not only the build-up of shore sand, but turbulence also serves to disrupt the dune ridge, to form an array of crests and long hollows or slacks. By erosion and deposition, the slack becomes progressively wider and on the landward side, it is bounded by the 'reretreating' scarp of the wedge. This is clad with a gently-sloping grassland on sandy loams stretching inland to fen, cultivation, peatland or bare rock. (This physiographical system has been studied in detail by William Ritchie and colleagues from whose work Fig. 15 has been adapted.)

The dunes and machair are open habitats, spread out for all to see, masked neither by water nor by scrub wood or tall herbs, due to grazing and exposure. There are three main zones; upper beach, dune and machair. If the upper beach has no sand, there are no dunes or machair. However, though most sandy beaches do have associated dunes and machair, Mather and Ritchie (1977) found that almost 22% of the beaches had machair but no dunes. In full development (which is usually achieved only in part at any one site) there is the following zonation from sea to island's core: foredune, mobile dune, fixed dune, machair, old hay-meadow, fen and loch, cultivation and heath. These zones are characterised by their landform, vegetation and fauna.

There are sharp contrasts. The dunes and machair are free-draining and though subject to drought, locally the land is flooded seasonally by the rising water table in deep slacks or by loch margins, and this is faithfully reflected in the flora and fauna. Other contrasts occur between the vegetation of calcareous loams of the machair and the acid, peaty gleys of the heathland known in the Outer Hebrides as 'blackland'. There are also contrasts between tilled and untilled machair and between different stages of natural recolonisation of ploughed ground. Striking contrasts are obtained by leaching of nutrients from the dune humps into the hollows where there is also enrichment by moisture, shelter and the manure of grazing stocks. More subtle effects are caused by induced deficiencies, where the uptake of essential elements by the plants is prevented by the high alkalinity of the soil.

Upper Beach and Foredunes

This is a dry, salty, sand-blasted, habitat between the high spring tide and the front of the main dune. Colin Welch and others have studied the shore beetles living in the rotting, weedy, jetsam of the upper shore at 24 sites in the Outer Hebrides. Twenty-two species were collected from six families of which 16 were Staphylinidae. The hydrophilid *Cercyon littoralis* was taken at 21 sites, and other dominants were the seaweed-frequenting staphylinids *Omalium riparium*, *Atheta vestita* and *Anotylus maritimus* and the weevil *Philopedon plagiatus*, which probably feeds on the roots of marram grass. Fifteen species were taken at Luskentyre, Harris and on the Monach Islands. The wrack-fly *Orygma luctuosa* and the shore-beetles *Cercyon littoralis* and *Micralymma marina* occur on both sides of the Atlantic.

The upper shore rings with the calls of breeding oyster-catchers and ringed plovers. In summer their eggs and young are camouflaged among the sandy shingle, while the parents draw the attention of the intruder with the 'broken wing' display. Arctic and little terns also nest there and greet the visitor with a sudden dive, bill-stab and high whistling *kee, keee-yahor kirri-kikki*. Gulls, hooded crows, starlings, rock-pipits and pied wagtails which nest in neighbouring habitats feed on the rich insect pickings of the upper shore and in the winter there are, amongst other migrants, turnstones, dunlins, sanderlings and curlews, which move in with the floodtide.

The saltmarshes occur in the transition between marine and

freshwater habitats and are often associated with the sand
dune-machair landscape, for example, at Luskentyre and
Northton, Harris, the Vallay Strand and Baleshare, North
Uist, and Iochdar, South Uist. However, saltings are usually
just within the reach of the highest spring tides (see Chapter 5).

Well separated clumps of marram grass, *Ammophila arenaria*, trap the beach sand and form isolated shaggy-topped
sandhills on the backshore. No other plant can keep company
with it in this exposed position. The rhizomes grow both horizontally and vertically to collect moisture from both rain and
deep groundwater, and this network of roots also holds the
sand fast. Marram thrives in mobile sand with each inundation
forcing upward growth and positioning the roots at greater
depth of sand with improved moisture. The lyme-grass *Leymus
arenarius* is an east and north coast species which is relatively
uncommon in the Hebrides, but where it does occur, it rein-
forces the marram in the mobile dunes. There is no obvious
reason for its low incidence in the west, though it is more sensitive to wind-exposure and sand-blast than marram.

In areas where the amounts of blowing sand are moderate to
light and which are very occasionally reached by the sea, the flat
sand at the foot of the main dune holds a community of sand
couch-grass (*Elymus farctus*) and the succulents sea sandwort

*A foredune with
marram grass at
Scarasta, Harris
(Photo J. M. Boyd)*

(*Honkenya peploides*) and sea rocket (*Cakile maritima*). Orache (*Atriplex* spp.) flourish where the beach pebbles have been blown clear of sand. In one such site in Benbecula we have seen the oysterplant (*Mertensia maritima*) with its spreads of blue-green fleshy leaves and deep blue flowers.

Dunes

The rampart of dunes facing the sea is usually mobile and the scarp face may be rutted by cattle and sheep with slips and slumpings of marram turf. These are the 'yellow' dunes in which the marram grass rises from freshly deposited sand, and nurses a thin plant community including red fescue (*Festuca rubra*), ribwort plantain (*Plantago lanceolata*), lady's bedstraw (*Galium verum*), bird's-foot trefoil (*Lotus corniculatus*) and wild white clover (*Trifolium repens*). Landward of the 'yellow' dune there is the 'grey' dune in which the density of the herb community has increased. The marram, somewhat thinner, rises from immobile sand masked by vegetation in which the sand sedge (*Carex arenaria*), common ragwort (*Senecio jacobaea*) and the moss *Rhytidiadelphus squarrosus* are added (p. 114).

The habitat is sufficiently clement for the snails *Helicella itala* and *Cochlicella acuta*, which are found throughout the machair, with the dune snail *Cepaea hortensis*. The 'grey' dune also has a thin community of soil invertebrates, some of which become concentrated in cow-pats which, when wet and fresh, are favourable niches for insect larvae, mostly flies and beetles, and the pioneering earthworms *Lumbricus rubellus* and *Bimastus tenuis*. When dry, red ants *Myrmica rubra* and *M. scabrinodis* are found in the dung. In the dune slacks the damper, more sheltered, and humid conditions support a green sward. These are oases in the austere duneland, often having a richness equal to or surpassing the machair. The slacks attract livestock for shelter, rest and pasture, and are often heavily manured. There is a sense of peace and prosperity in these sheltered hollows, bright with flowers and possessing thriving communities of insects, myriapods (the millipede *Cylindroiulus latestriatus*), snails, slugs (*Arion ater* and *Agriolimax* spp.) and earthworms (such as the *Lambricoides* spp.).

Rabbits (*Oryctolagus cuniculus*) have been introduced to most islands and they thrive in the easily dug, well-drained soils of the dunes. The juxtaposition of excellent burrowing habitat and the rich feeding grounds of the slacks is ideal, providing a short dash for safety from feeding areas when the silhouette of the buzzard (*Buteo buteo*) appears overhead. Rabbits probably have a significant effect on the development of the dunes

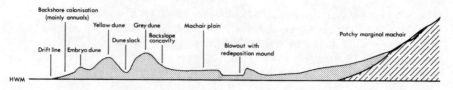

Backshore colonisation
(mainly annuals)

Yellow dune   Grey dune   Machair plain

Dune slack   Backslope concavity   Patchy marginal machair

Drift line   Embryo dune   Blowout with redeposition mound

HWM

Fig. 16
A transect across dune and machair from the sea's edge to the rock base of the island, showing the range of features described in the text (From Mather and Ritchie, 1977)

because they increase erosion, and they crop the vegetation close to the ground. It is also probable that they affect agriculture. In the Uists and Benbecula it is usual for sheep to be grazed on the dunes and machair whereas on Tiree, where there are no rabbits, cattle are also grazed on the machair, presumably because the lack of rabbits allows the kind of pasture growth more suited to cattle.

These more or less isolated assemblies of plants and animals in a relatively simple ecological setting have attracted biologists in the past. They possess finite resources, can become genetically separated for long periods, and endure different selective pressures resulting in varying frequencies of different morphs of the same species, as happens with the snails *H. itala* and *C. hortensis*. The ecology of each can be subtly different according to such factors as their differential tolerance to seasonal drought or flooding, and parasitism.

Though the dunes are a distinct landscape and ecological zone, they are a patchwork of biological communities some of which have the character of a desert, others of a fruitful land. In the transect of the dunes and the machair, the zonation of vegetation and fauna is as distinct as on the sea shore; the marine influence disappears when, one by one, the salt-tolerant, sandy species vanish from the sward. Landward of the 'grey' dune, there is the backslope (Fig. 16) which may be the clean sweep to a flat grassy plain or a tumult of hillocks, some still topped with wispy marram, which fade into the undulations of the machair plain. On the backslope the characteristic dune community changes to that of the machair, and marram and sand sedge disappear from the sward.

Dry Machair

Beyond the major divisions of upper shore, dunes and machair, there are many minor subdivisions which defeat description here. While marram is dominant in the dunes, it is not on the machair, yet the lady's bedstraw, ribwort plantain, bird's-foot trefoil and white clover are found throughout the entire system. It is therefore only after highly detailed study that the variability of the dune-machair system can be described. However, out of the list of flowering plants (Tables 6.1 and 6.2), there are some species which are constant in all machair systems. In addition to the four species mentioned above these are red fescue, yarrow (*Achillea millefolium*), creeping thistle (*Cirsium arvense*), buttercup (*Ranunculus acris/bulbosus*), eyebright (*Euphrasia* spp.), daisy (*Bellis perennis*) and the moss *Rhytidiadelphus squarrosus*. The dune slacks, which are flooded seasonally, have glaucous sedge (*Carex flacca*), silverweed (*Potentilla anserina*), creeping willow (*Salix repens*), marsh pennywort (*Hydrocotyle vulgaris*) and meadow grass (*Poa pratense*). The machair in June is a floristic idyll. Sunlit, fresh green meadows set by the blue sea are washed with the yellow of buttercup and trefoil and white snowdrifts of daisies and clover. In hay meadows and other ungrazed places there are waving stands of white gowans (*Chrysanthemum leucanthemum*), self-heal (*Prunella vulgaris*), yellow rattle (*Rhinanthus minor*), kidney vetch (*Anthyllis vulneraria*) and red clover (*Trifolium pratense*) among the grasses. The purple milk-vetch (*Astragalus danicus*), normally an east coast species, is found in Tiree hay meadows.

If machair is left ungrazed for a period of years, as it often is in burial grounds and airfields, the red fescue grows deep and rank, and eliminates nearly all other species, though ragwort (*Senecio jacobaea*) and knapweed (*Centaurea nigra*) survive in tall, isolated stalks. Such places demonstrate the importance of grazing in maintaining the diversity of the machair flora, though overgrazing often spoils the beguiling scene. Limited cultivation as happens on the Uists could, on the other hand, provide a valuable seed bed for dune annuals.

The machair flora varies from island to island and from place to place in the same island. Machair plant lists can be found in: Macleod (1948) in Barra; Vose *et al* (1957) in Tiree and Randall (1976) in the Monach Isles. Table 6.1 gives a list of the main species which constitute the floral spectacle and the botanical interest for which the machair is famous.

Table 6.2 gives a summary of the dominant species of plants in the dune-machair habitats in the Uists by Dickinson and Randall (1979). The Nature Conservancy Council (1986) has published details of 39 botanical sites in the Outer Hebrides, which show the rarer species and exemplary machair communities. For example, the one on the small island of Fuday, Barra is especially rich in orchids with uncommon species such as the small white (*Pseudorchis albida*), and at Uig Sands, Lewis the frog orchid (*Coeloglossum viride*) is found. The moss campion (*Silene acaulis*) is also found at Mangersta Sands.

The floristic richness of the machair, however, depends on the flowering opportunities of the pastures in the face of grazing and cultivation. Most plants which are palatable to sheep

Species	Habitats			
	d	dm	wm	fm
Marram grass *Ammophila arenaria*	*	*		
Sand couch-grass *Elymus farctus*	*			
Frosted orache *Atriplex laciniata*	*			
Sea rocket *Cakile maritima*	*			
Curled dock *Rumex crispus*	*			
Silverweed *Potentilla anserina*	*		*	
Daisy *Bellis perennis*	*	*		
Sea sandwort *Honkenya peploides*	*			
Ribwort plantain *Plantago lanceolata*	*	*		
Sea plantain *P.maritima*	*			
Wild white clover *Trifolium repens*	*	*	*	
Red clover *T. pratense*		*		
Lady's bedstraw *Galium verum*	*	*		
Red fescue *Festuca rubra*	*	*	*	
Sea kale *Crambe maritima*	*			
Wallpepper *Sedum acre*	*			
Oyster plant *Mertensia maritima*	*			
Moss *Rhytidiadelphus squarrosus*	*	*		
Liverwort *Peltigera canina*	*	*		
Moss *Hylocomium splendens*		*		
Moss *Thuidium delicatulum*		*		
Moss *Pseudoscleropodium purum*		*		
Moss *Hypnum* spp.		*		
Hogweed *Heracleum sphondylium*		*		
Meadow buttercup *Ranunculus acris*		*		
Bulbous buttercup *R.bulbosus*		*		
Lesser spearwort *R. flammula*			*	
Lesser celandine *R. ficaria*			*	
Wild carrot *Daucus carota*		*		
Lesser meadow rue *Thalictrum minus*		*		
Kidney vetch *Anthyllis vulneraria*		*	*	
Lesser burdock *Arctium minus*		*		
Ragwort *Senecio jacobaea*		*		
Yarrow *Achillea millefolium*		*		
Yellow rattle *Rhinanthus minor*		*	*	
Eyebright *Euphrasia* spp.		*		
Field gentian *Gentianella campestris*		*		
Purging flax *Linum catharticum*		*		
Milkwort *Polygala vulgaris*		*		
Primrose *Primula vulgaris*		*		
Harebell *Campanula rotundifolia*		*		
Frog orchid *Coeloglossum viride*		*		
Creeping bent grass *Agrostis stolonifera*		*		
Crested dog's tail *Cynosurus cristatus*		*		
Sand sedge *Carex arenaria*		*		
Carnation-grass *Carex panicea*		*	*	
Ragged robin *Lychnis flos-cuculi*			*	

Species	Habitats			
	d	dm	wm	fm
Cuckoo flower *Cardamine pratensis*		*		
Pennywort *Hydrocotyle vulgaris*		*		*
Vetches *Vicia* spp.		*		
Violets & pansies *Viola* spp.		*		
Self-heal *Prunella vulgaris*		*		
Marsh bedstraw *Galium palustre*		*		
Creeping willow *Salix repens*		*		
Marsh cinquefoil *Potentilla palustris*		*		*
Amphibious bistort *Polygonum amphibium*			*	
Common sorrel *Rumex acetosa*			*	
Bog stitchwort *Stellaria alsine*		*		
Common spotted orchid *Dactylorhiza fuchsii*		*		
Early marsh orchid *D.incarnata*			*	
Northern marsh orchid *D. majalis* ssp. *purpurella*			*	
Twayblade *Listera ovata*			*	
Sea pearlwort *Sagina maritima*			*	
Yorkshire fog *Holcus lanatus*			*	
Meadow grass *Poa pratensis*			*	
Jointed rush *Juncus articulatus*			*	
Sweet vernal-grass *Anthoxanthum odoratum*			*	
Field horsetail *Equisetum arvense*		*		
Autumnal hawkbit *Leontodon autumnalis*		*		
Marsh foxtail *Alopecurus geniculatus*		*		
Spike-rush *Eleocharis palustris*			*	*
Yellow flag *Iris pseudacorus*				*
Common reed *Phragmites australis*				*
Mare's-tail *Hippuris vulgaris*				*
Bulrush *Schoenoplectus lacustris*				*
Marsh marigold *Caltha palustris*				*
Water mint *Mentha aquatica*				*
Bogbean *Menyanthes trifoliata*				*
Fool's watercress *Apium nodiflorum*				*
Marsh ragwort *Senecio aquaticus*				*
Blue water speedwell *Veronica anagallis-aquatica*				*
Bottle sedge *Carex rostrata*				*
Greater tussock-panicled sedge *C.paniculata*				*
Soft rush *Juncus effusus*				*

Table 6.1 A list of species of plant from the dune-machair system taken from N.C.C. ed. Hambrey (1986), Dickenson & Randall (1979) and showing the distribution in dune (d), dry machair (dm), wet machair (wm) and fen/marsh (fm) habitats.

English	Scientific	Gaelic

1 Dune types

Active dune front
Marram grass — *Ammophila arenaria* — Muran
Hastate orache — *Atriplex prostrata* — Ceathramham–caorach
Sea sandwort — *Honkenya peploides*
Moribund dune front
Marram grass
Red fescue — *Festuca rubra*
Ribwort — *Plantago lanceolata*
Lady's bedstraw — *Galium verum*
Bird's foot trefoil — *Lotus corniculatus* — Adharc–an–diabhail
Wild white clover — *Trifolium repens* — Seamrag–gheal
Dune back
Marram grass
Red fescue
Lady's bedstraw
Ribwort plantain
Wild white clover
Ragwort — *Senecio jacobaea* — Buaghallan
Moss — *Rhytidiadelphus squarrosus*
Sand hill
Red fescue
Marram grass
Lady's bedstraw
Ribwort plantain
Wild white clover
Moss — *R. squarrosus* — Coinneach

2 Grassland types

Machair grassland
Red fescue
Meadow grass — *Poa pratensis*
Marram grass
Wild white clover
Ribwort plantain
Daisy — *Bellis perennis* — Neoinean
Bird's-foot trefoil
Moss — *R. squarrosus*
Dune slack
Carnation-grass — *Carex flacca*
Meadow grass
Red fescue
Silverweed — *Potentilla anserina* — Brisgean
Pennywort — *Hydrocotyle vulgaris* — Cornan–caisil
Moss — *R. squarrosus* — Coinneach

Table 6.2 Summary of the characteristics of machair vegetation in the Uists devised from Dickinson and Randall (1979) and showing the dominant species (in descending order in each habitat) in dune and grassland habitats of the dune-machair system.

The sea-pansy in South Uist (Photo J. M. Boyd)

and cattle have a greatly reduced opportunity of flowering, and thus of advertising their presence. We have walked the machairs of the Hebrides for almost forty years, and in summer the land has almost always been heavily grazed or cultivated pasture. In June 1988, however, while walking on ungrazed machair in Tiree amid countless flowering common orchids (*Dactylorhiza* spp.), we came across our first pyramidal orchid (*Anacamptis pyramidalis*)—a single lonely plant blooming gaily in utter isolation from its own kind. Never had we seen such a luxuriant orchid meadow. Yet, had it been in summer grazing, there would have been few orchids in evidence. Only in ideal flowering conditions which produced hundreds of thousands of the common species, did we see the single, shy rarity.

The fauna of the dune-machair system is nothing like so well-studied as the flora. However, while the ecological distribution of species is largely undescribed, a considerable list has been compiled from pitfall and ultra-violet lamp traps. In the 1950's, one of us described the distribution of earthworms and snails in ten dune-machair areas in the Inner and Outer Hebrides, and made comparisons between grazed and ungrazed machair on Tiree (Boyd, 1957). Sixteen species of earthworm were recorded and the same 16 on grass moor in different proportions, but only seven species on heather moors, all taken by the same methods. Everywhere *Lumbricus rubellus* was dominant over all others. In the dunes the sub-dominant

Machair in Tiree in June with bloom of buttercups, daisies and clovers (Photo I. L. Boyd)

was *Bimastus tenuis*; in the machair and cultivated soils *Allobophora caliginosa*, *Dendrobeana octohedra* and *L. castaneus* were also prominent; in the moorland *D. octahedra* and *B. eiseni* were the sub-dominants. These are not deep-burrowing worms and they do not raise large casts. They play a vital role in the aeration of the sandy loams without exposing sand on the surface. Locally, populations of *L. terrestris*, *Octolasium cyaneum* and *O.lacteum* raise large casts which are dispersed by the wind. Machair soils which have not been over blown by sand for centuries and which have never been tilled are organic moulds up to 20cms deep, resting on hard inorganic sand into which earthworms do not penetrate. These shallow, sandy soils are very vulnerable to drying-out, a process which can be accelerated in rainless summers by the activity of earthworms just as it can by the disturbance of rabbits and grazing livestock.

In his list of the non-marine invertebrates of the Outer Hebrides, Rodger Waterston has included species which live mainly or exclusively in sand dunes, but does not specify the habitat preferences—these may be found in the many papers which are cited in the references to his paper. However, in 1976 Dr Colin Welch and others conducted invertebrate surveys using pitfall and ultra-violet light traps from 18 sites situated mostly in the dune-machair habitat in the Outer Hebrides. In the pitfall traps a total of 155 species of beetle were caught of which 30 were Carabidae and of the remainder, half were Staphylinidae. Out of 31,000 beetles recorded about 10,000 were carabids dominated by the genus *Calathus*, especially *C. fuscipes*, with others prominent such as *Serica brunnea*, *Leiodes dubia* and *Silpha tyrolensis*, which are truly representative of a dry habitat, *Megasternum obscurum*, a scavenger of the litter layer, and *Tachyporus chrysomelinus*, a predator of aphids and other small insects which is more commonly found in lush wet habitats.

The data were complex in their interpretation. For example, the staphylinid *Xantholinus linearis* was taken from every site sampled with only 136 specimens, while the dung-beetle *Geotrupes vernalis* was taken from only three sites with 133 specimens. The survey yielded 25 species which were recorded from the Outer Hebrides for the first time, all of which have been recorded in Waterston's list. *Lathridius anthracinus* was recorded at Valtos, Lewis, the most northerly recording in Britain, and *Laemostenus terricola* and *Aleochara cuniculorum*, which live in rabbit burrows, had only been recorded once previously.

Welch (1983) also listed the Coleoptera of the Inner Hebrides. He found 937 species distributed over 15 of the best documented islands, compared with 605 species of beetle on Waterston's list for the Outer Hebrides. The list for the Inner Hebrides is compiled from 78 works, which gives some indication of the ecological background of the species, but again does not identify them to habitat. Our own work in Tiree concerned the dominant species of beetle caught in pitfall traps in grazed and ungrazed machair at Crossapol.

On the grazed ground the most numerous beetles by far were the Chrysomelids (*Longitarsus* spp.), though in biomass the catch was dominated by harvestmen, particularly *Phalangium opilio*. Such groups as *Calathus melanocephalus*, *Tachyporus* spp., *Aphodius* spp. (breed in dung-pats), *Longitarsus* spp., *Sitona* spp., *Apion apricans* and *P. opilio* seem to be favoured by the conditions on the grazed grassland. *Sitona* spp. and *Apion apricans* feed and breed on legumes such as *Trifolium pratense*.

The ungrazed machair had a soil fauna dominated by harvestmen and spiders and the carabid *Pterostichus niger*. Almost all the species caught in the traps showed marked differences between the grazed and the ungrazed ground, the one exception being the spider *Pachygnatha degeeri*. Other spiders were also greatly affected; *Lycosa pullata* was abundant on the ungrazed ground and almost absent from the grazings, while the opposite was the case with *L. tarsalis* and *L. monticola*. The green grasshopper *Omocestus viridulus* was much more abundant on the ungrazed ground. Ants nested and spent the winter in the ungrazed cover and went out onto the grazings in the spring.

The dunes can be an array of suntraps on summer days, giving strong insolation. The slacks can become infested with flies, the larvae of which are found in the soil, dung-pats or as parasites, such as the fly *Sarcophaga nigriventris* or the snail *H. itala*. Other winged insects are the meadow brown (*Maniola jurtina*), common blue (*Polyommatus icarus*), small tortoise-shell (*Aglais urticae*) and grayling (*Hipparchia semele*) butterflies. In the ultra-violet light traps, set mainly in machair areas in the Outer Hebrides, Welch caught 33 of the 367 species of Lepidoptera listed by Waterston for the islands as a whole. The common rustic (*Mesapamea secalis*), and the dark arches moths (*Apamea monoglypha*) were taken at every station, and were the most numerous species of the catch.

The belted beauty (*Lycia zonaria*) is abundant on the machair; the caterpillars feed on legumes and iris and the females are flightless, laying eggs on boulders, driftwood and fence posts. Welch found that numbers fell off dramatically from south to north in the Outer Hebrides. Some lepidopterists have read too much into the distribution pattern of the belted beauty, postulating land connections to explain the presence of the flightless females. However, as Peter Wormell has commented, the affinity of the gravid flightless females for wood has probably taken them to sea on small wooden craft and cargo. There is also the possibility of the females being carried to islands *in copula*. Nonetheless, the distribution in the Outer Hebrides against a constantly high presence of their food plants is interesting and worthy of further study.

The bumble bees *Bombus lucorum magnus*, *B. hortorum* and *B. muscorum liepeterseni* (formerly *smithianus*) are generally common on the machair. *B. distinguendus*, *B. ruderatus* and *B. lapidarius* are patchy in their distribution and possibly still extending their range in the Hebrides. The cuckoo-bee *Psithyrus bohemicus* and the fossorial bee *Colletes floralis* occur in both the Outer and Inner Hebrides, the latter burrowing in firm dune scarps, flying in sunshine and, in dull weather, remaining in its burrow with head protruding. *B. jonellus hebridensis* may be found on the machair, but is more numerous on heather.

Wet Machair

At the landward side of the machair plain the land often becomes marshy, with open water in the Uists, Benbecula and

Tiree forming chains of machair lochs. The seaward shores of these are sandy and part of the machair habitat, while the landward shores are part of the 'blackland' habitat with muddy, sometimes peaty margins often with bare rock and *Phragmites* fens.

Many species of the dry machair are still present in the wet communities. Red fescue and the sedges *Carex panicea* and *C. flacca* are dominant, with other prominent flowering plants such as lesser spearwort (*Ranunculus flammula*), the lesser celandine (*R. ficaria*), ragged robin (*Lychnis flos-cuculi*), cuckoo flower (*Cardamine pratensis*), marsh pennywort (*Hydrocotyle vulgaris*), marsh cinquefoil (*Potentilla palustris*), amphibious bistort (*Polygonum amphibium*), marsh bedstraw (*Galium palustre*), orchids (*Dactylorhiza purpurella* and *D. fuchsii* spp.), lesser twayblade (*Listera cordata*) and the autumnal hawkbit (*Leontodon autumnalis*). The field horsetail (*Equisitum arvense*) and the common spike rush (*Eleocharis palustris*) are also common.

The wet machair is often severely poached by cattle, at the margins of lochs or streams on ground which is seasonally flooded. Such areas may have dense stands of mare's tail (*Hippuris vulgaris*), bulrush (*Schoenoplectus lacustris*) and iris, or a community dominated by the marsh pennywort, common sedge, marsh cinquefoil and water mint (*Mentha aquatica*). The ditches and permanent marshes contain the water speedwells (*Veronica anagallis-aquatica* and *V. catenata*), marsh marigold (*Caltha palustris*), celery-leaved buttercup (*Ranunculus sceleratus*), fool's water cress (*Apium nodiflorum*), marsh willow herb (*Epilobium palustre*), bogbean (*Menyanthes trifoliata*) and others. In some areas the sedges *Carex rostrata* and *C. paniculata* and the rushes *Eleocharis uniglumis* and *Juncus effusus* are dominant. (The vegetation of the open waters is described in Chapter 10.)

The machair idyll is not only floral—in high summer it is full of bird song: the skylark; the cheeping of meadow-pipits; the wheezy *pee-wit, pee-wit* of lapwings; the liquid *toowe, toowe* of ringed plover; the shrill *klee-eep, klee-eep* of oystercatchers; the *tuuu . . . tuuu . . . tuuu* of redshanks; the trill of dunlin; the *chip-per, chip-per, chip-per* of snipe; the screech of terns and cries of gulls. The lapwing, oystercatcher and ringed plover are widespread, but are particularly attracted to nest in a diverse machair habitat of mixed cultivation and fallow stripes. The young are raised on the machair invertebrates and, in closely grazed areas, are particularly vulnerable to predation by gulls. Dunlin, redshank and snipe are hefted to the wet machair, nesting in grassy tussocks raised slightly above the damp substrate, where they find an optimal habitat with plenty of food and good cover in the marshy and trampled ground. The survey of waders on the machairs and blacklands of the Outer Hebrides by the NCC, the Wader Study Group and Durham University in 1983 found about 12,000 pairs of these six species. Lapwings were most numerous (*c.* 3,500) while oystercatchers, dunlin, ringed plovers and redshanks were all found in similar numbers (*c.* 2,000). Snipe were least numerous (*c.* 500) (see Part 3, Table VI in NCC 1986). The overall wader density on the land surveyed was 90 pairs per sq km. Similar data are not available for the Inner Hebrides, though a rather low estimate of 2,000–3,000 pairs of all species was made by Reed, Currie and Love (1983), which reflects the relatively smaller areas of machair in the Inner Hebrides.

In winter the machair is faded like a threadbare tapestry. Gone are the flowers and calling birds, but the apparently dead, buff-coloured flats belie the life within; some of it in hibernation in the soil, and some on the surface. It is a lean time for rabbits in their grazed-out, mossy warrens and hares range further to find food. However, in winter, when the mainland is frozen, the machair is an 'open' habitat for waders, and holds large numbers of lapwings, golden plover, curlew and snipe. In February 1975 an estimate was made of around 4,000 lapwings and 2,000 golden plovers, mostly in machair and blackland, in the Uists and Benbecula. Significant numbers of migrant waders visit the machairs in autumn and spring. Native grey-lag geese feed on machair and blackland all year round and are joined in winter by barnacle and Greenland white-fronted geese. It is a common sight on a winter's day on Islay and the Uists to see noisy flocks of geese lifting and settling over the sand dunes and machair in the cold watery sunshine.

Crofts and Farms

CHAPTER 7

Inbye and Blackland

In this book we place the agricultural habitats between those of the coast and the moorland, for that is where they are on the islands. Man has found his best opportunities for cultivation where the sandy ground grades into the peat, and his habitations and field systems have interrupted the natural transition from shore to moorland, providing a habitat for wildlife which borrows from each but which is distinct from both. In the crofting townships, the cultivated land, usually close to the crofthouse, is called the 'inbye', and in the Outer Hebrides it is called 'blackland' in contrast with the neighbouring machair, which is 'light' by comparison.

Crofts and farms consist of enclosed and unenclosed land. Generally speaking, the coastal habitats (dunes, machairs, and salt marshes) and the hill pastures are unenclosed; lands situated between these two are enclosed and have been cultivated. These historical patterns of land use (see p. 332) are described for the crofting system in the Uists by Professor J.B. Caird (1979), and for the farming system in Islay by Dr Margaret Storrie (1983). The enclosed lands are tenanted by individual crofters and farmers, whereas the unenclosed lands in the crofting system are the common grazings of the townships, in which each croft has a share, or in farming, are the grazing outruns of individual farms. Since the last war, the enclosed land has increased. Many machairs have been apportioned among the crofters of each township and fenced in separate fields. Also, patches of moorland have been fenced, fertilised and reseeded by both crofters and farmers. The ecology of the agricultural land has therefore been changed, and the more so through a change in practice, from mixed arable/livestock regimes to a grass-intensive/livestock husbandry.

Patterns of Land Use

The boundary between machair with its light sandy soil, and the hill with its dark, peaty gleys and podzols, is sometimes less

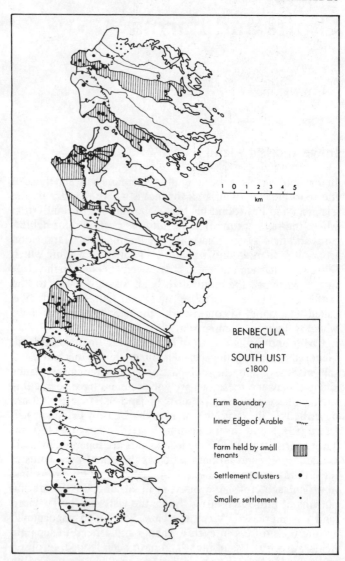

BENBECULA
and
SOUTH UIST
c1800

Farm Boundary	—
Inner Edge of Arable	ᴛᴛᴛᴛ
Farm held by small tenants	▥
Settlement Clusters	●
Smaller settlement	·

Fig. 17
Map of South Uist and Benbecula showing the boundaries of farms, c. 1800, transecting the islands from west to east (from Caird, 1979)

than 100 m. More often, it is extended by cultivation. Caird has shown that around 1800 the farms in South Uist and Benbecula transected the island from west to east, and each farm possessed the full range of habitats from sandy to peaty, exposed to sheltered and shore to hill top (Fig. 17). Later, many of these farms were sectioned into crofts, and in many crofting townships the land was tenanted in narrow strips aligned from shore to hill.

On the rocky break of ground between the machair and the

peatland, the croft house was built within the holding—before crofting times the houses were clustered in hamlets on the farms. The low rounded and thatched dwellings of earlier times have now been replaced by upstanding, gavelled, wide-windowed houses, usually built on the same site. The unfenced strips or rigs were worked in a 'run-rig' system of cultivation and husbandry, contained within a substantial dry-stone dyke, beyond which lay the hill grazings. In the growing season of corn and potatoes in rigs, the livestock were either transferred to the hill, enclosed on the inbye ground, or tethered on the rigs out of reach of crops, but from harvest to seed time, livestock had free run of the rigs. Today, fences have been erected between the rigs, and the run-rig system is largely in disuse. The hill ground also has long-disused *feannegan*, spade-

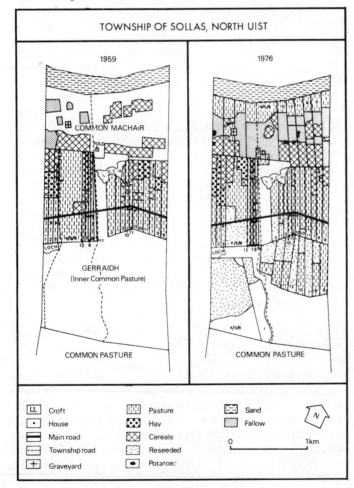

Fig. 18
Diagram of the crofting township of Sollas, North Uist, showing the detailed sectioning of land among the crofter's before and after the apportionment and reseeding of common grazings (from Caird, 1979)

cultivation mistakenly called 'lazy-beds' in English. This form of moorland cultivation, with its ridging and dressing of seaweed, greatly modified the machair-moorland transition, particularly in the Outer Hebrides. Today, only small patches of *feannagan* are worked, but the widespread ecological effects of past husbandry remain.

Caird (1979) has shown how the crofting system has run in the townships of South Boisdale and Sollas in the Uists. We see the sectioning of the habitat which has been wrought over the last two hundred years, and the diversity of use to which the township of Sollas has been put in the production of hay, cereals, old and new reseeded pasture, and potatoes (Fig. 18). While the crofting system was developing in the break-up of the mediaeval farms (Hunter, 1976), a non-crofting landscape of sporting estates and farms with industrial and servicing villages was created in the southern isles. Such a landscape was most highly developed in Islay, with clearance of much cotter settlement from the hill land to the villages, and by emigration. The agricultural habitats in Islay which have become so well known as the wintering grounds for geese which breed in Greenland (see Chapter 13), date from the mid-nineteenth century. Then the island changed hands, with dramatic reduction in the numbers of tenants, extensive drainage, and reorganisation of the field systems to provide arable land for the growing of barley for distilling and livestock for cheese-making. The new estates became sporting land with game-keepers, and the status of game species changed.

The farmlands around Stornoway in Lewis, on Skye, Raasay, Canna, Muck, Mull, Lismore, Islay, Jura, and Gigha are a different agricultural habitat from the crofts, and are more akin to the west mainland. While the fields of these farms are generally larger and more intensively worked than those in crofting townships, they are smaller than those on the mainland, though the farms in Islay bear comparison with those in Ayrshire and Galloway.

Agricultural Habitats

The inbye land is an integral part of the island ecology which has been neglected in comparison with machair and hill. The agricultural habitats have not attracted the naturalist, lacking as they do the num˙rs of species and variety of plant and animal communities posse˷ sed by the uncultivated land. However, the invertebrates are largely undescribed, and the difference between cultivated and uncultivated habitats in the Hebrides (except Islay) is far less than on the lowland mainland.

Exhaustively surveyed, the inbye would probably yield an inventory of plants and animals comparable to the machair. Many species which are common and of little interest in agricultural habitats on the mainland, are uncommon and of greater interest in the islands. For example, the three common species of white butterfly (*Pieris brassicae, Artogeia rapae, A. napi*) are often rare in the Hebrides and feed on Cruciferae in which the inbye abounds, notably as charlock (*Sinapis arvensis*) the weed of cereal crops. Also, species like bumble bees which feed on the machair, nest in the inbye and *vice-versa* for rock pigeons, which nest on the coasts and feed on the inbye. Buzzards, hen harriers, and short-eared owls breed on the moorland but include the inbye in their feeding range, and swallows may find few nesting sites outside the inbye.

The natural history of the inbye is, therefore, worthy of attention both for what it contains and for the contribution it makes to the ecology of the whole island and the archipelago. It is known for its undulating topography, variable soils, complicated wetland with much open and running water, and mosaics of cultivation and fallow in systems of small fields. Hedges are absent, and hedgerow trees almost unknown except in the sheltered sides of the Inner Hebrides. Nonetheless the inbye is, on the whole, a rich and varied habitat for wildlife.

The inbye has a colourful flora of little botanical interest compared to machair and moor, yet most of the species of both may be found somewhere within the agricultural scene. However, the agricultural character of the land is as attractive to the

Crofts at Tarskavaig, Skye, in September 1988 showing neat modern houses amid meadows of rough grass and rushes where once was cultivation. A view looking to the Cuillin Hills (Photo J. M. Boyd)

artist as it is off-putting to the naturalist. The brilliant daisy and buttercup meadows of lightly grazed pasture contain wild white clover, bird's-foot trefoil, eyebright, self-heal, ladies' bedstraw, harebell, tutsan, thyme, and grass of parnassus. Among the ungrazed mixtures of tall grasses (*Holcus, Agrostis, Deschampsia, Anthoxanthum, Cynosurus, Dactylis*) of old hay-meadows in early summer, are the swaying heads of hawkbits, gowans, corn marigolds, meadow sweet, yarrow, knapweed, ragwort, devil's bit scabious, wild parsley, wild angelica, iris, ragged robin, cuckooflower, and marsh marigold. The spikes of early and heathspotted orchids are frequent, particularly in the shelter of grassy ditches, and the lesser butterfly orchid is occasionally found in wet meadows.

These and many others wildly but shyly espouse the stands of crofter rye-grass, corn, and barley. A great deal of the wet blackland, which was at one time well drained and cultivated, has become choked with rushes and sedges. On the farms the flora is generally less varied due mainly to the reseeding, fertilising and heavy stocking of permanent grass. The grass-intensive regimes, with a short growing season in the Hebrides, reduce the botanical interest of the farmland, though it does make it more attractive for some birds and mammals, notably geese, starlings, pigeons, rooks, jackdaws, choughs (Islay), rabbits, hares, voles, fieldmice, moles and hedgehogs.

Farmland on Muck showing good grass and livestock with a shelter belt of trees (Photo J. M. Boyd)

The blackland is dotted with the houses of crofters and farmers providing an assortment of man-made niches not generally present in either machair or moor. These are domestic in character, but their insular situation confers a greater interest

upon them, than would be the case in mainland Britain; for example, in the distribution of breeding house sparrows, swallows, bats, and house mice. Mixed noisy flocks of migratory chaffinches, bramblings, greenfinches, twites and redpolls frequent the stackyards, and collared doves are now common. Around the croft and farmhouses there are beds of stinging and purple dead nettles, rose bay willow herb, docks and thistles which are good for birds and insects.

Throughout the year the blackland attracts large numbers of breeding redshank, lapwing and snipe and smaller numbers of oystercatcher, dunlin, curlew and common sandpiper. The wader survey of 1983–84 in the Uists showed about 100 pairs of waders per sq km, with redshank exceptionally numerous. The wetlands form a continuum with the machair and moorland lochs and streams, and have breeding mallard, teal, tufted duck, red-breasted merganser and occasionally shoveller. In winter there are large flocks of lapwing, golden plover and curlew in the bare fields, mixed sometimes with small assemblies of Greenland white-fronted, grey-lag and barnacle geese, and whooper swans (except in Islay, where the white-fronted are numbered in flocks of hundreds and the barnacle geese in thousands—see Chapter 13).

Corncrakes and Corn Buntings

Corncrake

In surveys conducted in 1968–72 and 1978–79, Dr James Cadbury (1980) showed that, between the two, there was a 56% reduction in the number of 10km squares in Scotland possessing breeding corncrakes (*Crex crex*). On the mainland the reduction was 89% in the east and 61% in the West Highlands, while in the Inner and Outer Hebrides, it was 33 and 3% respectively. In 1978–79, the Outer Hebrides held 260 pairs, the Inner Hebrides about 240 pairs, and Scotland as a whole, about 700 pairs (Table 7.1). Thus the Hebrides held about 71% of the Scottish population.

The corncrake breeds in the machair-blackland transition. Its grating call, drifting across the dusky landscape at sunset, is still one of the familiar sounds of mid-summer in Tiree and the Uists. Neighbouring cocks appear to 'talk' to each other; sometimes they call together but often one 'replies' to another. The migratory birds arrive in April from wintering grounds in Africa, and find their breeding habitat in the Hebrides not yet ready to receive them. Their breeding territories are in the grass and cereal crops and in tall mixed stands of weed species

Corncrake and corn bunting habitat among crofts in Tiree with tall, herb-rich hay meadows harvested in mid-late summer (Photo J. M. Boyd)

(see below), which by April have not yet grown long enough to provide sufficient cover for the birds. However, the iris flags are already well grown and receive the corncrakes, holding them until the hay, corn and weed coverts are grown and nesting begins.

In a survey of the habitat occupied by 190 calling corncrakes in the Inner Hebrides, Cadbury (1980, 1983) found 72% in mown grassland, 17% in rough vegetation, and 10% in marshes. Over three-quarters of those in mown grassland were in recent leys, or improved grassland. When nesting, they prefer the taller hay of the 'improved' leys, but when the chicks are at foot, they favour the less dense, herb-rich, 'natural' meadows.

A more recent study of corncrakes in the croftlands of the Uists by T.J. Stowe and A.V. Hudson (1988) has served to confirm many of Cadbury's observations in Tiree, and to define more precisely the habitat requirements of the species. Daily traces of radio-tagged cocks and hens were obtained. These showed that, while the cocks were sedentary in their calling sites at night, they wandered extensively during the day with much overlap; the hens also wandered widely before nesting, but thereafter settled to incubate and raise the brood of 8–12 eggs without assistance from the cock. Breeding lasts from May–August, and early-laying hens may be double-brooded, so a delay in cutting hay until July would therefore not be a ready solution to the problem of destruction of the birds. Stowe and Hudson, however, point to the requirement of the hay meadow beside areas of rough vegetation—beds of iris, hogweed, knapweed, nettles, reeds, rushes, and tall grass and herb communities on field margins, roadside verges, and around fenced installations are all valuable corncrake habitat. These features should be maintained in context with the hay meadow as escape routes for the birds when forced out by mowing *from the centre outwards*, and not as is traditionally done from the edge inwards. However, the greatest threat of all comes from a change in husbandry from hay to silage, and also from cattle to sheep, since spring grazing of nursing ewes in the inbye rather than on machair or hill reduces the nesting cover for corncrakes.

This well-established and successful pattern of behaviour of the corncrake is set in a diverse habitat of small, often rather weedy, unkempt fields (p. 132). Nowadays, however, the pattern is increasingly disrupted by the making of silage. The mowing of leys for silage in June kills corncrakes, and there is no doubt that if silage is generally made in preference to hay, the corncrake will suffer. The changes in agricultural practice which have wrought such damage to the corncrake in mainland Britain and Europe are now showing themselves in the Hebrides. Still, the changes are by no means uniform throughout the islands; the habitat, weather, and farming practice vary

Corncrake (Photo E. Hosking)

a lot from island to island, and there is a bounty scheme whereby crofters and farmers are encouraged to make hay rather than silage.

(a)

Area of Scotland	10km. sq. 1968/72	10km. sq. 1978/79	% Reduc'n occup. sq.
Inner Hebrides	54	36	33
Outer Hebrides	32	31	3
E Mainland	88	10	89
SW Mainland	67	20	70
NW Mainland	61	24	61
Orkney	30	27	10
Shetland	9	2	78
Scotland	341	150	56

(b)

Outer Hebrides		Inner Hebrides	
Lewis	31	Tiree	85
Harris/Bern'y	12	Skye	31–34
South Uist	83	Coll	28
North Uist	75	Islay	22–24
Benbecula	33	Colonsay	20
Other Sth. Is.	26	Small Is.	18–20
		Other Is.	31
Total	260	Total	235–242
Total for the Hebrides		495–502	
Total for Scotland		688–700*	

* +25 recorded on a single occasion and possibly breeding.

Table 7.1 The populations of breeding corncrakes in Scotland in 1968–72 and 1978–79 shown **(a)** by the numbers of 10km. sq. occupied in each survey period and **(b)** the numbers of regularly-calling corncrakes in the Outer and Inner Hebrides (from Cadbury, 1980).

Corn Bunting and Others

The corn bunting (*Miliaria calandra*) is also in decline in Scotland, but the reasons for this are less obvious than for the corncrake. The main breeding areas are in the coastal plains of cereal farming from Berwick to Buchan, and in the Hebrides, and it is scarce in other lowland farming areas along the

Solway, in the Lothians, Perth, Moray, Orkney and Lewis (Thom, 1986). Ideal habitat for both corncrake and corn bunting still exists in Tiree, where calm summer evenings are full of their callings. While numbers of breedings pairs have declined in or disappeared from other Scottish islands and in parts of the mainland, breeding populations still occur in the machair-inbye of Tiree, Coll, Uists and Benbecula, south Harris and north Lewis.

Corn bunting (Photo E. Hosking)

At the turn of the century, the species was plentiful in islands with machair-inbye land, but by the end of the 1930s it had ceased to breed in the Small Isles, was gone from Mull and Colonsay in the 1940s, and from Skye by the 1970s. Cadbury (1983) carried out biennial surveys in Tiree from 1971–79, and found 61–95 singing, mostly in small weedy fields of oats with margins dominated by hogweed. Dr D.B.A. Thompson informed us that in Tiree the corn bunting population declined in the early 1980s to less than 20 males, followed more recently by a slight increase. At present Tiree is the only island in the Inner Hebrides with breeding corn buntings. The ratio of calling corn buntings to corncrakes in Cadbury's survey was about one to one, though in 1971 it was two to one.

Current studies of corn buntings in the Uists and Benbecula by Des Thompson and Terry Burke indicate that the species has not declined: 160–180 singing males have been estimated in North Uist and 80–110 in South Uist and Benbecula. This could be because 'breaking-in' of uncultivated or neglected land under the Integrated Development Programme may have favoured the corn bunting. Fallow land and dunes are the preferred nesting areas, but fledglings occupy the standing cereal crops of the inbye, where there is better cover from predators and ample food.

The corn bunting is thoroughly promiscuous—in its most favoured habitats both males and females can have several partners. In Sussex, a polygamous male may have as many as nine females, yet in North Uist, Thompson and Burke found that the maximum number of females to one male is three, and that only one in three males were polygamous. The cocks are adept at defending their territories by singing from key vantage points, thus at once repelling other males and attracting females, and providing safe escort for them to and from the nest site during incubation. The largest birds have the most forceful songs and possess the richest territories. Peter McGregor and Michael Shepherd have shown that if the recorded songs of corn bunting cocks are played back to another holding territory, the song reaction of the resident is significantly more aggressive to a near neighbour's song than it is to that of a more distant cock (Thompson, pers. comm.). The Hebridean corn buntings in their open habitat, with their lower numbers and less complicated sex life provide especially good opportunities for research in the ecology and behaviour of birds.

Skylarks, meadow pipits, reed buntings and sedge-warblers are common breeding species. In the Outer Isles and Tiree the coverts of gorse and the niches provided by the human habitations offer breeding sites to a range of songbirds, and food and shelter for passerines on migration. In the Inner Hebrides and around Stornoway where there is more scrub and wood mixed within the crofts and farms, the communities of song-birds are enhanced by wren, dunnock, robin, whinchat, blackbird, song thrush, willow warbler, linnet and yellowhammer.

In total, the blackland-inbye of the crofts and the enclosed land of the farms make a major contribution to the natural history of the Hebrides. The invertebrates are largely undescribed, but it is clear from work already done that the fauna is probably as rich and possibly greater in biomass than that on machair and moor.

Woodlands

CHAPTER 8

Tree-growth in the Islands

The windswept nature of the Hebrides together with rain, flying sea spray, the grazing of sheep and deer and the burning of hill pastures means that conditions for the growth of trees are far from ideal. Yet pockets of woodland do occur, mainly in the sheltered glens of the Inner Hebrides. A major gradient of tree-growth occurs from the exposed western rim of the Outer Hebrides, Tiree and Coll to the sheltered glens and eastern aspects of Islay, Jura, Mull, Skye, Rum and Raasay, where conditions are favourable for production forestry. Small semi-natural woods and plantations occur in most of the Inner Hebrides with the exception of Tiree, where tree-growth is restricted to a few clumps of wind-twisted sycamores, elders, willows and hawthorns in the lee of houses or rock crevices. Natural woods occur on islands as small as Garbh Eileach, Bernera (Lismore) and South Rona, but there are none on the Treshnish Isles.

In the Outer Hebrides semi-natural scrub woodlands are usually restricted to islands in freshwater lochs, and in rocky defiles in the rolling country of peat bogs and exposed gneiss rock. The scrub woodlands that occur in lochs, such as at Loch Druidibeg, South Uist, but also on Lewis and Harris, show the potential for tree-growth in the absence of sheep, deer (only recently introduced) and fire, even where the exposure to wind and salt is high (see also p. 187). Before the advent of man and his grazing stocks, the Outer Hebrides probably possessed a wind-shaped scrub-forest of hardy, broadleaved trees to a height of 200m above sea level, and the ecology of the islands would have been different. However, pollen analyses of sediments in western Lewis show that no true woodland has developed in the relatively sheltered district around Little Loch Roag in the post glacial period (Birks and Marsden, 1979). In the Outer Hebrides trees are present on all the major islands, but are rare and usually much reduced in size. St Kilda, the South Barra Isles, Eriskay, Ronay, the Monach Isles, Berneray (Harris), Taransay, Scarp, Scalpay and Great Bernera are all treeless.

Mixed broadleaved and conifer woodland at Kinloch on the sheltered side of Rum. The woods contain Scots and Corsican pines, larch, Norway maple, lime, sweet and horse chestnut with native alder and birch (Photo J. M. Boyd)

'Policy' woodlands have been planted around most of the large houses, and have made a great contribution to the natural history of islands which would otherwise possess little or no woodland. These vary in character from the dwarf, contorted sycamore around such exposed lodges as Grogarry (South Uist) and Newton (North Uist) to the more sheltered, well-grown woods around Stornoway Castle (Lewis), Armadale Castle (Skye), Kinloch Castle (Rum), Canna House, Torosay Castle (Mull) and Islay House. The policy woods of Colonsay have over 200 species of exotic trees and shrubs.

Shelter belts, hedges and parkland have been planted and add much to the wooded aspect of many of the Inner Hebrides, notably on the well-farmed islands of Canna, Muck (p. 130), Lismore and Gigha, where the aesthetic and ecological effects of the trees are striking. Recent efforts to grow trees on a trial basis on the machair of Tiree failed because the trees were killed by wind and salt when they grew taller than the waist-high wind-shielding fence.

Commercial conifer plantations now cover extensive areas of the Inner Hebrides and there are also experimental plantations of spruce and pine on Lewis. Indeed there is probably more forest-covered land in the Hebrides now than since the beginning of man's widespread settlement of the Isles. Over the past fifty years, the spread of this new forestry, which has covered parts of mainland Argyll and West Inverness-shire, has

reached the Hebrides and the western limits of economic
growth, and in that short time commercial afforestation has
altered the character of Islay, Mull and Skye. Many of the old
birch, oak, hazel, ash and willow woods, which have been
planted through with conifers, though natural in appearance
today, were felled and coppiced in the 17th and 18th centuries to
make charcoal for the Lorne Furnace Company. Their furnace
at Bonawe, on the shores of Loch Etive, consumed much of the
timber yield from natural woodlands around the Firth of Lorne
and Sound of Mull. The First Statistical Account (1792–96)
mentions the sale of areas of natural woodland in Torosay parish, Mull, for iron-smelting and also woodlands at Portree and
Sleat in Skye being coppiced. Fifty years later in the New
Statistical Account, the landscapes of Skye, Mull, Islay and
Jura were beginning to show the effects of new coppice (presumably from the ravages of iron smelting) and of new plantations
of mixed broadleaf and conifer woods. About 1845 the main
plantations in Mull were at Torosay, Kilfinichen, Pennycross
and Torloisk, and on Skye they were at Portree, Kilmuir,
Strath and Sleat. There were others on Raasay.

One of the central questions concerning the history and
development of woodlands in the Hebrides is, did any plants
survive the last glaciation there, 12,000–13,500 BP (years before
present)? A silt deposit from Tolsta in Lewis, carbon-dated to
about 27,000 BP, contains the pollen of an open-herb vege-

*A native ash-hazel
woodland facing the
Sound of Sleat, Skye,
planted through with
conifers, which have
now been removed
(Photo J. M. Boyd)*

tation with willow and juniper. It also contains the Iceland purslane *Koenigia islandica*, which is today confined to Skye and
Mull and which is a plant of the Arctic. However, the evidence
of earliest post-glacial woodland in the Hebrides comes from
the pollen analyses by Dr John Birks and his colleagues
working in loch-bed sediments in Skye. In the late-glacial
period, about 11,500 BP, birch and hazel woods developed in
Sleat and Suardal; they may have regressed during the
readvance of the ice about 10,000 BP, but progressed again at
the beginning of the post-glacial or Flandrian period after
8,000 BP. Birch-hazel scrub was probably the pioneer
woodland community in the sheltered areas into which sessile
oak, ash, wych elm and holly became established as the climate
became drier and warmer. Woodland probably extended its
range well into the period of human settlement, which
commenced about 5,000 BP, and was probably at its maximum
at the end of the climatic optimum in the Sub-boreal about
3,000 BP. At this point, the climate became less favourable for
trees, and man had already started to clear the forest from the
major islands. Pollen research shows that forest cover in the
Hebrides today appears similar to that of 8,000 BP, when
much of the land, which has now been commercially afforested
in the sheltered islands, held mixed woods of birch, hazel, oak,
wych elm, aspen, willow, rowan, bird-cherry and holly, with
transitions from wooded to open ground in response to steep
gradients or exposure to wind, salt-spray and waterlogging of
the soil. There is evidence of past woodland on heather moor,
wet heath and shallow blanket mire, where the former forest
soils have been converted by long-term waterlogging to gleys,
podzols and peats. Since the last war, many such moors have
been afforested (see pp. 341–49). The mires which developed
on flat ground early in the post-glacial period, such as raised
mires, probably never had woodland.

Dean Monro (1549), Sibbald (1684), Heron (1794), Mac-
Culloch (1824) and the Statistical Accounts of 1792 and 1843 all
mention the presence of woods in the Inner Hebrides containing birch, oak, ash, hazel, rowan, wych elm, holly and willows.
During the climatic optimum of the Sub-boreal period
(3,000 BP) there were probably two types of woodland below
the 200m-contour: oak-ash woods on mixed organic and mineral soils in Islay and Mull and in local sheltered pockets on
Jura, Colonsay, Lismore, Eigg and Raasay; and birch-hazel
woods on the more extensive organic soils in the sheltered
aspects of the islands. The Hebrides have largely been beyond
the western limit of pine, although pine was probably present
on Mull, Rum and Skye at one time, and this contrasts with
Norway where pine grows close to the sea on outer coasts.

Native Woodland

Today, oak-ash woods in the more favoured areas of climate and soil have oak dominating in the acid soils and ash on the base-rich soils, with hazel, holly, hawthorn, wych elm, willow and alder all common; bird-cherry, aspen, guelder rose (*Viburnum opulus*) and blackthorn (*Prunus spinosa*) are uncommon while juniper is rare and gean is absent. The birch-hazel woods are on acid soils, in exposed situations, higher elevations, and on north-facing and generally wet slopes where oak and ash cannot live. In these arduous conditions they are joined by rowan, alder and willows, of which the rusty (*Salix cinerea* ssp. *oleifolia*) and eared willows (*S. aurita*) are more tolerant of exposure than the others.

The character of the native Hebridean woods (see p. 142–3) is marked aesthetically by their dwarf form as they cling close to valley and scarp, and ecologically by their oceanic and boreal species. To stand in the mature, broadleaved plantations at Bridgend, Torosay, Armadale and even as far west as Stornoway, is to stand in the woods of mainland Scotland, but to stand in native woods of Coille Mhor on Colonsay or Coille Thocabhaig in Sleat is to stand only in the Hebrides. The oceanic element in these woodland types includes flowering

Coille Thocabhaig, the native oak-birch/ash-hazel wood in Sleat, Skye, which is a National Nature Reserve (Photo J. M. Boyd)

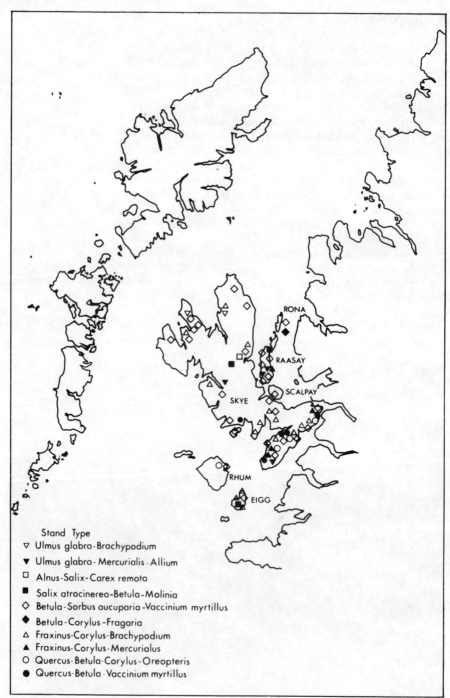

Stand Type

▽ Ulmus glabra-Brachypodium
▼ Ulmus glabra-Mercurialis-Allium
□ Alnus-Salix-Carex remota
■ Salix atrocinerea-Betula-Molinia
◇ Betula-Sorbus aucuparia-Vaccinium myrtillus
◆ Betula-Corylus-Fragaria
△ Fraxinus-Corylus-Brachypodium
▲ Fraxinus-Corylus-Mercurialus
○ Quercus-Betula-Corylus-Oreopteris
● Quercus-Betula-Vaccinium myrtillus

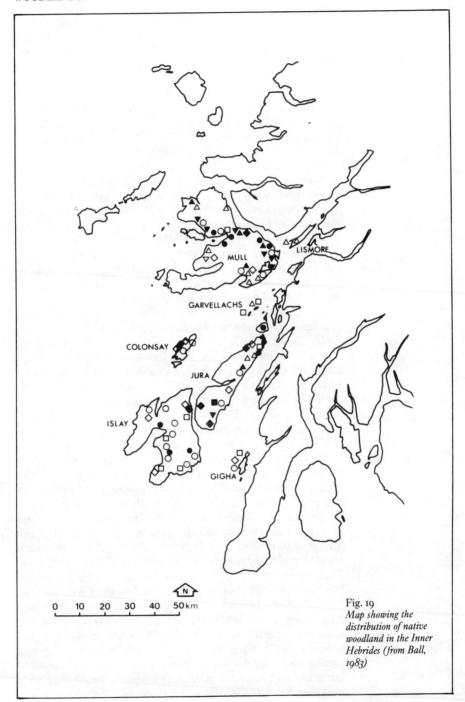

Fig. 19
Map showing the distribution of native woodland in the Inner Hebrides (from Ball, 1983)

plants such as the tutsan (*Hypericum androsaemum*), the climbing corydalis (*Corydalis claviculata*), the hay-scented buckler fern (*Dryopteris aemula*), the filmy ferns (*Hymenophyllum tunbrigense, H. wilsonii*) and the hard shield-fern (*Polystichum aculeatum*). The boreal element includes the globe flower (*Trollius europaeus*), melancholy thistle (*Cirsium heterophyllum*), enchanter's nightshade (*Circaea intermedia*), marsh hawk's-beard (*Crepis paludosa*), stone bramble (*Rubus saxatilis*), mountain melick (*Melica nutans*), the beech fern (*Phegopteris connectilis*) and the scaly male-fern (*Dryopteris affinis*).

These woods are influenced by the grazing of sheep, cattle and occasionally goats, which encourages growth of bracken, purple moor-grass, sweet vernal-grass, Yorkshire fog, creeping soft grass, bents and fescues with false brome and tufted hair grass on base-rich soils. Other common species are wood sorrel, wood anemone, honeysuckle, common violet, germander speedwell, bugle, yellow pimpernel (*Lysimachia nemorum*), and primrose. Also present are the lady fern (*Athyrium felix-femina*), the narrow buckler fern (*D. carthusiana*) and the lemon-scented fern (*Oreopterus limbosperma*).

The Hebridean woods are festooned with lichens, some holding as many as 200 species. Coille Mhor on Colonsay and Coille Thocabhaig in Sleat have had respectively 132 and 129 species of epiphytic lichens recorded (Rose and Coppins 1983). Coille Mhor has the Lobarion community of many species luxuriant upon oak, and also well developed on hazel and ash, while the Graphidion communities coat the smooth bark of hazel. The acid bark of birch holds the *Parmelietum laevigatae* association of many species, and the Usneion communities, containing five species of *Usnea*, are found on willows.

The damp, mild, oceanic conditions of these native woods favour the growth of mosses and liverworts on the trees and the shaded rocky floor. Barks of oak, birch, alder, hawthorn, rowan and conifers are acid while those of ash, wych elm, sycamore, hazel, willows and elder are alkaline. The spongy bark of elder is particularly favourable to mosses and liverworts, and *Metzgeria fruticulosa, Tortula viresens* and *Cryphaea heteromalla* are confined to elder in the Inner Hebrides (Corley 1983), while *Ulota calvescens* and *Zygodon conoideus* are confined to hazel. Several *Orthotrichum* spp. are confined to trees with alkaline bark, and the acid-bark community also includes *U. drummondii* on alder, *Dicranum fuscescens* on oak and *Plagiochila punctata* on sheltered birch stems. Basalt and limestone boulders and scarps provide different woodland substrates from gneiss, granite and Torridonian sandstone for mosses and liverworts, but many species of the genera *Hylocomium, Thuidium, Dicranum* and *Rhytidiadelphus* are prominent in the woodland floor whatever the substrate, and those of *Hypnum, Isothecium, Frullania* on the tree trunks are also ubiquitous. *U. phyllantha* and *F. dilatata* are salt-tolerant and occur on eared willow close to the sea. Twigs have *U. crispa* and rain-tracks, *M. furcata.*

Ash-elm-hazel woods occur on calcarous soils on Jura, Garbh Eileach, Lismore (Bernera), Mull, Eigg, Skye and Raasay. Two types are recognised; one occurs on base-rich, free-draining soils with false brome, water avens (*Geum rivale*), sweet woodruff, enchanter's nightshade, sanicle and wild strawberry; another grows on alluvial loams with dog's mercury, ramsons (*Allium ursinum*), hedge woundwort, herb Robert, red campion and common nettle. Wych elm is often absent, and the ash-hazel stands have the analogues of the above wych elm woods, one typified by the abundance of false brome and the other by dog's mercury. These have admixtures of hawthorn, holly, bird-cherry, blackthorn and dog rose (*Rosa canina*), and bracken, wood sorrel, wood anemone and wild hyacinth are ubiquitous. In wet areas the ash-wych elm-hazel grade into alder-willow carr.

Alder-willow woods occur on soils developed from alluvium, which is flushed with mineral-rich ground water. Alder grows closely together with rusty willow and the shrubby eared willow on the fringes and in the glades. Where the substrate is more acid and less flushed, the alder may be replaced partially by birch. The wet floors of such woods support the remote sedge (*Carex remota*), in abundance with a characteristic wet com-

Wood anemone (Photo J. M. Boyd)

munity including marsh pennywort, yellow iris, meadowsweet, marsh-thistle (*Cirsium palustre*), marsh hawk's-beard, wavy bitter-cress (*Cardamine flexuosa*), marsh ragwort (*Senecio aquaticus*), hemlock water-dropwort (*Oenanthe crocata*), purple loosestrife and rushes. These woods are seldom extensive but they have a widespread distribution on Gigha, Islay, Jura, Garvellachs, Mull, Skye and Raasay.

Oak-birch woods occur on well-drained brown earths and podzols derived from acid rocks. On low ground where oak has been felled or on higher and north-facing slopes which are too cold and sunless for oak, the woods become birch-rowan on mixed mineral-organic soils and birch-hazel on predominantly organic soils. These woods occur on all the large islands of the Inner Hebrides and, unless they occur within forestry deer-fences, are heavily grazed. The ungrazed birch-oak has a floor of blaeberry and the grazed, of wavy hair-grass, moss carpets and hard fern (*Blechnum spicant*). The woods have a bright-flowering community including common cow-wheat (*Melampyrum pratense*), goldenrod (*Solidago virgaurea*), honeysuckle, tutsan, foxglove, primrose, wood-sorrel, wood-anemone and wild hyacinth. The lightly grazed birch-hazel woods have a ferny floor with *Oreopteris*, *Dryopteris* spp., *Athyrium* and *Phegopteris* spp. When heavily grazed, bracken or a community including sweet vernal-grass, bents, fescues, pig-nut (*Conopodium majus*), yellow pimpernel, bugle and enchanter's nightshade becomes common.

In exposed and north-facing aspects of mountain and island, where conditions are hard, the ash, oak, wych-elm, hazel, and alder stands are progressively replaced by birch. At the limits of native tree growth, only birch with eared willow and rowan remain, but the gradation to that limit is different depending on the soil type. The birch is mainly *Betula pubescens*; although *B. verrucosa* is present in the Hebrides, its distribution is as yet unstudied.

The leached mineral soils, or podzols, have a birch-rowan association which may contain scattered aspen, hazel and willow, but juniper is rare. The floor is dominated by blaeberry, bracken, purple moor-grass, bents, sweet vernal-grass, tormentil, wavy hair-grass, hard fern and devil's bit scabious. These woods do not occur on soils derived from basalt or in limestone localities but are otherwise widely distributed. The birch-hazel association on the brown earths is the most common native woodland in the Hebrides, and is recorded on all the islands where woodland occurs. It also possesses hawthorn, blackthorn or sloe, holly, aspen, bird-cherry and guelder-rose, though this is rare. The woodland floor is dominated by bracken, or a grass association (sweet vernal-bents-fescues-false brome), with water and wood avens, common valerian, wild strawberry, enchanter's nightshade, lesser celandine, yellow pimpernel, ferns, sedges and the ever-present primrose, sorrel, anemone and bluebell.

On the flushed gleys, peaty gleys and peaty podzols in gneiss, schist, granite, quartzite and sandstone islands, there is willow and birch. The rusty and eared willows are mixed with birch in similar manner to alder in the alluvial soils. This wood can either be a pioneer of new woody cover on moorland or a relict of erstwhile high woodland—the latter still retaining many of the epiphytic lichens, mosses and ferns of native high forest which the former do not possess. The floor is dominated by purple moor-grass, jointed rush (*Juncus articulatus*), and the mosses *Polytrichum* and *Sphagnum*. Many of the species of ground flora in alder-willow woods (above) are also present in these woods which occur on all islands possessing tree-cover. Pioneer phases of the birch-willow woods are particularly well seen in Eigg and Gigha and have many wet-heath plants such as the cross-leaved heath, bog asphodel, bog myrtle (*Myrica gale*), devil's bit scabious, tormentil, marsh cinquefoil, star sedge and flea sedge (*Carex pulicaris*).

In the Outer Hebrides native woodland is confined to islands in lochs and a few rocky ravines. The largest wooded islands occur in the freshwater lochs of South Uist, with smaller stands of low scrub as at Lochs Laxavat, Ard and Iorach and Loch Orasay in Lewis. The most important ravine woodland is at Allt Volagir near the north shore of Loch Eynort, South Uist. This is a dwarf wood which is so sparse as hardly to merit the term 'woodland'. However, in a habitat so exposed and bereft of trees as the Outer Hebrides, these wooded areas have a biological interest well beyond their physical size. The largest of the island woods is in Loch Druidibeg where the canopy consists of birch (*B. pubescens*), rusty and eared willows and rowan and is up to 3–4m tall. One island has a dense cover of *Rhododendron ponticum*, another has planted firs (*Abies* sp.) and there is another tiny birch-rowan wood beside Loch Spotal. These woods have an undercover of the dog rose (*Rosa canina*), brambles (*Rubus* sp.) and honeysuckle. In some of these woods hazel, aspen and juniper are present and there is a fern-rich ground flora.

The Allt Volagir wood is perhaps the most interesting native wood in the Outer Hebrides since it is regarded as a relict of the woodland which was once extensive before the advent of human settlement and animal husbandry changed the face of the islands. There is a canopy of birch, alder, grey willow, hazel, rowan and aspen, with an under layer of eared willow, juniper, holly, bird-cherry, ivy and *Rubus* sp. and a ground flora

A native wood at Allt Volagir, South Uist, containing at least eleven species of tree and a community of woodland plants (Photo J. M. Boyd)

of wood sorrel, wild angelica and bluebells with mosses, lichens and liverworts. An ash sapling has been seen, and over 60 species of vascular plant have been recorded from the wood which has been made a Site of Special Scientific Interest by the Nature Conservancy Council.

Plantations

The only example of high-canopied woodland in the Outer Hebrides occurs at Stornoway, where, about 1850, James S. Matheson began to create wooded policies around the Castle he had built overlooking the town and harbour. As was the custom in the sylvicultural and horticultural enterprises of the 19th and early 20th centuries, soil was imported from the mainland to supplement the poor native peaty gleys and podzols, and a wide variety of exotic species were used. In the Inner Hebrides, on existing brown earths in Skye, Mull and Islay, noble woodlands developed; the woods have grown well as far west as Stornoway and are greatly cherished by Lewis people for their gentle beauty and the relief they give to their otherwise bare landscapes. Peter Cunningham has studied and enjoyed these woods and their birds since the war, and states:

In the course of time and with considerable foresight and planning a magnificent collection of native and exotic trees and shrubs grew up around the castle, so distributed that no part of the woodlands seem ever without leaf and colour.

The plantations include spruces, firs, cypresses, pines, common beech, copper beech, elm, wych elm, sycamore, ash, oak, laburnum, whitebeam, plum, maple, berberis, azalea, fuschia and rhododendrons. To these can be added the native species which have volunteered their presence in the woods and a large and varied ground- and epiflora. The epiflora (mainly lichens) of the Stornoway and Rodel woods is described by Riedl (1979), who found the trees heavily encrusted by at least 58 species of lichen, while the forks of the trees are festooned by many species of moss and the hard fern.

There is a small plantation at Northbay, Barra, containing 13 species of tree and shrub and harbouring breeding goldcrests. It is a fine covert for migrant birds, and the same can be said for small stands at Grogarry, South Uist; Newton, North Uist; Horgabost and Borve, Harris; Voltos Glen and Glen Tolsta, Lewis. Experimental plots of conifers by the Forestry Commission at Balallan and Valtos have been followed by more extensive plantations of lodgepole pine (*Pinus contorta*) and Sitka spruce (*Picea sitchensis*) at Garrynahine (600 ha.) and Aline (200 ha.) in Lewis. In North Uist other experimental plots by J.P. Sutherland of the North of Scotland College of Agriculture have shown that the most successful exotic species of tree were the grey alder (*Alnus incana*), lodgepole pine, mountain pine (*Pinus mugo*), and native goat willow and wych elm. The best exotic shrubs were *Escallonia macrantha*, *Olearia albida*, *O. macrodonta*, *Phormium tenax* and dwarf mountain pine. Strangely, the list does not include sycamore (*Acer pseudoplatanus*) which by its very presence in existing plantations is one of the best trees for shelter in the Hebrides. These plantations give to the Outer Hebrides a range of habitats and species which might otherwise be absent. James Matheson, the Forestry Commission and other landowners who created these woodlands mainly for shelter, amenity and timber, have made a significant contribution to the conservation of nature as well as providing shelter for people and livestock.

The Inner Hebrides have plantations comparable to those of the mainland, again roughly divided into those of long-standing—mainly in broadleaves and conifers in the 'policies'

A spruce plantation at Braes, Skye, showing regeneration of native trees and bushes by the roadside (Photo C. Maclean)

of large houses or around villages—and commercial, coniferous plantations which are now extensive in Islay, Jura, Mull, Skye, Raasay and Scalpay (Skye). The extent of plantation woodland now greatly exceeds that of the native woodland and, though much of the recently-planted land probably carried native woods in the past, the new plantations have substantially changed the environment of the Inner Hebrides. On balance, that change has so far helped to diversify the environment, though the benefit to nature conservation would be enhanced with the greater use of broadleaf species, open space in the plantations of spruce and lodgepole pine, and the retention of old birch, oak, ash, hazel and willow for regeneration within the deer-fences.

The early plantations date back to the first half of the 19th century, and trees of that period still survive in many of the old policy woodlands. The most popular and successful broadleaf was sycamore, but oak, elm, beech (*Fagus sylvaticus*) and Norway maple (*Acer platanoides*) were widely used with the conifers, Norway spruce (*Picea abies*), European larch (*Larix decidua*), Scots pine, Corsican pine (*Pinus nigra*) and Douglas fir (*Pseudotsuga menziesii*). Despite many of these woodlands having been exploited for their best trees, and used over the last century as shelter for game and livestock, many old trees remain, providing habitat for a variety of wildlife. It became fashionable at one time to collect species of exotic trees in arboreta, so many Hebridean policy woods still contain fine specimens of *Thuja, Araucaria, Cedrus, Abies, Chamaecyparis, Tilia, Hippocastanea, Acer* and even palms and bamboos from subtropical regions.

Woodland Fauna

The plantations in Mull and Skye are dominated by lodgepole pine (50%) and Sitka spruce (40%). Larch has been used for amenity and fire protection (9%) and all others, including broadleaf species, amount to 1%. The moorland habitat gradually changes through growth stages of the plantations. In the five years after fencing, planting and cessation of burning, the grasses become rank, and there is often a spread of heather. The moorland waders may have abandoned the plantation, but songbirds such as the meadow pipit, skylark and wheatear may still remain and be joined by the predatory kestrel, short-eared owl, hen-harrier, fox (Skye only), weasel (except on Islay and Jura) and stoat, feeding on the thriving populations of voles in the luxuriant ground vegetation.

Next comes the 'thicket' stage (from 5–10 years), when the moorland birds have been replaced by willow warblers, whinchats, stonechats, robins, dunnocks, linnets, song thrushes and starlings feeding on the enriched supply of seeds, shoots and insects. By the beginning of the 'pole' stage, from 10–20 years, the canopy has completely closed and the thicket species are replaced by those of the 'mature' stage, 20 years or over, including chaffinches, greenfinches, chiffchaffs, siskins, redpols, goldcrests, blue tits, coal tits, great tits, blackbirds, wood pigeons and sparrow hawks. The number of species of bird increases during the growth stages of the forest but declines when the canopy closes tightly, and thinning of the forest at intervals of 10 years enhances the habitat for deer, birds and insects, as does the maintenance of open space with margins of birch, oak, ash, hazel and willow which have a good epiflora and insect fauna. Berry-bearing trees such as rowan, holly, elder, hawthorn, blackthorn or sloe, guelder rose and juniper are attractive to birds in the roadsides, fire-breaks, stream banks, lochsides and glades. Often the forestry fence encloses old broadleaf woodland which is retained unplanted and managed for natural regeneration. A good example of this occurs near Leitir–Fura, in south-east Skye, where a species-rich, ash-hazel wood within the forestry fence is now being cleared of the young coniferous underplantings, and the development of a mixed woodland by the Nature Conservancy Council on Rum, specifically to encourage a wide variety of

Roe deer fawn in the heather of open woodland (Photo J. M. Boyd)

wildlife, is described in Chapter 15. The woods at Stornoway Castle are the main focus of woodland fauna in the Outer Hebrides, and possess the following species of breeding bird:

English	Scientific	Gaelic
Skylark	Alauda arvensis	Uiseag
Grey wagtail	Motacilla cinerea	Breacan-baintighearna
Pied wagtail	M. alba	Breac-an-t-sil
Dipper	Cinclus cinclus	Gobha-uisge
Wren	Troglodytes troglodytes	Dreathann-donn
Dunnock	Prunella modularis	Gealbhonn-garaidh
Robin	Erithacus rubecula	Bru-dhearg
Whinchat	Saxicola ruberta	Gocan
Blackbird	Turdus merula	Lon-dubh
Song thrush	T. philomelos	Smeorach
Mistle thrush	T. viscivorus	Smeorach-mhor
Sedge warbler	Acrocephalus schoenobaenus	Uiseag-oidhche
Whitethroat	Sylvia communis	Gealan-coille
Chiffchaff	Phylloscopus collybita	Caifean
Willow warbler	P. trochilus	Crionag-ghiuthais
Goldcrest	Regulus regulus	Crionag-bhuidhe
Spotted flycatcher	Muscicapa striata	Breacan-sgiobalt
Blue tit	Parus caeruleus	Cailleachag-cheann-gorm
Great tit	P. major	Currac-baintighearna
Treecreeper	Certhia familiaris	Snaigear
Buzzard	Buteo buteo	Clamhan
Corncrake	Crex crex	Traona
Lapwing	Vanellus vanellus	Curracag
Snipe	Gallinago gallinago	Naosg
Wood pigeon	Columba palumbus	Smudan

English	Scientific	Gaelic
Collared dove	*Streptopelia decaocto*	
Cuckoo	*Cuculus canorus*	*Cuthag*
Jackdaw	*Corvus monedula*	*Cathag*
Rook	*C. frugilegus*	*Rocas*
Raven	*C. corax*	*Fitheach*
Starling	*Sturnus vulgaris*	*Druideag*
House sparrow	*Passer domesticus*	*Gealbhonn*
Tree sparrow	*P. montanus*	*Gealbhonn-nan-craobh*
Chaffinch	*Fringilla coelebs*	*Breacan-beithe*
Greenfinch	*Carduelis chloris*	*Glaisean-daraich*

One of the interesting features of this community of breeding birds is that many of them are at the extreme edge of their range, in particular the whinchat, chiffchaff, willow warbler and treecreeper. Even the garden warbler (*Sylvia borin*) and the wood warbler (*Phylloscopus sibilatrix*) have been recorded in summer. On Lewis many of the moorland birds commute daily or seasonally to and from the Stornoway woods, such as herons, kestrels, merlins, peregrines, hooded crows, ravens and starlings. In winter the dunnocks, robins, thrushes, tits, and finches move from the wood into the gardens of the town; Stornoway with its sycamores and shrubbery is but an urban extension of the neighbouring woodland habitat. The common winter migrants are blackcap (*Sylvia atricapilla*), fieldfare (*Turdus pilaris*), redwing (*T. iliacus*), waxwing, (*Bombycilla garrulus*), brambling (*Fringilla montifringilla*) and a few woodcock (*Scolopax rusticola*), goldfinch (*Carduelis carduelis*) and redpoll (*C. flammea*). No other woodlands in the Outer Hebrides have the same depth and variety of woodland habitat as the Stornoway woods, and few of these species breed elsewhere. However, the long-eared owl (*Asio otus*), the heron and the hooded crow nest on the wooded islands in the lochs.

Bramwell and Cowie (1983) quoting mainly from Taylor (1981), list 42 species of bird, 23 mammals, 3 amphibians and 3 reptiles which are found in the woodlands of Skye, Mull, Jura and Islay. None of these are rare but the distributions on these islands is interesting. Of the 73 vertebrates on this list, 51 were present on all four islands; 6 on three; 10 on two and 6 on one (3 questionable). The last are the brown long-eared bat (*Plecotus auritus*), red squirrel (*Sciurus vulgaris*), fox (*Vulpes vulpes*) and the smooth newt (*Triturus vulgaris*) all on Skye, and the bank vole (*Clethrionomys glareolus*) and polecat/ferret (*Mustela furo*), on Mull.

The nightjar (*Caprimulgus europeus*), which is at the extreme

limit of its range in the Hebrides, has declined in Britain and
has ceased to breed regularly in the Hebrides. It was last
reported from Mull and Jura (1968–72). The great spotted
woodpecker (*Dendrocopos major*) has colonised Jura, Mull and
Skye since 1953 with single birds seen on Islay and Rum, and
the green woodpecker (*Picus viridis*) has bred on Mull since
1979. The robin and redstart (*Pheonicurus phoenicurus*) are
restricted to wooded islands but the latter is absent from Raasay, Canna and Eigg. Breeding fieldfares and redwings have
not yet been recorded from the Hebrides. Willow warblers are
common in all forms of woody cover, but the whitethroat,
blackcap, wood warbler and chiffchaff favour extensive scrub
or tall, mixed woodland with a scrub understory on Skye, Eigg,
Rum, Mull, Jura and Islay.

The goldcrest has colonised the islands that have conifer
plantations, as has the coal tit. The goldcrest is the initial coloniser and adjusts its numbers and distribution in the build-up
of the dominant coal tit. The blue tit is widespread but the great
tit is patchy becoming periodically absent in some of the small
islands like Muck. The chaffinch is abundant and widespread
in all island woods and the siskin, redpoll, bullfinch and
crossbill have all found suitable habitat in the plantations and
native woods. The crossbill in the Hebrides depends on maturing spruce plantations and a wide range of size and age classes
is to its advantage. The siskin, which was noted as absent from
the Hebrides by Baxter and Rintoul (1953), has now also
successfully colonised spruce plantations on Skye, Rum, Eigg,
Mull, Islay and occasionally Raasay and Canna (Thom, 1986).
Bullfinches breed regularly on Skye, Raasay, Mull and Islay
and intermittently in Eigg, Rum and Jura. The tree sparrow is
not necessarily a woodland bird in the Hebrides, breeding as it
has done in the past in treeless habitats such as St Kilda and
Tiree; it still breeds sporadically on Islay, Tiree, Canna, Skye,
Lewis and North Rona.

The fauna of Hebridean woodlands has not been systemati-
cally studied, but the birds, butterflies and moths are reasonably well known. The invertebrates in general are poorly
recorded and many rewarding opportunities await the invertebrate biologist in the study of these woodlands. A variety of
habitats is present because of the wide range of woodland
types, and the new woods created by the Nature Conservancy
Council on Rum provide an especially good opportunity to follow the development of woodland communities in the Inner
Hebrides over the next fifty years. There is already a good
record of colonisation of these woods by Peter Wormell (1977)
and others, and on Canna by Dr J.L. Campbell (1984) over the
past fifty years.

The wood ant (*Formica aquilonia*) is a recent coloniser of the Hebrides and was recorded at Mudalach Wood, on the Skye shoreline of Loch Alsh, in 1975 and 1984. Arboreal insects are well represented in the Hebrides. Even islands where woodland is restricted to isolated patches of scrub on crags or on islands in lochs, there are relict populations of woodland insects. On Rum, for example, there are 130 species of lepidoptera whose larvae feed on trees. Mull has a number of species of lepidoptera typical of deciduous woodland which are present in ancient woodland relicts on the adjacent mainland, such as the marbled brown (*Drymonia dodonaea*) which is typical of oak woods and the scarce prominent (*Odontosia carmelita*) which is typical of mature birch woods.

Colonisation by insects of newly planted woods occurs continuously. Within eight years of planting oak trees at Harris on the south-west of Rum, three species of gall wasp specific to oaks had colonised—the nearest natural oaks were five miles away. Conifer plantations have also brought colonists with them; the pine weevil (*Hylobius abietis*) and several species of bark and wood-boring beetles, plus the pine beauty moth (*Panolis flammea*), the pine carpets, *Thera firmata* and *T. obeliscata*, and the barred red (*Hylaea fasciaria*) are all present. The tawny-barred angle (*Semiothisa liturata*), another coniferous species, is present in the policy woods of Colonsay, and the giant wood wasp (*Uroceros gigas*) occurs in coniferous plantations in the Inner Hebrides together with its parasite, *Rhyssa persuasoria*, the largest of British ichneumon flies.

The purple hairstreak (*Quercusia quercus*), a true forest butterfly living in the canopy of oaks, is found in Coille Mhor in Colonsay together with the vapourer moth (*Orgyia antiqua*). Relict populations of these insects may have survived in this native wood remote from the charcoal burning which ravaged most other oak woods in the 18th and 19th centuries (Wormell 1983). The speckled wood (*Pararge aegeria*) is now found on Islay, Jura, Mull, Eigg, Rum and Canna and many species are likely to be introduced by the attachment of eggs to imported wood. Wormell (1983) mentions geometrid moths with flightless females from woodland habitats which are found in the Hebrides, such as the mottled umber (*Erannis defoliaria*) in Rum and Canna. However, some may occur naturally in solitary situations, since the larvae of the northern winter moth (*Operophtera fagata*) and the scarce umber (*Agriopis aurantiaria*) moths have been found on isolated birches in remote rocky clefts on Rum.

Moorland Habitats

The main road (A865) through the Uists forms the boundary
between the blacklands and moorlands over many miles.
Travelling north from Daliburgh to Lochmaddy, you see on
the right open hill ground rising to the summits of the islands,
and on the left enclosed croftland, often known as the
blacklands, stretching away towards the machair and the sea. In
the previous chapters we have examined all the left-hand area,
and now we turn to the right. This embraces the hill-country
which stretches from the sea shore to the mountain-tops in
some islands. Over most of the coast of the Hebrides there is
little or no effect of blown sand and the moorland borders with
the upper shore. On the rocky west coasts exposed to the force
of the Atlantic, such as on Mull of Oa, Islay; Ceann a' Mhara,
Tiree, Tangaval, Barra; Mangersta, Lewis; and Ruaival, St
Kilda, the moorland facing the prevailing winds is affected by
wind-driven spray, while on the sheltered east coasts this effect
is minimal and the peatland, characteristic of the interior of the
islands, lies hard upon the shore habitats, as around the east
coast sea-lochs of the Outer Isles and the lee coasts of the Inner
Isles.

The effect of sea spray on moorland habitats is described in
Chapter 5 on salt marshes; here we look in detail at the moorland ecosystem which covers most of the islands and which has
been used over the centuries as open-range grazings for sheep
and cattle, as a source of peat for fuel, as a sporting range
mainly for wildfowl, red deer, salmon and trout and more
recently for forestry. The hill ground has its own ecological
zonation which relates mainly to the patterns of waterlogging,
exposure and altitude. Though bare and barren in aspect, there
is in fact considerable variety in a habitat which ranges from the
flat expanses of monotonous deep peat in central Lewis to the
comparatively dry, thin-soiled slopes of the mountainous
islands, especially the base-rich massifs of Skye, Rum and
Mull. Lewis is estimated (DAFS, 1965) to have 595 sq km of
peat to an average depth of 1.5m while the moorlands of Tiree
have no workable peat.

Peat formation depends on rainfall, temperature, topography and country rock. By far the largest land area of the Hebrides has a rainfall, temperature regime, and topography conducive to peat formation, which has continued at different rates during successive climatic periods (see p. 59). The plant communities which have given rise to the peat have also changed. Forest has been very sparse or absent from the Outer Hebrides, Tiree and Canna. The Hebridean peat has therefore been generated by the plant communities of mire, rather than of woodland. Vascular plants and mosses maintain the peat blanket today.

Andrew Currie (1979) has identified the following moor and hill habitats, not all of which are present on each island but which are found throughout all the islands.

Moor	Hill
Sub-maritime heath and grassland	Upland acid heath and grassland
Lowland acid heath and grassland	Upland blanket peat
Lowland blanket peat	Montane flush and snowfields
	Cliff
	Scree
	Boulder field
	Summit

Lowland Heath

Lowland acid heath and grassland is the most extensive habitat of the Hebrides; it merges with other habitats and its dominant species are found over most of the moorland. There are also variants of this acid heath which reflect the degree of waterlogging; the dry areas tend to have more heather while the wet areas have more grass, sedge and rush. Also, in the setting of the Hebrides, species such as red fescue, sea plantain and thrift can be found throughout the altitudinal range of heath from the coast to the mountain tops. Conversely, the arctic-alpine species *Dryas octopetala* occurs on calcareous heaths near sea level in Skye and Raasay.

The plant communities of the acid heaths and grasslands are the main component of the vegetation of the Hebrides which contrast with the calcareous communities of machair and dunes where soil conditions are very different. In general, this is dark country of heather, purple moorgrass, deer grass with

Mountain avens to be found in Skye and Rum (Photo J. M. Boyd)

Sphagnum moss and common cottongrass in the rank wet ground. The proportion of heather to grass is a function of the intensity of grazing and burning as well as the waterlogging of the land. Within the forestry fences on Skye, heather has returned to ground where the land is free from sheep, deer and fire and has generally had better drainage. On the low moorland margins, the influence of sea spray or blown sand brings greenery to the sward with infiltrations of *Festuca-Agrostis-Holcus* communities, which also occur with the moorland around sites of past human settlement such as brochs, derelict crofts, sheilings and sheep folds. Similarly, on the high moorland margins, the effects of altitude, improved drainage and more readily available minerals are shown by spreads of wavy hair grass and mat grass in the moorland patchwork. In the basalt and gabbro country of the Inner Hebrides, where conditions are less acid than on the gneiss, the upper moorlands also possess much sweet vernal, viviparous fescue, and bent grasses.

The following plants determine the character of moorlands:

English	Scientific	Gaelic
Ling	*Caluna vulgaris*	*Fraoch*
Cross-leaved heather	*Erica tetralix*	*Fraoch-frangach*
Bell heather	*E. cinerea*	*Fraoch-a'-bhadain*
Blaeberry	*Vaccinium myrtillus*	*Dearcan-fithich*

English	Scientific	Gaelic
Creeping willow	*Salix repens*	
Purple moor grass	*Molinia caerulea*	Fianach
Deergrass	*Trichophorum cespitosum*	
Common cottongrass	*Eriophorum angustifolium*	Canach
Star sedge	*Carex echinata*	
Common sedge	*C. nigra*	
Pill sedge	*C. pilulifera*	Seisg
Carnation grass	*C. panicea*	
Green-ribbed sedge	*C. binervis*	
Viviparous fescue	*Festuca vivipara*	Feur-chaorach
Creeping soft grass	*Holcus mollis*	
Wavy hair-grass	*Deschampsia flexuosa*	Moin-fheur
Early hair-grass	*Aira praecox*	
Creeping bent-grass	*Agrostis stolonifera*	
Common bent-grass	*A. capillaris*	
Velvet bent-grass	*A. canina*	
Heath grass	*Danthonia decumbens*	
Heath rush	*Juncus squarrosus*	
Soft rush	*J. effusus*	Luachair-bhog
Sharp-flowered rush	*J. acutiflorus*	
Bulbous rush	*J. bulbosus*	
Field wood-rush	*Luzula campestris*	Learman
Heath wood-rush	*L. multiflora*	
Common dog-violet	*Viola riviniana*	Dail-chuach
Common milkwort	*Polygala vulgaris*	
Heath milkwort	*P. serpyllifolia*	
Slender St John's wort	*Hypericum pulchrum*	Achlasan-Chaluim-Chille
Tormentil	*Potentilla erecta*	Leamhnach
Round-leaved sundew	*Drosera rotundifolia*	
Long-leaved sundew	*D. intermedia*	Lus-na-fearnaich
Great sundew	*D. anglica*	
Sheeps' sorrel	*Rumex acetosella*	Ruanaidh
Heath speedwell	*Veronica officinalis*	Lus-cre
Lousewort	*Pedicularis sylvatica*	Lus-nam-mial
Common butterwort	*Pinguicula vulgaris*	Mothan
Harebell	*Campanula rotundifolia*	Butha-mu
Heath bedstraw	*Galium saxtile*	
Devil's bit scabious	*Succisa pratensis*	Greim-an-diabhail
Mouse-eared hawkweed	*Hieracium pilosella*	Lus-na-seabhaig
Bog asphodel	*Narthecium ossifragum*	Bliochan
Heath-spotted orchid	*Dactylorhiza maculata*	Urach-Bhallach
Bracken	*Pteridium aquilinum*	Raineach
Mosses	*Sphagnum cuspidatum* *S. imbricatum, S. rubellum, S. fuscum, S. subsecundum, S. papillosum, S. magellanicum*	
Lichens	*Cladonia uncialis* *C. impexa*	Crotal

*Bog asphodel (Photo
J. M. Boyd)*

The zoology of the acid moorland systems is generally less well known than their botany, one exception being the avifauna. The extreme exposure and heavy rainfall, combined with acidic, often waterlogged, soil conditions and a small range of species of plants, limits the diversity of invertebrates living there. However, the species which do occur, such as the midges (*Culicoides impunctatus*), are often present in profusion. Midges are especially abundant on peaty islands where small stagnant pools provide perfect breeding grounds, and clegs, or horse flies (*Tabanidae*), are another biting insect of these areas. Cattle, sheep, deer and, on Rum, ponies are all driven off the moorlands by these insects on still summer days, the red deer and sheep taking to the high ground while the cattle retire to the shore. Six species of clegs are found in the Hebrides, and their larvae are the predators of the larvae of other insects.

Some large and beautiful moths occur on the moorlands. By day, from April to August, the male emperor moth (*Saturnia pavonia*) may be seen flying quickly in an almost straight line over heather moorland. The female, however, which is even larger than the male, flies only at night, and during the day she produces a scent which can attract males from many miles. The caterpillars are equally spectacular and feed mainly on heather. Throughout the spring and summer there is a succession of hairy caterpillars of lasiocampid moths, such as the drinker (*Philudoria potatoria*) on purple moor-grass, fox (*Macrothylacia rubi*) and the northern eggar moths (*Lasiocampa quercus callunae*) on heather, which provide food for the cuckoo (*Cuculus canorus*), a common summer visitor to Hebridean moorlands.

Other day-flying moths on moorlands are the little eye-catching burnet moths with their bright scarlet underwings, which appear to have a somewhat localised distribution. For example, we have never seen burnets on Tiree despite many years of observation, though the six-spot burnet (*Zygaena filipendulae*) is common on the moorlands of most of the Inner Hebrides. We have also seen the Scottish race of the transparent burnet (*Z. purpuralis caledonensis*) on southwest Rum. It is concentrated in the Inner Hebrides, where it occurs on south-facing slopes, with wild thyme (*Thymus drucei*) upon which the larvae feed. It has been recorded from the Tertiary basalt habitats of Skye, Canna, Rum, Eigg, Muck, Mull and also Kerrera. The five-spot burnet (*Z. lonicerae*) occurs on Talisker Point, Skye where it feeds on legumes in the grass heath, and the slender Scotch burnet (*Z. loti scotica*) is confined to the Inner Hebrides with colonies on Mull and Ulva (Wormell, 1983).

Butterflies of the moorland include the meadow brown (*Maniola jurtina*), the small heath (*Coenonympha pamphilus*), the large heath (*C. tullia*), the dark green fritillary (*Argynnis aglaja*) and the small pearl-bordered fritillary (*Boloria selene*). The winter moth (*Operophtera brumata*) is present on moorland on Rum, where its larva has adapted to feeding on heather.

Flies, beetles, moths, butterflies, saw-flies, pondskaters, dragonflies, collembola, harvestmen and spiders sustain low densities of insectivores such as the meadow pipit and skylark, with the wheatear, stonechat and wren on the more broken ground with tall shrubs of gorse, heather and willow and some bare rock. In the spacious, flat mires (see below) the songbird community may be reduced to less than one or two pairs of meadow pipits per hectare. Red-throated and black-throated divers breed on moorland and hill lochs, the latter much scarcer than the former. The red-throat breeds on all the main islands except Colonsay, Tiree and Barra, while the black-throat breeds in Lewis and North Uist. There are also scattered breeding waders on the moors. Most of these feed on the shores and wet machairs and include common sandpipers, dunlin, lapwings, golden plovers, greenshanks, snipe and curlew (Inner Hebrides). Breeding densities of golden plover

Red-throated diver
(Photo D. MacCaskill)

on moorlands of the Outer Hebrides are generally less than one pair per sq km except on Lewis where, locally, they might be twice as numerous. The moorlands of Eigg, Islay, Jura, Mull, Rum, Raasay, Skye, Lewis, Harris and the Uists hold small populations of red grouse with black grouse on Colonsay, Islay and Jura. The raptors include the short-eared owl, hen harrier, sparrowhawk, buzzard, golden eagle, kestrel, merlin and peregrine. Herons, which feed on the weedy sea-inlets, often nest at moorland sites of scrub-covered islands in lochs, and ravens, hooded crows and gulls are common—they scavenge and breed on the moorland which also possesses breeding colonies of Arctic skuas on Coll and Lewis. Frogs occur on Skye and Mull but not on the Outer Hebrides, although they may have been introduced there.

Bogs and Mires

The 1980s will be remembered in the annals of Scottish natural history for the research into peatlands in Caithness and Sutherland, which accompanied the campaign by conservation bodies to safeguard these great mire systems from drainage and afforestation. The resulting publication, *The Flow Country: the peatlands of Caithness and Sutherland* (NCC, 1988) has seven authors, two editors, and fifty other contributors (mostly scientists). It has almost 350 references to other publications and it took 18 months to produce. In its introductory sections there are fine illustrated accounts of the development, classification and distribution of mire systems among which are those of the Hebrides, particularly in Mull and Lewis. The mire is an organic landscape with features ranging from the bold to the subtle, from the macro- to the micro-habitats. The whole system is termed 'blanket mire complex' and the parts, 'mire units'. However, in the Hebrides, with the exception of central Lewis, the blanket mire complex is not extensive, and we have adopted the established British practice of describing the mire units according to the hydromorphological features, of which 'blanket mire', 'raised' and 'valley' mires are represented in the Hebrides.

Fig. 20
Map showing the distribution of deposits of deep peat in the Hebrides and west mainland (from The Flow Country—The peatlands of Caithness and Sutherland, *1988,* Nature Conservancy Council)

The Callanish Stones, Lewis (Photo J. M. Boyd)

Within the lowland moorland there are blanket mires and more localised raised and valley mires, which are discrete systems of great interest. About 80% of the Lewisian platform north of the road from Leurbost to Garynahine is covered by deep peat. Peat formation commenced about 6,500 years ago in the 'Atlantic' period, and built-up 5m depth in places such as at Callanish where the megaliths were exposed by clearance of the peat mat in the 19th century. In the remainder of the Hebrides peat is extensive, but is generally neither so deep nor so continuous as on Lewis and is interspaced with tracts of drier heather moorland and bare rock. The inter-relationships of microtopography, water levels and patterns of vegetation of bogs in the Hebrides and comparisons between these and other British bogs are described by Goode and Lindsay (1979); Lindsay, Riggall and Bignal (1983); Ratcliffe (1977).

Blanket and Raised Mires

Blanket and raised mires are ombrotrophic, receiving all their water and nutrients from rainfall on the mire surface. The undisturbed blanket mires have spacious flats, usually of many sq km, which rise by about 1m in 1km from the edge to the crown of the bog. Raised mires are of lesser extent, and are generally flat with boundary streams. These flat surfaces have a

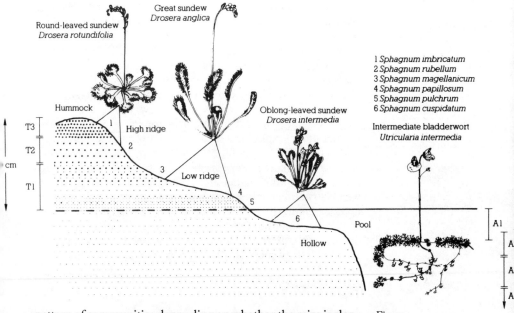

Fig. 21
A section of the pool and hummock showing the zonation of the Sphagnum *mosses and the sundews in the microlandform (from* The Flow Country—The Peatlands of Caithness and Sutherland, *1988,* Nature Conservancy Council)

pattern of communities depending on whether the mire is sloping in one direction (valleyside), or on all sides (watershed); the presence or absence of pool and hummock systems and of hollows; and on the nature of the water table, which about 90% of its time is normally within 5cms of the surface.

Though the entire body of the mire is waterlogged for most of the year, in summer the surface dries differentially causing local changes in the vegetation, which means that the bog vegetation is patterned by the seasonal variation of water levels. Bog biologists describe the habitats as *hummock, high ridge, low ridge, hollow* and *pool* (Fig. 21). In the broad, there are permanently waterlogged hollows and pools dominated by *Sphagnum* spp., mainly *S. cuspidatum*, purple moor grass, white-beak sedge, mud sedge (*C. limosa*), long-leaved sundew (*D. intermedia*), and bogbean. This community contrasts with that on swells of the bog with ridges and hummocks which, though waterlogged in winter, are drier in summer and dominated by tall purple moor-grass, deer grass, heather, cross-leaved heath, bog asphodel, common cottongrass, the hummock-forming *Sphagnum rubellum* and the wooly-fringe moss (*Rhacomitrium lanuginosum*) on the driest parts. There is an intermediate community identified by the growth-form of the moor-grass in clumps, cushions of *Sphagnum magellanicum* and a greater abundance of the white-beak sedge.

At the crown of mires, which have not been drained or otherwise changed by grazing and burning, there are pool and hummock systems. On the surface there seems little pattern, but when viewed from the air such systems are seen to be composed of an infinite variety of shapes. In absolutely flat watersheds in the blanket mire the pools and lochans may be rounded, but in others, on slight slopes of the very shallow 'valleys', the long axes of the pools and hummocks lie along the line of contour. This is due to water flowing at right-angles to the slope towards the edges of the bog where the outflow streams occur. These bog structures are delicate and sensitive to microtopography and changes in hydrostatic conditions within the bog as a whole. If, as often happens, the peripheral areas of a blanket mire are drained, the internal pool systems of the mire might be changed. These subtle widespread effects which sometimes transect ownership boundaries, take years to appear, and in the past have gone unappreciated.

Large cushions of *Sphagnum* are typical of blanket mire conditions, with the frequency of each species differing throughout the wet-dry successions. Bogbean thrives in dense mats in

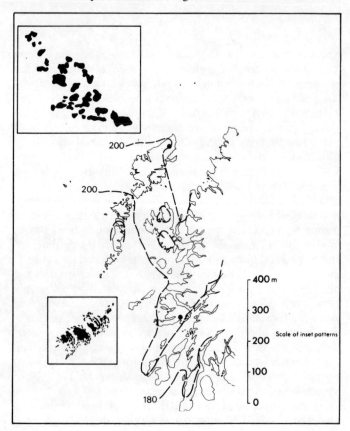

Fig. 22
Diagram showing the pattern of pools and ridges which distinguish the bogs in Lewis and Mull with annual average number of 'wet days' 1951–60 from British Rainfall *(from* The Flow Country—The peatlands of Caithness and Sutherland, *1988, Nature Conservancy Council)*

A bog in Glen Brittle, Skye (Photo I. L. Boyd)

the deep pools in association with sedges, cotton grass and the many-stalked spike-rush (*Eleocharis multicaulis*), while the submerged peat surfaces are covered by filamentous algae (*Batrachospermum* sp. and *Zygogonium* sp.) and the leafy liverwort (*Pleurozia purpurea*). The shallower pools have bog asphodel, sundew and bog pondweed (*Potamogeton polygonifolius*). The *Calluna-Molinia-Narthecium* transitions to the drier areas of the bog have much wooly-fringe moss and antler lichen (*Cladonia* spp.). The driest areas occur on peat mounds and are dominated by heather, crowberry, cotton grass, and the mosses *Pleurozium schreberi* and *Hypnum cupressiforme*. In eroding peat haggs the wooly-fringe moss abounds together with heather, purple moor-grass, common cottongrasses and the fir clubmoss (*Lycopodium selago*).

One of the best examples of blanket mire in the Hebrides is in the flow country at Achmore in central Lewis. This displays the full range of features, with lochans and extensive pool systems. Though grazed and burned for many centuries, these bogs, plus two on Islay, still retain pristine features which elsewhere have largely been destroyed by drainage and peat extraction. We have walked to the pool systems in Duich Moss (Eilean na Muice Duibhe), Islay in hard winter weather, and the frozen lochans at the crown of the bog were spread like white tablecloths. There are other very good examples of near-pristine blanket mire at Glac na Criche, Sanaigmore, Islay—now much reduced from its original size but possessing a striking abundance of black bog-rush (*Schoenus nigricans*)—and at Moineach Mararaulin on the watershed between Glen Brittle and Grunagary Glen, Skye—now almost surrounded by conifer plantations. Glen More, Mull has a fine raised mire between the Coladoir River and the A849 road. The pools and hummocks are well developed on two slightly sloping tongues of mire; as the slope steepens, small drainage channels appear and the pool systems vanish.

Valley Bogs

Valley bogs receive much of their water as run-off from the surrounding countryside, and this carries soil-enriching minerals. This type of bog is particularly frequent on the undulating, loch-studded country between Lochs Roag and Erisort in Lewis. They often merge with blanket mires on neighbouring higher ground, but are usually in small rock basins (<15 ha), and are much wetter than blanket mires because the water moves to the centre of the valley eventually draining away by a water track in the axis of the valley. These tracks are not streams but form definite channels up to 5m wide, sometimes deep and meandering with sparse, open vegetation and a bed of soft, organic detritus often stained red with oxides of iron. Water seeps rather than flows, but there is greater movement and nutrient-loading than in other parts of the bog. The tracks have filamentous algae (*Zygogonium* sp.) and a low, *Carex*-dominated fen with *Sphagnum subsecundum*, mud-sedge, bog pondweed and bogbean. Deergrass, white-beak sedge, slender sedge, sundew and bog-rush are abundant within the water tracks, with common cottongrass on the margins. Table 2 of Goode and Lindsay (1979) shows the changes in the flora of the valley mires in Lewis from the water track to the drier margin. Fifty-four species of bog plant were recorded, 26 in the water

track, 25 in the *Carex-Sphagnum* lawns and 42 in the hummock
and hollow habitats. The popular impression is of the mire as a
dull, wet wasteland when it is in fact a wonderful tapestry
whose beauty and interest is open only to those few naturalists
who now carry a lens and have knowledge of grasses, sedges,
rushes, mosses and lichens. The mire often also acts in the
service of man as the sponge which retains the rainfall and
regulates the supply of water to stream, river, reservoir,
industry and household.

Towards the lower end of the water tracks, the *Carex* fen,
dominated by bottle sedge and slender sedge (*C. lasiocarpa*),
thickens in response to increased nutrients. The white water-
lily, lesser spearwort, marsh cinquefoil, horsetail and the
mosses *Sphagnum recurvum* and *Polytrichum commune* thrive in
the enrichment. The lower reaches of the water tracks resemble fen hollows with greater diversity of species, particularly on
the basalt plateaux of Skye and Mull, where the bedrock is
base-rich and of a higher nutrient status than the Lewisian
gneiss. *Sphagnum* hummocks in the water tracks usually hold
sundews, bog asphodel, deer grass, bottle sedge, common
butterwort, occasionally pale butterwort, lesser clubmoss
(*Selaginella selaginoides*) and the few-flowered sedge (*Carex
pauciflora*). In the dry tops of the hummocks there is heather
and bell heather, milkwort and tormentil. On the margins of
the tracks the hummocks coalesce, become larger and merge
into the context of the mire. White-beak sedge is often characteristic of the margin between the richer valley mire and the
surrounding blanket mire which is ombrotrophic. The extreme
wetness of the valley mires protects them from the adverse
effects of burning and heavy grazing, but they are more vulnerable to drainage than are blanket mires.

Plants which characterise the mires of the Hebrides (wetter
(w), intermediate (i), and drier facies (d) of the mire flora) are:

English	Scientific	Gaelic	Facies type
Bog mosses	*Sphagnum palustre*		w
	S. recurvum		w
	S. subsecundum		w
	S. inundatum		w
	S. subnitens		w-i
	S. cuspidatum		w
	S. tenellum		w-i
	S. papillosum		w-i
	S. magellanicum		w-i
	S. rubellum		w-d
Bogbean	*Menyanthes trifoliatus*	*Luibh-nan-tri-bheann*	w
Great sundew	*Drosera anglica*	*Lus-na-fearniach*	i-d

English	Scientific	Gaelic	Facies type
Round-leaved sundew	D. rotundifolia	} Lus-na-fearnaich	i-d
Oblong sundew	D. intermedia		w-i
Deer-grass	Trichophorum cespitosum		i-d
Purple moor-grass	Molinia caerulea	Fianach	i-d
Common cottongrass	Eriophorum angustifolium	Canach	w-d
Hare's-tail cottongrass	E. vaginatum		d
Many-stalked spike-rush	Eleocharis multicaulis		w-i
Bog asphodel	Narthecium ossifragum	Bliochan	i
Common butterwort	Pinguicula vulgaris	Brog-na-cuthaige	i
Cross-leaved heath	Erica tetralix	Fraoch-frangach	i
Heather	Calluna vulgaris	Fraoch	d
Crowberry	Empetrum nigrum	Caora-fithich	d
Marsh cinquefoil	Potentilla palustris	Coig-bhileach-uisge	w
Tormentil	P. erecta	Leamhnach	d
Water horsetail	Equisetum fluviatile	Clois	w
Lesser spearwort	Ranunculus flammula	Glas-Leumhnach	w
Bog pondweed	Potamogeton polygonifolius	Linne-lus	w
Black bog-rush	Schoenus nigricans		w-i
Bottle sedge	Carex rostrata	⎫	w
Common sedge	Carex nigra	⎪	i-d
Bog sedge	C. limosa	⎬ Seisg	w-i
Slender sedge	C. lasiocarpa	⎪	w
White-beak sedge	Rhynchospora alba	⎭	i
Mosses	Polytrichum commune	⎫	w
	P. alpestre	⎪ Coinneach	w
	Pleurozium schreberi	⎬	d
	Racomitrium lanuginosum	⎭	d
Lichens	Cladonia impexa	⎫	d
	C. uncialis	⎬ Crotal	i-d
Algae	Zygogonium	⎭	w
	Batrachospermum		w

Agricultural development in Britain over the last two millenia has removed much of the widespread, primaeval mire, and in recent years, forestry has also made claims upon the remaining mire systems. The conservation of bogs has thus become a *cause célèbre* in Britain, and Duich Moss in Islay has been at the centre of the public debate. The proposal to extract peat from the bog by Scottish Malt Distillers was opposed by conservation bodies on the grounds that such a development would seriously damage one of the last undisturbed blanket bogs in the Hebrides which is also the winter roost of the rare Greenland white-fronted geese, and the outcome of the controversy was a shift of the peat extraction to another bog in Islay which has no significant interest. It is a good measure of the success of nature conservation in Britain that the safeguard of habitat still popularly regarded as good-for-nothing wasteland has been so successfully accomplished at Duich Moss.

Montane Communities

The lowland heaths with their in-lying mires reach up the island hills and merge with sub-montane grass heaths of bents, fescues, sweet vernal and mat grasses on well-drained slopes with a lot of exposed rock. Variations in the grassy mantle reflect those of climate and substrate. The mountain tops of the Hebrides have a limited range of species compared with the mainland; the Outer Hebrides possess only 29 of the 118 species of montane vascular plants in the British flora, though the Inner Hebrides has a montane flora similar to the West Highlands, possessing 93 species. In general, the mountain tops are too wind-blasted, rugged and limited in summit area to develop extensive montane communities, though spacious summits do occur in the larger of the Inner Isles. Often, therefore, the botanically interesting montane communities are placed on broad terraces or in gullies well below the summits. Snow-patch vegetation is poorly represented and widely scattered in comparison with the mainland, though it occurs more frequently on Jura, Mull, Rum and Skye than on North Harris.

The gabbro and basalt summits are more base-rich than those of granite, gneiss and quartzite, but this difference is not greatly reflected in the plant communities as it is at the lower levels, where more mature soils have been generated. The ultra-basic rocks of Rum, though magnesium-rich, are low in calcium and have a poor flora. The summit habitats are dominated by a heath of wooly-fringe moss with montane and Arctic-Alpine sedges, rushes and herbs. These summit habitats are islands within islands; outliers of the Arctic-Alpine plateau of mainland Scotland which are still being colonised by the montane species. For example, the lady's mantle (*Alchemilla wichurae*), rock whitlowgrass (*Draba norvegica*), Alpine rock-cress (*Arabis alpina*), and rock sedge (*Carex rupestris*) and creeping cudweed (*Gnaphalium supinum*), Alpine cinquefoil (*Potentilla crantzii*), Alpine pearlwort (*Sagina saginoides*) and *Sibbaldia procumbens* have been found in Skye but in none other of the Hebrides. Similarly, the spring sandwort (*Minuartia verna*) is recorded only from Mull, Alpine penny cress (*Thalspi alpestre*) only from Rum and the bog bilberry (*Vaccinium uliginosum*) only from Jura.

The thin, wind-clipped, procumbent mantle of plant life on the rocky summits possesses its own muted beauty when seen on a fine summer's day. So wonderful are the outward views from the high-tops of the Cuillins and Paps on such days that the carpets of moss, lichen and sedge go unnoticed underfoot, yet this wafer-thin veneer of life is as subtle in its ecology as in its colours of grey, greens and ochres. The rock surfaces are encrusted with lichens, and some areas near the summits have especially interesting communities. Take the wet heaths of the endemic mosses *Campylopus shawii* and *Myurum hebridarum* in North Harris, which will only grow where there are over 220 wet days per annum, and the crags of Coire Uaigneich, east of Blaven in the Black Cuillin of Skye, which contain an extensive north-west facing outcrop of Jurassic limestone with a rich flora including tall herbs such as Alpine rock cress, Alpine mouse-ear (*Cerastium arcticum*) and rock whitlowgrass. The Cuillin of Rum possesses a maritime grassland with fescues, bents and hair grasses created and maintained by a vast nesting population of burrowing Manx shearwaters. On Rum, the moss-campion (*Silene acaulis*), northern rock cress (*Cardaminopsis petraea*), the two-flowered rush (*Juncus biglumis*) and the arctic sandwort (*Arenaria norvegica*) are to be found on scattered ridges and terraces of the gabbro hills, with the Alpine penny-cress and the snowy saxifrage (*Saxifraga nivalis*) on the basalt, while on the neighbouring granite top of Orval there is a stoney fjellfield holding a heath in which the Alpine-clubmoss (*Lycopodium alpinum*) is locally dominant with wooly-fringe moss, sedges and rushes. The basalt escarpment of The Storr and Quirang in Skye is one of the finest upland botanical sites of the Hebrides with a fine range of species-rich, montane communities on ledges, dry and sunlit rocks, wet and shadowy gullies, steep slopes with screes below cliffs and summit ridges. Both it and the Black Cuillins are SSSIs (Sites of Special Scientific Interest). Saxifrages (*S. hypniodes, S. aizoides, S. oppositifolia, S. nivalis*) and mountain avens occur in a bright

The alpine clubmoss which forms a carpet on the summit of Orval, Rum (Photo J. M. Boyd)

and diverse flora which also includes the rare Iceland purslane *Koenigia islandica*, also found on Mull. There are also fern-rich niches with the green spleenwort (*Asplenium viride*), brittle bladder-fern (*Cysopteris fragilis*), holly fern (*Polystichum lonchitis*) and the mosses *Mnium orthorhynchum* and *Pohlia cruda*.

The species lists for the montane vegetation of the Hebrides are given by Currie (1979) and Currie and Murray (1983). Within the montane elements of the Hebridean flora there are, in addition, the following species which characterise the northern montane (nm), Arctic-subarctic (as), Arctic-alpine (aa) and Alpine elements (a) in both the Inner and Outer Hebrides:

Alpine scurvy-grass	*Cochlearia alpina* nm
Variegated horsetail	*Equisetum variegatum* nm
Interrupted clubmoss	*Lycopodium annotinum* nm
Alpine hair grass	*Deschampsia alpina* as
Eyebright	*Euphrasia frigida* as
Northern yellow rattle	*Rhinanthus borealis* as
Chickweed willow-herb	*Epilobium alsinifolium* aa
Alpine willow-herb	*E. anagallidifolium* aa
Three-leaved rush	*Juncus trifidus* aa
Three-flowered rush	*Juncus triglumis* aa
Trailing azalea	*Loiseleuria procumbens* aa
Alpine meadow-grass	*Poa alpina* aa
Glaucous meadow-grass	*Poa glauca* aa
Alpine bistort	*Polygonum viviparum* aa
Holly fern	*Polystichum lonchitis* aa
Whortle-leaved willow	*Salix myrsinites* aa
Alpine saw-wort	*Saussurea alpina* aa
Scottish asphodel	*Tofieldia pusilla* aa
Mossy cyphel	*Cherleria sedoides* a*

*Requires confirmation from the Outer Hebrides.

The animal ecology of the Hebridean uplands is mainly unknown, though many species have been recorded. The beetles are the best studied group of upland invertebrates, but even so their distribution is still incompletely understood, and even less is known of their ecology. Species once thought typical of the Cairngorm plateau and the highest mainland peaks are now known from the Skye Cuillins, the Paps of Jura and the higher peaks of Mull and Rum. The ground beetle *Nebria nivalis* is one such example, a predator of other invertebrates around the margins of permanent snowfields over which it will forage at night. It is found in company with *N. gyllenhali*, a common and widely distributed upland species. Other typical upland beetles include *Leistus montanus, Patrobus septentrionis, Arpedium brachypterum, Geodromicus longipes, Mycetoporus baudueri, M. monticola, Boreophila islandica, Atheta tibialis* and *A.*

nitidiuscula. The flightless weevil, *Otiorhynchus arcticus*, a common montane species, also occurs in the dunes of Kilmory on Rum, but is generally distributed throughout the Outer Isles. Similarly, *Ocypus hibernica*, presently known in the Hebrides only from South Uist, is an example of the many montane species which occur at low altitudes in the Outer Hebrides. At least five species of dung beetles (*Aphodius* sp.) have been found exploiting deer dung in the Hebrides, of which *A. borealis* is a true montane species. There is little information about the spiders of the uplands but *Meioneta nigripes*, *Theridion bellicosum* and *Entelecara errata* are known to occur.

The Hebrides have a number of rare upland microlepidoptera including *Scrobipalpa montanus*, a leaf miner on the mountain everlasting on Rum, *Nepticula dryadella*, on mountain avens, *Catoptria furcatellus*, on grasses of the high screes and erosion terraces, and *Epinotia nemorivaga*, on bearberry (*Arctostaphylos uva-ursi*) on Coll. However, as with many of the invertebrate groups, this list is probably limited more by the number of expert naturalists who have looked for different species in these parts than by the diversity of the fauna.

The invertebrates on the high tops also include flies and spiders, which are the thinly distributed food of the rock pipit throughout the Hebrides, and ring-ouzel in the Inner Isles. Ptarmigan bred in the Outer Isles until about 1924 and also formerly bred on Rum where it still occurs occasionally. Small breeding populations still survive on Skye, Mull and Jura, feeding on the shoots and fruits of crowberry, bearberry, creeping and dwarf willow and the occasional insect and spider. The raven and the golden eagle occupy the high-top range of all the mountainous islands as well as much of the lower moorland and coastal habitats. Though the eyries are usually at low level, often near the sea—in Skye the golden eagle has been known to nest on flat ground—these birds can rise from their nests and, in a matter of minutes, soar high above the summits on the lookout for prey and carrion. Red deer and sheep occupy the mountain tops of Harris, Skye, Mull and Jura from time to time in settled weather and the carcases of those that die provide food for eagles and ravens. Ptarmigan and mountain hares, although scarce, are also prey of the golden eagle; the mountain hare can be seen on Lewis, Harris, Skye, Raasay, Scalpay and Mull. On Rum, the montane zone contains thousands of breeding Manx shearwaters which have made the tops green and rich in fauna, thus attracting wheatears. The shearwaters provide food for brown rats and both fall prey to the eagle.

Inland Waters

The inland waters of the Hebrides are modest compared with those of the mainland. With the exception of the waters on machair and limestone, the catchments are generally small, of low altitude and poor in nutrients. However, they are a major component of the ecosytem and contribute much to the character and natural history of the islands. The soft bugling of the whooper swans on the machair loch on a still, crisp winter's day is a thrilling sound, while in the long twilight of a summer's day, the sedge warbler calls from the reed bed, its scoldings interspersed with sweet, musical passages. In wet weather the islands' lochs overflow and join the burns rushing downhill in wind-whipped cascades, often ending over a precipice to the sea. This is in sharp contrast to long, warm dry spells when hill streams are reduced to a whisper, and blue damselflies have their courtship on sunny, heathery banks and the red-throated divers perform their high-flying ritual between the hill lochs and the sea.

Physical and Chemical Conditions

On the 1:63,360 O.S. maps, there are some 7,580 lochs in the Hebrides; 1,542 in the Inner and 6,038 in the Outer Isles (Table 10.1). The Outer Hebrides comprise 1.3% of the land area of Great Britain, but have 15% of the area of standing water. Ninety-seven per cent (7,408) of the lochs in the Hebrides are less than 0.25 sq km in area and 98% (5,977) of those in the Outer Hebrides are in nutrient-poor catchments. The largest lochs by area are: Langavat on Lewis (8.9 sq km, 67.6 million cu m); Suainaval, also on Lewis (2.4 sq km, 80.5 million cu m, 65.7 m deep). Lochs are most numerous on the platform of impervious gneiss of the Outer Isles and on the plateau basalts and hard quartzites of the Inner Isles. The landscapes of central and north Lewis and North Uist are a patchwork of lochs and lochans; the sea inlets of North Uist almost connect at high tide with the inland waters while, at the ebb, the frontier between the sea and the fresh waters becomes separated by wide expanses of sand or wrack (see over).

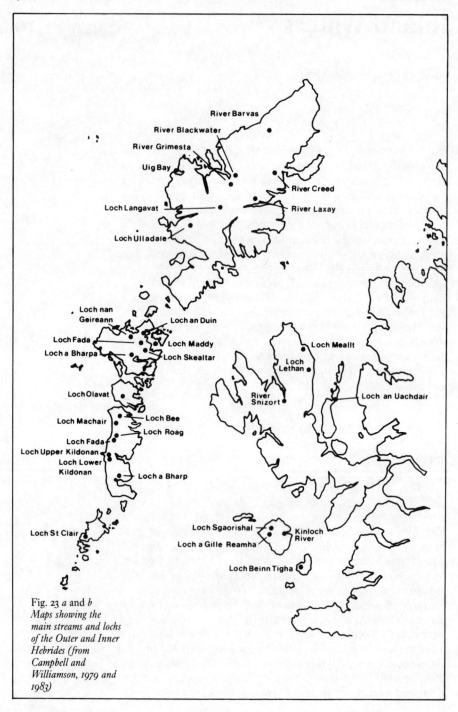

Fig. 23 *a* and *b*
Maps showing the
main streams and lochs
of the Outer and Inner
Hebrides (from
Campbell and
Williamson, 1979 and
1983)

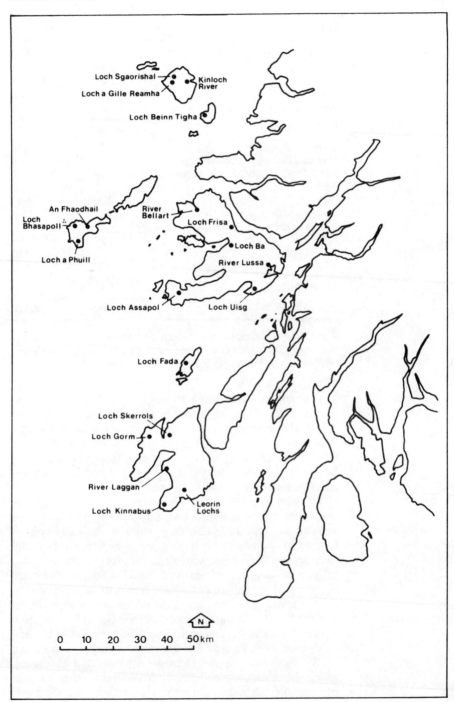

Islands	Lochs	Streams
Lewis and Harris	4,136	1,030
North Uist	914	122
Benbecula	325	43
South Uist	650	106
Barra	13	74
Outer Hebrides	6,038	1,375
Skye	307	632
Raasay, Scalpay, South Rona	62	65
Rum, Eigg, Canna, Soay, Muck	129	108
Tiree, Coll, Ulva, Iona	117	66
Mull	226	351
Colonsay, Oronsay	17	34
Lismore, Kerrera, Seil, Luing, Scarba, Shuna	25	65
Jura, Gigha	390	132
Islay	269	162
Inner Hebrides	1,542	1,615
Total for the Hebrides	7,580	2,990

Table 10.1   The numbers of lochs and streams in the Hebrides taken from O.S. maps by Waterston *et al.*, (1979) and Maitland and Holden (1983)

The running waters are short and fast-flowing, except on the flat platforms of mire and through cultivated land and machair. The total number of streams entering the sea, as marked on the O.S. map, is 2,990 (1,375 Outer, 1,615 Inner Hebrides) these are the conflux of 19,347 stream segments (9,240 Outer, 10,107 Inner). In the Inner Hebrides, there are 10,550km of streams covering an area of some 22 sq km.

The rain from the ocean is like very dilute sea water, containing dissolved substances acquired from the atmosphere and the sea, and these find their way into the water system. During its journey through mire, meadow, stream, loch and river back to the sea, the water becomes further charged with substances acquired from the land. Though there are numerous trace substances which enrich these fresh waters, the two which more than any of the others govern their quality as a medium for life, are sodium chloride (salt) obtained from the sea, and calcium carbonate (lime) obtained from shell-sand or alkaline rocks such as limestones. The influence of the sea on the freshwater of the Hebrides is illustrated by Fig. 24, which shows that, while there is little difference in the calcium content of fresh waters from the Outer Hebrides, the Inner

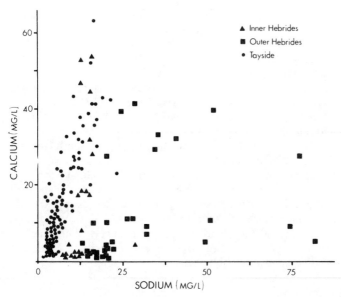

Fig. 24
Plots of calcium against
sodium values for
various waters in the
Outer Hebrides, Inner
Hebrides and Tayside
to illustrate the
gradient, from the outer
rim to the central
mainland, of ions
derived mainly from
sea spray (from
Maitland and Holden
1983)

Hebrides and mainland Scotland, the sodium content (indica-tive of salt) is highest in the exposed Outer Hebrides. The influence of salt and lime on the habitat has already been men-tioned in Chapters 5 and 6 respectively, in the descriptions of saltmarshes and machair. Now we deal with the effects of these and other solutes on the biota of inland waters. In this chapter we are concerned with the running and standing waters which lie above the limits of Ordinary Spring Tides but which are still charged with substantial quantities of salt.

Freshwater Vegetation

In Table 20 of *A Nature Conservation Review*, 139 species of vascular plant are listed for open waters in Britain; 86 of these have been recorded from the Outer Hebrides and a greater number from the Inner Hebrides, for which a comprehensive check-list is not available (Currie 1979; Currie and Murray 1983). There is a group of species which is more or less con-fined to north and north-west Britain: quill-wort (*Isoetes lacus-tris*), spring quill-wort (*I. echinospora*), the white water-lily (*Nymphaea alba*), awlwort (*Subularia aquatica*), water starwort (*Callitriche hermaphroditica*), creeping forget-me-not (*Myosotis secunda*), marsh bladderwort (*Utricularia intermedia*), water lobelia (*Lobelia dortmanna*), slender-leaved pondweed (*Potamogeton filiformis*) and floating and small bur-reeds

(*Sparganium angustifolium* and *S. minimum*). There are three species rare to the British flora and possessing Irish-American affinities, namely: American pondweed (*Potamogeton epihydrus*) in the Outer Hebrides; slender naiad (*Najas flexilis*) in the Uists, Benbecula, Mull, Colonsay and Islay; and the pipewort (*Eriocaulon aquaticum*), which is confined in the British Isles to Skye, Ardnamurchan and western Ireland. The rare Shetland pondweed (*Potamogeton rutilus*) is found in the Outer Hebrides and Tiree.

Loch Druidibeg (loch of the little starling) in South Uist is at the centre of an inland-water system which embodies most of the estuarine, brackish and freshwater habitats of the Outer Hebrides. Much of this system has been designated an SSSI and National Nature Reserve by the NCC (see also pp. 380 and 388), and includes alkaline, neutral and acid lochs on machair, blackland and moorland habitats respectively. The range in chemical character of the freshwaters of the Loch Druidibeg NNR is shown in Table 10.2.

Loch	pH	CaCO$_3$	Na	Ca	Cl	SO$_4$	Habitat
Stilligary	7.58	104.8	22.6	39.7	29.8	20.8	machair/alk*
a'Mhachair	7.70	62.4	18.9	28.0	33.4	16.8	machair/alk
an Roag	6.60	4.6	21.1	2.6	37.6	11.5	brackish
Fada	6.60	8.4	20.8	3.6	34.1	12.9	blackland/neut**
Eilein	7.63	25.6	15.1	10.5	22.0	12.1	blackland/neut
Rigarry	7.00	14.0	13.3	4.2	20.6	12.1	blackland/neut
Druidibeg (West)	7.23	33.2	18.7	10.9	29.8	10.9	moor/neut-acid
Druidibeg (Mid)	6.30	3.8	12.8	4.4	21.3	9.2	moor/neut-acid
Hamasclett	6.00	0.8	13.6	1.7	22.0	8.0	moor/acid***
A. na h'Achlais	5.82	1.8	13.1	1.3	20.6	10.9	moor/acid
Teanga	5.56	0.6	12.0	1.1	22.0	9.3	moor/acid

*   machair/alkaline = eutrophic/mesotrophic
**   blackland/neutral = mesotrophic
*** moor/acid = oligotrophic

Table 10.2   The range of character in the main lochs in Loch Druidibeg and neighbouring lochs measured by Waterston and Lyster (1979) in April–May 1977:

Fig. 25
Map showing the lochs of South Uist referred to in the text (from Waterston and Lyster, 1979). N.B. Grogarry Loch = Loch a'Mhachair

It is often difficult to categorise Hebridean lochs according to their richness, because of the large influence of the sea on their chemical composition; most are anomalous in whatever trophic category they fall. Probably the only truly eutorphic loch in the Outer Hebrides is Loch a'Chinn Uacraich on Benbecula.

Professor David Spence gave a list of 66 species of macrophytes from 33 lochs in the north of South Uist (Spence *et al.*,

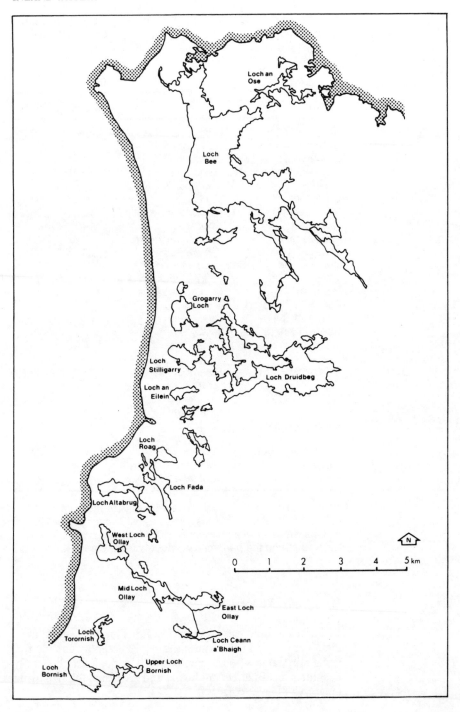

Loch an
Ose

Loch
Bee

Grogarry
Loch

Loch
Stilligarry

Loch an
Eilein

Loch Druidbeg

Loch
Roag

Loch Fada

Loch Altabrug

West Loch
Ollay

Mid Loch
Ollay

East Loch
Ollay

Loch
Torornish

Loch Ceann
a'Bhaigh

Loch
Bornish

Upper Loch
Bornish

N

0   1   2   3   4   5 km

1979) including the widest possible set of ecological conditions from brackish-fresh waters in the Outer Hebrides (Table 10.3).

Species		Lochs	% Freq
Marsh marigold	Caltha palustris	10	30
Common sedge	Carex nigra	18	54
Stone-wort	Chara spp	14	42
Many-stalked spike-rushes	Eleocharis multicaulis	9	27
Common spike-rush	E. palustris	17	51
Marsh pennywort	Hydrocotyle vulgaris	12	26
Quill-wort	Isoetes lacustris	14	42
Jointed rush	Juncus articulatus	7	21
Bulbous rush	J. bulbosus	23	69
Shore-weed	Littorella uniflora	27	81
Water lobelia	Lobelia dortmanna	21	63
Water mint	Mentha aquatica	8	24
Alternate-flowered water milfoil	Myriophyllum alterniflorum	27	81
Spiked water milfoil	M. spicatum	15	45
Common reed	Phragmites australis	7	21
Pondweeds	Potamogeton gramineus	23	69
	P. natans	21	63
	P. perfoliatus	11	33
Lesser spearwort	Ranunculus flammula	18	54
Unbranched bur-reed	Sparganium emersum	9	27
Awlwort	Subularia aquatica	9	27

Table 10.3 Twenty-one dominant species found in over six (20 per cent) of the 33 lochs surveyed by Spence et al. (1979) in the Uists. The total number of lochs in which each species was found and the percentage frequency are given.

Brackish Waters

Electrical conductivity of water is a function of the amount of dissolved solids in the water; sea water is highly conductive, while rain water is poorly conductive. The quality and quantity of solutes has an effect on the pH and the distribution of living creatures (Table 10.4).

Loch	1	2	3	4
Conductivity	2,573	13,235*	22,490	33,900
pH	8.1	8.8**	8.5	9.6***
Species				
E. palustris	+			
N. alba	+			
P. australis	+			
P. natans	+			
P. perfoliatus	+			
P. praelongus	+			
Callitriche sp.	+			
M. alterniflorum	+	+		
Chara sp.	+	+		
L. uniflora	+	+	+	
P. gramineus	+	+	+	
Enteromopha sp.	+	+	+	
F. ceraniodes	+	+	+	+
R. spiralis		+	+	+
Chaetomorpha sp.		+	+	+
Ectocarpus sp.		+	+	
Polysiphona sp.			+	+
F vesiculosus			+	+
Codium fragile				+
Halidrys siliquosa			+	
A. nodosum				+
Ceramium rubrum				+
Cladophora sp.				+

1   Loch Ceann a' Bhaigh (Ollay-Eynort system)
2   Loch Bee
3   Loch Roag (Howmore system)
4   Loch an-t-Saile (Bee system)
*   Average of range: 9,860–16,610
**   Average of range: 8.5–9.45 pH units
***   Average of range: 9.20–9.95 pH units
+   Found by Spence et al.

Table 10.4   The distribution of macrophytes in four lochs in South Uist having conductivities greater than 1,000 ls/cm (at 25°C) arranged in decreasing order (Spence, et al., 1979).

This choice of lochs illustrates well the front between the fresh water and marine systems. The green alga (*Enteromorpha*) occurs at the fresh water-marine interface, because above the level of *Enteromorpha* the species are predominently fresh in character, while below that level they are marine. Indeed a three-tier distribution is detectable in which those above the starworts (*Callitriche*) are positively fresh, those between the starworts and the plant limp (*Ectocarpus*) are brackish, and those below the plant limp positively saline.

Loch Ceann a' Bhaigh is connected to the sea in Loch Eynort. It has remained relatively fresh in character with beds of common reed, white water lily and pondweeds, but *Fucus ceranoides* is a sure indicator of saline conditions. The other extreme is Loch Bee, the largest brackish lagoon in the Hebrides, which is up to four times as salty as Ceann a' Bhaigh and has almost lost its fresh water communities. Around fresh water inlets there are hardy stands of pondweed (*Potamogeton gramineus*), spiral tasselweed, shore-weed, alternate-flowered water milfoil (*Myriophyllum alterniflorum*) and lesser spearwort. Elsewhere, Loch Bee is brackish to marine in character with abundant *F. ceranoides* and bladder wrack. Serrated and knotted wracks, 'bootlace' (*Chorda filum*), sea lettuce (*Ulva lactuca*), *Enteromorpha* sp., and the threads *Codium tomentosum* and *Cladophora glomerata* grow in the vicinity of the sea inlets. Lochs Roag and an-t-Saile are distinctly brackish. Loch Obisary is brackish, with small specimens of the marine mussel (*Mytilus edulis*) on the fronds of the pondweeds in the shallows. This is a very unusual loch because it has a small, shallow inlet from the sea and it is quite large and deep. This means that there is full strength sea water at depth, and almost fresh water at the surface.

Edith Nicol (1936) was the first to describe the brackish habitats of the Hebrides in detail. In twelve brackish water systems, she identified 108 species: 59 marine, 25 brackish and 24 fresh water, as well as seven species of euryhaline fishes; permanently there is the common goby, flounder, fresh water eel, three-spined stickleback and 9-spined stickleback, and occasionally thick-lipped grey mullet and sand smelt. The marine species disappear when the salinity becomes <25 ppt (parts per thousand); brackish communities are centred in salinities of 25 ppt and gradually decline to <5 ppt when fresh water communities become established. The snails, *Lymnaea peregra* and *Skeneopsis planorbis*, are at the fresh and marine ends of the salinity gradient respectively, and the edible mussel occurs throughout. Mysids, gammarids and hydrobiids all have a species in fresh waters and show a remarkable succession of tolerance along the salinity gradient.

The hydroids (*Gonothyrea loveni*, *Clava multicornis*) and the snails (*Littorina littorea* and *L. mariae*) occur on rocky shores with *Fucus ceranoides*, while the flatworm (*Procerodes littoralis*), the bryozoan (*Bowerbankia gracilis*) and the isopod (*Jaera nordmanni*) live under stones. Other isopods (*Idotea chelipes* and *Sphaeroma hookeri*), the amphipods (*Gammarus duebeni* and *G.*

zaddachi), and spire-shells (*Hydrobia ulvae, H. neglecta, H. ventrosa* and *Potamopygrus jenkinsi*) occur in mats of pondweed, spiral tassel and algae. The ragworm (*Nereis diversicolor*), the cockle (*Cerastoderma glaucum*) and a dwarf form of the sand-gaper (*Mya arenaria*) are widespread in the silt, but the Baltic tellin and the sandhopper (*Corophium volutator*) occur locally. The opossum shrimps (*Praunus flexuosus* and *Neomysis integer*) and the common shrimp (*Crangon vulgaris*) keep company on the silt surfaces.

There are a few freshwater species which reach into the low saline levels of the brackish system. *L. peregra*, water bugs (*Nepa cinerea, Sigara sahlbergi, S. scotii*), dragonfly nymphs (*Ischnura elegans, Enallagma cyathigerum, Sympetrum nigrescens*, and *Libellula quadrimaculata*), beetles (*Gyrinus caspius, G. substriatus, Haliplus confinis, Donacia versicolorea*), caddis larvae (*Leptocerus* sp., *Triaenodes* sp., *Limnephilus* sp.), and the crustaceans (*Eurycercus lamellatus, Daphnia pulex, Cyclops strenuus* and *Diaptomus laticeps*) have been found in salinities of 3 ppt.

Moorland Waters

Loch Druidibeg lies in an ice-hewn saucer in the gneiss platform. Its extensive, complex coastline and small islands are the breeding haunt of native grey-lag geese. Eastward of Druidibeg are Lochs Hamasclett, Teanga, Airigh na h'Achlais and Spotal, filling small valleys in the foothills of Hecla which Waterston reports as having a significant fauna with, among others, bryozoans, hydra, snails and caddises. These are typical

Loch Druidibeg, South Uist, a National Nature Reserve and wetland site of international importance (Photo J. M. Boyd)

of countless little lochs scattered throughout the islands which
have brown, acidic waters low in nutrients. Around their margins there is an assortment of water-plant communities whose
composition reflects local conditions of exposure, depth of
water, texture of the lochbed, inflow of streams as well as the
background acidity and poverty of the waters. Shore-weed,
water lobelia, water horsetail and spike-rushes grow sometimes in mosaics, sometimes in bands parallel to the margin,
while in sheltered, deeper waters there are the pondweeds and
the white water lily which, on the dark mirror of Loch Hamasclett, is startling in its beauty. The fine sediments in the deep,
quiet waters also support dense beds of the alternate-flowered
water milfoil and, in the shallower water near the shore, the
quill-wort. E.M. Lind (1952) studied lochs in South Uist and
Rum and found that machair and moorland lochs alike were
generally poor in phytoplankton with *Eudorina elegans, Botryo-
coccus braunii, Ceratium hirundinella* and *Staurastrum* spp.
dominant. (However, machair waters can be so rich in phytoplankton in summer as to possess a 'bloom'.)

Loch Druidibeg itself is bedded on the acid gneiss and fed
from the east by streams from a peaty hinterland. In the West,
though, it is bounded by green base-rich pastures and there is a
distinct increase in acidity from west (pH 7.2) to east (pH 6.0,
see above for Loch Hamasclett). Druidibeg also has a great
variety of shorelines; some are sheltered and silty, while
exposed shores are gravelly, stony and scoured by wave action.
In the most sheltered silty places there are boggy margins.
These are usually poached by cattle, which graze the stands of
common and beaked sedges, carnation grass, bulbous, jointed
and spike-rushes and the common reed interspersed with
pennywort, brookweed (*Samolus valerandi*) and bog pimpernel
(*Anagallis tenella*). This contrasts with the community on the
ungrazed margins of the islands with royal fern (*Osmunda rega-
lis*), water horsetail and beaked sedge. The off-shore shallows
have submerged stands of shore-weed, water lobelia, lesser
spearwort and bulbous rush, and as the water deepens, these
are replaced by quill-wort, awlwort and the pondweeds
(*Potamogeton gramineus, P. praelongus, P. perfoliatus*). Although
the shores are grazed, and wave-action limits the accumulation
of organic sediments and the growth of floating and shore
vegetation, there is a greater diversity of plant life in Loch
Druidibeg than its bleak moorland surroundings suggest.
This, however, is in keeping with its large size, complex shape
and the neutral to acid range of its waters.

The fauna of moorland waters in the Inner Hebrides is
reviewed by Maitland and Holden (1983) and in the Outer
Hebrides by Waterston *et al.* (1979). The dominant species of

zooplankton in lochs on Lismore and Rum were the copepods *Diaptomus glacialis, D. laciniatus, Cyclops strenuus,* and the cladocerans *Daphnia hyalina* and *Bosmina coregoni.* Waterston and Lyster (1983) listed and named the zooplankton in a comprehensive list of the invertebrates of the Loch Druidibeg system. *D. hyalina* is probably the most abundant zooplankter, and in Loch Fada, North Uist, R.N.B. Campbell found eight cladocerans and two copepods.

The rocky shores have hydra (*Hydra vulgaris*), a shrimp (*Gammarus duebeni*), sponges (*Ephydatia, Euspongilla* and *Heteromeyenia*), molluscs (*Lymnaea peregra, Armiger crista, Ancylus fluviatilis* and *Pisidium* spp.), bryozoans (*Plumatella* spp., *Fredericella sultana, Cristatella mucedo*), leeches (*Glossiphonia* spp., *Theromyzon tessulatum, Haemopis sanguisuga* and *Helobdella stagnalis*), worms (*Eiseniella tetraedra* and *Lumbriculus variegatus*), caddis larvae (*Polycentropus flavomaculatus, Limnephilus* spp.), bugs (*Salda littoralis, Saldula saltatoria* and *Velia saulii*), beetles (*Haliplus confinis, Hydroporus palustris, Ilybius fuliginosus, Gyrinus substriatus, Orectochilus villosus* and *Dryops griseus*), sponge-fly larvae (*Sisyra fuscata*) and alder-fly larvae (*Sialis lutaria*).

The weedy shores have a similarly diverse but different community with *Gammarus duebeni,* cladocerans, copepods, corixids, beetles, fly (midge) larvae and six species of the bivalve *Pisidium.* The weed beds in deeper water have hydroids

Lochain Dubha beside the A851 east of Broadford, Skye. A fine dubhlochan, of which there are a great number in the Hebrides, with reedy and sedgy margins and natural, dwarf woods on the islands (Photo J. M. Boyd)

(*Hydra vulgaris*), worms (*Stylaria lacustris*), cladocerans (*Alona, Alonella, Peracantha, Eurycercus*), molluscs, corixids (*Arctocorisa germari, Sigara* spp.), bugs (*Notonecta glauca* and *Nepa cinerea*), caddis larvae and the larva of the moth *Nymphula nympheata*. The larvae of the beetles *Donacia versicolorea* and *D. simplex* feed respectively on the floating pondweed and floating bur-reed. The main species of fishes in moorland waters are brown trout, eels, three- and nine-spined sticklebacks and occasionally sea trout and salmon and on Islay, Skye, Raasay, and Lewis there are lochs containing arctic charr. The common frog, common toad and the palmate newt are widespread in the Inner Hebrides. Grimsay is the only known site where the palmate newt has been recorded in the Outer Hebrides and there is also one established toad population on Great Bernera, Lewis. Adult frogs have recently been released on South Uist. Some doubtful records exist for the smooth newt on Scalpay (Skye) and Canna, and the crested newt has been recently introduced to Skye from the mainland.

Machair Waters

West of Loch Druidibeg lies blackland and machair, the ecology of which is described in Chapters 6 and 7 respectively. In many islands, freshwater lochs are situated on the shell-sand landward of the dunes, and on the line of contact between the sandy platform and the rocky core of the island (p. 110). Many of these lochs receive their waters from the peaty hinterland and drain to the sea through sand-silted channels, but in some there is little channelled inflow or outflow, and water flux is by seepage. The beds of these shallow, machair lochs are of calcareous sand with some organic silts, and the whole loch is well mixed and aerated by wave-action. Fluctuations of the water table result in the drying out of the shallows in summer and the inundation of wet machair at other times of year. Heavy stocking and cultivation of the surrounding pastures contributes to the high nutrient status of these waters, common in the southern Outer Hebrides and Tiree. A pale green 'bloom' on the machair lochs in summer is usually caused by the prolific growth of unicellular algae, possibly caused by the local enrichment of nitrogen from agricultural fertilisers and excrement from waterfowl.

In the shallows, stonewort and slender-leaved pondweed (*Potamogeton filiformis*) predominate together with the alternate-flowered water milfoil, maritime water crowfoot (*Ranunculus baudotii*), water mint, marsh cinquefoil, marsh pennywort, bogbean, iris, lesser spearwort and marsh

marigold. Dense beds of common reed occur where the swamp
is deep and cattle do not have access. Where the reeds grow in
standing water with open spaces they are accompanied by
common spike-rush (*Epipactis palustris*) and bulbrush
(*Schoenoplectus lacustris*). In the outer shallows, there are mixtures of bulbous and spike- rushes and, in the deeper waters,
spiked water milfoil, and pondweeds (*P. natans, P. praelongus,
P. perfoliatus* and *P. gramineus*). Lochs Stilligary, a'Mhachair,
Bornish and Ollay in South Uist are good examples of machair
lochs which have been studied (Spence *et al.*, 1979; Waterston
and Lyster 1979). The lesser water plantain (*Baldellia ranun-
culoides*) flowers at the waters edges in Loch a'Mhachair.

No other brackish-fresh water studies in the Hebrides are as
comprehensive as those on the lochs in South Uist (R.N.B.
Campbell 1986), but studies have been done on the brackish
waters of North Uist (Nicol 1936), phytoplankton in five lochs
including one on Lismore (Brook 1964), fresh water communities of lochs in Raasay (Heslop Harrison 1937, and Spence
1964), Skye (Vasari and Vasari 1968 and Birks 1973) and Islay
(Birks and Adam 1978). There are also many floras for individual islands including inland-water species, but knowledge is
patchy, generally thin and in need of integration and extension.

The main zooplankters in the machair lochs are the cladocerans *Daphnia hyalina, D.longispina, Bythotrephes longima-
nus, Holopedium gibberum, Bosmina coregoni, Polyphemus
pediculus, Leptodora kindtii* and *Diaphanosoma brachyurum* and
the copepods *Macrocyclops albidus, Cyclops agilis, C. strenuus* and

*Loch a'Phuill, Tiree,
is a fertile machair loch
with a sandy bed and
large stocks of
invertebrates, trout and
wildfowl (Photo
J. M. Boyd)*

Diaptomus weirzejskii. Neomysis integer, a mysid, can also be found.

On the loch bed there are no sponges or flat worms as in the moorland lochs, but there is a dense and varied fauna, and most of the taxa mentioned above for the moorland waters are also present in the machair lochs, though in greater numbers. In addition to these, *Hydra vulgaris* and the bryozoans are abundant under stones, leeches are common—especially in the haunts of waterfowl—and there are many species of mollusc dominated by *Potamopyrus jenkinsi, Lymnaea peregra* and *Pisidium* spp. distributed in beds of weed or in silt. The larvae of the mayflies *Caenis moesta* and *C. macrura* (also known as the fisherman's curse) are found in the silt and emerge in millions in early summer, providing a surfeit of food for trout. Another, *Cloeon simile*, emerges from the beds of weeds. There are many species of case-bearing caddis larvae, corixids and water beetles, including an aquatic weevil *Litodactylus leucogaster*, amongst submerged water milfoil. Midges (chironomids) are abundant, but only a few have been identified from adults. The dragonflies are *Ischnura elegans, Enallagma cyathigerum, Pyrrhosoma nymphula* and *Sympetrum nigrescens*. Waterston *et al.* (1979) described the free-swimming microfauna over the lochbed, which included 4 species of cladoceran, 9 copepods and 13 ostracods; food in plenty for trout, eels, three- and occasionally nine-spined sticklebacks and flounders.

Rivers and Streams

Most of the plant species mentioned in the description of the Loch Druidibeg system are common and widespread throughout the Hebrides. Accordingly, these surveys provide a wholesome appreciation of the ecology of brackish, machair and moorland waters within the physical and chemical ranges of these islands. However, the highly acid reaches with pH values below five as found in the dark, peaty lochs, or dubh lochans, of the mires are not well represented in the Druidibeg system, nor does it contain the range of running waters found in the Hebrides, which, though possessing a restricted flora and fauna, remain comparatively unstudied except for their migratory fish.

The rivers of Lewis, Harris, Skye, Rum, Mull, Jura and Islay are short, often torrential in character and usually devoid of vegetation. Where the rate of flow declines, the communities resemble those of associated fresh water lochs. Hill streams have a rapid and continuous rise and fall in response to rainfall, and the beds are scoured clean of sediment. The machair

streams also rise and fall, but in more gradual response to the
rise and fall of the water table—the ground water reservoir in
the dune-machair platform. In summer drought, the hill
stream becomes a bare pebble bed linking deep cisterns of
clear rather lifeless water, while the machair streams become
ribbons of sand and pools luxuriantly overgrown with iris,
fool's water cress (*Apium nodiflorum*), alternate water milfoil
and water horsetail. Streams and drains in all parts are often
stained red by the oxides of iron leached from neighbouring
podzolic soil. Many lochs and streams have been modified,
sometimes with disastrous results, to enhance their stocks of
sedentary and migratory fish (see below). The catchments of
the main rivers of Rum, for example, were manipulated last
century to provide a run of sea trout and salmon at Kinloch, but
the scheme was abortive, testimony to man's misjudgment of

*The Ord River, Sleat,
Skye, is typical of the
small, short, unpolluted
streams of the
Hebrides, with runs of
sea-trout and gorges
holding fragments of
native woodland
(Photo J. M. Boyd)*

nature, because a dam ruptured and the Kinloch River was scoured of the gravels necessary for spawning beds.

In the few streams which have been studied in the Hebrides, the fauna was dominated by insect larvae and molluscs. Rodger Waterston described the shallow metre-wide stream running from the hill through arable land and machair to the sea at Borve in Barra: the hill-stream reach had 10 species of water beetle, 5 caddises, a bug, 2 flies, 2 snails and a species of leech. In the mid-reach over rocks with the moss *Fontinalis*, there were limpets (*Ancylus fluviatilis*), midge and caddis larvae, stoneflies (*Leuctra fusca, Amphinemura sulcicollis, Chloroperla torrentium*), a mayfly (*Baetis rhodani*) and a beetle (*Dryops griseus*). The silted, slow-flowing stretches overgrown with water cress, water crowfoot, marsh-wort and water milfoil had abundant *Gammarus duebeni*, molluscs, water beetles, midge and crane-fly larvae, caddises and corixids, including the minute water boatman *Micronecta poweri*.

Balfour-Browne (1914) recorded 23 species of water beetles from 12 streamlets in Lewis and Harris: (*Haliplus* spp., *Hydroporus* spp., *Agabus* spp., *Helophorus* spp., *Ilybius* and others) of which only *A. paludosus* and *A. guttatus* were regarded as true stream species. The pearl mussel (*Margaritifera margaritifera*) occurs in some of the rivers, and Loch Cravadale, of Harris, where it was first noted by Martin Martin (1703).

Fish

There are seven indigenous species of fresh water fish in the Hebrides: Atlantic salmon (*Salmo salar*), trout (*Salmo trutta*), arctic charr (*Salvelinus alpinus*), three-spined stickleback (*Gasterosteus aculeatus*), nine-spinned stickleback (*Pungitius pungitius*), European eel (*Anguilla anguilla*) and brook lamprey (*Lampetra planeri*), though this last may be absent from the Outer Hebrides. Four species have been introduced to the Inner Hebrides: rainbow trout (*Salmo gairdneri*), American brook charr (*Salvelinus fontinalis*), pike (*Esox lucius*) and perch (*Perca fluviatilis*). Attempts to introduce the American brook charr and the rainbow trout to the Outer Hebrides have been unsuccessful, and rainbow trout populations in the Inner Hebrides are maintained by stocking only. The flounder (*Pleuronectes flesus*), sand smelt (*Atherina presbyter*)—which often shoals with sticklebacks—and the thick-lipped grey mullet (*Crenimugil labrosus*) are found in brackish waters and, temporarily, in fresh waters, with the flounder sometimes going far upstream. Sturgeon (*Acipenser sturio*) and the allis and twaite shads (*Alosa alosa* and *A. fallax*), sea bass (*Dicentrarchus labrax*) and the common goby (*Potamoschistus microps*) are also recorded from fresh waters in the Inner Hebrides (Maitland and Holden 1983).

The inland fish stocks of the Outer Hebrides are probably more representative of the original colonisers of the islands in the melt-waters of the Pleistocene ice. Only migratory, euryhaline species could live in both salt and fresh waters and run upstream from the sea as the land emerged from the ice-sheet, held back only by unscalable waterfalls (except for eels). Salmon have remained anadromous (spawn in fresh waters and feed at sea), trout have become divided into an anadromous form, the sea trout, and a non-migratory form, the brown trout, and the fresh water eel is catadromous (spawns at sea and returns to fresh waters). In contrast, the arctic charr, which must have arrived in the Hebrides as an anadromous species, is now confined to a few fresh water lochs with no migratory stock. Three-spined sticklebacks have also formed anadromous and non-migratory stocks.

The fish of the inland waters of the Hebrides are described by Campbell and Williamson (1979 and 1983), (Table 10.5).

Island/Fish	1	2	3	4	5	6	7	8	9	10	11	12	13	14	15	16	17
Skye	*	*	*	*		@	*	*		*			*				
Scalpay		*	*				*										
Raasay		*	*				*	*		*							
South Rona							*										
Soay						@	*										
Rum	*	*	*				*	*		*	*						
Canna							*										
Eigg			*		*		*										
Muck							*										
Coll			*				*	*	*	*	*						
Tiree			*				*	*	?	*	*						
Mull	*	*	*		*	@	*	*	*	*	*						
Lismore			*				*	*									
Kerrera			*				*					?					
Seil	*	*				@	*	*		*							
Easdale						?	?										
Luing						@	*										
Scarba						@	?										
Shuna							*										
Colonsay			*				*	*		*							
Garvellachs							*										
Jura	*	*	*				*	*		*	*						
Islay	*	*	*	*		@	*	*	*	*			?	*	*		
Gigha			e			@	*			*							
North Rona						?											

Island/Fish	1	2	3	4	5	6	7	8	9	10	11	12	13	14	15	16	17
St Kilda							*										
Harris	*	*	*			@	*	*									
Lewis	*	*	*			@	*	*			?						
Pabbay (Harris)						@											
Monach Isles							*	*									
North Uist	*	*	*	*		@	*	*	*	*	*	?					
Benbecula	*	*	*				*	*	*	?	*						
South Uist	*	*	*			@	*	*	*	*	*						
Barra	*	*	*				*	*	?								
Berneray (Harris)		o					*	*		*							
Totals																	
Outer Hebrides	*	*	*	*		@	*	*	*	*	*	?	?				
Inner Hebrides	*	*	*	*	*	@	*	*	*	*	*	*	*	*	*		
Mainland+	*	*	*	*	*	@	*	*	*	*	*	*	*	*	*	*	*

1 Salmon   2 Sea trout   3 Brown trout   4 Arctic charr   5 American brook charr   6 Rainbow trout   7 European eel   8 3-spined stickleback   9 Spined stickleback   10 Flounder   11 Thick-lipped grey mullet   12 Sea or river lamprey   13 Brook lamprey   14 Pike   15 Perch   16 Minnow++   17 Common carp

* present;   @ an introduction, not an established population;   + Lochs Morar, Shiel and Awe, carp in Kintyre;   ++ *Phoxinus phoxinus*;   e recently extinct;   o introduced into Loch Bhruist in 1988.

Table 10.5   The distribution of brackish-freshwater fish is given by Campbell and Williamson, (1979 and 1973) for the Outer and Inner Hebrides and it has been supplemented by information on the distribution of fish in the Outer Hebrides supplied by R.N.B. Campbell.

Salmon 'run' (return to the rivers) in the Outer Hebrides from late February into the summer, with a peak in July, although this will depend on the level of the rivers. The main river-loch systems are the Rivers Barvas, Blackwater, Grimersta and Laxay in Lewis, Amhuinsuidhe, Laxadale and Obbe in Harris, Skealtar in North Uist, and Howmore, Kildonan and a'Bharp in South Uist. There is a spring run of salmon in two systems of the Outer Hebrides which are more typical of the much larger Scottish east-coast rivers than the summer runs in the West Highlands and the Inner Hebrides. In the Skealtar, angling can begin in late February, and by the end of May over 40 salmon can be landed at an average weight of 6.5kg with some individuals over 13kg. Grilse, the early maturing phase of the salmon which have probably spent only one year at sea before returning to the spawning river, weigh from 2 to 5kg and run from late May onwards. Peak angling catches of grilse on the Skealtar occur in late July-early August, averaging 2.7kg in weight. However, salmon farming on this river has recently affected catches.

In the Outer Hebrides between 3,700 and 5,900 salmon are caught by anglers every year. There are small bag-net salmon fisheries in the Inner Hebrides, particularly off Skye, which to some extent will affect the catches of salmon in the river-loch systems, yet substantial catches have been recorded from some of these systems. During the 1970s, for example, between 1,200 and 5,000 salmon were caught each year in the systems of the Sligachan and Snizort district of Skye. Slightly greater numbers have been recorded from the Ba, Pennygowan and Lussa districts of Mull, and many fewer from Islay, where good catches are still recorded from the River Laggan but not on the River Sorn.

Mills and Graesser (1981) briefly described the rivers in the Hebrides which have stocks of salmon for angling. In the Inner Hebrides these are confined to the larger islands, and they do not have as high a sporting reputation as those of the mainland or the Outer Hebrides. This is reflected in the relatively poor information given about their stocks. Menzies (1938) tagged and released 94 salmon at bag nets off Soay; of the 22 recaptures, one was taken on Skye, 3 on the west coast of Scotland and 18 on the north and east coasts. This indicates that stocks of fish frequenting the west coast may be in passage to the north and east coasts. However, other tagging at Ardnamurchan showed that the majority of fish recaptured were caught within 64km of the tagging point. The salmon disease Ulcerated Dermal Necrosis (UDN) has been known in the Hebrides in the past, occurring when salmon and sea trout were held back in the sea by drought and low stream flows. A few outbreaks of UDN have been reported from the River Aros, Mull and the River Sorn on Islay, but it is believed that the disease does not flourish in the acid fresh waters that characterise the major river-loch systems in the Hebrides.

The lochs of Harris and the Uists used to have excellent sea trout angling, and the fish are larger and more numerous in the fertile machair waters than in moorland habitats. This is easily seen by comparing the stocks of the Lower Kildonan and Howmore situated on the machair with Loch a'Bharp in the moorland, all in South Uist. Nall (1930) suggested that the Howmore-Lower Kildonan sea trout are typically fast-growing, short-lived and spawn few times, compared with those elsewhere on the west coast, which grow slowly, live longer and spawn more often. The spawning performance of the Howmore sea trout resembles more that of the distant River Tweed than it does that of the much nearer River Ewe in Wester Ross. Nall (1932, 1934) also found that the growth of sea trout in North Uist was similar to the fast-growing Howmore stock and that those from Harris and Lewis resembled the slow-growing Loch a'Bharp stock.

Though sizable runs of sea trout do not occur until July, the angling season opens in February, when good fish occupy estuaries and tidal races feeding on sand-eels, young herring and elvers in season. There has been a dramatic decline in catches of sea trout, with fairly constant angling on the three South Uist lochs, compared with salmon which have remained fairly steady in numbers:

Years	sea trout	salmon
1962–66	564	50
1967–71	236	41
1972–76	81	66

The average weight of sea trout in these years was 1.13kg with the largest fish usually weighing between 3.5 and 4.5kg, though the largest sea trout caught was 6.4kg.

Brown trout are widespread, but unlike eels are not present on many smaller islands such as St Kilda, Mingulay, Canna, Muck and Scarba, because these islands do not possess sufficiently permanent or extensive enough stream and loch systems to support a population. They have a highly varied diet. Small and large trout have roughly the same dietary range, except the smaller trout take the smaller-sized end of the spectrum of prey including cladocerans, copepods and other micro-crustacea, insect larvae, pupae and nymphs, amphipods, molluscs, small fish and in the few waters in which they occur, palmate newts. In moorland systems with acid waters and very low stocks of invertebrates, such as those on the gneiss, granite, Torridonian sandstone and quartzite in the Outer Hebrides, Jura and Islay, the few trout which survive are large and almost entirely piscivorous, feeding on charr. This sometimes leads anglers to seek the large cannibalistic 'ferox' trout to be found in some of these dark lochs, which have ample spawning beds, poverty of invertebrate food, but shoals of charr. In the Outer Hebrides 'ferox' occur in Loch Langavat, Lewis, where conditions are right for piscivorous trout.

The status of the brown trout populations in lochs depends, therefore, on the balance which is struck between the rate or recruitment of young fish to the population, and the amount of food available. The balance is achieved differently even in somewhat similar lochs. For example, in both the main machair lochs on Tiree, Lochs a'Phuil and Bhasapol, there are high

stocks of invertebrates, but the former has much more extensive spawning beds than the latter. This results in Loch a'Phuil
having a large population of medium-sized, rather thin fish
while Loch Bhasapol possesses fewer larger-sized fish in good
condition and the same comparison can be obtained in South
Uist between the rich Lochs a'Mhachair and Upper Kildonan.

Rainbow trout have been introduced to the Hebrides but
have been unsuccessful in permanent establishment. The
rapid growth of trout-farming on the west coast of Scotland has
resulted in escapes from netted pens in lochs, including at least
one loch on Mull, and American brook charr introduced late
last century to Loch Beinn Tighe on Eigg and a few small lochs
on Mull are still extant. None of these lochs have trout,
however.

Arctic charr occur in Lochs Fada, a'Bharpa and the Loch
Skealtar system on North Uist, Lochs Langavat and Suainaval
on Lewis, an Uachdair on Raasay, Mealt on Skye and Kenna-
bus on Islay. However, there are still other suitable waters on
Lewis and Skye in which charr might be found where they may
be sympatric with brown trout feeding almost exclusively on
plankton. In Loch Mealt though, there are no trout and the all-
opatric charr feed on organisms normally taken by trout
including sticklebacks and stickleback egg clumps.

The three-spined stickleback is widely distributed and
occurs in three forms, roughly associated with tidal pools, open
waters, and streams and ditches. There are several forms: *trachurus* the rough-tailed, which is found in brackish habitats and
is anadromous, *leiurus* the smooth-tailed and the intermediate
semiarmatus which are all found throughout the Hebrides.
However, *anomalus*, which lacks pelvic spines and has a varying
number of dorsal spines, has been found only on North Uist.
The nine-spined stickleback is less widely distributed than the
three-spined and is restricted to shallows with abundant aquatic vegetation; they are much more common in the Outer Isles
than in the Inner, where they have been found on Islay, south-
west Mull and in Loch Claid on Coll.

Elvers born in the Sargasso Sea in the western Atlantic make
the astounding journey to the fresh water systems of Europe,
arriving in the Hebrides in April and May. They are ubiquitous
in inland waters, even in small systems such as on St Kilda and
the Monach Isles which contain no other fish, with the possible
exception of sticklebacks. The movement of eels into the
estuaries and stream systems is often marked by the appearance of predatory herons, gulls and otters. The eels, which may
spend over 30 years in fresh water before migrating to spawn
and die, feed on molluscs, crustaceans, insect larvae and
nymphs. Apart from a few eel traps, which killed otters as well

as eels (see p. 106), there has been no large scale exploitation of eels in the Hebrides.

Brook lampreys have only been reported from the Inner Hebrides, although both the river lamprey and the sea lamprey are probably more widespread than the records show. The only record of a river or a sea lamprey is from a small stream on Kerrera, but the presence of these primitive fish is only readily recorded during the spawning season in the spring or early summer. Otherwise, tell-tale marks on salmon in Skye which have been parasitised by lampreys suggest their presence— though this does not tell us where the parasitism occurred during the long migrations of the Atlantic salmon—and parts of a lamprey were also recently recorded in North Uist in the regurgitated meal of a heron.

Perch and pike occur only as introduced species to a few lochs in northern Islay and form the only populations of coarse fish in the Hebrides. Pike feed on young trout, and efforts have been made to eliminate them from Loch Skerrols by treating the loch with a piscicide.

Reptiles and Amphibians

Like coarse fish, reptiles and amphibians have also found great difficulty in bridging the marine barrier (Table 10.6). Although the reptiles—adder, slow worm and common lizard—depend on fresh waters only to a very small degree, the amphibians— palmate and smooth newts, common frog and common toad—require fresh waters for breeding and live in moist, fresh habitats.

Island/Species	1	2	3	4	5	6	7	8
Skye	*	*	*	@	@	*	*	*
Raasay	*	*	*		*	*	*	*
Scalpay	*		*		*		*	*
Soay							*	*
Eigg			*			*	*	
Rum			*			*		
Canna					?	*		
Coll			*					
Tiree								
Mull	*	*	*			*	*	*
Kerrera							*	*
Iona							*	
Lismore			*					
Jura	*	*	*			*	*	*
Garvellachs			*				*	*

Island/Species	1	2	3	4	5	6	7	8
Luing		*			N	N	*	*
Scarba	*							
Seil								
Shuna								
Islay	*		*				*	*
Colonsay		*	*					
Gigha						Y	*	*
South Uist							*	
North Uist			*					
Lewis	?	*						
Harris	?	*						
Inner Hebrides	*	*	*		*	*	*	*
Outer Hebrides		*				*	*	
West Mainland	*	*	*		*	*	*	*

1 Adder   2 Slow worm   3 Common lizard   4 Crested newt
5 Smooth newt   6 Palmate newt   7 Common toad   8 Common frog

* present;   @ introduced but not established;   N newt of unknown species;   Y young (tadpole).

Table 10.6   The distribution of amphibians and reptiles in the Hebrides compiled by R.N. Campbell.

Many species predate the populations of toads, frogs and newts. These include fish, gulls, herons, mergansers, crows, otters and feral mink. In 18 years of study of brown trout food in north Scotland, Niall Campbell has not found tadpoles in the stomachs, though frogs were commonly found in spring. It is therefore all the more remarkable that American brook charr have been found gorged on both tadpoles and small frogs in Mull.

Waterfowl

The inshore, coastal and inland waters of the Hebrides are a rich and varied habitat for many species of water bird. The wildfowl (swans, geese, ducks, grebes and divers) are described in greater detail in Chapter 13 (Table 13.6), since they have had a special place in the natural history of the islands for well over a century, and today hold much that is of special interest in science and conservation. Many species commute between the shore and inland waters, or between the rich machair lochs, which are feeding and nursery areas, and the poor moorland lochs which provide sequestered breeding sites. In winter, the communities of waterbirds are different from those in summer and spring, and autumn sees migrants—particularly on the busy, weedy shallows of protected shores, and the machair lochs, often still 'open' when mainland fresh waters are frozen. The maintenance of sufficiently high water levels in the machair lochs, particularly in dry summers, is vital for the waterbirds. These levels are affected by drainage for agriculture and therein lies a conservation problem (p. 270).

Mammals

In the Hebrides the otter is mainly a marine species and is widespread on all the islands except perhaps distant outliers like St Kilda and North Rona, where it has not so far been recorded. It is described in Chapter 5. Mink (*Mustela vison*) has recently been introduced to Lewis and Harris, possibly as escapes from mink farms at Steinish and Dalmore, which were both closed in 1961. They are thought to have spread through the islets in the Sound of Harris and are now colonising the southern Outer Hebrides. The water vole (*Arvicola terrestris*) has been recorded in Skye and Islay, and the water shrew (*Neomys fodiens*) in Skye, Raasay, Pabay (Skye), Mull, Kerrera, Garvellachs and Shuna.

The inland waters of the Hebrides are probably second to none in Britain as a refuge for wildlife. Unlike many parts of mainland Britain, the waters are unpolluted from agricultural seepage or industrial effluent, and they possess many unique features. However, they are fragile, and require careful and sympathetic management if they are to maintain their diverse qualities.

PART II

Studies of Islands and Species

CHAPTER II

The Seabird Islands

Seabirds are part of the very fabric of the Hebrides; the call of the sea-mew is heard in the lore and music of the Gaelic people, and that of the kittiwake can be heard in Mendelssohn's *Fingal's Cave*. In their cliff-bound home or over the awesome spaces of ocean, their natural gifts of flight are not only amazing in the physical sense, but also very beautiful, sometimes humorous and occasionally bizarre.

The west coast of Scotland has long been famous for possessing one of the richest seabird communities in the world. This reputation is based on accounts of a limited number of spectacular but remote breeding stations during the summer. Recent counts suggest that there are roughly a million breeding pairs, about a third of the total for Britain and Ireland, a tenth of that of western Europe and a twentieth of that of the cooler part of the Atlantic and adjacent seas.

Thus begins a key paper by Bourne and Harris (1979) to which this chapter largely refers, and provides a review of the literature from Harvie-Brown and Buckley (1888; 1892) to 'Operation Seafarer' (Cramp *et al.* 1974) and the ornithological atlas (Sharrock, 1974). Since then Thom (1986) has brought the records up-to-date in *Birds in Scotland*, and a Seabird Colony Register is in preparation by the Seabird Group of NCC.

There can be no full understanding of seabirds without first having a knowledge of climate and hydrography and of the ecology of the sea, the seashore and the coasts, and this we have covered in previous chapters. There are essentially three types of seabird according to feeding habits: firstly, the coastal species such as the gulls, cormorants and terns, some of which lead a semi-terrestrial life, frequent freshwaters and feed at sea within a few kilometres of the shore; secondly, the off-shore species such as auks, kittiwakes, skuas and gannets, which have a marine existence (except for breeding sites); thirdly, the

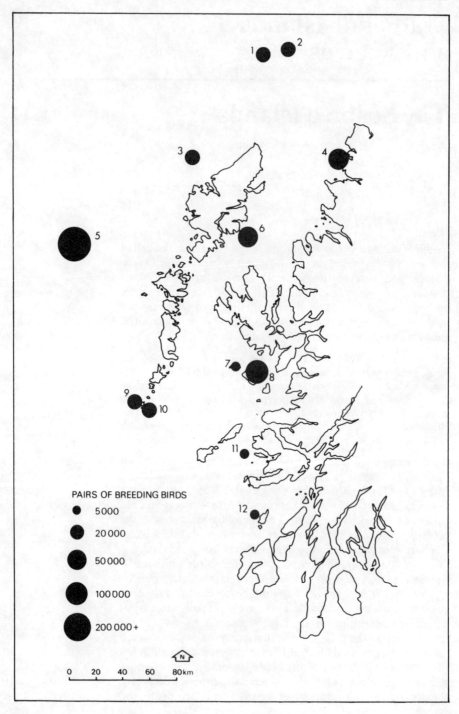

PAIRS OF BREEDING BIRDS

● 5000

● 20000

● 50000

● 100000

● 200000+

0   20   40   60   80km

Stac an Armin (190m) viewed from the summit of Boreray (380m), St Kilda holds about 12,000 pairs of gannets on its spire (Photo J. M. Boyd)

pelagic species such as the petrels which range widely from inshore waters to the vast expanses of ocean many hundreds of miles from land. Exceptions to this are the kittiwake (*Rissa tridactyla*) which is off-shore and oceanic in habit while all the other gulls range off-shore but are mainly coastal; the black guillemot (*Cepphus grylle*), which is coastal while all the other auks are off-shore; and the red-neck phalarope (*Phalaropus lobatus*), which is for most of the year a pelagic species ranging the oceans far from land, yet it breeds and raises its young in coastal freshwater habitats.

The Hebrides provide ideal seabird breeding habitat. Remote and varied coastlines lie within easy reach of feeding grounds at sea, the superlative cliffs of St Kilda heading a list of

Fig. 26
Map of the main seabird islands of the Hebrides. 1 Sula Sgeir, 2 North Rona, 3 Flannans, 4 Handa, 5 St Kilda, 6 Shiants, 7 Canna, 8 Rum, 9 Mingulay, 10 Berneray, 11 Treshnish, 12 Colonsay

first-class habitats for vertical cliff-nesting species such as kittiwakes, guillimots and shags, among which Mingulay and
Berneray in the Barra Isles, the Shiant Isles and Handa in
Sutherland are most notable. St Kilda also has spacious cliff
terraces with much talus, and similar cliffs are also found in the
Shiants and Treshnish Isles, affording nesting spaces for
borrow- and crevice-nesting species such as puffins, Manx
shearwaters, storm petrels, (Leach's Petrels also at St Kilda,
Flannan Isles, North Rona and Sula Sgeir), razorbills and
black guillimots. There is enormous scope for surface-nesting
gulls and terns throughout the Hebrides, but gannets which
may be ledge- or terrace-nesters are confined to large, long-
established sites at St Kilda and Sula Sgeir, and small,
recently-established colonies on the Flannans and Shiants.
There is an almost endless set of options for breeding sites for
all species of British seabird, yet so few of them are taken up,
possibly because of poor food supply and predation.

The Islands

The seabird islands are shown in p. 202 and the distribution of
species within them in Table 11.1

Species Islands	fulmr p	manx s p	st pl	lh pl	gnnt p	corm p	shag p	ac sk p
North Rona	3738	0	pt	pt	0	0	126	0
Sula Sgeir	6532 i	0	pt	pt	9143	0	10	0
Flannan Islands	4734	0	pt	pt	414	0	336	0
St Kilda	62786	pt	pt	pt	50050	0	52	0
Lewis & Harris	16407	0	0	0	0	47	1368	48
Uists & Benbecula	1055	0	pt	0	0	105	55	6
Monach Islands	593	0	0	0	0	13	25	0
Barra *	486	0	0	0	0	0	0	0
Ming'y & Berneray	10457	0	pt	0	0	0	721	0
Shiant Islands	6816	0	0	0	1	? 0	1777	0
Skye & outliers #	3730	?	?	0	0	76	1677	0
Rum	581	116000	0	0	0	0	14	0
Canna Eigg Muck	1078	1085	0	0	0	0	1815	0
Coll Tiree Gunna	1510	0	0	0	0	1	140	47
Mull & outliers @	1773	pt	pt	0	0	42	578	0
Jura & outliers X	87	0	0	0	0	7	192	54
Colonsay & Oronsay	869	0	0	0	0	0	118	0
Islay	1469	0	0	0	0	0	393	0
Gigha & Cara	117	0	0	0	0	0	247	0
Summer Isles	1008	0	pt	0	0	0	108	0
Handa	3474	0	0	0	0	0	256	30

	gt sk p	bh gl p	cm gl p	lbb gl p	hg gl p	gbb gl p	kwe p	sh tn p
North Rona	14	0	0	2	80	733	3943	0
Sula Sgeir	0	0	0	0	13	3	1031	0
Flannan Islands	0	0	0	4	11	168	2779	0
St Kilda	54	0	0	154	59	56	7829	0
Lewis & Harris	36	140	292	260	1776	1258	2430	0

	gt sk p	bh gl p	cm gl p	lbb gl p	hg gl p	gbb gl p	kwe p	sh tn p
Uists & Benbecula	0	153	85	7	487	64	0	0
Monach Islands	0	57	61	10	78	52	0	0
Barra *	0	0	41	0	176	20	0	0
Ming'y & Berneray	6	0	2	94	405	170	8614	0
Shiant Islands	6	0	0	51	164	127	1864	0
Skye & outliers #	0	24	235	518	2896	344	1914	0
Rum	0	0	15	80	379	50	2213	0
Canna Eigg Muck	0	0	139	86	2142	160	1057	0
Coll Tiree Gunna	0	817	344	225	2899	267	1060	0
Mull & outliers @	0	2	276	80	2921	526	337	0
Jura & outliers X	0	197	280	931	2183	114	17	0
Colonsay & Oronsay	0	63	67	27	933	38	5646	0
Islay	0	17	361	407	1520	93	563	0
Gigha & Cara	0	26	194	355	818	56	0	0
Summer Isles	0	0	7	7	299	109	0	0
Handa	66	0	6	2	54	31	10732	0

	re tn p	cn tn p	ac tn p	le tn p	glmt i	rzbl i	b glmt i	pffn i
North Rona	0	0	0	0	17104	1038	54	5500
Sula Sgeir	0	0	0	0	24746	580	?	500p
Flannan Islands	0	0	0	0	21926	3160	6+	4400
St Kilda	0	0	0	0	22705	3814	17	230501
Lewis & Harris	0	114	762	13	1238	853	2172	273
Uist & Benbecula	0	114	508	50	0	0	302	0
Monach Islands	0	92	122	26	0	0	292	0
Barra *	0	43	60	0	0	0	61	0
Ming'y & Berneray	0	0	0	0	30881	16893	12	3570p
Shiants	0	0	0	0	18380	10948	31	77000p
Skye & outliers #	0	110	1291	0	2494	1151	2967	367
Rum	0	0	0	0	3644	471	122+	50p
Canna Eigg Muck	0	26	284	0	6873	2273	272	1086
Coll Tiree Gunna	0	403	76	79	727	289	13	1
Mull & outliers @	0	785	224	0	4775	322	224	1068
Jura & outliers X	0	537	326	0	0	27	112	0
Colonsay & Oronsay	0	40	724	0	13541	1450	397	0
Islay	0	15	638	15	2522	1239	555	0
Gigha & Cara	0	15	32	0	30	17	177	4
Summer Isles	0	67	67	0	0	63	86	0
Handa	0	8	4	0	98686	16394	?	803

Table 11.1   Populations of seabirds in the Hebrides. Numbers of all species except the auks and the fulmars on Sula Sgeir are *breeding pairs*. All the auks are *individuals*, except for four colonies of puffins which are *breeding pairs*. i = individuals; p = pairs; pt = present; * = Pabbay to Eriskay; # = South Rona, Raasay, Scalpay, Pabbay, etc; @ = Treshnish Isles, Iona, Ulva, Staffa, etc; X = Scarba, Luing, Lunga, Shuna etc. Harris and Lewis are separated from the Uists and Benbecula by the main channel of the Sound of Harris. Fulmr = fulmar, s = shearwater, pl = petrel, st = storm, Lh = Leach's, gnnt = gannet, corm = cormorant, sk = skua, ac = arctic, gt = great, gl = gull, bh = black-headed, cn = common, lbb = lesser black-backed, hg = herring, gbb = greater black-backed, kwe = kittiwake, tn = tern, sh = sandwich, re = roseate, le = little, glmt = guillemot, rzbl = razorbill, pffn = puffin. [These data are from the Seabird Colony Register (Compiler: Dr Clare Lloyd) of the Nature Conservancy Council's Seabird Group. Many of the data from the remote outliers were provided by the Seabirds at Sea Team of NCC.]

St Kilda

In Chapter 16 we describe the seabirds of the St Kilda group of islands, which have contributed to the declaration of these islands as a World Heritage Site. Here, we place St Kilda in the context of the other seabird islands of the Hebrides. The largest seabird assembly in one island—including its outliers—occurs on Boreray in the St Kilda group. Boreray (384m) and its two gigantic stacks, Stac an Armin (196m) and Stac Lee (172m), hold the largest assembly of North Atlantic Gannets (*Sula bassana*) in the world. There is a total of 50,000 pairs, with 13,500 on Stac Lee and 11,900 on Stac an Armin (Murray and Wanless, 1986), and they also have major colonies of kittiwakes, guillemots, razorbills, puffins, fulmars, Manx shearwaters, storm petrels and Leach's petrels, bringing the total number of breeding seabirds to well over 100,000 pairs. The other islands have somewhat smaller totals and no breeding gannets. St Kilda as a whole, though, with 320,000 breeding pairs, probably possesses over one-third of all the seabirds breeding in the Hebrides and about 11% of those breeding in Britain and Ireland. Seventeen species of seabird, including eider (*Somateria mollissima*) and red-necked phalarope have bred at St Kilda this century—the largest list for any British seabird colony. To sail close to the perpendicular walls, massive rock bastions, dark sinister caves and spectacular arches and rock pillars, all echoing with the calls of a myriad of seabirds, is to behold one of the natural wonders of the British Isles. The more adventurous captains take their ship between Stac Lee and Boreray and at the point of transit the sky is full of gannets, to port are the overhanging flanks of the stack and to starboard the mighty west wall of Boreray which appears caught in a snow storm of kittiwakes and guillemots, the drama heightened by gannets in hundreds diving into the wake of the ship as the disturbance brings fish to the surface.

The Shiants

The Minches have good stocks of pelagic fish and the Shiants are placed in the midst of rich feeding grounds for off-shore species of seabird—hence the large colony of puffins (77,000 pairs) and good numbers of guillemots (9,000 pairs). This is St Kilda in miniature, but without the rarer pelagic species—the Manx shearwater and the two small petrels. Neither does it possess an established gannetry. In 1984 a single nest was built on Eilean Mhuire and in 1985–86 single nests were also built on Garbh Eilean, but breeding has not yet been proved. The puffins are largely housed in a large talus slope on Garbh Eilean which is reminiscent of the Carn Mor, the now famous puffin-shearwater-small petrel site at St Kilda. The Shiants possess a rare and wonderful atmosphere, and from the summits there is a fine panorama of islands and distant mountains. The little house on Eilean an Tigh has been the base for many school expeditions which go there to study the seabirds and the eco-system of a remote island.

North Rona and Sula Sgeir

The Flannan Islands, Sula Sgeir, North Rona, Mingulay and Berneray all hold about the same number of breeding seabirds, between 24,000 pairs (Sula Sgeir) and 31,000 pairs (North Rona), and any one of those hold more than the rest of the Outer Hebrides (22,000 pairs). This is because of their consistently high stocks of guillemots, of an order similar to St Kilda (24,000 pairs) (Bourne and Harris, 1979). Sula Sgeir is but a rocky ridge 750m long and 250m wide, and every part of it seems tenanted. There are probably 13 species, and a remarkably sharp boundary exists between the tightly packed gannet grounds and guillemot stances and the open pattern of the fulmar grounds, with each sitting bird beyond 'spitting distance' of its neighbour. The stench of bird manure, rotting fish and fulmar oil is everywhere and the wild calling of thousands of piscivorous throats is deafening.

In the midst of this melee stand the low, dry-stone bothies of the gannet-hunters from Ness in Lewis, who come to the rock annually to take 2,000 *gugas* (young, unfledged gannets) to salt as food for the local people. This harvest of *gugas* is taken under licence; elsewhere in Britain the gannet is fully protected. In 1985, Stuart Murray counted 9,100 occupied nests of gannets on Sula Sgeir, and despite the off-take of over 20% of the young and the construction of a small lighthouse and helipad on the rock by the Northern Lighthouse Board, numbers seem to be steady at about 9,000 pairs. Murray noted that though the area on which the helipad now stands was not occupied by gannets when it was built in the early eighties, there were some 68 nests there in 1985!

North Rona has 13 species of breeding seabird. It is a major site for the guillemot (*c.* 2,000 pairs), storm petrel (order 3) and Leach's petrel (order 3). The 80 pairs of Arctic terns on the perched storm-beach on Fianuis are unusual for the distant outliers, and the colony of 730 pairs of great black-backed gulls is the largest in Britain. It is also a wonder that over 2,500 pairs of puffins—preferred prey for these gulls—have survived on this small 130ha. island.

The first account of the colonies of small petrels was by Ainslie and Atkinson (1937) and they were graphically described by Fraser Darling (1939) and Robert Atkinson (1949). Atkinson's youthful adventure in hitching a lift in a Stornoway drifter to North Rona and making some absolutely new discoveries in the biology of these little, exceedingly wild and remote species caught the imagination of young island-going naturalists who succeeded them in the exploration of the outliers of the British Isles. It is a wonderful experience to stand in the ruins of the Rona village—or the *cleitean* on Boreray—through the three dark hours of a June night and witness the arrival of the small petrels at their nests. Both ground and sky are alive with darting forms and the swish of wings; the soft, rhythmic purring and crooning of the stormies in their burrows ends in a distinct *hiccough*, while the Leach's in their bounding flight have a whirring call ending in a loud *wicka, wicka*.

Mingulay and Berneray

Mingulay and Berneray each have nine species of breeding seabird. Barra Head, which is another name for Berneray, is the most southerly point in the Outer Hebrides round which a sea-current flows from the Sea of the Hebrides. This current of in-shore water meets the westerly movement of ocean water south-west of Barra Head, and on this 'front' there is a rich food supply for seabirds. It is to be expected, therefore, that the southern isles of Barra should hold good breeding stocks of off-shore species, and accordingly there are 8,600 pairs of kittiwakes, 8,500 of razorbills and 15,500 of guillemots on Berneray and Mingulay. There are few puffins (3,600 pairs) compared with the Shiants (77,000), which are situated close to the largest concentrations in the Hebrides of Norway pout (*Trisopterus esmarkii*), a favourite food of puffins.

Small Isles

The major seabird island of the Inner Hebrides is Rum, which comes second to St Kilda in order of magnitude. However, Rum is greatly different in character to St Kilda since it owes its eminence to a single species—of the 120,000 pairs of 12 species of seabirds breeding on Rum (Wormell, 1976), 116,000 are

Manx shearwaters, nesting high on the mountain tops and hidden in burrows during hours of daylight. They emerge from and visit their burrows at night with a great cacophony of screeching, crowing and crooning from both the air and the ground. The Norsemen named one of the peaks tenanted by the shearwaters 'Trolaval', after the goblins who called so strangely in the night. (The survey of this vast shearwater 'conurbation' across the Rum cuillin is described in Chapter 15.) Otherwise Rum holds few other seabirds for its size—about 1,800 pairs of guillemots, 1,100 kittiwakes, 500 each of razorbills, fulmars and herring gulls and six other species with less than 100 pairs (Table 11.1).

Canna, Eigg and Muck also hold small populations of Manx shearwaters; Canna has about 1,000 pairs. During the day large numbers of shearwaters can be seen from the ferries around the Small Isles, Coll and Tiree, and on summer evenings large 'rafts' are present in the Sound of Rum, awaiting nightfall and subsequent flight to nesting grounds on the high tops. Canna may have storm petrels, and has the largest colonies of shags (1,000 pairs) and herring gulls (2,100 pairs) in the Hebrides.

Treshnish Isles and Others

The Treshnish Isles hold 14 species (Table 11.1) including three pelagic species—fulmar, Manx shearwater and storm petrel. There are also about 2,000 pairs of guillemots and 500 of puffins. A visit to the Treshnish Isles and Staffa on a bright, warm June day is glorious to the naturalist. The setting of seabirds on the pillared basalt walls, green-mantled terraces and among cushions of sea-pinks is idyllic, very different from the awesome seabird-thronged abysses of St Kilda, Mingulay and Handa. Colonsay and Oronsay have colonies of kittiwakes (5,600 pairs) and guillemots (6,500 pairs), while Tiree has small colonies of fulmars, shags, 6 species of gull, 3 species of tern, razorbill, guillemot and black guillemot. Coll has no cliff-nesting seabirds, but holds a small colony of Arctic skuas.

Handa

Handa is not strictly in the Hebrides, but the seabirds that breed there feed in Hebridean waters. The vertical galleried sandstone walls of Handa are ideal for guillemots, of which there are 50,000 pairs, and to a lesser extent razorbills (8,200 pairs) and kittiwake (5,300 pairs), but not for puffins (400 pairs). The concourse of guillemots nests close to large stocks of herring, mackerel, sprat and Norway pout (Bailey *et al.*) in the north Minch.

The large islands of Lewis and Harris, the Uists and Benbecula, Barra, Skye, Mull, Islay and Jura all possess small straggling colonies, though there are many hundreds of miles of coastline bereft of any breeding seabirds. For example, the north coast of Skye with the Ascarib Isles in Loch Snizort and the Rhinns of Islay both face 'fronts' with good supplies of fish and have many small colonies, but on the other hand the east coasts of both the Outer and Inner Hebrides possess very few breeding seabirds.

The Species

Fulmar

The stronghold of the fulmar is St Kilda, where there are 62,800 pairs. It is thought that it has nested there for over 800 years (Fisher, 1966) and has only come to occupy most of the coasts of Britain and Ireland in the last century. The spread is believed to have stemmed not from St Kilda, but from a genetically distinct race which colonised Foula from Iceland and Faeroe in 1878. One theory is that the Icelandic race has the ability to breed in small groups or isolated pairs, while the St Kilda race requires the local stimulation of large, dense assemblies for successful breeding. Another theory connects the spread with the warming of the North Atlantic over the last hundred years, and another with the spread of offal from the whaling (at the turn of the century in Shetland and Harris) and the fishing industries attracting fulmars into areas hitherto unoccupied by them. In truth, no one knows. In the Hebrides it is not quite ubiquitous, not breeding on much of the east coast of Harris and North Uist, the west coast of South Uist and all of Benbecula, the east and south coasts of Skye from Staffin to Loch Scavaig, on South Rona and Raasay, the east coast of Mull from Ardmore Point to Carsaig, Lismore and the isles in the Firth of Lorne, Jura and East Islay from Bunnahabhain to Port Ellen (Thom, 1986). Why such long stretches of the coast should remain unoccupied is a mystery, though the fulmar seems much less attracted to sheltered than to exposed coasts. It is particularly numerous in highly exposed isles with adjacent, rich, turbulent seas, such as St Kilda, Mingulay, North Rona, Sula Sgeir, Shiants and Handa.

Professor G. M. Dunnet and colleagues (1978, 1979, 1982), working on Eynhallow in Orkney, showed that fulmars are about ten years old before they breed, by which time only about 6% return to the native colony. The survival rate for adults is about 97%, which shows the great hardiness of this inhabitant of the tempestuous coasts.

Manx Shearwater

The Manx shearwater is one of the most numerous seabirds in the Hebrides; more numerous than the fulmar, gannet, herring gull, kittiwake and razorbill, but less so than the guillemot and much less than the puffin. Yet shearwaters are an uncommon sight in most of the Hebrides. It is known that the birds disperse widely to distances of up to 200km from nest sites in foraging flights, and increase in numbers within 10km of breeding islands during the late afternoon and into the evening, when large 'rafts' of often over a thousand birds form off-shore on the sea's surface, awaiting nightfall.

  The major colonies are on Rum and St Kilda, with smaller centres on Canna (Swann in Campbell, 1984), Eigg, Muck (Dobson, 1985), Treshnish Isles, and at Gallan Head in Lewis.

A Manx shearwater caught in the lap of a night visitor to Carn Mor, St Kilda (Photo J. M. Boyd)

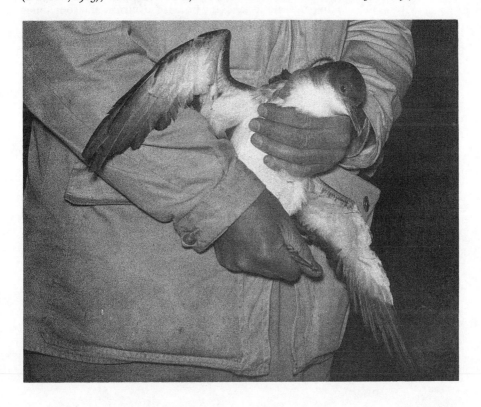

Shearwaters are, therefore, most numerous in the Sea of the Hebrides, and can be seen from ferries serving the islands from Oban and Mallaig, their dark shapes and swerving, gliding, skimming flights are unmistakable compared with the straight missile-like trajectory of the auks. The passage to St Kilda also features the shearwaters in great numbers, and the sooty shearwater (*Puffinus griseus*) and great shearwater (*Puffinus gravis*), both of which breed in the South Atlantic, are seen occasionally around St Kilda. Cory's shearwater, which breeds in the Mediterranean and from Azores to the Cape Verde Islands, has been seen off Islay, North Uist and Lewis, and the little shearwater (*Puffinus assimilis*) was seen off Islay on 30th June 1974. Rings on Manx shearwaters breeding in Scotland have been recovered from South American waters and the Gulf of Mexico—a juvenile was found off Argentina, 9,830km from its nest site eight weeks after the ring was fixed.

A midnight visit to the summits of Hallival and Askival on Rum, or Carn Mor on St Kilda to hear the home-coming of the shearwater host is an exciting experience. Their weird haunting call comes in surges upon the wind; the incoming birds arriving with rising shrieks of *kukroo-kukroo-kukroo*, ending with the strike of the bird at the burrow and sometimes on the lap of the observer. They are wild and vicious, and their barbed beaks will tear unwary hands.

Small Petrels

The storm petrel breeds at nine sites between Sanda and North Rona, and it is also a widespread breeder in Orkney and Shetland (Thom, 1986)—breeding is suspected at six other sites. Only two colonies are thought to exceed 100 pairs: St Kilda (>10,000 pairs) and Priest Island, Summer Isles (*c.* 10,000). The only other large colony in Scotland is on Foula (1,000–10,000). However, the actual numbers present at all sites are largely unknown. Breeding probably occurs on the outliers on the west of the Outer Hebrides from Monach to Loch Roag and in the Sound of Harris—we heard one calling from a burrow at Shillay, Harris in September 1953. Also, breeding is suspected on Canna and the Shiants. They are unlikely to be found on islands possessing rats, and ringed birds show that many colonies may be visited by young birds before they settle to breed. In summer, birds ringed in Scotland have been caught in Norway, Faeroe and Iceland and in winter, off the African coast from Liberia to Natal.

Leach's petrel breeds at St Kilda, Flannans, North Rona and Sula Sgeir; the only other breeding records in Britain and

Ireland are in recently established sites at Foula (1974) and
Ramna Stacks (1980). Both species of small petrel have a pro-
tracted breeding season—we have heard them at Carn Mor in
April and at North Rona in October. The single white egg is
usually incubated from early June and the last young go to sea
in November. Until 1955, knowledge of small petrels was confined to the works of Atkinson and Ainslie (1937), and Darling
(1940) referring to North Rona. Possibly the largest colony in
Britain which contains both species of small petrel is on Carn
Mor, Dun and Boreray at St Kilda (Boyd, Tewnion and
Wallace, 1956). The difficulties of measuring the size of such
colonies are formidable, yet the assembly of Leach's at St Kilda
can be reliably assessed in thousands, in hundreds on the Flannans, North Rona and Sula Sgeir, and in tens at other sites.
There are single old records of Wilson's Petrel (*Oceanites
oceanicus*) from June (1891), and the white-faced petrel (*Pelago-
droma marina*) from Colonsay (1897).

Gannet

Wanless (1986) estimated a world population of gannets occupying 263,200 nest sites (pairs), of which 223,400—85%—are
in the East Atlantic, and Scotland has 131,800, 59% of which
are at 12 sites. St Kilda alone has 50,100 nest sites, and the
Hebrides as a whole has 59,220 nest sites. There are three
Gannetries: St Kilda, Sula Sgeir (9,100), Flannans (410)
(Table 11.1, and p. 203); however, gannets from Ailsa Craig
(21,500) and Sule Stack (4,000) fish in the Hebrides. They do
no overfly isthmuses, so there are daily passages mainly of St
Kilda birds round the Butt of Lewis, through the sounds of the
Outer Hebrides to and from the feeding grounds in the Minches and the Sea of the Hebrides. In like manner birds from
Ailsa Craig fly round the Mull of Kintyre and through the
Sounds of Islay and Gunna to the Sea of the Hebrides and
beyond.
    The gannet usually feeds by plummeting from a height of 20
to 30m into the sea, catching its prey on the dive and usually
swallowing the fish before it surfaces. It feeds mostly on pelagic
fish—mackerel, herring, sprat—which are most plentiful in
the Minches and the Sea of the Hebrides (Bailey *et al.*, 1979).
There are also feeding grounds around St Kilda where shoals
of mackerel and sand-eels break the surface of Village Bay on
calm mid-summer evenings. In winter Scottish breeding gannets move south, mostly to the Bay of Biscay, but some reach
tropical West African water and others enter the Mediterranean. In January they head northward again, returning to the

breeding islands in February and March in preparation for egg-laying in April, though some stay in British waters all winter.

The gannet has been increasing in numbers during this century, maybe as a result of a relaxation in hunting, though the colonies which are still harvested in the Vestmannaeyjar group in Iceland, Mykinesholmur in Faeroe, and Sula Sgeir are stable or increasing in numbers. New colonies are forming, even though the ability of the gannet to establish new colonies may be limited by social factors. It is thought (Nelson, 1978) that until a threshold of pairs — 20–35 — has been established, there is insufficient social stimulation for successful breeding. However, when this threshold has been reached, as it now has in the Flannans though not in the Shiants, the colonies increase rapidly. It is also known that young gannets may not return to their birth colony when they settle to breed. The steady state of the Sula Sgeir colony points to this, and ringed birds from the Bass Rock and Ailsa Craig (the only substantial ringing-sites for gannets in Scotland) have been found in Icelandic and Norwegian colonies.

Cormorant and Shag

The cormorant is distinguished from the shag by its larger size, heavy bill, white cheeks and chin, white thigh patches in breeding birds, and white breast in the immature birds. It lacks the crest possessed by the breeding shag, and is a much rarer bird than the shag in Britain. The cormorant is limited as a breeder to a few well-separated sites while the shag is widespread as a breeder in many sites, and almost ubiquitous as a fish-hunter in the Hebrides. Whereas the cormorant breeds on open sites with full exposure to the elements, the shag nests in caves, overhung cliff-bottoms, and in crevices under boulders on cliff-terraces immediately above the sea. The cormorant feeds mostly on bottom-feeding fish in shallow water and freshwaters, while the shag feeds on fish in the water column, and almost exclusively at sea.

There is a regal look to the cormorant as it stands tall in its rookery. The shag on the other hand, looks sinister and almost bizarre, as it perches erect in the Stygian gloom of its sea cave, merging with dark rock and shadow. However, when the shag emerges into the sunshine, it displays the finest vestments; its iridescent dark-green and black plumage has the sheen of silk. Both species are known as *scarbh* (scarv) in Gaelic.

In the Outer Hebrides, the cormorant has two main breeding sites; at Loch an Tomain (*c.* 100 pairs), a freshwater loch in North Uist, and on Stockay (*c.* 13 pairs) in the Monach Isles. Other small colonies exist in Loch Roag, Lewis, and in South Uist and Barra. Bourne and Harris (1979) stated that *c.* 380 occupied nests can occur in the Outer Hebrides, Thom (1986) stated that there are 240 pairs in West Inverness and Argyll. Most of these are in the Inner Hebrides scattered in small groups on the west coast of Skye, Rum, Ross of Mull and Mull of Kintyre. In Tiree cormorants have recently used Ceann a'Mhara as a perching site, and they are frequently seen at sea and on the freshwater lochs. About 16% of the Scottish population breed in the Hebrides. In winter, cormorants disperse in coastwise movements to other sectors of the British and Irish coasts, but a few from Scotland reach points ranging from Spain to Norway.

In contrast to the patchy occurrence of the cormorant, the shag is present on the bird islands usually in tens, occasionally in hundreds, and in Canna there are four large and many small breeding colonies with about 1,000 pairs in total. Numbers fluctuate greatly from year to year and in Canna counts in 1970 and 1971 were 200 and 1,900 pairs respectively, but 800–900 is a recent average size (Swann in Campbell, 1984). Only about 100 birds remain around Canna in winter, and ring returns show that the rest disperse throughout the Hebrides, mostly to the Outer Isles. Of all shags ringed, 70% have been recovered within 100km of the site of ringing; only 1% of Scottish rings have been recovered from France and Norway. The *scarbh* is still shot illegally for food in the Hebrides and often dies in fishing nets.

Skuas

The skuas are uncommon in the Hebrides in comparison with Orkney and Shetland; they are boreal species breeding on a NE-SW front of declining numbers from Unst, Shetland, to Jura. The great skua or 'bonxie' has extended its breeding range SW in the last 30 years and now breeds in North Rona (14 pairs), Lewis (*c.* 30 at 3 sites), St Kilda (54), Mingulay (6), and Handa (66), and there have been recent records of breeding on the Shiants and the Summer Isles. The Arctic skua breeds in small groups of up to 20 pairs in the moorlands of Lewis, North Uist, Benbecula, Coll and Jura. The dark phase predominates, and pairs are occasionally of dark and light birds.

The skuas are pirates, chasing gulls, gannets, terns and auks to a point when the hapless victim disgorges the contents of its crop, upon which the skua swiftly stoops. They are also predators of other seabirds, killing adults and pillaging eggs and nestlings. The bonxie can kill a bird as large as a gannet, and is the boldest of birds in defending its own nest-site against an intruder sheep and sheep dogs can be harried and cowed by the diving bonxies and chased from the nesting area. Nearby, there are usually pools at which the bonxies bathe, preen, and stand with raised wings, cackling. They rise to meet the intruder barking loudly and then suddenly swoop in attack, sometimes striking the head with their feet before climbing away with a guttural *tuk-tuk-tuk*. Though the birds are unlikely to cause injury to a person, the onslaught takes nerve to resist, and usually results in a hasty, head-down retreat. In the Northern Isles the two species often nest on the same ground, and on Noss in Shetland the nesting area of the bonxie is extending at the expense of the arctic skua. Such competition may also occur in the nesting areas north of Gress in Lewis. The young of both species are great wanderers; ring returns from Scottish great skuas range from Greenland and Spitzbergen to the Mediterranean, Cape Verde Islands and the coasts of New England and Brazil, and ring returns from Arctic skuas are similarly well distributed, but there is a concerted movement to the Mediterranean and West Africa as far south as Angola in winter. Over 100 (presumably immature birds) have been seen off North Uist in May.

The Pomarine skua (*Stercorarius pomarinus*) is an oceanic species which breeds in arctic USSR, winters in the tropical Atlantic, and occurs on spring passage in the Outer Hebrides in flocks ranging from a few birds to over 1000. The long-tailed skua (*Stercorarius longicaudus*) nests in the Scandinavian arctic, and also occurs in spring passage in the Outer Hebrides, where, off Balranald in North Uist, 271 were counted on a day in late May and 390 between 18th and 25th May 1983.

Gulls

The herring gull is the 'sea-gull' of common usage; its voice is the familiar reminder of the seaside to the urban dwellers, and its gliding flight in the slip-stream of the ship is the fascination of ferry passengers. However, its clamouring flocks at rubbish dumps and fishing stations and its foul disregard for buildings, vehicles and boats is the scourge of the burghers of Stornoway, Portree, Tobermory and Port Ellen. Herring gulls have been suspected of spreading disease, especially *Salmonella*, and contaminating domestic water supplies. There are *c.* 3,500 pairs of breeding herring gulls in the Outer Hebrides, of which *c.* 1,800 are in Lewis and Harris. Bourne and Harris (1979) estimated *c.* 1,800 occupied nests of herring gulls, *c.* 1,100 of lesser black-

backed gulls, 221 of great black-backed gulls and 27 of common gulls in 18 sites on the moors of Lewis.

Herring gulls and lesser black-backed gulls at Mallaig harbour (Photo J. M. Boyd)

The herring gull is a commensal species nesting within easy flying distance of human settlement where it is a scavenger. There are comparatively few herring gulls at the outlying stations of St Kilda (<100 pairs), Flannans (<30), North Rona (*c.* 80), Sula Sgeir (*c.* 13), though the Inner Hebrides are more densely occupied, with all the seabird islands holding over 100 pairs and Canna *c.* 800. The lesser black-back is less of a scavenger and seems more at home in the outliers. When St Kilda was first occupied by the army, the camp swill was dumped daily at the jetty in Village Bay to the accompaniment of a noisy cloud of gulls. Most of these were herring gulls with fewer lesser black-backs, single Iceland gulls (*Larus glaucoides*) and glaucous gulls (*Larus hyperboreus*). This did not however result in an increase in the size of the gull colonies. The lesser black-backs became established in the mid-fifties before the army arrived with a subsequent increase in their breeding in the 1970s but with little change in the herring gull.

In autumn, there is a south-easterly movement of herring gulls from the Hebrides to the conurbations of Strathclyde and the Moray Firth, with a return movement in spring. We have seen a wing-tabbed herring gull off Tiree in June which had been caught at the Bishopriggs rubbish dump in Glasgow in the previous winter. The lesser black-back is much less numerous than the herring gull. In the Outer Hebrides there are c. 500 pairs of lesser black-backs, a migratory species which overwinters in the western Mediterranean and West Africa. Lesser black-backs breeding in Faeroe and Iceland move through the Hebrides in large numbers in spring and autumn.

The great black-back, unlike other species of gull, does not nest in dense colonies, and where there are many nesting together such as on North Rona, the nests are usually well-separated. It seems to be much more sensitive to disturbance than the other species, and often nests in solitude on spacious moorland, remote headlands, surf-grit islets, the tops of stacks inaccessible to sheep and man, but within easy access to feeding grounds.

There are c. 2,600 pairs of great black-backs breeding in the Outer Hebrides, and North Rona is the headquarters, with c. 730 pairs. This is an astonishing number in such a small island (130 ha.) for a bird of solitary nesting habit. However, conditions are probably ideal—an uninhabited, seldom-visited island with sheep and good nesting colonies of kittiwakes and auks, 19km from the gannetry and auk colonies on Sula Sgeir and close to commercial fishing grounds. In Lewis the largest colony (125 pairs) is on Druim Mor facing Broad Bay. In the other islands the great black-back breeds in tens, with the largest assembly (c. 100 pairs) in the Inner Hebrides on the Treshnish Isles. After breeding, there are roosting flocks sometimes hundreds strong including many immatures, which disperse southward into Ireland and the British mainland in winter. Few go further.

The common gull (*Larus canus*) is far from 'common' in the Hebrides, where the Outer Hebrides are thought to have c. 600 pairs. It does not breed in the outliers, and breeds in tens in the Inner Hebrides. Even the large islands may not have more than 100 pairs. Tiree, a favourable island, has usually 50–100 pairs. In winter the birds disperse southwards to Ireland and lowland Scotland, where they are joined by others from many parts of Scotland to form flocks many thousands strong.

The black-headed gull (*Larus ridibundus*) breeds throughout the main chain of the Outer Hebrides, Tiree, Coll, Colonsay, Jura, Islay and Gigha, but not in the outliers, Skye, Raasay, the Small Isles and Mull. It is a highly gregarious species, which nests in close proximity to human settlement, feeding on agricultural land, the microcrustacea of the shore, domestic and fishery litter, and nesting in swampy fens and bogs. In the Outer Hebrides there are >400 pairs in well scattered sites throughout the islands, with the largest colony (>200 pairs) at Loch Stiapavat, Lewis. Tiree and Coll can have over 700 pairs in several colonies in good years, but here as elsewhere, the colonies are disturbed by visitors and at least one has been destroyed by drainage. In winter the black-head is moulted with only a dark ear spot remaining, and the birds disperse southward to Ireland and the British mainland providing recruits for the wintering flocks on the Clyde and Solway coasts.

The kittiwake (*Rissa tridactyla*) is a gull in a class of its own; it is an off-shore, oceanic feeder. The Hebrides hold some 42,000 breeding pairs, 18,500 in the Outer and 23,500 in the Inner Hebrides. The headquarters of the kittiwake is at Handa, St Kilda and Berneray, which both hold *c.* 9,000 pairs. Where they occur, they nest in thousands. However, in some of the Inner Hebrides they are in hundreds but very seldom in tens. It is this highly gregarious, dainty gull which enlivens the seabird islands with its snow-white plumage, delicate flight, spectacular nest site and musical chorus.

Counts at St Kilda and Ailsa Craig show that over the two decades from 1959–79 numbers fluctuated greatly. The reasons for this are complex, but probably related to the availability of sufficient food for chick survival over sustained periods of years. The immature kittiwake is particularly handsome, with a dark W across the outstretched wing, and a black tip to the tail. It spends two years at sea before returning to breed in the third year. During this time, and also in winter as adults, they wander great distances across the Atlantic and into the Mediterranean.

The Iceland gull (*Larus glaucoides*) and the glaucous gull (*L. hyperboreus*) are winter visitors, and occasionally present as immatures in summer; the little gull (*L. minutus*), Sabine's gull (*L. sabini*), the ring-billed gull (*Larus delawarensis*—first recorded in Scotland in South Uist, 1981), Ross's gull (*Rhodostethia rosea*) and the ivory gull (*Pagophila eburnea*) have been recorded recently as vagrants in the Hebrides.

Terns

The Arctic tern is by far the most numerous tern in Scotland, and about 65,000 pairs (90%), breed in Orkney and Shetland. By contrast, only about 5,000 pairs breed in the Hebrides, two-thirds of them in the Outer Hebrides. The colonies are short-lived. In Tiree the total number of arctic terns (*c.* 400 pairs) has probably not changed greatly over the past 30 years, yet they have changed greatly from year to year in any one locality. After an absence of many years, they suddenly settle to breed at an old breeding site, and will be gone in the following year or two. The largest concentrations are probably on the Monach Isles (900 pairs in 1979), Coll and Tiree (*c.* 400), Treshnish Isles (*c.* 300) and on the isolated islet of Heiskeir (Oigh-sgeir) off Canna.

The terns are elegant, slender birds of white and pale grey plumage with black heads and a delicate, pulsating flight. They fiercely defend their vulnerable nests and young against intruders; rats, cats, dogs, otters, mink, crows, gulls and man are vigorously attacked by the swooping, screeching birds. Flashing past the head, the tern jabs home its sharp bill, some-times drawing blood. The little tern (*Sterna albifrons*) is, in our experience, the fiercest of all, but they have little defence against the persistent predator. When breeding, they feed mainly on sand-eels, and during the day the birds are absent from the colony, fishing at sea. The Scottish terns travel to the West African coast for the winter. Arctic terns travel far into the southern hemisphere; some were recorded off Natal in November having travelled 10,000km in four months.

The common tern is in fact, far less 'common' than the Arctic tern. In the Outer Hebrides there were thought to be about 750 pairs in 1980, and in the Inner Hebrides there are small colonies of usually less than 30 pairs in Tiree, Coll, Treshnish, Colonsay and Handa. However, there are probably more than meets the eye, since this species can very easily be mistaken for the Arctic tern from which it differs by having a black tip to its bill. As in Orkney, there are probably over 2,000 pairs in the Hebrides compared with over 11,000 in Shetland. The little tern breeds in many colonies of a few pairs through-out the length of the Outer Hebrides (90 pairs) particularly in the Monach Isles (26) and Eoligarry, Barra (12). The Inner Hebrides has similar small colonies in Tiree, Coll, Islay and Gigha. One pair of Sandwich Terns (*Sterna sandvicensis*) nested in the Monach Isles in 1978, but there is no other breeding record from the Outer or Inner Hebrides. Roseate terns (*Sterna dougallii*) have been sighted in both Inner and Outer Hebrides between May and July, and a pair was present at Balranald, North Uist in May 1969. The black tern (*Chli-donias niger*) and the white-winged black tern (*Chlidonias leu-copterus*) have occurred in the Outer Hebrides as vagrants in June 1978 and May 1964 respectively.

Auks

These are the guillemots, razorbills and puffins which are adapted both for flying and for swimming penguin-like in pur-

*Puffin (Photo
J. M. Boyd)*

suit of their prey. They are splendid black (or sooty-brown) and
white, frock-coated birds, occupying the sea-cliffs and cliff-
terraces. They occur in great numbers and though highly gregarious at their nesting sites, disperse widely in small numbers
over a vast expanse of sea. Scotland holds 80 and 90%
respectively of the British and Irish populations of guillemots
and puffins. The observed occurrence of auks at sea in the
Hebrides in summer and winter is shown in Fig. 11.5 (Bourne
and Harris, 1979).

The stronghold of the guillemot (*Uria aalge*) is in the
Northern Isles (207,000 birds *not pairs*), and the Hebrides,
including Handa and the Mull of Kintyre (103,000). In the case
of the razorbill (*Alca torda*) and the puffin (*Fratercula arctica*) the
weightings are reversed (Cramp *et al*, 1974). However, in 1988
c. 270,000 guillemots were counted in the Hebrides (Table
11.1). The most important sites for auks are in the outliers, the
Shiants and Handa, but the weightings of the species at each
island are different depending on the proximity of feeding

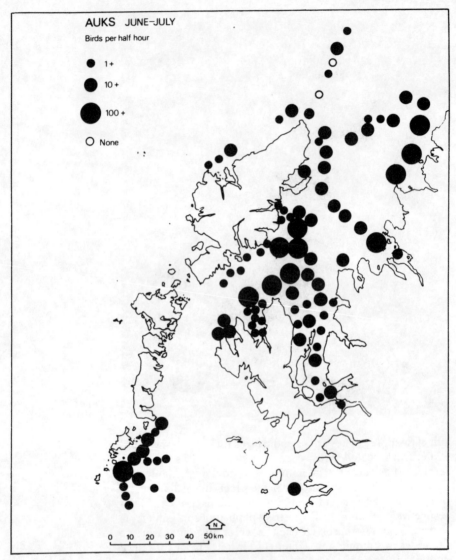

AUKS JUNE–JULY

Birds per half hour

● 1 +

● 10 +

● 100 +

○ None

Fig. 27 *a & b*
The seasonal distribution of auks at sea in the Hebrides (from Bourne and Harris, 1979)

grounds and the nature of the cliff habitat. Let us compare Handa and the Shiants. Both have similar feeding grounds in the Minch, but they have a very different cliff ecology. The former having horizontally stratified sandstone in vertical, galleried cliffs, ideal for guillemots and razorbills, but poor for puffins, and the latter having vertically-jointed basalt with talus and green terraces which, though only moderately favourable for guillemots and razorbills, is ideal for puffins.

Guillemots nest on flat or slightly bevelled ledge systems,

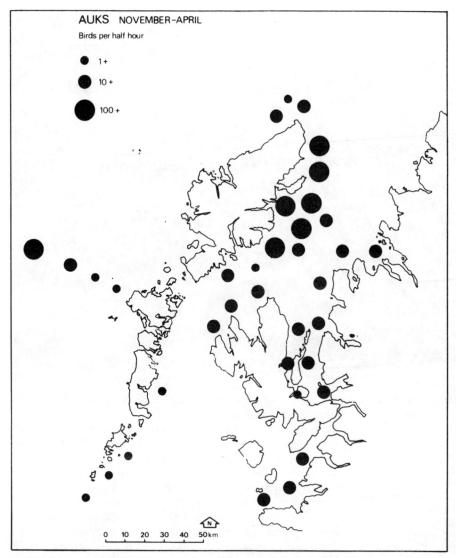

AUKS NOVEMBER-APRIL

Birds per half hour

● 1+

● 10+

● 100+

and razorbills in clefts in cliffs, crevices under talus, and burrows. Their eggs are top-shaped so that when disturbed they do not roll from the ledge, but sit-up and spin on the spot. The puffin on the other hand is a burrow- and crevice-nester. It is seen at its densest on Dun, St Kilda, which is for the most part a single great puffin terrace.

There are three races of guillemot, two of which occur in the Scottish waters. *Uria aalge hyperborea* breeds in the Arctic and is a winter visitor; *U.a.aalge* the black northern race and *U.a.al-*

*Guillemots (Photo
J. MacGeoch)*

bionis the sooty-brown, southern race breed in Scotland, the
latter predominating in the Hebrides. There is also a north-
south gradation of the 'bridled' form, which has a white eye-
ring. In Shetland >20% are 'bridled', in the Hebrides >10%
and in the south of England only 1%. The razorbill (*A. torda*) is
of the race *islandica*, breeding from Iceland to Brittany, and the
puffin (*F. arctica*) is of the race *grabae* breeding from the Faeroe
Islands and southern Scandinavia to France.

   Guillemots and razorbills have been increasing in numbers
in recent years in Scotland, and this has been seen in Canna
and Tiree. During the 1950s, the puffin population on Hirta, St
Kilda declined and fringe colonies entirely disappeared while
dense colonies became noticeably depleted (Harris, 1984).
During this period, puffins may not have decreased in other
islands of St Kilda which were densely stocked, and the species
was increasing elsewhere in Scotland. After a period of stabi-
lisation the population on Hirta is again increasing by about
4% per annum. Such fluctuations are probably related to a
decline in the preferred food of the puffin in the established
fishing areas, which is reflected in chick survival. In 1959, widespread mortality of puffin chicks occurred on Hirta; on Dun

alone there were estimated to have been at least 8,000 dead, and autopsies showed death by starvation (Boddington, 1960).

Guillemots ringed in the Hebrides, mainly on Canna, have been found as juveniles in the North Sea, but adult recoveries have been mainly from southern England, with a few from France and Spain. Razorbills from the Hebrides do not appear in the North Sea, but probably move southward in company with the guillemots. Puffins disperse widely in all directions in winter; two chicks ringed on Sule Skerry on consecutive days were recovered in the following December as far apart as Newfoundland and Tenerife.

The black guillemot (*Cepphus grylle*) or 'tystie', is comparatively rare; the Scottish population was estimated as about 7,500 pairs in 1969–70, with 530 in the Outer Hebrides and possibly about 1,000 in the Hebrides as a whole. Recent counts on Skye and the Monach Isles indicate that these are substantial underestimates. In 1988, 7,900 birds were counted in the Hebrides, but the apparent increase may be related to a much more assiduous survey in recent years. Unlike the guillemot, which is concentrated in large, well separated breeding colonies, the 'tystie' is present on most islands in small nesting groups of seldom more than 10 pairs but sometimes, as at Shillay in the Monachs and Belnahua in Lorne, 20 or more. They disperse locally in autumn, acquiring their winter garb and seldom travelling more than 100km from the nest site. The little auk (*Alle alle*) is a winter vagrant in the Outer Hebrides and the extinct great auk (*Pinguinis impennis*) was last recorded at Stac an Armin, St Kilda in July 1840.

CHAPTER 12

The Seal Islands

Seals have great public appeal and are protected by popular acclaim, despite the complaints of fishermen and fish farmers about the damage they do to their trade. Remote, strange animals, they fascinate many people, and their apparent wide-eyed innocence strikes a chord of sympathy in the human mind. Fraser Darling wrote (1939):

the great seals are the people of the sea and it is not to be wondered at that Gaeldom should have invested them with half-veiled but occasionally irruptive humanity.

In Britain there are two species of seal: the grey seal (*Halichoerus grypus*) and the common seal (*Phoca vitulina*). The grey seal breeds in the Hebrides between September and November. Pupping occurs above highwater mark at traditional sites where bulls hold a kind of territory which can extend into the sea, but is more usually well above the shore. Mothers and pups stay ashore during nursing, but part when the mother is mated

Common seal (Photo J. M. Boyd)

at the end of the short nursing period. The common seal pups in June and July, and birth and nursing of pups takes place on inter-tidal sand and rock and in the sea. The grey seal pup may drown if it enters the sea before it is weaned and has moulted its thick, white, natal coat known as *lanugo*, whereas the common seal pup sheds its lanugo *in utero* and is born with its sea-going coat, so swims immediately with its mother.

The full-grown grey seals are distinctly larger than any common seals. The dark, broad forehead and large muzzle of the grey seal bull distinguish it from the grey seal cow, which has a steel-grey head and back, a shorter muzzle and cream-coloured blotching on the chest and belly, although some females can also be quite dark. The literal translation of the scientific name for the grey seal is the 'Roman-nosed sea pig', and this is probably a concise and apt description of the species. In the common seal there is less difference between the sexes, and both have shorter muzzles than greys with a smaller, more rounded head and body colour varying from dark brown to fawn, often spotted all over. There is an overlap in the appearance of the juvenile greys with adult commons, and the best diagnosis of species is in the arrangement of the nostrils: in the grey they are well-spaced ventrally, while in the common they are V-shaped. There is also a difference in the type of coastline that the two species inhabit. The grey seal likes exposed coasts and is at home around the outlying islands, while the common prefers sheltered coasts, and because of this is called the 'har-

Grey seal bull fresh from the sea in his breeding territory on the sheep-grazed pastures of Shillay, Sound of Harris in September 1953 (Photo J. Donaldson)

bour seal' in other parts of the world. In the Hebrides the grey seal is often found sharing sheltered waters with the common seal, but the common seal is very seldom seen in the surf-bound habitats of the grey seal, though it does occur in very exposed sites in Shetland and Tiree.

Seals and the Hebrideans

Ron Mor, the great seal, is part of Gaelic lore. The mysticism which surrounds the grey seal is described by Seton Gordon (1926):

Among the people of the isles these great seals have always been regarded as half human. It is said that the clan MacCodrum had affinity with the seals, and at the annual seal battue in autumn an old woman of the clan was always seized by violent pains out of sympathy with her kinsfolk of the sea that were then being murdered in their surf-drenched home.

Today, with the decline of local fisheries and the statutory protection of seals, there is less contact between people and seals and the mystical traditions have faded. In historical times there was never a widespread tradition of seal hunting in the Hebrides, though the hunter-fishermen from mesolithic to medieval times probably hunted seals as the Scandinavians and Eskimos have always done. Seals provided meat, oil and hides for the islanders, but these commodities have been superseded in time by home-produced agricultural products, imported rubber and leather ware, fuel oils, bottled gas and pharmaceuticals. The first account of seal hunting in the Hebrides is by Martin (1703) in North Uist:

On the Western Coast of this Island lyes the Rock Cousmil (Cousamul) . . . still famous for the yearly fishing of Seals there, in the end of October . . . the Parish Minister hath his choice of all the young Seals and that which he takes is called Cullen Mory, that is Virgin Mary's seal . . . When the crew are quietly landed, they surround the Passes, and then the signal for the general attacque is given from the Boat and so they beat them down with big staves . . . giving them many blows before they are killed . . . I was told also that 320 Seals, Young and Old, have been killed at one time in the Place.

During the height of the human population in the mid-19th century, after the collapse of the kelp industry when poverty and malnutrition were rife, seal hunting probably became a widespread necessity. In 1844, North Rona became uninhabited and the build-up of the large grey seal assembly there probably dates from that time (Boyd, 1963). By 1880, there were enough seals breeding on Rona to attract hunters, who also visited Sula Sgeir to take gannets (see p. 207). Similarly, when St Kilda was evacuated in 1930 and the Monach Isles in 1944, breeding colonies of grey seals became established, and we believe that the increase in the grey seal population in the Hebrides, recorded in the second half of this century, began in the middle of last century following the withdrawal of man from the outlying islands both as a resident and as a visiting seal-hunter. Since the Conservation of Seals Act, 1970, grey seals have been killed in the Hebrides to protect fisheries and fish farms and, under licence, to supply a small craft industry in seal skins which has now declined. In 1977, an unsuccessful attempt was made by the Department of Agriculture and Fisheries for Scotland to reduce substantially the number of seals breeding on Gasker and the Monach Isles by a licensed Norwegian sealer; 324 adult seals were killed but bad weather caused the operation to be abandoned.

Size and Distribution of the Grey Seal Population

The Sea Mammal Research Unit of the Natural Environment Research Council surveys the grey seals on their breeding grounds each year. The estimated number of grey seals in Great Britain in 1985 is given in Table 12.1.

Stock	Year	Pup production	Population size	Probable status
Inner Hebrides	1985	1,700	7,500	Unknown
Outer Hebrides (incl. N. Rona)	1985	10,900	42,500	Increasing
Orkney	1985	6,900	26,900	Increasing
Shetland	1983	1,000	3,500	Unknown
L. Eriboll & Helmsdale	1984	900	3,100	Unknown
Farne Isles	1985	860	4,400	Stable*
Isle of May	1985	800	4,000	Stable*
SW Britain	1982	850	3,000	Unknown

* These stocks are shown separately as equivalent all-age populations which have some degree of exchange.

Table 12.1   Status of the grey seal in Great Britain in 1985 (NERC, 1987)

About 24,000 grey seal pups are probably born annually on the coasts of Great Britain, with perhaps another thousand in Ireland (Hewer, 1974), of which 12,600 (about half) are born in the Hebrides (including North Rona). From knowledge of the

population age structure, the total number of seals can be estimated from the number of pups born. This shows that about
53% of grey seals in Britain live in the Hebrides making up
one-third of the world population.

A glance at the map (Fig. 28) shows that isolation and lack of
disturbance by man has a strong bearing upon the distribution
of the grey seal in its choice of breeding sites. Almost without
exception in the Hebrides, the colonies are on small seldom-
visited islands, though these may be within sight of an inhabited shore across a narrow sound as at Nave Island (Islay),
Eilein Ghaoideamul (Oronsay) and Gunna (Tiree). The
breeding distribution is shown in Table 12.2. In recent years,
the grey seal population has increased at 3–7% per annum in
the Hebrides, depending on the colony. However, a recent epidemic of a distemper-like disease amongst seals in Europe may
have temporarily reduced this rate of increase.

Island	1961	1968	1976	1981
Outer Hebrides				
Monach Isles	50	200	2575	
North Rona	2600	2200*	2500	
Gasker	1094	1400	2340	
Shillay	150	200	690	
Coppay	80	150	515	
Haskeir	113	—	385	
Causamul	84	200	270	
Deasker	17	—	75	
Outer Hebrides	4200	4350	9350	
Inner Hebrides				
Treshnish Isles				755
Oronsay+				745
Gunna				235
Nave Is. Islay				105
Others #				100
Inner Hebrides				1940

* Boyd and Campbell, 1971
+ Eilein nan Ron and Eilein Ghaoideamal (Oronsay)
# Jura (40), Rum (30) and a few on each of Canna, Coll, Tiree and
Skye.

Table 12.2   Estimates of production of grey seal pups in the
Outer Hebrides in 1978 (Boyd, 1961; Bonner, 1976; Summers,
1978) and the Inner Hebrides in 1981 (Vaughan, 1981).

When we began our work on grey seals in the Hebrides we
inherited from Fraser Darling the concept that the stocks on
the various breeding islands were biologically (genetically)

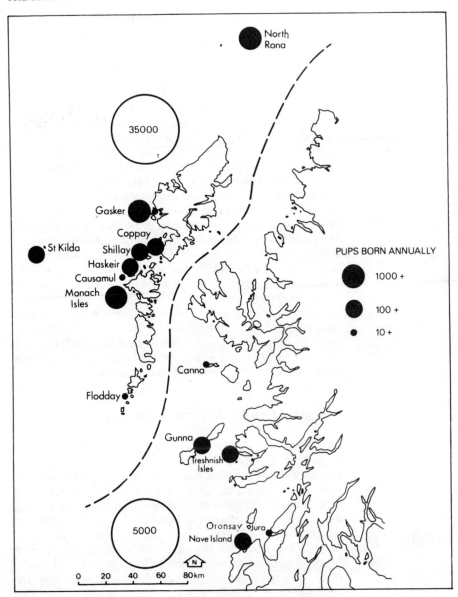

Fig. 28
*Distribution of grey
seal breeding grounds
in the Hebrides (after
Summers and
Harwood, 1979 and
Vaughan, 1983)*

separate; he drew attention to differences in the coat colour of
the stocks that he studied at the Treshnish Isles and North
Rona. The programme of work that started for the Nature
Conservancy at North Rona in the late fifties, and which has
been continued by us and others ever since, has shown that
there is probably little, if any, such separation and that, while

the choice of breeding grounds seems to be mainly confined to the long-established sites listed in Table 12.2, there is inter-change between them. Young bulls and cows branded on North Rona have subsequently been found breeding on the Monach Isles, and from this it has been estimated that at least 8% of the seals on the Monach Isles are of North Rona stock (Harwood, Anderson and Curry, 1976).

Further evidence of recruitment to breeding islands of 'out-side' offspring is found in the rate of increase in the size of the assembly on the Monach Isles. In the period 1961–76, the number of pups born there increased steadily from 50 to 2575 per annum, which would have been impossible without recruitment from other islands. However, some degree of separation probably exists between stocks in different sectors of the British coast. For instance, the timing of the breeding season differs in different sectors; the first pups to be born each year are on the coast of South Wales in September while the last are born at Scroby Sands, Norfolk, in December. The spread of births in the Hebrides, including North Rona, is from the beginning of October to mid-November. However, there is an earlier start by about a week in the more southerly assem-blies on the Treshnish Isles and Oronsay, where the peak of pupping occurs about 2nd October, than on North Uist and Harris, where the peak is about 7th, and on North Rona, where the peak is later still, occurring about 10th October.

The Breeding Cycle of the Grey Seal

The breeding cycle of the grey seal which, before Fraser Dar-ling's time fifty years ago was a mystery, is now well known. During the spring and summer, the nursery islands hold few seals and the breeding grounds above high watermark have none at all. Where the seals from all the breeding islands go at this time is largely unknown. However, judging by reports of marked young seals from North Rona, the dispersal may be over 650km from the breeding site; sightings range from Donegal (530km), to south-east Iceland (750km) and south-west Norway (720km). However, the young seals may not necessarily follow their seniors to these distant shores; they may wander far from the 'normal' range or be carried far by sea currents. The population probably scatters from all the breeding islands to favourite feeding grounds where they can quickly make good their loss of condition through breeding, though most of them probably remain within 150km, since although they leave the breeding islands *en masse* in October and November, many return there to moult in January and

February. Both bulls and cows occur in these moulting assemblies, but the late winter is a particularly important time for the cows; the fertilised ovum forms a blastocyst and remains dormant in the uterus for about 3 months after mating, becoming implanted in the wall of the uterus. Seals, together with other sundry species such as the roe deer and the eastern spotted skunk, are unusual in having delayed implantation, the end of which roughly coincides with the time of moult. In a few weeks, the seals will have changed their coats and be off again to their hunting, the females with their growing embryos.

During the summer dispersal, seals from different breeding islands must come to share the same feeding grounds. The bulls are first to begin the return to the breeding grounds, gathering from late July onwards on rocks which, earlier in the year, were occupied by the moulting assemblies.

By late August, the bulls have been joined by cows on the rocks adjacent to the breeding grounds; they are heavily pregnant, and usually closer to the water than the bulls. They also sleep less soundly, and will be the first to slip into the water at the slightest sign of danger. There is much fidgeting and calling in soft, haunting voices. At North Rona the resting rocks are on Gealldruig Mhor and Loba Sgeir, which are the thresholds of the nursery grounds on Fianuis and Sceapull.

The build up in the numbers of bulls and cows occurs synchronously. Breeding bulls will normally weigh between 250 and 300kg and are over 2m long. Only the prime bulls will be successful at retaining a position on the breeding grounds, where competition for a place can be fierce. Few bulls under the age of 10 will win through and, even when old enough,

Grey seal bull's head showing the wide dark eyes and the vibrissae on the muzzle and forehead said to detect movements of prey in the sea (Photo J. M. Boyd)

sheer physical size is important. Bulls must also bring ashore significant body reserves, because the most successful will stay for up to 8 weeks without leaving to feed or drink. This is a significant drain on their resources and few will probably manage to defend a position on the breeding grounds for more than 3 or 4 years running. Throughout the breeding period the aim of a grey seal bull is to station himself in those areas of a colony where females are most likely to give birth, feed their pups and come into oestrus.

At North Rona, the gullies on Fianuis are a narrow main access for a heavy traffic of lumbering adults. The seals here are more densely packed, and in a constant state of agitation with much fighting of bulls and bickering and snapping of cows. By the middle of October this is a foul ghetto of the seals' own making—a muddy quagmire and a string of septic pools dotted with the pathetic bodies of bloated pups. Even more pathetic are the starving orphans with puss-filled eyes, con-trasting with the fat, fluffy youngsters on the wide space of the hinterland where the turf remains intact and conditions are better.

From the Fank (sheep fold) Brae above the promontory of Fianuis it is possible to watch the seals closely, out of range of scent and sight. Among the many bobbing heads around the east landing on the sheltered side, there is one looking intently inland, often stretching to see the other seals already ashore. The dappled silvery throat and short nose shows it to be a cow, possibly about to deliver her first pup. In a few moments she is ashore and desperately hauling herself clear of the surf breaking upon her back and splaying upon the slabs in front of her. Her wet, blue-grey back shines like polished steel. An embattled bull—dull by comparison—hurrying to escape an adversary, inspects her as she makes her way up the slabs. A quick snap and lunge sees him off to the sea. It is now obvious that she is pregnant, and she is clean and fresh compared with the other seals which have been ashore for a week or more. Her bulk is due less to her unborn pup than to the thick layer of blubber fat she is carrying to see herself and her pup through the 18 days of lactation.

At the top of the shore rocks she sees the other seals already distributed over the swards ahead. She is cautious, moving one lurch at a time, looking anxiously around her and sniffing the air. A fracas close-by frightens her and she quickly turns towards the sea, but, reassured, resumes her progress inland. Finding her way barred by other cows warding her off as she approaches their pups, she is compelled to zig-zag through the colony in a series of minor conflicts until, eventually, she reaches 'clear' ground at the old bothy by the storm beach,

which flanks the cliff-top on the west side. She has traversed
the peninsula and has reached the far fringe, almost on the
western, cliff-bound coast. However, she has found her pupping spot and lies quiet awaiting her time of delivery. This
journey from the sea, though arduous, is not a record; a few
bulls and cows breed on the ridge at the top of the Fank Brae
from where we are observing, about 40m above and 450m from
the sea.

Births are rarely seen; that is mainly because of the visual
disadvantage of most observers in viewing the herd from the
flat, but also because of the rapid delivery of the foetus in a few
minutes, sometimes even in seconds. the first indication of a
birth at North Rona is a noisy scuffle of gulls over the afterbirth
during which a bird is sometimes maimed by the reactive cow.
A few hapless great black-backed gulls stalk the colony drag-
ging broken wings.

After an hour our attention returns to the cow by the bothy
and we find a thin yellowish pup lying beside her; she has
succeeded in warding-off the gulls which, having devoured the
afterbirth, linger on the ruined bothy, still hopeful of having the
pup as well. The pup is helpless, though it instinctively nuzzles
at the mother searching for a nipple. The touch of the infant on
her flank makes her keel over on one side to expose her belly
and pivot round to present her nipples to the pup. She may also
appear to guide the little one towards her nipples by waving her
flipper. The two nipples, normally inverted in the streamlining
of her body for swimming, are then everted and the pup atta-
ches and sucks in the first hour of its life. Feeding occurs about
five times in 24 hours at regular intervals. The seal cow's milk
has a fat content of 50% compared with the 3.5% of the dairy
cow, and the pup probably drinks this rich milk as fast as it is
produced by the mother; it weighs about 14kg at birth and 40kg
when weaned about 17 days later—putting on over 1.5kg per
day! This increase in weight is achieved by little growth in
length from 82cm at birth to 90cm at weaning; most of the
weight increase is caused by a thickening layer of blubber
under the skin. Needless to say, the cow loses weight by about
4kg per day and at time of weaning, she is barely two-thirds of
her weight on coming ashore, about 170kg. In contrast to her
plump condition on arrival in the colony, she departs lean,
almost skinny, but not before she has been mated by one or
more of the bulls.

From our observation post on Fank Brae it is possible to pick
out the bulls from the cows; they are fewer (1 in 10 in the dense
colony) larger, and generally darker in colour. They are well
spaced through the colony and do not lie closely packed as they
would on the offshore rocks. On the fringes of the colony, and

in the sea immediately offshore, there are many other bulls ready to move in and take the place of tired bulls. Bulls, unlike cows, continue to grow in size through life and the older, bigger bulls probably occupy the breeding grounds early in the season.

Bulls first come into breeding condition when they are 5 or 6 years old, and most of them are dead by the time they are 15; a few live longer but rarely over 20 years old. Cows also attain puberty when five or six years old, but live longer than bulls; most are dead by the time they are 20, but a few live longer occasionally to over 30 years and sometimes, though rarely, over 40.

There is an air of reluctant toleration of each other among the resident bulls. Each keeps its distance but does not miss an opportunity of extending its chances of mating and of challenging the advance of neighbouring bulls or intruders. These encounters follow a pattern: the lumbering intruder halts when he sees the territory holder advancing; lowering his head flat along the ground and opening his mouth showing his teeth, he hisses; the challenger may do likewise, the two may then advance, and an energetic clash can follow with contestants snarling and gripping each other by the folds of skin on the neck, flipper and tail. The fight is usually short-lived but, despite the toughness of the skin in these animals, some deep wounds can be inflicted. Fights to the death probably never happen. Usually, however, the challenge does not come to blows and the challenger makes off back to the sea or to a safe distance.

An intruding challenger which has come to the rear of the colony by a fringe route passing further and further from the sea can find himself in deep trouble. In the heat of the moment he has turned into the colony, to find himself surrounded by resident bulls, and he chooses the shortest route to the sea. This is a savage gauntlet of running fights with perhaps six or more big bulls, ending with a headlong plunge into the sea. We have seen a bull which had fallen to its death over a cliff, probably as a result of such a chase.

Copulation commences with the cow coming on 'heat' towards the end of the nursing period, some 15–18 days after giving birth. A day or two may pass before she will allow the bull to mate. He will grasp her by the neck but only to facilitate his successful mounting, and afterwards they will lie quietly for up to 15 minutes. Mating also takes place in the sea. In the deep channels at Eilein nan Ron, Oronsay, there is evidence of bulls holding 'territory' in sheltered waters opposite small pupping beaches. During coition, the pair are submerged, only surfacing to breathe.

During the 18-day nursing period the pup has grown rapidly, and partially moulted its thick birth coat. By the end of the first month of life it has little or no white fur and is clad instead in its short, sea-going coat. The female pups have blue-grey heads and backs with light underparts, often with faint grey flecks. The males are dark grey, sometimes jet black, with faint grey flecking on flanks and belly. Wide-eyed, they face the world with pulsing nostrils, trembling vibrissae and tiny glistening teeth set in a delicate pink mouth; the milk teeth are shed *in utero*. Without warning, they are deserted by their mothers, and at little more than a fortnight old, they have to fend for themselves.

Grey seal cow and recently born pup on North Rona. The pup's white coat is cast during the nursing period and before it puts to sea (Photo J. M. Boyd)

Pup mortality is high. If the little ones survive the ravages of the gulls, the bites of jealous, quarrelsome cows, infection and the crushings by both bulls and cows, they face the hazards of sea-going without the guidance and protection of parents. Well equipped as they are with a sleek, waterproof and heatproof coat and layer of blubber, provisioned with nourishment to see them through the learning-to-feed period, and having the instincts to avoid danger and defend themselves against an enemy (try handling one!), many perish in their first year. About half of the pups born never live to see their first birthday.

Mortality of pups is much lower on colonies like the Monach Isles, Shillay (Harris) and the Treshnish Isles (<12%)— where the seals pup on clean sand or wave- and rain-washed

rocky platforms—than on North Rona or Gasker (>20%)
where the turf soon breaks and where infection may be har-
boured in the soil.

Conservation and Management of the Grey Seal

The increase in numbers of grey seals, which can be traced
back to the last century, still continues. The fishing industry
claims that seals cause significant damage to fisheries through
predation on catchable stocks of fish, codworm parasites and
damage to fishing gear. The situation is made more serious by
the decline in available fish stocks in areas frequented by seals,
but for reasons other than seal predation; the continuous
exploitation of fish stocks by man over the last century, with
ever greater efficiency in fishing technology. Parrish and
Shearer (1977) estimated that 65,000 tonnes of fish (£15–20 million at 1974 prices), were 'lost to seals' annually in the UK.
About 85% is attributed to grey seals (55,000 tonnes), of which
about 28,000 tonnes may be taken in the Hebrides. However,
these estimates were obtained using highly dubious
measurements of the grey seal diet and food requirements. In
1981, the Sea Mammal Research Unit (NERC) produced a
more realistic estimate of fish consumption by grey seals. It
seems that 60% of the diet may be sand-eels, while cod, whiting, saithe, pollack, haddock, ling and many other species make
up the remaining 40%. They estimated that, on average, a grey
seal will eat about 5 kg of fish each day, which means that the
British grey seals eat 84,000–215,000 tonnes of fish each year. It
would, of course, be unrealistic to translate this figure into an
estimate of financial loss to the fishing industry because the
great majority of fish eaten by grey seals probably have no
commercial value.

The case put against the seals by certain fishermen and fish
farmers whose stations are continuously visited by persistently
roguish seals is irrefutable, and the fishermen are legally
entitled to defend their stations in a humane way by shooting
the intruders with a rifle. However, this raises another problem, because there are now many fish farms in the sea lochs of
the Hebrides and all these will defend their nets against seals.
Killing is neither regulated nor monitored, so this could be a
major new source of mortality for seals that could affect their
populations.

In 1977, NERC advised on how to stabilise grey-seal stocks
in Britain at the mid-1960's level, and how to maintain a
sustainable pup harvest with maximum gain in scientific
information. Since the grey seal is polygamous, little or no con-

trol of numbers can be achieved by culling bulls; measures of control can only be applied by culling pups and adult cows or a combination of both. Such operations on the breeding grounds causes disturbance, the escape of many cows to sea and the desertion and orphaning of suckling pups. Highly organised operations in ideal weather may achieve the desired objective, but operations are often disrupted by storms resulting with difficulties in seamanship, shooting, taking samples from the dead seals, recording and disposal of carcasses. Considering the Outer Hebrides and Orkney as a single stock, the NERC scientists stated that the population could be reduced to the desired mid-1960s level by either culling 6000 pups and 6000 cows in one year with a pup cull of 6000 thereafter, or in a sliding scale of annual culls up to a ten-year period with 4000 pups and 700 cows annually with 4000 pups annually thereafter. The effects of such culls on the population, however, are unpredictable since there is no way of making a consistent choice of animals to be killed; while older cows may hold their ground and be shot, younger cows may put to sea at the sound of the first shot and not return during the culling operation.

The shooting of hundreds of cows and pups annually in the National Nature Reserves of North Rona and Monach Isles which, together with the small seal islands off Harris, Treshnish Isles and Oronsay are Sites of Special Scientific Interest under the Wildlife and Countryside Act, should require quite irrefutable scientific justification. So far, despite strenuous efforts by fishery biologists, a directly significant connection between grey seals and the general status of available commercial fisheries has not been proven (except locally—often by common seals). The suggested cull to a level of the mid-1960s will logically reduce the number of fish taken by grey seals, but is unlikely to cause any significant rise in the general income of fishermen.

Common Seal

The distinction between grey and common seals has rarely been made in the literature of the Hebrides, though Martin (1703), referring to the Outer Hebrides, states:

those (seals) on the east side, who are of lesser stature (than the grey seal), bring forth their young in the midle of June

This is a clear identification of the common seal. Today, they still frequent the sheltered eastern coasts and sounds of the Outer Hebrides, and also are widespread in the Inner Hebrides (Vaughan, 1983). They are very confiding, and provide an exciting spectacle for sightseers on ferries, yachts and tripper-boats around Gigha, in the Firth of Lorne, Loch Linnhe and the Sounds of Mull, Iona and Sleat. Ferry passengers are likely to see common seals in summer in the rock-bound approaches to Port Ellen, Islay; Arinagour, Coll; Canna Harbour; Castlebay, Barra; Lochboisdale; Lochmaddy; Tarbert, Harris; Stornoway and in crossings of the Sounds of Barra, Eriskay and Harris, Kyle of Lochalsh and Kylerhea where the Forestry Commission have built a hide to observe seals and otters. The common seal is mainly of dark brown appearance, but due to a varying intensity of light speckling can vary in colour from almost uniform dark brown to light fawn or, more rarely, creamy white.

The bulls are somewhat larger than the cows, but this is not as obvious as in the grey seal; adult bulls are 1.5 to 2m long and cows, 1.3 to 1.5m. They weigh about 100kg. The breeding biology is still unclear; scientists cannot examine this species as they do the grey seal, since pupping and mating does not take place in quick succession while ashore. Common seal pups are born on tidal strands in the Hebrides between mid-June and mid-July; at birth they are about 85cm in length and weigh about 9kg. Suckling lasts from four to six weeks, bringing the pup's weight to about 26kg at weaning, and the cow comes into oestrus at the end of lactation. The moult probably takes place in August. Like the grey seal, common seals have a delayed implantation of the fertilised ovum (blastocyst) of about 12 weeks, and a gestation period of 8 months.

Though the haul-outs of common seals are reasonably well known, little is known about the numerical status of the species; unlike the grey seal it has not been possible to count the common seal pups and to calculate from that the total population. However, they are so widely distributed and generally present in small numbers, particularly on sheltered coasts, the Hebrides must hold many thousands. Common seals in the Hebrides remained largely unaffected by the epidemic of a distemper-like disease in 1988. In company with grey seals they have been hunted since prehistoric times and bones have been recorded from archeological sites (Clark, 1946). Before the Conservation of Seals Act (1970), there was no protection for the common seal in Britain, but in historical times it is unlikely that many were taken before the use of the rifle. In the decade 1971–81, an average of 240 common seal pups were killed annually in the Hebrides under a commercial licence, in addition to others of all ages that have been legitimately shot by fishermen and fish farmers protecting their nets and cages.

The movements of common seals probably depend much on

local conditions. While many probably feed along the sheltered shores of sea lochs, they will also move many miles out to sea to feed. Observations of common seals in Orkney showed this to be the case—individuals will make foraging trips to sea of several days duration, and we have observed large seasonal fluctuations in numbers of common seals at sites in the Hebrides. While observers at Davaar Island (Campbelltown), Ronachan (Kintyre), Isle Oronsay (Skye) reported large numbers of common seals in spring and summer, those at West Kilbride and Head of Ayr (Ayrshire), Carradale (Kintyre), Lough Foyle, McArthur's Head (Islay) and Lady's Rock (Lismore) reported large numbers in autumn and winter. Some of these changes may be local redistributions, but more distant seasonal movements cannot be ruled out. The numbers present at a site will also change according to the state of moult of the population, and these factors have to be included in any estimate of population size derived from one-off counts of seals at haul-out sites.

At some sites, common seals patrol the sheltered coasts, sea-lochs and inner sounds, usually singly. They tend to feed at high tide; the rest of the time is spent sleeping on the leeward side of rocks, safe from disturbance but conveniently close to their radius of hunting. Occasionally they are joined by grey seals and while juvenile greys may mix with the commons, the adults usually remain apart on other skerries. Many such situations are in the path of migratory sea-trout and salmon, and within easy reach of salmon-fishing stations and fish farms. There is little wonder, therefore, that the common seal has a particularly bad reputation and is shot on sight when it ventures near such installations.

The seals of the Hebrides have given both of us that sense of wonderment in nature without which there is no driving force in biology, and provided us with a rousing professional challenge. We were initially inspired by the work of our late mentor and friend Sir Frank Fraser Darling on North Rona and Treshnish before the last war (Boyd, 1986), and in the fifties and sixties the late Professor H.R. Hewer, whose book *British Seals* (1974) in this series is the standard work on the subject. In the seventies and eighties we worked with W.N. Bonner, C.F. Summers, Sheila Anderson, Mike Fedak and the late R.W. (Bill) Vaughan, who tragically lost his life while studying seals in the Wash. The sense of companionship which attended the work, which was focused to a great extent on North Rona, the Monach Isles and the Harris islands, still lives on. However, despite our best efforts, the seals still hold many of their secrets close to themselves.

Islay

Many things combine to make the Hebrides a very special place for the naturalist: the flowers of the machair islands; the seabirds of St Kilda; the red deer of Rum; the grey seals of North Rona—the geese of Islay. Indeed, Islay is the wildfowl island *par excellence*, with a great extent and variety of coastal and wetland habitats. There is an agricultural tradition in Islay possibly dating back to Bronze Age times, and this saw great expansion in the Middle Ages to the population maximum in the early 19th century, since when farming has replaced crofting-type landuse. Today, Islay resembles the Highland-Lowland fringe of the Scottish mainland, with good-sized tenant farms on estates of declining size and prosperity. In the last century, the estates have been managed as sporting land *inter alia* for wildfowl, with protection of the wildfowl grounds for private shooting. The main overwintering stocks consist of: up to 22,000 barnacle geese (*Branta leucopsis*), 7,000 Greenland white-fronted geese (*Anser abliforns flavirostris*), 3,000 eider (*Somateria mollissima*), 1,500 scaup (*Aythya marila*), 800 teal (*Anas crecca*), 500 wigeon (*Anas penelope*), 100–500 each of mallard (*Anas platyrhynchos*), shelduck (*Tadorna tadorna*), less than 100 greylag geese (*Anser anser*) and pochard (*Aythya ferina*). Since the wildfowl grounds of Islay are of national and international importance (many of the wintering species breed in other countries), the NCC has notified them as SSSI's (p. 245) and has devised a scheme for compensating farmers for the grazing of geese within the SSSI's; also the RSPB runs the farm of Aoradh at Gruinart as a wildfowl reserve (p. 338 & 341) in the heart of the barnacle goose ground (the geese of Islay became a *cause célèbre* in nature conservation in the mid-1980s).

Barnacle Goose

From mid-October to mid-April, barnacle geese that nest in East Greenland occupy north-west Scotland and Ireland.

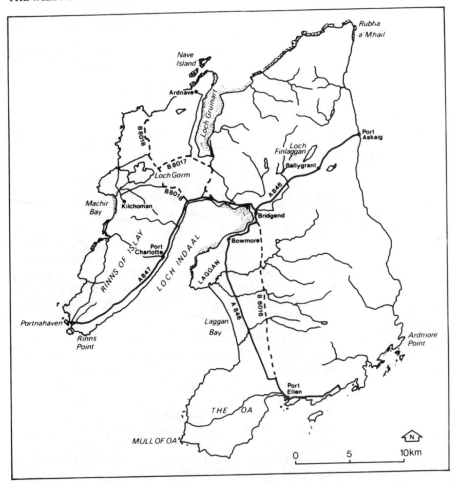

Fig. 29
Location map of Islay

These form a population of about 30,000 birds, distinct from those that nest in Spitzbergen, which spend the winter on the Solway. The main body occupies the Hebrides, with small well-separated flocks on south Orkney and the mainland seaboards of Sutherland, Wester Ross and Argyll. The headquarters of the species is in Islay, and at the peaks of numbers in November and March the island may hold over 27,500, almost 90% of the Greenland stock (Table 13.1), which for a short time in autumn, assembles in Islay before dispersing to Ireland and other wintering grounds in the Hebrides (Easterbee *et al.*, 1987). Clearly, Gruniart, which in autumn may hold *c.* 74% of the stock, is a focal point in the annual migration of the Greenland barnacle geese, and is a very important area in their conservation (p. 245).

Island Group	March 1973	March/April 1978	March/April 1983	March 1988
Islay	15,000	21,000	14,000	20,200
Treshnish Isles	420	610	620	378
Tiree/Coll	145	390	620	550
Barra Sound	335	455	375	431
Isay (Skye)	295	290	250	245
Monach Isles	640	760	640	715
Harris Sound	980	1,330	1,555	1,007
Shiant Isles	450	420	420	532
Scotland	19,740	28,060	20,820	26,957
Ireland	4,400	5,760	4,430	7,594
Total	24,140	33,820	25,250	34,551

Table 13.1 Number of Greenland barnacle geese counted in aerial surveys of their main haunts (Ogilvie 1983a and *in litt.* 1988—the figures are rounded by Thom, 1986 and are not peak counts).

The barnacle geese in Islay are distributed throughout the pasturelands, which have been improved by agriculture over the centuries, and which have been used in recent decades in modern grass-intensive husbandry, supporting herds of dairy and beef cattle. However, a decline in dairy husbandry in the 1980s has probably affected the distribution of the geese. Concentrations are centred on Gruinart, Bridgend and Laggan, between which there is probably much exchange. A large number of birds that roost at Gruinart use the Loch Gorm area for feeding (p. 243 & opposite).

The population has been counted annually in November, after the main influx of birds has arrived from Greenland, and in March/April before the main exodus departs to their Arctic breeding grounds. In the 1960s and 70s, counts in January showed a slightly smaller population in mid-winter, possibly caused by winter mortality through shooting and natural causes, followed by some immigration into Islay from elsewhere. After the shooting season in February and March, the pastures of the Hebrides are at the lowest point of annual productivity, and at this time, the improved fields of Islay are clearly more attractive to between 2,000 and 3,000 geese than the threadbare, withered machairs and sheep-walks of neighbouring islands and the mainland coast. Before making the long flight to Greenland and entering upon the rigours of the breeding season, the geese require a build-up of body condi-

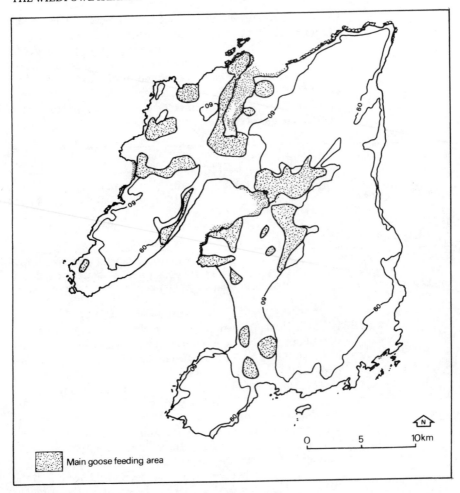

Fig. 30
*Map showing the main
goose wintering grounds
in Islay (from Ogilvie,
1983)*

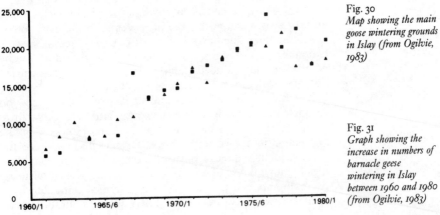

Fig. 31
*Graph showing the
increase in numbers of
barnacle geese
wintering in Islay
between 1960 and 1980
(from Ogilvie, 1983)*

tion which, in the southern Hebrides, can best be achieved in the reseeded and fertilised cattle pastures of Islay.

Between 1961 and 1981 the number of barnacle geese wintering in Islay increased from about 6,000 to 20,000 (Ogilvie, 1983b). The data are plotted in Fig. 30, and five key counts of the 20 given by Ogilvie are shown in Table 13.2, which also gives data on recruitment, total Greenland population, and the percentage of that total wintering in Islay.

Winter	Nov	Mar/Apr	Change	% young	Greenland	% Islay
1961–2	5,800	6,800	+1,000	10.7	14,000	41.4
1965–6	nc	8,300	—	11.2	20,000	45.0
1972–3	17,300	15,000	−2,300	12.1	24,000	71.2
1977–8	19,600	21,000	+1,900	4.9	33,000	65.2
nc = no count						

Table 13.2   Four key counts of barnacle geese in Islay in November and March/April 1961–81, showing numbers on Islay, percentages of young in Islay, percentages of the total Greenland population in Islay, and data on changes in numbers (after Ogilvie 1983b).

The annual population on Islay is the total number of survivors of the previous year, including first-year young. Mortality is measured by subtracting the current autumn total, *excluding* first-year birds, from the autumn total of the previous year, *including* first-year birds. Over twenty years the average annual mortality was 9.6% which corresponds with 10% for the Spitzbergen population on the Solway. Though there was some immigration to Islay in the course of each winter, there has been no significant regional redistribution of stocks throughout this twenty-year period. Recruitment, therefore, is measured by the percentage of first-year birds present in the flocks, and has averaged 14%. The higher value of recruitment over mortality is consistent with a population which has increased by a factor of three in 20 years. In the early 1980s, recruitment declined mainly because of poor breeding success and increased shooting. This resulted in a decline in the population, but reduced shooting in recent years has caused numbers to return to the high levels of the 1970s.

Bag-records in the 1960s and early 1970s, show 500–700 barnacle geese shot by estates in winter, and to that total must be added those shot by farmers and others. However, as the population increased in the 1970s, farmers became more and more strident in their complaints of damage done to their grazings by huge flocks of geese, so the shooting season for geese (1st September to 31st January) was extended until 20th February below high-water mark. There was also an increase in

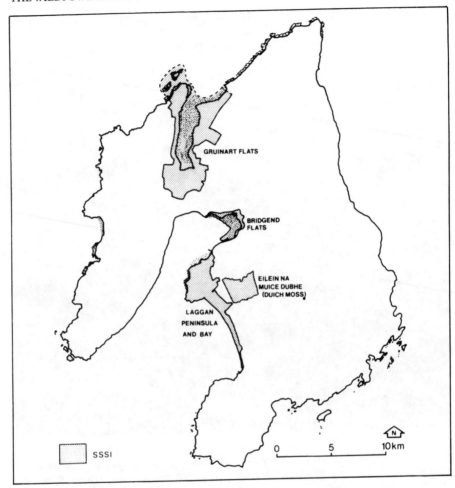

Fig. 32
Map showing the SSSIs on Islay which are of special interest because of wintering wildfowl, particularly barnacle and white-fronted geese which breed in Greenland (Updated from Kerr and Boyd, 1983)

shooting intensity by the estates to between 1,200 and 1,400 annually. This helped their tenant farmers by reducing actual numbers and dispersing the very large flocks from fertilised and reseeded fields. The estates also let the shooting to a few hotels, and there was extra income to be had from shooting by visitors. In the mid-1980s, the NCC notified the main goose grounds of Islay as three SSSIs, including part of the new RSPB Reserve at Aoradh (Fig. 32), and there followed a scheme to compensate farmers for the grazing of geese on their land situated within the SSSIs at Gruinart, Laggan and Bridgend. Outside the SSSIs, farmers obtain licences to shoot, or otherwise move, barnacle geese from their land, hopefully into the SSSIs. While this arrangement does not give full protection to the barnacle goose, the species is unmolested in its

Barnacle geese in flight in Islay (Photo Morley Hedley)

favourite grounds. Unfortunately however, the scheme is not satisfactory to all farmers, especially those whose improved fields are close to the boundaries of the SSSIs, but outside them, and do not qualify for compensation.

Greenland White-fronted Goose

The world population of the white-fronted goose (*Anser albifrons flavirostris*) breeding in West Greenland and wintering in Britain, now amounts to about 21,000 birds. During the autumns of 1982–84, the numbers in Britain increased under protection—1982: 7,200; 1983: 8,200; 1984, 9,490; 1985; 11,026; 1986; 10,809. Islay held 45–56% of the British stock (20–25% of the world stock) in November 1986 with a wide scatter of smaller concentrations notably in Tiree/Coll, Kintyre and Galloway (Table 13.3).

Island Group	Nov 1982	Nov 1983	Nov 1984	Mar/Apr 1985
O. Hebrides	89	99	114	15
Skye/Sm. Is	96	98	106	108
Tiree	372	357	620	750
Coll	343	435	441	179
Islay	3, 250	4,592	5,256	4,715
Other Areas				
NE Scot'd	457	315	376	518
N. Argyll*	158	193	243	181
S. Argyll	1,723	1,342	1,659	1,635
Galloway	595	683	633	713
England	33	1	10	13
Wales	73	93	76	88
Totals	7,189	8,188	9,490	8,997

*Data do not include those of Tiree/Coll nor of Islay all of which are given separately; they include data from Kintyre where 1,276 and 940 were counted in November 1982 and 1983 respectively; they also include 118 and 134 respectively from Loch Lomond.

Table 13.3   The distribution of Greenland white-fronted geese in the Hebrides in 1982–85 compiled from Thom 1986 and Stroud (1985).

The increase in numbers in Scotland from 4,000–5,000 in the 1950s to 7,000–8,000 in the 1980s has been accompanied by a decline in Ireland from about 15,000 to 8,000–9,000, of which 5,000–6,000 are on the Wexford Slobs, (Ogilvie 1983b). This decline is attributed mainly to the draining of bogs, widespread disturbance, and shooting. In Islay, the white-fronts are scattered widely over the island, frequenting a different range to the barnacles, but overlapping with them. While the great barnacle goose flocks roost far out on the tidal flats and on secure land such as Nave Island, the white-fronted spend the night mainly on lochs and bogs. During the day they move in small flocks composed of family groups of up to a few hundred individuals. They feed on stubbles and rush-meadows, and are sometimes seen among the barnacle geese on improved pastures.

In the period 1966–82 the white-fronted goose population fluctuated between 2,500 and 4,000, with percentages of first-year birds ranging from 4.6 to 26.1 (Ogilvie, 1983b). The average rate of recruitment from 1962–86 was 14.8% per annum, while the average rate of loss was 10.5% per annum. How many of these recruits might be immigrants from Ireland

Locality	1981/82	1982/83	1983/84	1984/85	1985/86	1986/87
Oa	540	758	865	1,232	1,286	1,128
Ardtulla	0	0	0	95	0	27
Gruinart	322	114	415	884	633	70
Gorm	232	197	454	390	349	675
Rhinns	396	657	504	217	802	1,641
Laggan	527	444	646	777	1,005	740
Glen	475	174	350	340	60	345
Kilmeny	1,096	1,535	1,358	1,321	2,197	1,860
Totals	3,588	3,879	4,592	5,256	6,332	6,486

Table 13.4   Autumn distribution of white-fronted geese in Islay in the eighties (Stroud 1984, 1985 unpublished).

A large flock of barnacle geese taking off at Gruinart Flats which lie within an SSSI and partly within an RSPB Reserve (Photo Morley Hedley)

is unknown. Today, the white-fronted goose is completely protected in Scotland, but since licences can be obtained for shooting other species of geese, and the white-fronts often live close to barnacles and greylags, many are probably accidentally shot. Illegal shooting of white-fronts in the small, widely scattered flocks throughout the Hebrides still continues.

The danger to this race of geese by the reclamation of moorland for forestry, and the extraction of peat for industrial purposes, posed a threat to the future of stocks in Islay, as it has done over many years in Ireland. In 1985–86, development and conservation interests were brought into conflict in Islay over

the proposals to extract peat for distilling from Eilean na Muice Dubh (Duich Moss), a main roost of white-fronted geese. Another proposal to afforest moorland on the Rhinns, used by white-fronts, was also in contention. These issues of white-fronted goose conservation on Islay assumed national and international importance, because Duich Moss and much of the Rhinns are SSSI's, and the white-fronted goose is a species protected under the Wildlife and Countryside Act and European Council of Minister's Directive on the Conservation of Wild Birds. These two factors effectively brought the conservation of the white-fronts and their wintering areas in Islay within the sphere of British domestic law, and in 1987 political pressures resulted in the distillers seeking and obtaining sufficient peat for their purposes in another less prestigious bog on the island.

Greylag Goose

With the thousands of wintering Greenland barnacle and white-fronted geese on Islay, there are a few hundred greylag geese (*Anser anser*), which arrive in early October and depart in early April. There is no recent breeding record of greylag in Islay, the breeding stronghold in the Hebrides being in the Uists and Benbecula. Boyd and Ogilvie (1972) thought that the greylags in Islay belonged to the indigenous native stock from north-west Scotland and were not Icelandic birds; this was based on the similar observed percentages of young birds in stocks from Islay and north-west Scotland. Greylags have never been numerous in Islay (Booth, 1981) and have been in steady decline since the 1950s when 500–600 birds frequented the fields and saltings around Islay House—now there are less than 100 in the same localities.

Tiree, Gunna and Coll

Goose-watching was a common activity of ours on a winter's day in Tiree. Starting on the Reef, we walked along the east bank of An Fhaodhail. On the left there were two square kilometres of rush meadow and fields of improved pasture and stubble; on the right rocky heath, fringed with small green fields of cattle-grazed pasture. Our quest for geese in such habitat was short-lived for, as we came in sight of the ruins of Odhrasgair, we put up a flock of about 40 Greenland white-fronts calling wildly to all their kith-and-kin across the flats towards Balephetrish and Kenovay. The ponds and watercourses held whooper and mute swans, teal, mallard, pochard, tufted duck and goldeneye, and the noise of the white-fronts sent a wave of unrest throughout the populace.

By the time we had reached the road at Balephetrish, we had counted over 300 of them—most of the stock wintering in Tiree (Table 13.3), and there were about 30 greylags in small groups among the white-fronts. However, there was no sign of barnacle geese until we had climbed Balephetrish Hill. Turning our backs upon the spacious rushy flats in the centre of the island, we were now in a different habitat—a ragged ribbon of green grass between sea and moor, running away as far as the eye could see to Coll. There, about 500m away, in their typical Hebridean setting of sea-meadows above the Atlantic breakers, grazed a tight pack of about 150 barnacle geese.

We were standing at the southern limit of the barnacle goose range in Tiree, Gunna and Coll. If we were to walk northwards we would drive them all before us and obtain little idea of the size of the population. Therefore we decided to drive to Miodar on the Gunna Sound and walk southward by the shores of Salum and Vaul. The barnacles which forage on Tiree flighted in the afternoon to roost on Gunna and we had them flying towards us. Hidden in the rocky country, there was great excitement as the flocks came flying low overhead, rearing upwards as we suddenly came into their view.

In recent winters, 400–600 barnacle geese have roosted on the Gunna roost. Some move northward to Ballyhaugh on Coll and others to the north coast of Tiree as far south as Saltaig to feed. The 300–400 white-fronted geese occupy the wetlands, stubble and improved pastures across the waist of Tiree from Balephetrish Bay to Hynish Bay, and about 100 greylag geese occupy a wide area of western Tiree between Loch Bhasapol and Loch a'Phuil and eastward to Kenovay—a few pairs of greylags have bred in Coll since the 1930s (Boyd, 1958) and are increasing, with a report of breeding in Tiree in 1986. White-fronts are fully protected and barnacles are also protected but can be shot under licence by farmers and crofters to protect crops. There are no sporting licences for these species, but greylags may be shot between 1st September and 31st January, which provides a loophole for the unscrupulous shooter. For example, two tame Canada geese (*Branta canadensis*), possibly visiting from Colonsay, which we observed in April 1986 in Tiree, were shot on the ground in the following winter by a foreign visitor. This species, like greylags, may be shot without licence, but such an incident is indicative of the low prevailing level of sportsmanship to which the protected species are exposed in remote places by some shooting parties.

The Uists and Benbecula

From the late 1950s to the late 1960s, those of us in the Nature Conservancy who had the job of setting up and managing the Loch Druidibeg National Nature Reserve in South Uist, had the memorable experience of staying with Mrs Annie Flora MacDonald on the shores of the loch. Having been the wife of a famous gamekeeper, possessing the 'second sight', and having been in service at Balmoral, 'herself' was a person of outstanding Gaelic character. We breakfasted at her kitchen window, where we could see the native greylag flighting in the misty autumn sunrise.

About 20–30 pairs of greylag which had nested on the islands and neighbouring moorland of Loch Druidibeg during the summer, had produced as many fledged goslings, and these were augmented by about the same number of juveniles of the same stock, not yet paired. The whole flock roosted on Loch Druidibeg, and in the morning flew in noisy gaggles just above the crofthouse roofs to settle for the day in the stubbles and stooks from Dromore to Howmore. In those days this was the stronghold of the native greylag in Britian, and it was for this reason that the Reserve was created initially, with the breeding islands and neighbouring shores of Loch Druidibeg owned and managed by the Conservancy as a strict wildlife sanctuary. Since then, the special interest in the Reserve has been extended to include the entire succession of species and habitats from the sandy shore to the peat moorland (see p. 388). (It is a pity though that the boundaries were not extended to run from the western to the eastern shores of South Uist, thus encompassing the sheltered, rocky, weed-infested shores, without which a comprehensive nature reserve in the Outer Hebrides is incomplete.)

In a survey of 1968–72, Newton and Kerbes (1974) found some 60 pairs of greylag geese and less than 20 on nearby moorland, producing between 30 and 53 broods. Most of the broods hatched among the heather of the willow-, birch-, rowan- and juniper-wooded islets, and were soon on the loch after hatching. However, Loch Druidibeg itself with its heathery, sedgy margins has poor feeding for goslings compared with the rich green pastures beside the nearby machair lochs. Thus the broods were quickly led along the watercourses to Lochs Stilligarry and a'Mhachair, where they stayed until fledged.

During and after the last war, the native greylag stock were used to supplement the stocks of crofthouse birds with the eggs hatched under broody hens. Numbers of breeding pairs declined but nesting continued at Loch Druidibeg where they were accorded some protection by the estate, and a few pairs continued to breed in North Uist and Lewis.

In the past twenty-five years though, the picture has changed; the greylags are no longer concentrated in and around Loch Druidibeg. From that centre, and with the protection of the breeding sites afforded them there, they have colonised many of the inland loch-systems in the Uists and Benbecula. Currently there are 2,500–3,000 native greylag geese in Britain, with 500 to 700 breeding pairs (Owen et al., 1986), of which 230–243 pairs (c. 1,860 birds of all ages) are in the Uist and Benbecula (Pickup, 1982), up to 30 are in the Sound of Harris, 10–15 are in Lewis, c. 15 are in the Summer Isles, 2–9 are in Coll, and one and two pairs are in Canna and Rum respectively (Thom, 1986). The main breeding concentration is now located on the loch-riddled landscape and east coast islands of North Uist. Paterson (1987) has updated the census in the Uists (Table 13.6), and estimated the breeding population as 156 pairs, which does not indicate a serious decline since 1982 because Pickup's data included unconfirmed reports, while Paterson's did not.

Island	February	August
North Uist	805	812
Benbecula	65	147
South Uist	301	336
Total	1,171	1,295

Table 13.5   The numbers and distribution of greylag geese in the Uists in 1986.

In winter, some of the native greylag may leave the Outer Hebrides, for example to Tiree and Islay, and those that remain are joined by migrants, possibly from north-west Scotland or Iceland. Flocks of up to 200 migrating greylags pass through the Hebrides, pitching onto headlands, off-shore islets and coastal marshes.

Over the turn of the century until the Second World War, South Uist held the main stock of geese wintering in the Hebrides, and the lodges at Grogarry and Askernish were in the midst of excellent wildfowling grounds. Guns were posted across the bent hills at right angles to the shore, awaiting skein upon skein of barnacle geese in their daily flights along the seaboard from roosts to feeding areas and back. There were also other shooting lines posted to intercept white-fronts and greylag flying into the stubbles and cattle pastures, and shooting of both geese and ducks from 'blinds' along the chain of machair lochs from Loch Bee to Loch Hallan. Then there were many thousands of barnacle and white-fronted geese but now there are only a few hundred of each species (Tables 13.3 and 13.5), more of the former than the latter. The main barnacle goose flocks in the Outer Hebrides are in the Barra Sound (*c.* 400), Monach Isles (*c.* 700), in Harris Sound (*c.* 1,200) and Shiant Islands (*c.* 500). The white-fronted geese have declined in numbers with only 70–80 in small flocks on South Uist remaining.

Swans

The Uists and Benbecula hold the main concentrations of swans in the Hebrides and are one of the densest breeding areas in Scotland, with over 20 pairs per sq km. Some 400 Mute swans (*Cygnus olor*), a moult flock of fully-grown, non-breeding birds, spend the summer on Loch Bee. The habitat is ideal—the shallow machair lochs and associated reed beds and marshes provide excellent nursery grounds. Mutes with collars attached at Loch Bee in 1979 have later been seen as far south as Kintyre and County Derry (Spray, 1982) and in Tiree between 1982 and 1987. They breed in small numbers in Lewis, Barra, Tiree, Coll, Jura, Islay, and Gigha (Thom. 1986). In autumn, many hundreds of whooper swans (*Cygnus cygnus*) pass through the Hebrides from Iceland to Ireland, and we have spent some wonderful days on North Rona in October with swans (and geese) passing. At the other end of the Hebrides, at Balephuil, we often see the return April flight northward of whoopers. From Ireland they come in tight flocks just above the breakers, rise over the dune rampart and settle on the coastal lagoon of Loch a'Phuil, with much musical calling to and from the residents. In mid-October 1981, Chris Spray counted 359 whooper swans wintering in the Uists and Benbecula with probably about 450 in the Outer Hebrides as a whole. In the Inner Hebrides, the main whooper ground is in Tiree with 100–120 in January, and only a few birds on passage in Islay. A few well-separated whoopers, mostly with non-lethal injuries, spend the summer in the Hebrides. Pairs have bred successfully in Benbecula (1947) and Tiree (1977–9).

Ducks

Table 13.6 shows the distribution of breeding swans, geese and ducks in the Hebrides. Eider (*Somateria mollissima*), Mallard (*Anas platyrhynchos*) and red-breasted merganser (*Mergus serrator*) are the most numerous and most widely distributed of the ducks. The eider usually nests within easy distance of the sea or estuaries for transfer of small ducklings to rearing areas, and is absent from the interior of the largest islands—Lewis, Skye, Mull and Islay. The mallard and merganser breed throughout the islands, but not on the high hilltops and in the remote outliers—there are no breeding records of these species from St Kilda or North Rona. Shelduck are widespread in the Uists and Harris, and occur locally elsewhere, except in central and north Lewis where breeding has not been recorded. Where they occur together, eider are usually seen in tens and shelduck in pairs.

The breeding distributions and numbers of other species of duck are much more discontinuous than the foregoing, and with the exception of teal (*Anas crecca*) others are comparatively rare as breeders though common enough in passage or wintering. For example, wigeon, tufted duck (*Aythya fuligula*), pochard (*A. ferina*), pintail, (*Anas acuta*), gadwall (*A. strepera*) and shoveler (*A. clypeata*) breed mainly in North Uist. There are a few pairs of pintail and shoveler in South Uist, Benbecula and Tiree; and two old records of gadwall in Tiree and shoveler as an irregular breeder in Islay (Ogilvie, 1983; Ogilvie and Atkinson-Willes, 1983; Cunningham, 1983; Thom, 1986).

Island	Species of Wildfowl																	
	1	2	3	4	5	6	7	8	9	10	11	12	13	14	15	16	17	18
Lewis			+		+	+		+	*						*		*	
Harris			+		+			+	*						*		*	
North Uist	*		*		+	+	+	*	*	+	+	+	*	+	*		*	
Benbecula	*	+	*		+	+		*	*	+			*		*		*	
South Uist	*		*		+		+	*	*	+		+	*		*		*	
Barra	?				+			+	*						*		*	
Skye			+		+	+		+	*	o		+	+		*		*	+
Raasay									*						*		*	
Small Isles					+			+	*						*		*	
Coll	+		+		+	o		?	*						*		?	
Tiree	+	+			+	?	+	*	*	+	+	o	+		*	o	*	?
Mull	+				+				*				+		*		*	
Jura					+			+	*						*		*	
Islay	+				+			+	*				+		*	+	*	?
Colonsay			+	+				?	*				?		*		*	
Gigha	+				+	?		?	*				?		*		?	
Lismore	+								*						*		?	

* widespread   + scarce   ? possible breeder   o record before 1950

1 Mute swan   2 Whooper swan   3 Greylag goose   4 Canada goose   5 Shelduck   6 Wigeon   7 Gadwall   8 Teal   9 Mallard   10 Pintail   11 Shoveler   12 Pochard   13 Tufted duck   14 Scaup   15 Eider duck   16 Common scoter   17 Red-breasted merganser   18 Goosander

Table 13.6   Distribution of breeding swans, ducks and geese in the Hebrides, compiled from Hopkins and Coxon, 1979; Ogilvie, 1983; Ogilvie and Atkinson-Willes, 1983; Cunningham, 1983; Thom, 1986.

Machair in bloom with daisies, buttercups and clovers at Balinoe, Tiree (Photo J. M. Boyd)

'The Devil's Footprint'—a flooded and beautifully vegetated kettle hole at Laig, Eigg (Photo J. M. Boyd)

Spotted orchids stand proud in sheltered ditches and tall herb meadows (Photo J. M. Boyd)

The lady's bedstraw is one of the dominant flowers of the dunes and machair (Photo J. M. Boyd)

The grass of Parnassus is a star on the dark grass heaths of Sanday (Photo J. M. Boyd)

The transparent burnet moth, Rum (Photo I. L. Boyd)

Stornoway Castle woods and the River Creed in April 1970 (Photo J. M. Boyd)

A fold of Highland cattle with herdsman in the rough bounds of Glen Harris, Rum (Photo J. M. Boyd)

Eroded Jurassic sandstone at Elgol, Skye with Loch Scavaig and Gars-Bheinn (880m) (Photo J. M. Boyd)

Thrift among lichen covered rocks on Ceann a'Mhara, Tiree (Photo I. L. Boyd)

Sunset on Traigh Bhi (Travee), Balephuil, Tiree (Photo I. L. Boyd)

The zonation of wracks on a sheltered rocky shore showing the sharp boundaries between species (Photo T. A. Norton)

Common sea-urchins inhabit the lower shore and the laminarian zone below low-tide mark (Photo T. A. Norton)

Puffin with sand-eels (Photo D. MacCaskill)

Mixed colonies of kittiwakes and guillemots on an undercut cliff, Mingulay, Barra Isles (Photo J. M. Boyd)

The North Atlantic gannet with chick about six weeks old on Stac an Armin, St Kilda (Photo J. M. Boyd)

In the St Kilda gannetry—view from Boreray to Stac Lee (163m) with Hirta and Soay in the background (Photo J. M. Boyd)

A weaned grey seal pup weighing about 45kgms in its first sea-going coat on North Rona (Photo I. L. Boyd)

Female golden eagle with young at cliff-ledge eyrie beside rowan tree (Photo D. MacCaskill)

Tobermory, Mull, showing the village at two levels; the waterfront buildings are on a raised beach with a perched sea-cliff behind them, and the upper village on the cliff top (Photo J. M. Boyd)

Islets and skerries on the north-east tip of Coll looking across the Sea of the Hebrides to Rum (Photo J. M. Boyd)

The Machair Islands

CHAPTER 14

Tiree and the Uists

About 6,600 years ago, when man first moved into the Hebrides, the islands had still to take on their present shape. The hard rock had already been moulded by the ice, but further changes in the shorelines were ahead. Drifts of gravel and sand, and deposits of peat, changed the appearance and nature of the islands. The natural history, land-use economy and culture of many of the islands on the outer fringe of the Hebrides from Lewis to Oronsay was greatly influenced by influxes of white, shell-sand from the sea which was blown inland to form a thick carpet on exposed western coasts. *Machair*, the Gaelic word for the grassland ecosystem which has formed on this sand, is uniquely apt, because nowhere else are there meadows quite like these. This grassy plain contrasts sharply with the generally dark, peaty and rocky interiors of the islands, and between the two the cottages of crofters and small farmers are often built. The machair also provides grazing for livestock and rich hay meadows in an otherwise agriculturally poor environment.

We have already given an account of the maritime system which results in the creation of machair (Chapter 6), and now we consider this environment; how it has evolved in relation to management by man and what it has to offer in both an aesthetic and a practical sense.

At 138m above sea level, the summit of Beinn Hynish is the highest point on Tiree. Yet, from this relatively low point (now holding a huge-domed radar station) there is a clear view to Barra, Skye, Mull, Islay and the horizon of the wide Atlantic broken only by the stack of the Skerryvore lighthouse. Tiree is the most remarkable machair island of all. It is 17km long by between 1–10km across, and shaped like a loin chop (Fig. 34). Mather, Smith and Ritchie (1975) have calculated that of the 77 sq km of land surface, 25.8 sq km (33.5%) consists of dunes and machair compared with 10% in South Uist. The remainder consists of 41.5% of raised beach surfaces (cultivation, heath and open water) and 25.0% of rock (bare rock, heath and open water).

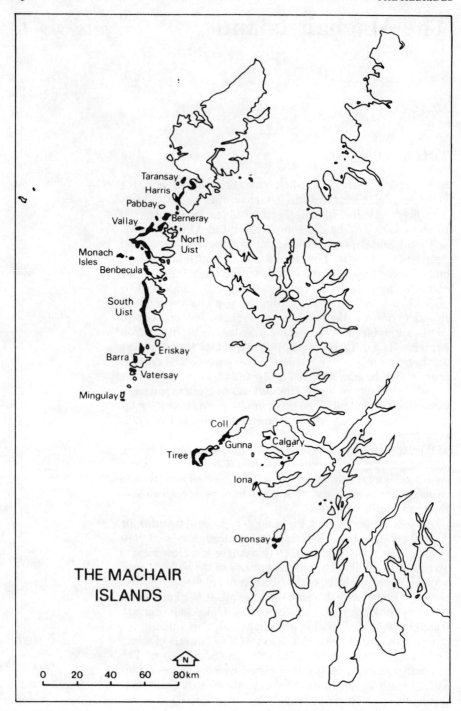

Taransay
Harris
Pabbay
Vallay
Berneray
North
Uist
Monach
Isles
Benbecula
South
Uist
Barra
Eriskay
Vatersay
Mingulay

Coll
Gunna
Calgary
Tiree
Iona

Oronsay

THE MACHAIR
ISLANDS

N

0   20   40   60   80 km

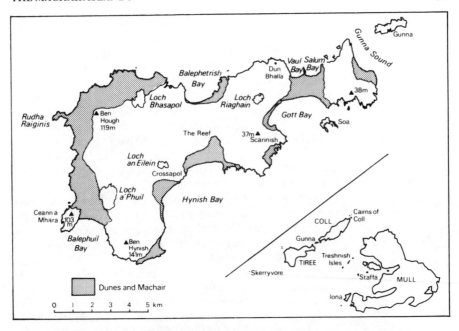

Fig. 34
Map of Tiree

One can see how the rocky ridge stretching from the Cairns of Coll to MacKenzie's Rock, 5km south-west of Skerryvore, must have presented a barrier over which ice from the Caledonian plateau moved with great force. The ice waxed and waned over the period of general retreat and ultimately disappeared, but there were adjustments to the level of the land and sea caused by loss of the ice burden (see Chapter 1 for a description of the post-glacial isostatic uplift and sea level changes). This created the raised beaches of the Hebrides. Seventy-five per cent of Tiree is a raised tidal platform, strewn with glacial debris dropped by melting ice and later rearranged by the sea and wind. Much of the shell sand present in the Hebrides, which makes up most of the beach/dune/machair systems, is of ancient origin. During the post-glacial period, molluscs and crustacea were once abundant in the seas surrounding the Hebrides and it is the remains of the exoskeletons of these animals which account for a significant proportion of land in the Hebrides today. It is thought that little new sand is now being added and that localised erosion is balanced by localised accretion.

From Beinn Hynish the natural pattern of vegetation is obvious; the dark heathland of the rocky interior constrasting with the light, fresh greens of the machair grasslands and saltings by the shore. Hollows in the gneiss rock platform have given rise to small acid lochs, but Loch a'Phuil and Loch

Fig. 33
Location map of the
machair islands, those
islands which possess
large amounts of shell
sand in beaches and
dunes and have
machair grassland

Bhasapol, placed between the dunes and the hard core of the island, are alkaline machair lochs (see Chapter 10).

The dunes and machair have grown in parallel with human settlement of the islands; there are signs of wind-blown sand particles in intertidal peat at Borve on Benbecula from 5,700 years ago, and within the many layers of sand and debris laid down chronologically over the millenia, there are also the remains of human settlement. The five main interludes are Neolithic, Beaker, Iron Age, Viking/Medieval and Historical, and sites such as Rosinish on Benbecula, Udal on North Uist and Northton on Harris possess most if not all of these interludes of occupation. Other sites have the remains of Iron Age 'wheelhouses', under- and over-lain by blown sand. Such single-interlude sites are on low machair plains, while the multiple sites are on higher machair plains and hills. The wheelhouse sites are often waterlogged or collapsing at the front from coastal erosion.

The sandy drift is usually well stratified. Starting at the bedrock, there are usually several metres of layered sand and sandy soil. Each layer contributes to the record of ecological history; layers of pure sand indicate periods of windblown transgression of sand and instability of the land surface while organic soil indicates time of stability and growth of vegetation. If waterlogged at sometime these layers may be dark-coloured and peaty in texture. Staining may also arise from the water-table oscillating through the contact surfaces of peaty soils and white sand, thus causing the sand particles to become stained by the peaty water. Within these strata man's artifacts occur, and can be used to age different horizons in the sequence.

The Mesolithic sites in the Hebrides are not on machair because there was probably little or no machair about 6,500 years ago. The earliest inhabitated sites on machair are Neolithic, situated on the glacial till, going back to about 5,800 BP and lasting until about 4,400 BP. These are overlain by Bronze Age (Beaker) occupations dated between 3,500 and 2,500 BP, which are in turn overlain by Iron Age occupations between about 2,500 and 1,500 BP. The uppermost strata are from the Viking/Medieval and historical periods when, in other parts of the islands, the beehive houses, duns and blackhouses were built in places where the soil was shallow and the country rock exposed. It is always fascinating to look at erosion faces in the machair dunes, especially in the lower dark layers of ancient organic soil, for ancient human litter such as shaped stones, fragments of pottery and bone, animal teeth, shells and, if lucky, pieces of flint. The complexity of machair soil sections is shown in Fig. 35 where those from Rosinish and Northton are shown (Ritchie, 1979).

Fig. 35
Machair
stratigraphy—sections
of machair soil at
Rosinish, Benbecula
and Northton, Harris
showing the periods of
human occupation
(from Ritchie, 1979)

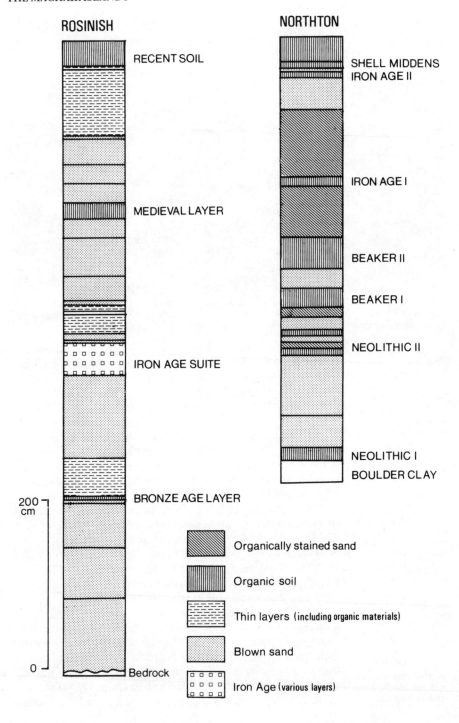

ROSINISH

RECENT SOIL

MEDIEVAL LAYER

IRON AGE SUITE

BRONZE AGE LAYER

200
cm

0   Bedrock

NORTHTON

SHELL MIDDENS
IRON AGE II

IRON AGE I

BEAKER II

BEAKER I

NEOLITHIC II

NEOLITHIC I
BOULDER CLAY

Organically stained sand

Organic soil

Thin layers (including organic materials)

Blown sand

Iron Age (various layers)

Dun Bhalla at Vaul, Tiree showing the internal diameter of Iron-age dun/farm now grass-covered, and the surviving base of the cavity wall into which there is a low entrance, in 1988 (Photo J. M. Boyd)

The history of Dun Bhalla the Iron Age fort-farm on Tiree is known in detail from the excavation and studies of Dr Euan Mackie. Tiree has a score or more of small forts which were constructed from the Iron Age into Viking times. They are thought to have served as defences against raiders, and were used by a pastoral people who herded their livestock and grew their crops on the machair. The people who lived in eastern Tiree at the time of Dun Bhalla were Iron Age farmers living in wooden homesteads. The Dun was built in the first century BC, probably by new settlers who brought with them stone-building craftsmen. It was built on a headland backed by spacious ranges of dunes, flats of machair and heath, some of which might have held scrub woodland. The excavation shows, however, that the 30ft high building survived for only about a century; in the second century AD it was much reduced in height, and converted into a farm. Tiree, for the time being at least, had come upon more peaceful times.

Returning to Beinn Hynish, the hill possesses three duns, several field systems of different occupations placed one upon another, stone alignments and green knolls suggesting ancient domestic or ceremonial sites, turf dykes, ruined blackhouse-type dwellings, and ditches from the time when the hill was cleared of cottars to create a large sheep farm at Hynish. The modern boundary dykes and fences mark the common grazings

Fig. 36
Map showing the distribution of machair in the Uists and Barra (from Ritchie, 1986)

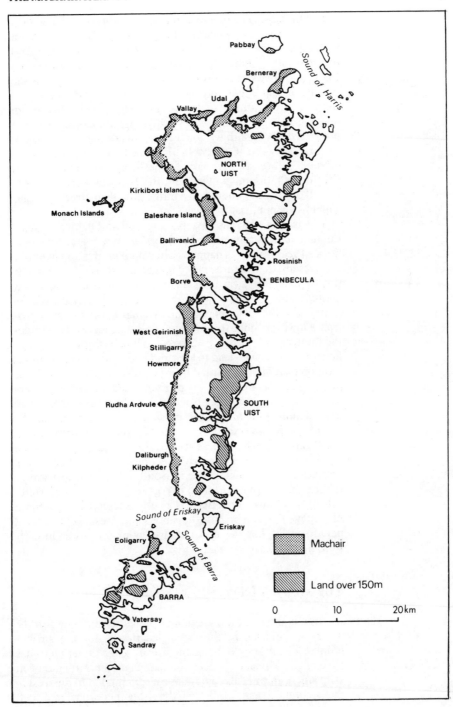

of five townships settled by crofters last century and managed today by their descendants. In the 6th century AD, Saint Columba arrived at Iona from Ireland and founded (563 AD) the monastery there. It was subsequently destroyed by the Vikings on five occasions between 795 and 986 AD, with the murder of the abbot and monks in 806, 825 and 986 AD. If such was the treatment of the monastery by Norsemen, one can imagine that the treatment of other island communities that possessed any wealth was no less drastic, though no record of such has survived. Tiree probably had a thousand years of agriculture before the arrival of the Columban monks, who regarded the island as Tir Iodh, the Land of Corn. In those far-off days of sail, there was a traffic directly between the isles which does not exist in today's jet age.

The machair islands have been grazed and cultivated since the first settlers arrived in the Hebrides. When grazing continues all year round, as happens when both rabbits and livestock are present, the pastures fail to flower and set seed. Eventually this depletes the swards of many species of plant, especially annuals, and encourages the spread of moss. It may also lead to thinning of the turf, opening the machair to the threat of erosion. However, since the machair ecosystem has evolved under the influence of grazing livestock, too little grazing can also be detrimental as it will lead to long and rank grass which provides little opportunity for annual herbs to survive. Occasionally, as in old hay meadows or in grazings used mainly for over-wintering cattle, a balance is maintained between the potential degradation of the machair by erosion on the one hand and the loss of species diversity and productivity on the other. The best effects are seen where there are no rabbits, such as at The Reef on Tiree, or where the hay meadows are so close to the crofthouses, as at Kilpheder in South Uist, as to discourage rabbits. The rabbit-infested, overgrazed, wind-eroded south side of Ben Eoligarry in Barra is an object lesson in the amount of damage that can be done by rabbits and livestock but which, paradoxically, has the prettiest display of primroses in early June that we have seen anywhere.

The Monach Isles

If Tiree is the most remarkable of the larger machair islands, the Monach Isles fit the same description for the smaller islands. The first sight that many visitors to the Outer Hebrides have of the Monachs is from the passenger aircraft landing at Balivanich, Benbecula. They appear about 14km to the west in the lap of the ocean, while from the shore they are 12km distant

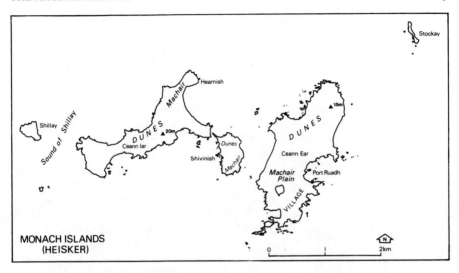

Fig. 37
*Map of the Monach
Islands*

and appear as a rampart of pale sand dunes, above which rises
the stalk of the disused lighthouse. It is understandable therefore, that the islands also carry the old Norse name Heisker,
meaning Bright Rock; in the morning sunshine the cream-
coloured sand-hills and the milk-white surf create an unmis-
takably bright impression. When ashore, the islands in summer
are a blaze of flowers; daisies, bird's-foot trefoil, white clover,
buttercups, eyebright, sea-pansies and many others. The
Monach Isles, like Tiree, are emergent humps of gneiss, which
are in this case tilted slightly to the west. The Monach platform
was probably joined to North Uist before and during the post-
glacial adjustments of sea level. Now the depth between the
islands is from 10–40m over a varied seabed of solid rock, boulders and sand. This shallow shelf is exposed to the full force of
the Atlantic, and there is a build-up of breakers around the
islands which absorbs energy from the swell before it reaches
the shore of North Uist. It is on the outer reaches of this shelf
that the power of the seas around the British Isles is at its
greatest and where, at some future time, wave energy generators may be placed.

   The Monach Isles (Fig. 37) consist of about 577 ha. of hum-
mocked landscape, covered mostly by low dunes with high
ridges, a machair plain with lochan and marshes plus sandy,
pebbly and rocky shores with shingle ridges. The dunes are
from 8–15m above sea level and the flat machair is less than 8m
above sea level. There are two main islands, Ceann Ear ('East
End', 193ha.) and Ceann Iar ('West End', 135ha.), joined at low
tide by a sandy, tidal flat including the islet of Shivinish (28ha.).
This group of three is separated from Shillay (16 ha.) by deeper

water. Shillay, which has the lighthouse, and Stockay (3ha.) are both rocky. The little archipelago is 7.5km from east to west and 3km from north to south, and has been used for grazing live-stock, arable agriculture, fishing and probably also for the hunting of seals and seabirds.

Dean Monro wrote in 1549 that Heisker belonged to the Nuns of Columnkill, and there is a tradition of a nunnery on Shivinish and a monastery on Shillay where a beacon was maintained. Bleau's Atlas (1654) shows two places of worship on 'Hekskyr or Na Monich', and there is a record of a cargo of barley-meal being sent from Heisker to Ballachulish in 1692 for the starving and destitute MacIans following the massacre of Glencoe. The prosperity of the islands was confirmed by Martin in 1695, who mentions fertile soils, corn and black cattle. The Monach Isles had probably been settled for cen-turies, but are now deserted. There was probably once a crossing from Piable in North Uist to the Monach Isles, and the inhabitants left a legend that their last crossing of the land bridge was made about 1650 by a girl taking a heifer to a bull. This coincides with the tradition of the inundation by sea and sand of the island village of Baleshare on the neighbouring coast of North Uist.

In the late 19th century there was a 'run-rig' system (see pp. 127, 332) of 10 crofts on Ceann Ear and the other two main islands were common grazings. The land was cultivated for three years with a rotation of barley, oats and potatoes. Sea-weed was used as manure, and the land was then left fallow for several years. The crops were unfenced, so herdsmen kept the stock and at night animals were gathered and enclosed. For the remainder of the year they ranged freely. The land or 'scat' was sectioned in shares to each crofter who was also allocated a number of grazing animals ('souming') on the common. Corn was kiln-dried and milled in hand querns. The 'souming' in the 1930s for each of the three surviving crofter families was 8 cows, 2 horses and 24 sheep. Ceann Iar and Shivinish has no dry-weather freshwater supply, so cattle were therefore removed in summer while sheep grazed the islands all year round. There was no fuel, so peat was brought from North Uist and later coal was imported by the lighthouse tender. Culti-vation ended in 1947, five years after the last family left.

Fishing was important in the economy of the community. Each family usually had a 10m open boat with sails and oars for fishing and to carry livestock, peats and merchandise. Fin-fish caught in summer were wind-dried and salted, and latterly there was creel fishing for lobsters and crabs. Periwinkles, bivalves and limpets provided food from the shore. Kelp (wind-dried wrack) was burnt in winter on simple hearths and the potash was exported in the spring. Now all this activity has ceased—although Heisker is still used for grazing sheep by a farmer from North Uist—and about 10 boats, mostly from Grimsay, work the lobsters, and the old schoolhouse is used as a bothy by the fishermen. The islands are owned by Countess Granville, except for Shillay which belongs to the Commissioners of the Northern Lighthouses. The entire group is a National Nature Reserve and Site of Special Scientific Interest managed jointly by the owners, tenants and the Nature Conservancy Council.

One of us (JMB) first went to the Monach Isles in the early 1960s from Gramsdale Benbecula, in an 8m open boat of a type used by Uist fishermen for a century or more—in fact the six-oared Highland boat which took Martin to Heisker and St Kilda in 1695 was probably an antecedent of this type of craft built in Grimsay. After navigating the sandy shallows of Oitir Mhor and breasting the ocean swell over the bar of Beul an Toim, our Grimsay skipper hoisted sail. In a lively, well-listed fashion, we made for Heisker; in the age of the power-boat this was a pleasure in itself and also a rerun of medieval history. For two hours we shared the wind with fulmars, terns, gulls, auks, gannets and cormorants, before landing at Port Ruadh with a more heightened sense of achievement than if we had been driven there by an engine-powered boat.

On going ashore, the place is alive with birds; gulls, terns, shelducks, eiders, red-breasted mergansers, oystercatchers, ringed plovers, rock pipits, pied wagtails and starlings. Above the shore is the low eroded dune crest from which one can look across a flat machair plain to an encirclement of shaggy dunes. The succession of seaward and landward dunes, which we described in Chapter 6, is absent on the Monach Isles due to their small size. The axes of the islands are roughly parallel with the prevailing south-west wind, which has probably caused the downwind sides of the islands to be blown clear of sand to form one of the finest ranges of dunes in the Hebrides, at the north end of Ceann Ear. These high dunes fill the landscape to the north of the machair plain with rock outcrops, upon which the scattered village ruins stand stark. Everywhere there are rabbit burrows and the occasional sprinkling of sturdy looking cattle, and the green meadows are misted with white and yellow daisies, wild white clovers, buttercups and trefoils.

Dr Roland Randall (1976) described seven main plant communities on the Monach Isles: (1) mobile dune with marram grass; (2) stable dune with marram and sand sedge; (3) flat dune with marram, sand sedge, daisy, ribwort and mosses; (4) machair with no marram but with sand sedge, daisy, red fescue, ribwort, plantain, yarrow, eyebright and lady's bedstraw; (5) sand-sedge pasture with red fescue, daisy, ragwort and yarrow; (6) sea pink sward with sea plantain, sea milkwort and red fescue (salting) and (7) peaty sedgeland with common sedge, white clover, red fescue, Yorkshire fog, marsh pennywort and silverweed (see also Table 6.1, p. 116). Other more localised communities occur such as on the strand line with sea spurrey, sea arrow grass and salt-marsh grass; wet slacks have sedges, jointed rush and silverweed; fens have spike rush, mare's tail, sedges and cotton grass; Stockay has tall herb stands with cow parsnip; heaths have ling, creeping willow and devil's bit scabious; vegetated cobble has cleavers *Galium aparine* and the lochs have pondweeds, water milfoil and water crowfoot. The stands of undisturbed machair are rich in clovers, and the disturbed ground has much perennial rye grass. Perring and Randall (1972) have recorded 257 species of plant on the Monach Isles, and since then another has been found, the rue-leaved saxifrage (*Saxifraga tridactylites*). Other species of special note are the oyster plant (*Mertensia maritima*), adder's tongue (*Ophioglossum vulgatum*), field gentian (*Gentianella campestris*), water whorl-grass (*Catabrosa aquatica*), small sweet grass (*Glyceria declinata*) and the greater tussock-sedge (*Carex paniculata*). The black oat (*Avena strigosa*) is a relict cultivar and the northern marsh yellow-cress (*Rorippa islandica*), which is a common plant of the summering grounds of the barnacle goose in the Arctic, is also present in this, one of the Scottish wintering grounds. Other northern species are also found on the Monach Isles; for example the oyster plant, which is a northern species, grows beside the southern bog pimpernel, and similarly, continental species such as the mountain everlasting, water dropwort and the frog orchid occur in an otherwise oceanic community.

The ruined village is situated at the southern end of the machair plain close to the lochs. In 1815 about 100 people and 1,000 cattle and sheep were thought to have lived on the Monach Isles, but this was reduced to one family in the early 20th century. However, recovery was quick, because by 1846 there were 39 inhabitants, and by 1867 there were between 80 and 90 with 75 on Ceann Ear, this number remaining static until the 1914–18 War. In 1886 there were 8 crofter and 6 cottar families, and about the turn of the century there were about 60 children at school. The crofter families lived in clusters of buildings including house and steadings enclosed in a stack yard, whereas the cottars had solitary cottages, and were probably squatters eeking out an existence in fishing, beach-combing for shell-fish, kelp burning and helping crofters. By the mid-1920s there were 10 families, and in 1939 only two remained, those of John and Alexander MacDonald, plus the lightkeepers. In 1942 the lighthouse was closed, and in 1943 the MacDonalds left. During the period 1942–49 the family of Peter Morrison of Grimsay lived on Ceann Ear, but after this the Monach Isles had no permanent inhabitants.

Machair—A Natural Heritage

The machair islands are valued pieces of Britain's natural heritage which have seen large changes in the last two centuries. The human population was greatest on the machair islands between 1821 and 1841; in 1831 there were 4,453 inhabitants on Tiree compared with 760 in 1981, similarly, in 1821, 4,971 people lived on North Uist, but by 1981 the total was 1,670. There was a similar decline on South Uist although numbers there have been kept high by the presence of army personnel. The height of the population coincided with the peak of the kelp industry, and followed the reorganisation of estates. In some of these estates many small tenancies, involving runrig cultivation and common grazings with houses in clusters, were changed to crofts with enclosed arable land, common grazings and houses well separated on the enclosed land. By 1830, however, the kelp industry was waning, the estates were in poor financial straits and the population was far in excess of the islands' resources. On Benbecula and South Uist, the land that had not been assigned to crofts was cleared, and the clearances of tacksmen (leasees) and cottars (sub-tenants or squatters) continued when the estates passed from Clanranald to the Gordons of Cluny in 1838. Poverty was rife, and many cottar families emigrated to Canada and Australia.

At this time agricultural improvement took on a new pace, with a subsequent loss of parts of the machair and hill-grazings of the crofting township to extend new farms. By 1850, nine-tenths of the population was concentrated on less than one-third of the land of South Uist, and it was at this time that the main drains were dug that no doubt changed the character of the wetlands. Later, the Crofters' Act of 1886 gave security of tenure to the crofter-tenants, and in 1897 the Congested Districts Board was empowered to resettle or encourage estates to resettle crofters on farms. Thus by 1924 those lands that had been largely cleared of tacksmen and cottars were apportioned into crofts and resettled. The present crofting pattern of land-tenure dates from about the 1820s, but was not complete until about the 1920s. In the past 30 years, many machairs, which had been common land for cultivation and grazing, have been apportioned to individual crofts, fenced and cultivated.

The influence of this turbulent socio-economic history on the wildlife of the machair islands is unrecorded. However, there are accounts which indicate that at times of high human population the machair grasslands may have become extensively unstable, and drifted into dunes. About 1811 James Macdonald wrote of South Uist and Barra:

In winter, and even until the middle of May, the western division or machair, is almost a desolate waste of sand; and this sand encroaches rapidly the next division, namely that of lakes and that of firm arable ground.

Also, describing the Monach Isles about 1815 Captain Otter stated,

the whole surface of Ceann Ear (the main arable land) was denuded of soil.

These descriptions are probably exaggerated, but it is almost certain that the socio-economic changes of the times were accompanied by some ecological changes which have contributed to the consitution of the valued machair habitats of today. The fact that many of the features of the machair result from human activity over the centuries does not detract from its value as a habitat for wildlife; most landscapes in Britain have a significant man-made component, and the modern attitude is that the human component is often not at all bad. In fact, some habitats are so far from being natural (i.e. unaffected by man) that it is positively detrimental to the wildlife they contain to allow them to look after themselves. To retain floristic variety, grasslands such as machair often require moderate grazing, and many of the stages between arable and ley provide fine mosaics of wild flowers and nesting sites for waders and songbirds. Cultivation and heavy grazing or rabbit-infested machairs on the other hand can cause widespread blowing sand in place of pasture. Deep drainage lowers the water table, makes the dry dunes drier, shrinks the machair lochs and dries out dune slacks, marshes and fens, all rich in wetland flowers, waders and wildfowl. Reseeding and the use of concentrated fertilisers and herbicides on old pastures, eliminates the highly diverse mixture of grasses, sedges and tall herbs. The wildlife of the machair has been created and maintained by traditional crofting agriculture, so it follows that large-scale changes in crofting can carry with them corresponding changes in the wildlife.

Most of the population of the corncrake (*Crex crex*) breeding in Britain, nests in the Hebrides, and it has become the symbol of conservation among the crofts of the machair islands. When the birds arrive in spring, they find cover in the early growth of yellow iris from which they move to nest in the young stands of barley, oats and hay ideal for them and their chicks. The cutting of the crops does not generally start until late July when the young are already mobile and able to avoid the mower, and in most cases, the hay meadows are alongside the strands of cereals or have marshy margins with iris, meadowsweet and common reeds which provide excellent escape cover for the crakes. Tiree has some of the finest corncrake habitat, and in the gloaming of a July day, a walk along any township road guarantees the sound of calling corncrakes from the dewy hay, barley, irises and reeds, the ratchety voice of the bird belying its beauty of shape and plumage (see pp. 131–4).

The distribution of machair in the Hebrides is seen in Fig. 33, which also shows the spot distribution of SSSIs containing machair habitat. The Integrated Development Programme (IDP) in the Outer Hebrides, which saw investment in agriculture, has, perhaps predictably, run its course without significant damage to the machair. However, it provided the stimulus for a flurry of research activity in 1983, when predictions of doom for the machair in the wake of updated agricultural practices, were rife. The concern which this created and the surveys which accompanied it has resulted in an enormous increase in our knowledge of the machair flora and fauna and their relationship to agricultural practice. In 1982–85 the NCC, with the support of the Environmental Directorate of the EEC and the co-operation of the RSPB, Wader Study Group, SWT and others, carried out a study of the environment implications of the IDP, and the results are contained in a tri-partite report *Agriculture and Environment in the Outer Hebrides* (Hambrey, 1986) and numerous separate published papers. An Agricultural Development Plan is now in progress in the Inner Hebrides, and much of the knowledge and experience gained in the IDP, particularly in the interactions of agriculture with nature conservation in crofting areas, will accrue to this new scheme.

CHAPTER **15 Rum—An Island Nature Reserve**

The road to the isles immortalised in song runs 'by Ailort and by Morar to the sea'; it is effectively the A830 between Fort William and Mallaig, and the trail of tourists and fish-freezer juggernauts. Where the road turns sharply west at the high point at Back of Keppock there is a serene view; the western skyline holds the cuillins of both Skye and Rum, and often this is the traveller's first sight of the isles.

The centre piece is Rum (10,684ha.) which, as the drive proceeds north to Mallaig, gradually appears from behind the heights of Eigg and then stands proud of all other land, an elegant sweep of peaks blocking sight of Canna and the Uists. For a long time it was called the 'forbidden island', partly because of its sad history of clearance of its native Gaelic people in the 1820s when the island was owned by the Maclean of Coll, and partly because of the exclusive use of the island by the three wealthy familes who owned Rum from 1847–1957. They used the island as a sheep run, and after reintroducing red deer from 1845, as a sporting estate. Access between the mailboat and the island was by the owner's private boat, and the island afforded no inn to the casual visitor. Since 1957, when Rum was purchased as a National Nature Reserve by the Nature Conservancy, the ferry between the mainland and the island is still operated by the owner who also provides accommodation and campsites for visitors. Though visitors now make bookings for lodgings, increasing numbers arrive from yachts and tripper-boats from Mallaig and Arisaig, and none are turned away. Though certain restrictions have been applied in the interests of wildlife research and management over the last 30 years by the Nature Conservancy and its successors since 1973, the Nature Conservancy Council, the island is now far from being 'forbidden'. Indeed the *bona fide* visitor is invariably welcomed and asked to observe the rules which make the island available to people, without loss or damage to wildlife.

From Mallaig, Rum resembles an oceanic volcano whose shape speaks of wild and rugged scenery, and whose texture

appears sometimes gentle, and sometimes hard and sharp. In fact, Rum is an eroded Tertiary volcano and the other Small Isles are built mainly of lava and ash. The great magma chambers and vents of Rum have thrust their way through the existing crust of Mesozoic and Palaezoic rocks, and subsequently have been shattered and eroded by ice, sea and weather over tens of millions of years. What now remains are the cold, solid innards of the volcano, consisting mostly of basic (gabbro) and ultra-basic (peridotites and allivalites) igneous rocks within a frame of much older Torridonian sandstone, part of which is under the sea to the west.

Rum ponies at the Bullough Mausoleum in Glen Harris, Rum. A small herd (c. 25) of ponies run wild on Rum, but are selectively bred and some are used to bring deer carcases off the hill (Photo J. M. Boyd)

As the mailboat crosses the Sound of Rum, the visitor becomes aware of the awesome character of the island — gone is the gentle, distant silhouette and in its place is the massive, wild reality of Rum. The lower half of the Rum cuillin shows the dark-red Torridonian frame and the upper half, the dark-grey basic and ultra-basic core. It has the scenic grandeur and general ecology of the bare, deer-forest country of the north-west Highlands, but it is more varied because of its unusually wide range of rocks and soils, its responses to sea spray and weather, and to the presence of 116,000 pairs of Manx shear-waters nesting in the mountain tops.

At the landing place in Loch Scresort, Rum rises steeply from the village of Kinloch to the summit of Hallival (723m) which leads to the summit of the island, Askival (812m). The

Fig. 38
Location map of Rum

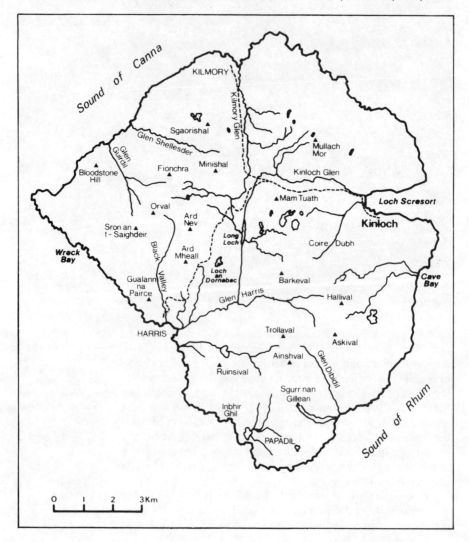

cluster of cottages in the wooded precincts of Kinloch Castle are today's statement of human habitation and landuse which goes back to prehistory, while the panoramic view from the top of Askival is unsurpassed for its inner whorl of surrounding peaks, and its mountainous and island-spattered outer circumference. Here, the naturalist with an eye for country can see an exciting field of exploration; the Inner Hebrides merge with the mainland massifs and the Outer Hebrides stand aloof, but each island is a microcosm awaiting discovery. Rum is now the most celebrated of them all as a centre of research, and one of the best documented islands in Britain. The vegetation and flora have been described by Eggeling (1965) and Ferreira (1967), the insects by Steel and Woodroffe (1969) and Wormell (1982), birds by Bourne (1957) and Love (1984), red deer by Clutton-Brock, Guinness and Albon (1982) and geology by Emeleus (1980). Also, a natural history of Rum has recently been edited by Clutton-Brock and Ball (1987).

The human history of Rum has been told by John Love (1983, 1987) and probably starts with the Mesolithic hunter-fishermen of about 6,600 years BC. There is a charcoal hearth and shell/bone midden at Bagh na h-Uamha (Caves Bay), in a situation characteristic of that used by these earliest settlers. That was in the Atlantic period when the climate was as moist as it is today, but over 2°C warmer. Rum was probably clad in a wild mixed forest on the lower ground from sea level up to 200m, dense on the sheltered side, and thin on exposed faces. There was probably a thinning of the forest on to the higher ground without a definite treeline, and the high tops were probably as clear of trees then as they are today. Without any appreciable human effect, the character of the maritime forest and heath would reflect solely the influence of natural factors of wind-blow, drainage, salt-spray, fire by lightening and the browsing and grazing of red deer and invertebrates. The ancient fauna may have become isolated there when the land and ice bridges disappeared at the end of the Quaternary ice age 10,000 years ago, or it may have arrived on rafts of storm-swept timber in which the sea and shores probably abounded. The field mouse, brown rat and pygmy shrew may have reached Rum naturally on such flotsam, but they may have come first by boat, possibly in Viking times (Berry, 1983); the pipistrelle bat probably reached the island naturally. This vision of the pristine state of the island is not just an idle dream; it is important to bear in mind when coming to decide the objects of management of Rum today, as a nature reserve.

The history of Rum therefore is a *vignette* of the Hebrides as a whole since the time of the first settlers; it plumbs the depths of human history in Scotland and holds the relics of

successive cultures, while its rocks and soils range from the
acid to the ultra-basic and the entire span of geological age
from the Palaeozoic to Recent. Its ecology embraces habitats
from the very exposed to the sheltered and from the sea shore
to the mountain tops, and it has it own unique inventory of
plants and animals bound in a discrete ecosystem. Few small
islands in Europe are more attractive to the naturalist than
Rum as a nature reserve and a base for ecological research.

The Volcano

The Rum volcano dates back to the early Tertiary (Palaeocene)
when, some 60 million years ago, Greenland and Europe
began to drift apart and a great deal of volcanic activity occurred in north-west Britain (see p. 38). The volcano was probably
once a conical pile of cinder and lava possessing erupting
craters and many NW–SE fissures which issued lava over
about 10 million years. There were two main periods of
eruption: the first predated the central volcano, and its relics
occur in Eigg, Muck, and eastern Rum around Allt nam Ba and
Beinn nan Stac; the second postdates the centre, and its relics
are found in western Rum in Orval, Bloodstone Hill and
Fionchra, and in Canna and Sanday. In the ensuing 50 million
years, about 1km of the overburden has been removed by erosion which was very severe in the four ice-ages of the Pleistocene (*c.* 600,000 to 10,000 years ago). It was then that the
island as we know it today was created, firstly as a *nunatak* protruding above the vast ice-sheet covering NW Europe, and
later, when the ice melted, as a marine island in an arctic sea.
Rum was probably high enough to have its own glaciers, which
in the latter stages of the glaciation served to push aside the
on-coming massive ice from the Caledonian plateau to gouge
the valleys now drowned by the Sounds of Eigg, Rum and
Canna. The cover having been stripped away, the roots of the
volcano are again laid bare to the atmosphere in a complex of
rocks and volcanic structures, affording a generation of geologists an unending field of study.

The oldest rock on Rum is the gneiss in the vicinity of the
Priomh Lochs, and the massifs of Ainshval and Sgurr nan Gillean. Though the contact between the gneiss and the Torridonian sandstone usually indicates an Archaen land surface (see
p. 33), the outcrop of the former is extraordinary. Because of
volcanic activity, most of the gneiss is placed out of context
within the ring fault which encircles most of the intrusive rocks
in the roots of the volcano. Such a land surface probably exists
under the Torridonian sandstone which occupies the northern

Fig. 39
*Geological map of Rum
(from Emeleus, in
Clutton-Brock and
Ball, 1987)*

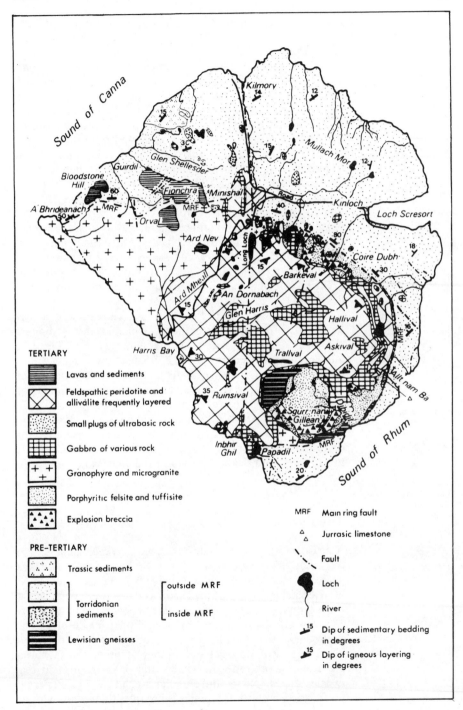

TERTIARY

	Lavas and sediments
	Feldspathic peridotite and allivalite frequently layered
	Small plugs of ultrabasic rock
	Gabbro of various rock
	Granophyre and microgranite
	Porphyritic felsite and tuffisite
	Explosion breccia

PRE-TERTIARY

	Trassic sediments
	Torridonian sediments [outside MRF] [inside MRF]
	Lewisian gneisses

MRF Main ring fault

△ Jurrasic limestone

─·─ Fault

⬤ Loch

River

15 Dip of sedimentary bedding in degrees

15 Dip of igneous layering in degrees

and eastern parts of the island (Fig. 39). Between the old Torridonian and the young Tertiary rocks which make up the bulk
of the island, there are middle-aged Triassic sediments which
have been derived from the weathering of the Torridonian
in a distant era of erosion. These are the sandstones and
limestones—'cornstones'—of Monadh Dubh, and similar
rocks of Jurassic age occur at Dibidil and Beinn nan Stac.

The much younger volcanic intrusion occupies the whole of
the south-western sector, and is separated from the volcanic
rocks by a complex ring fault that takes a convoluted course
from Camus na h-Atha near Bloodstone Hill through Orval to
the Kinloch-Kilmory-Harris watershed and from thence in a
rough semi-circle through Meall Breac, Cnapan Breaca,
Dibidil and Papadil. The emplacement of the granophyre of
Orval and Ard Nev and other structures (felsite plugs, explo-
sion breccias, tuffisites, basalt dykes and sills) came before the
ring fault, but the ultrabasic and gabbros occurred afterwards,
cutting and metamorphosing the existing rocks along the line
of the fault. The structure, growth and decay of the volcano is
described by Emeleus (1983, 1987).

The ultrabasic rocks of Hallival and Askival are well known
for their layered appearance; they look like 'bedded' sedimentary rocks. This is caused, it is thought, by injections of magma
into deep chambers of the volcano. Some of this magma would
be expelled and some retained at intervals of time which
allowed for very slow cooling and separation of heavy and light
minerals. The residue of each injection is represented by a
layer, the lower part of which is rich in denser, faster-settling
olivine and the upper part in feldspar. Thus in a sequence of
partial eruptions of the contents of the magma chambers,
fifteen layers of thickness varying from 50 to 150m have been
formed.

The Forest

A main objective of the nature reserve is to recreate a habitat
resembling that which existed in Rum before the island was
made treeless by man, and to achieve this, the managers must
have a reliable picture of the island as it was 2,500 years ago at
the beginning of the Iron Age. This has been done by the study
of pollen and plant remains from bogs. Following the clearance
of the ice in the Boreal period (10,000–7,000 BP) a forest of
birch, pine, willow, hazel and juniper occupied the sheltered
glens and slopes, and the glades and open range held bog
myrtle, sedges, grasses and club mosses. The following period
until 2,500 BP saw the climatic optimum, with maximum forest

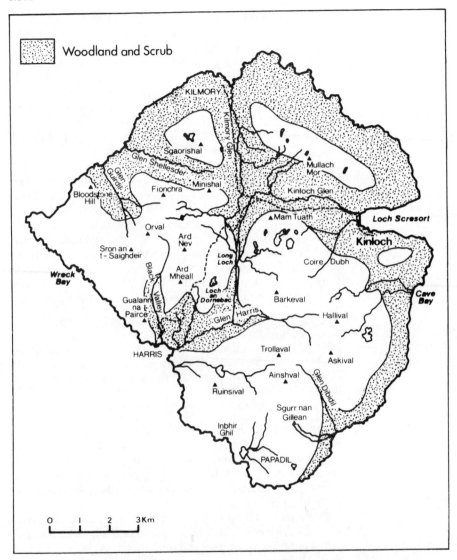

Woodland and Scrub

cover including oak, ash, alder, rowan and wych elm. The
maximum extent of the primaeval forest is shown in Fig. 40
(after Ball, 1987).

When the Iron Age people were rearing their stock around
Dun Bhalla in Tiree, others were settled in Rum and busy felling and burning the forest to make way for their livestock. At
the same time the climate became cooler and wetter with a
sharp increase in bog moss, bracken, alder, willow and juniper
and a decrease in oak and wych elm. Such fluctuations had

Fig. 40
*Forest map of Rum
(from Ball, in
Clutton-Brock and
Ball, 1987)*

taken place before 2,500 BP, but then there had not been farmers with metal axes! The long-term decline of the forest had begun, and was assisted on its way by the Norse invasion of the 8th century. Felling, burning, grazing and cultivation continued and by medieval times the island was almost treeless. It is clear that the medieval people of Rum had no sense of the forest as a vital resource of shelter for stock, a source of timber for fuel and for building houses and boats.

The peak human population on Rum was about 400, and occurred in the early 19th century (Love, 1987) when there must have been only a very few trees remaining, in inaccessible gullies. After the last copse was felled in 1796 (Ball, 1987), a tree must have been a curio to the native-born Rumach; something worth walking far to see. The island remained treeless for about 50 years until, in the 1850s, the new owners planted the large sycamores, beeches and elms which stand today behind the Post Office on the site of the old Kinloch House (now demolished). Plantations were extended around Kinloch Castle and Loch Scresort in the early years of this century. Following an assessment of these woods Martin Ball states:

Altogether 120 tree species have been catalogued (for Rum) and, though the woods do not resemble the natural forest, they have enabled many woodland plants to survive, including attractive carpets of bluebell, wood sorrel and buckler fern, and many species of epiphytic lichen and moss which depend on shade and high humidity. Some more local woodland plants, including wood anemone and wood sedge are now extinct outside the Kinloch woods.

In 1958, following the declaration of Rum as a National Nature Reserve, the current reafforestation of the island was begun, with the removal of sheep and the setting-up of small, deer-fenced plantations in Kinloch, Kilmory and Harris Glens, Guirdil, and in 1,400ha. of the sandstone hills to the north and south of Loch Scresort.

Since 1960 well over half a million trees of 20 different species have been raised in a nursery at Kinloch and established out of reach of deer and other livestock. Native trees of West Highland stock—pine, birch, alder, ash, oak, wych elm, rowan, aspen, willows, holly, bird cherry, hawthorn, blackthorn, whin and broom—were planted on the ploughed and unploughed land and given rock phosphate fertiliser in moorland habitats most favourable to each. In habitats exposed to high winds and salt spray, lodgepole pine (*Pinus contorta*) from North America was used as a 'nurse' for the native trees. Unfortunately, early growth was retarded by a fire which swept through north-east Rum in March 1969, but the ecology of the plantations is now greatly different to that of the open hill. After

25 years of respite from grazing, and the subsequent growth of trees, there are now extensive new woodland and moorland communities of native species which have been unrepresented on Rum for many centuries.

Already a woodland flora is shyly making its presence felt under the young trees where once there was heather and moor grass—honeysuckle; hard, mountain and buckler ferns; wavy and tufted hair grasses; bluebell; angelica; wood sorrel; primrose; wood violet; self heal, pignut; germander speedwell and blaeberry (Ball, 1987). When Rum lost its forest it also lost its woodland fauna, that assemblage of diverse creatures each specialised for life in one or more of the vast number of nooks and crannies of the forest. It is impossible to create an 'instant' flora and fauna for the new woodlands—such a thing has to develop in time; for example many insects live on dead wood, which in nature is usually provided by old, decaying trees, of which there are as yet few on Rum. However, since the first woods were established at Kinloch 80 years ago, 20 species each of arboreal Heteroptera and aphids and over 130 species of moth—the caterpillars of which feed on trees or shrubs—have been recorded. There are also many gall-forming sawflies, wood-boring beetles including the long-horn (*Asemum striatum*), ichneumon flies including the persuasive burglar (*Rhyssa persuasoria*), which is the parasite of the giant woodwasp *Uroceros gigas*. One leaf-miner moth (*Phyllonorycter maestingella*) on Rum has as many as six ichneumon parasites, showing how advanced the colonisation of the woodlands have become. The northern winter moth, which has flightless females, is also present, indicating perhaps that there has been sufficient woody habitat in the past to maintain a population (Wormell, 1987).

One-hundred-and-ninety-four species of bird have been recorded on Rum, of which 87 have bred on the island and over 50 now do so regularly (Love and Wormell, 1987). The Common Bird Census of 1974 found 23 species breeding in the mature woods around Kinloch: woodcock (2 pairs), common sandpiper (1), woodpigeon (10), collared dove (6), cuckoo (3), grey wagtail (2), pied wagtail (1), wren (18), dunnock (14), robin (43), blackbird (28), song thrush (17), mistle thrush (2), willow warbler (28), goldcrest (21), spotted flycatcher (1), long-tailed tit (6), coal tit (7), blue tit (9), treecreeper (4), hooded crow (2), house sparrow (6) and chaffinch (43). With the growth of the young plantations in recent years, this woodland community has been augmented in numbers, and by a few pairs each of whinchat, grasshopper warbler, whitethroat, garden warbler, wood warbler, chiffchaff, greenfinch, siskin, bullfinch and reed bunting. The blackcap may also breed there.

The recreation of the forest habitats of Rum is therefore well on its way, but will require to continue for many decades and to be extended westward into the glens of Kinloch, Kilmory and Shellesder. The grand vision of wild and mountainous Rum to some extent restored to its former wooded state, with the return of much of its wildlife naturally regenerating after centuries of deprivation, may not yet be an idle dream.

Red Deer

It was Fraser Darling who in 1933 first saw the scientific challenge in the study of red deer (*Cervus elaphus*) in the Scottish Highlands and Islands. Rum was his first choice as a centre for his deer study but Sir George Bullough, then the laird, refused him permission, and he carried out his pioneer research in Wester Ross. As if in posthumous irony to Sir George, who died in 1939, the Deed transferring Rum from the Bullough Family to the Nature Conservancy as a National Nature Reserve in 1957 bore the signature of F. Fraser Darling (as a member of the Conservancy). It therefore took over 20 years for the work he had started at Dundonnell (so well described in *A Herd of Red Deer*) to be recommenced by a succeeding generation of researchers, this time on Rum!

The life history of red deer has been traditional knowledge in the Highlands for centuries. In Scotland the red deer was originally an inhabitant of the forest, as it is today in continental Europe. However, as the Caledonian forest was destroyed progressively over many centuries from the Iron Age onwards, the red deer were probably reduced in numbers, and became well adapted for survival in the bare, almost treeless mountain country. Following the breakdown of the clan system after the Risings of 1715 and 1745, the clearance of the remaining forest and cottar communities to make way for sheep in the late 18th and early 19th centuries, and the establishment of the large sporting estates in the 18th and 19th centuries, the deer became more and more of a sporting asset to the landowner. In ancient times, the deer were hunted in the forest with bow and arrow and on the open hill by driving them into traps, and later, on the estates before the days of the rifle, deer-hounds were used to pursue and kill the deer. After the introduction of the rifle, the entire style of hunting was changed to stalking and killing of selected individuals. Stags possessing fine antlers (12 tynes is 'royal', 14 'imperial' and 0, 'hummel') became prize animals sought after by stalkers as 'trophy heads', so in a historical sense, the stalkers employed by the estates and their employers were the first paid observers of red deer. It was their traditional

knowledge as part of the lore of the Highlands that fired
Cameron to write *The Wild Red Deer of Scotland* (1923), and
Fraser Darling, as one of the first Leverhume Research Fel-
lows, to carry the work into the era of modern science in 1933.

*Rutting stag in Rum
(Photo T. H. Clutton-
Brock)*

On Rum the loss of forest and the increase in people and
domesticated stock (cattle, goats and ponies, as well as sheep)
resulted in the extermination of red deer in the 1780s. A flint
arrowhead found on Hallival indicates that deer may have been
hunted there in Stone Age times, and in Glen Duian there is a
deer trap similar to that described by Dean Monro in 1549,
which may have been used by the people in Glen Harris in
medieval times. Red deer were reintroduced to Rum in 1845
after the ownership of the island passed from the Maclean of
Coll to Lord Salisbury, and later to a Campbell family (Love,
1980). Further introductions of English park deer took place
later, to 'improve the stock' on Rum and the Bulloughs, who
acquired the island from the Campbells in 1886, maintained
the deer population between 1,200 and 1,700, and culled
annually some 40 each of stags and hinds. When the island

passed to the Nature Conservancy in 1957, sheep were removed and the deer population was held at a level of about 1,500, with a one-sixth cull of both stags and hinds. However, it was not found possible to maintain such a level of cull on Rum, where there is no recruitment from neighbouring underculled estates. Culls ranging from one-seventh to one-tenth of the population in April proved more appropriate, depending on the size of the population. On the mainland where immigration is possible between estates, the experience and results gained from the one-sixth cull on Rum were later employed by the Red Deer Commission (Annual Reports 1961–75) in their advice to deer-forest managers throughout Scotland.

The seasonal rituals of stags and hinds take place on Rum as they do in all other deer forests. There are five different desig-nated sectors of the population, with little exchange of hinds but much exchange of stags during the rut (p. 283 & 377). One of these sectors, the North Block, has been kept quiet and free from culling since 1972. In 1971 there were 60 hinds over one year old in this block and by 1983 that number had increased to 179. Stag numbers remained constant at 130 until 1980, when they decreased to 97 in 1983. In the ten-year study only two hinds left the block despite the reduction of the population in the neighbouring blocks by culling, though some on the edges of the block wandered further afield without becoming detached. As their numbers increased above 15 hinds per sq km, so the age at which hinds first conceived a calf changed from two to three years and the percentage of calving by 'milk' hinds (with a calf of the year at foot) dropped from 80 to 40%. Winter mortality of calves increased greatly from about 5 to about 35% of the total number of calves born in the previous summer. This resulted in a fall in the calf/hind ratio from 50 to 25 calves per 100 hinds.

As hinds increased, so the date of the rut became later and the performance of stags became affected. Stags were predis-posed more to the stresses of high densities of hinds and accompanying food shortage than the hinds themselves. As hind numbers increased so the mortality of male calves and knobbers (male yearlings) rose more rapidly than in females, and growth of young males was more retarded than in females. In adult stags the mean age at death of those surviving for over three years fell from 14 to 10 years, while that of hinds remained constant between 12 and 14 years. The sex-ratio is therefore changed with an increasing bias in favour of hinds, proving that it is unwise to increase the number of hinds in order to provide a sustained stock of large stags. High stocks of hinds are associ-ated with low performance of stags resulting in higher stag mortality and poor antlers (Fig. 41). Paradoxically, this goes

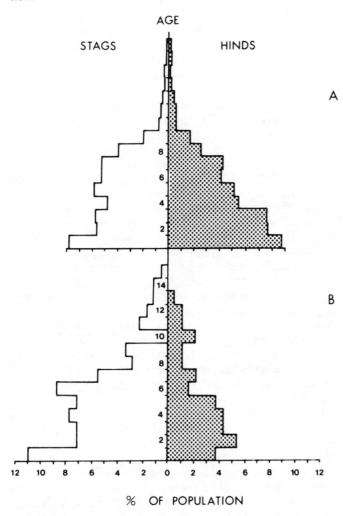

AGE

STAGS HINDS

A

B

% OF POPULATION

Fig. 41
(a) Year class percentages in the red deer population of Rum on 1st June 1957 reconstructed from subsequent deaths and estimated survivors up to May 1966. (b) Percentages of animals in different year classes in the North Block (of Rum) in 1971 (from Clutton-Brock, Guinness and Albon, 1982)

against the grain of traditional management of deer forests, where hind densities are allowed to increase to well in excess of optimal levels.

We have described this mechanism of natural control of deer numbers in some detail so as to convey an impression of the intricacy of the process and the finery of the research which has been done by the Large Mammal Research Group of Cambridge University—the full body of which is described by the principals Tim Clutton-Brock, Fiona Guinness and Steve Albon in *Red Deer: behaviour and ecology of two sexes* (1982), and *Red Deer in the Highlands* (1989), which are the very worthy successors to Fraser Darling's *A Herd of Red Deer* (1937), and which have a world-wide significance in the fields of population ecology and sociology in large herbivores.

Over 15 years the research team in the North Block has studied the entire lifespan of many individual deer in both sexes, and the build-up and decay of social groups. Hinds occur in groups of up to twenty related deer; each group having a matriarchy lead by old hinds and possessing kindred females and immature stags. The juvenile hinds remain with their mothers, aunts and cousins for life in the mother's home-range or an overlapping range. By contrast, the young stags leave the hind group at two years old and wander for another two years before settling with other stags on their own ground usually apart from hinds. These stag groups have less cohesion than the hind groups and gradually dissolve in autumn at the onset of the rut, when one by one the stags move to their rutting areas, often over a distance of several miles, to the other side of the island. There the roaring contests take place, and Rum echoes with the sound of their deep, throaty voices. They often come to blows with antlers locked, occasionally inflicting severe injuries; an old stag might have fought forty to fifty rutting battles in his life and sustained many scars. However, continuous fighting for a harem, though very much in the character of the dominant stag, is not in his best interests. Firstly, he stands a good chance of injury, and secondly, he expends valuable energy which is vital to see him through the cold famine of winter. Stags that can maintain the highest rates of roaring tend to be dominant.

During the winter between November and March the plane of nutrition on Rum falls and the deer starve; though they still graze the withered vegetation they get little nourishment. In April the first flush of green comes to the sea-meadows by the shore, and there lean animals often graze in mixed herds. The early spring nourishment provided by the draw-moss on the wet heaths of moor-grass, deer hair grass and cotton grass is also attractive in April; the first green shoots of these grasses and sedges are palatable, but not so their stiff grown leaves. The rapid increase in food in April and May is accompanied by the casting of antlers and the onset of growth of the new antlers in 'velvet'.

As spring passes into summer the deer move to rush meadows and to higher ground; away from biting flies they peacefully graze the grassy out-washed fans and gulleys, upwards to the mountain tops. The basalt hills of Bloodstone and Fionchra and the limestones of Monadh Dubh have excellent greens frequented by deer in summer, and when the highest pastures on the island over the shearwater grounds on the summits of the cuillin take growth in early summer the deer also move there. In June, the hinds drop their calves, usually choosing habitat with deep cover of grasses, rushes and heather, and in August the stags cast the 'velvet' from their antlers, which then harden and become both the symbols and weapons of challenge. As summer passes to autumn there is a resurgence of growth in the sea-meadows, to which the deer return to complete their provisioning before the rut and the first storms of winter, and the last nutritious food of the year is found among the heather.

The detailed story of the red deer of Rum has been pieced together over 30 years by a succession of workers whose names are written in the extensive literature which the study has yielded. There is no doubt that the fundamental biology of red deer (and other related species) has been greatly advanced by this work, and our enhanced understanding of the processes which govern their life should enable us to manage red deer in a variety of ways—from the truly wild animal of the mountain to the domesticated deer of farm or park.

Sea Eagles

It is testimony to the wild, shy character of the golden eagle (*Aquila chrysaetos*) that it has survived the persecution of centuries in Britain, and now enjoys full protection. By comparison, the white-tailed eagle or sea eagle (*Haliaetus albicilla*) is by nature much more confiding to man, and was exterminated in Britain at the beginning of the 20th century. The last pair nested in Skye in 1916.

In the past the sea eagle lived in the Hebrides in ecological conditions very similar to the present day but with important exceptions. These include persecution by shepherds, gamekeepers and collectors, and though the illegal killing and taking of eagles and their eggs has been greatly reduced, persecution of today is in constant scrutiny by the RSPB, police, and the general public. Also, the ability of eagles to raise young is inversely related to concentrations of pollutants in their food. Coastal eagles feeding on seabirds and fish may accumulate damaging amounts of these toxic substances (eg DDT and PCBs), which did not exist in former times when the sea eagles bred in the Hebrides. In 1968, George Waterston and Johan Willgohs of Bergen, who believed a reintroduction of the sea eagle to Scotland would be a great triumph for wildlife conservation, made an unsuccessful attempt at reintroduction on Fair Isle. A much more sustained effort over several years was clearly required.

The decision by the Nature Conservancy Council in favour
of the reintroduction of the sea eagle to Scotland was therefore
a finely balanced one to which Lord Dulverton gave crucial
support. The project was started on Rum in 1975. For eleven
years an annual batch of eight-week old nestlings was collected
under licence in Nordland by the Norwegian naturalist Harald
Misund, and transported by the Royal Air Force from Bodo to
Kinloss, Moray. From thence the birds were taken to Rum for
rearing and release into the wild under licence by the project
officer John Love. From the beginning the project was a fine
example of teamwork between the Nature Conservancy
Council, Royal Society for the Protection of Birds, Royal Air
Force, World Wide Fund for Nature, Scottish Wildlife Trust,
Institute of Terrestrial Ecology, and the Norwegians. It is
described in *The Return of the Sea Eagle* (Love, 1983).

J. A. Love releasing a young sea-eagle for its first flight in the wild on Rum. Between 1975 and 1985, 82 young sea-eagles were released from this rock above Loch Dornabac (Photo J. M. Boyd)

The Bodo district in Norway is very reminiscent of the
seaboard of West Inverness. The view that we described of
Skye and the Small Isles from Mallaig closely resembles that of
the sea-eagle islands Landegode, Helligvaer and Bliksvaer

from Bodo. The ecology is also similar in detail, but there is a difference of about 10° of latitude, with different day-lengths and breeding conditions. The confiding nature of the sea eagle is evident, when they can be seen scavenging in Bodo harbour, and nesting in accessible sites close to human habitation. They also nest at high density, as on Karlsoyvaer where the birch woods are similar to those on the Garvellachs, Raasay and South Rona. Nests are found in crevices on high vertical cliffs and pine trees above the fjords in sites typical of golden eagles in Scotland. The species prospers in Nordland, and the few young taken for the Rum project (single birds were taken from eyries possessing two eaglets) pose no threat to the sea eagle in north Norway.

If the birds could be given living space in the Hebrides the portents of reintroduction were good. However, there were a number of other unanswered questions to be put beside that concerning the toxic effects of pollutants. Would people with guns, traps and poisons in Scotland kill these huge, often low-flying and rather fearless birds (wingspan up to 3m, weight up to 7.25kg)? Would ravens, crows, greater black-backed gulls and fulmars (which seriously oiled one of those released in Fair Isle) harrass and cause the death of the newly fledged eagles? Would the resident golden eagles prevent the young sea eagles establishing feeding and breeding territories? Would the techniques of rearing and release cause the young birds to be 'imprinted' on their handler and have difficulties in forming successful breeding pairs in the wild?

The first batch of four young almost brought the project to a halt. The single male died before release, and of the three females reared and released one was later found dead under an electricity cable in Morven. The remaining two survived. Fortunately the project was budgeted for five years based on the fact that the birds were unlikely to breed in the first six years of their lives. The doubts of the critics and the jibes of the cynics were not strong enough to stop it, and since then it has gone from strength to strength. The techniques of transportation, caging, feeding, handling, release, provisioning and observing the birds in the wild all improved with experience. The project was extended, and over the period 1975 to 1985, 85 young eagles from Norway were transferred to Rum. Three died in captivity and 82 (43 females and 39 males) were released at the same rock beside the road above Loch an Dornabac. Seven (3 males and 4 females) died soon after release and a few others may have died unnoticed. Sadly, two were poisoned, one of which was four years old and approaching breeding condition.

The young eagles remain in the vicinity of the release site for a few weeks, and a few have settled in the Small Isles. Others have wandered far: south to Ireland, north to Caithness and throughout the Hebrides. The first birds were ready to breed in 1980–81; in 1980 birds were seen carrying sticks; in 1981 a crude nest was built close to the site used by sea eagles a century before, and between 1982 and 1984 there were several breeding attempts each year which failed because of infertile or broken eggs. This was possibly to be expected in young birds breeding for the first time, however. Other breeding pairs may have gone unrecorded. In 1985 at least four pairs attempted to breed, and the first Scottish-bred sea eagle for almost 70 years flew in the Hebrides. In 1986, two more were fledged, in 1987, three and in 1988, two. In 1988, eleven pairs (about a quarter of the birds reintroduced) attempted to breed, and in 1989, three pairs reared five young. The total number of Scottish-bred birds fledged so far is 13. All the birds are young; with growing numbers in breeding condition and with growing experience of the birds in breeding, prospects of a successful reintroduction are good.

The return of the sea eagle to the avifauna of Britain is on its way. Unlike the osprey which returned naturally, the sea eagle has been physically brought back by a scientific and technical endeavour. In the minds of those of us who conceived and ran the project, there was never any doubt that the qualities of the Rum National Nature Reserve as the point of introduction were the best in the country and that we would require to keep the supply of recruits coming from Norway for at least five years. In the event the recruitment continued, thanks to Captain Misund, for ten years and was discontinued on the year of the fledging of the first Scottish sea eagle in the new population. The project proceeds with the care and protection of breeding pairs towards a viable population by the end of the century.

St Kilda—Island of World Heritage

One of the pleasures of visiting St Kilda is to walk contemplatively through the ruins and meadows of the old village (Fig. 43). Even to those who know little of its history, the sight of the place instils a sense of wonder, while to those who are well-read on St Kilda, the place is positively haunted, with, in every direction, the signs of a vanished race of people.

To the few surviving natives, the St Kilda of their childhood will never return. Even to those of us who knew the deserted islands in the early 1950s when the sad sight of the derelict village was eased by an all-pervading sense of wilderness, the place is not the same. Today the sights and sounds of the modern army garrison and the stream of summer visitors tend to dispel the sequestered quality of the St Kildan experience of those former days. However, many more are now able to enjoy St Kilda, and it is still a pleasure to take the Keartons' book *With Nature and a Camera* (1897) to St Kilda to relish Richard's

Fig. 42
Location map of St Kilda

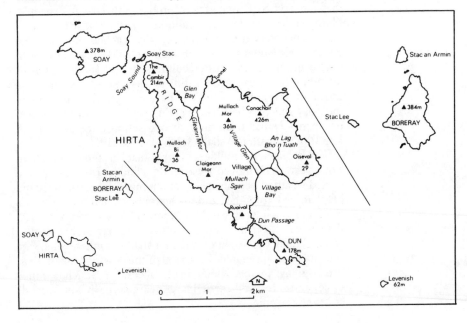

description and to stand in the exact spot of Cherry's photographs, placing again the St Kildans upon their island.

On small lonely isles, people and wildlife live in a microcosm; that's what makes them attractive to archaeologist, historian and scientist alike. St Kilda is at once superb in natural and cultural qualities succinctly stated in the *Nomination of St Kilda for inclusion in the World Heritage List* (Secretary of State for Scotland, 1985). Its 'world' status in wildlife heritage results from its vast seabird populations, its indigenous fauna of mice and wrens and its Soay sheep. However, the natural history of the islands is inextricably intertwined with the history of the St Kildans over many centuries; to appreciate the wildlife, one must also appreciate the people.

The St Kildans

Who were the first St Kildans? We can only make an informed guess. As the Stone-age and Bronze-age peoples moved northward into the Hebrides, from 6,600 to 2,400 years ago, so more and more islands became settled. It is logical therefore that in due time, a people accustomed to sea-going in small craft and blessed with an ameliorating climate, would reach St Kilda, but the spread of human settlement throughout the islands may have taken many centuries to accomplish. Cottam (1979) points to the absence of neolithic artifacts, indicating that the first St Kildans were probably Bronze Age people. However, he gives a word of caution on datings of artifacts at St Kilda since very little bronze actually reached these remote outliers. He suggests that, though St Kilda may have been visited by the hunter-fisher cultures (for seals and seabirds, including the great auk), it did not become settled until the arrival of pastoralists, who may have brought the ancestors of the Soay sheep. The earliest dating (radio-carbon) of human occupancy comes from boat-shaped settings of stones in An Lag Bho'n Tuath in Village Glen, *c.* 3,850 BP.

The Bronze-Age builders of the Callanish stone circle about 3,600 years ago enjoyed a warm, dry climate. Long periods of settled weather were probably much more dominant in island life than they are today, and the 80km passage from the Harris Sound or Loch Roag would be a much less daunting prospect than it has been in historical times. Further archaeological research may shed light on the first shadowy inhabitants, who probably long-predated the arrival of the Norsemen with their ocean-going vessels which made access to St Kilda much easier and safer, and carried larger cargoes of livestock, foodstuffs and people.

The history of St Kilda is written somewhat inscrutably upon the face of the islands in many generations of stone and turf structures and, less conspicuously, in soils, vegetation and fauna. The Village Glen and Gleann Mor are the main centres, but structures are present throughout Hirta even on the most unlikely cliff terraces and on all the other islands. Stac an Armin has many 'cleits' (drystone huts used for drying hay, turf and birds) and other structures, and Stac Lee has a small stone shelter tucked into its south-west wall. However, it is to the village that we must look for the testament of St Kildan culture. The modern intrusion of the army installations has been strictly limited from the beginning in 1957 to localities at the eastern end of the Village Area, the beachhead, the summits of Mullach Mor and Mullach Sgar and in the route of the road linking all those sites. It is one of the great achievements of the NTS, NCC and the army that, despite the disruption caused by military activity in such a small island, so little of its antiquities have been damaged or lost. The National Trust for Scotland has also reconstructed the church, schoolroom, factor's house, feather store and five cottages, and has consolidated the walls of other cottages, blackhouses and byres, 'cleits' and walls. The manse is now used as the Sergeant's Mess. In outward appearance none of the buildings have been changed from the pre-evacuation time prior to 1930.

Village Glen is a reliquary containing the artifacts of almost four millenia: boat-settings of stones, stone circles, cairns and

The 'Hardrock' operation of 1957 showing the tented camp in the Village meadows and a landing craft discharging on the beach. A construction squadron of the Royal Air Force built the Army base on Hirta, St Kilda in 1957–58 (Photo J. M. Boyd)

platforms dating from the Bronze Age to Christian times: the remains of an earth house or 'souterrain' possibly from the Iron Age about 1,700 years ago, denotes another cultural epoch which in turn was replaced by a new immigrant people who built round corbelled houses with separate living and sleeping compartments. The Calum Mor House in the Village, the Amazon's House in Gleann Mor and the Staller's House on Boreray together with many other corbelled remnants, may have belonged to this period.

The Norse influence came at that time, and though many of the place names are Norse and there have been Norse artifacts found on Hirta (notably two oval brooches indicating a woman's grave of the 10th century AD), the occupancy of St Kilda by Viking settlers was possibly light enough not to have displaced the native communities. Though the St Kildans may have from time to time been reduced or even expelled by disease and starvation over the centuries, the Norse names and the corbelled-building culture lived on into medieval times, when the main settlement was located at Tobar Childa under Glacan Conchair where a few medieval houses survive (one with a beehive sleeping chamber) among more recent 'cleits'. A causeway ran from the landing place (where the feather store was built in the 19th century) to Tobar Childa. This is the village that Martin saw when he visited Hirta in 1695.

In the 1830s the Rev Neil Mackenzie persuaded the St Kildans to build a new generation of houses in the pattern of the Hebridean *tigh dubh* or blackhouse along a new causeway some 200m nearer the sea. He also had a head-dyke built around the village and had the land between the Amhuinn Mor and the glebe sectioned into 19 runrig strips (Fig. 43). This signalled the end of the corbell-building, and thereafter all 'cleits' and drystone buildings were built with perpendicular walls exemplified by the large 'cleits' immediately behind the 'street.' However, the 1830s conformation of houses in the village street was short-lived, for in the 1860s the laird had 16 three-roomed, gavelled cottages built between the blackhouses, many of which thereafter became byres or stores. The present church and manse were built in the 1830s, the factor's house and the feather store in the 1860s and the schoolroom in 1898.

The evacuation of St Kilda is one of the social ironies of this century, and is best described by Tom Steel in *The Life and Death of St Kilda* (1975). The native community had possibly survived (with some enforced breaks in occupancy because of epidemic and starvation) for over 2,000 years and failed by 25 years to see its 'salvation' with the arrival of the Armed Services in 1956. In truth, the events at St Kilda in the past 30 years would have served to modernise the entire scene of *any* existing

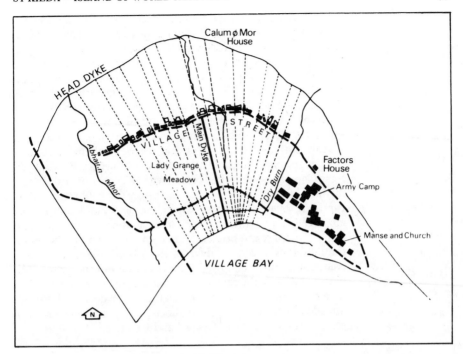

native community, and much of old St Kilda that now remains, could easily have been swept away.

As it is, the human scene has changed. For the few ancestral Gaelic-speaking families, there are now unnumbered short-term individual inhabitants. For the old culture, the remains of which are skilfully curated by the National Trust for Scotland, there is the 'high tech' of the army, upon which most other visitors to St Kilda ride pick-a-back. Nonetheless, when one is on one's own with the seabirds in the vastness of cliff, cave and stack, one is back in old St Kilda—in that timeless place where the frailty of human life is seen against the enduring rock of ages.

Fig. 43
Map of the Village of St Kilda in 1860 showing the unenclosed strips of land running from the shore to the head dyke with the cottage of each strip placed along the 'street' (St Kilda Handbook, National Trust for Scotland)

The Rock of Ages

St Kilda is a freakish little archipelago of four cliff-bound islands (Fig. 42)—Hirta (638ha., summit 420m), Soay (99ha., 378m), Boreray (77ha., 384m) and Dun (32ha., 175m)—about 70km west of the Outer Hebrides. There are also numerous stacks of which Stac an Armin (196m) and Stac Lee (172m) are by far the largest. Boreray and the two great stacks are a satell-ite group some 6km to the north-east of the main cluster of

islands. The islands are the eroded fragments of a Tertiary volcano, thrust through the Precambrian and Mesozoic rocks at
the edge of the Hebridean shelf some 60 million years ago.
Fig. 44 shows a simplified geological map of the islands
(Harding *et al.*, 1984). A mass of granite (the hills of Conachair
and Oiseval in east Hirta with the remainder drowned in the
Boreray Passage) is emplaced in a context of older gabbro (west
coasts of Hirta and Dun, Glen Bay and all of Soay, Boreray and
the great stacks). The gabbro and the granite are rocks of
sharply contrasting character, and between them there is a
zone of rocks of intermediate character known as the Mullach
Sgar Complex—dolerites veined with microgranite (well seen
in the Quarry), breccias, and inclusions of gabbro, possibly
ruptured from the crust when the granitic magma was
emplaced. The boundary between the granite and mixed rocks
of the Complex can be clearly seen on the storm beach and in
the buildings and head dyke of the village; the pale cream-
coloured granite occupying the eastern end of the beach and
hinterland while the remainder is made up of grey mixed rocks.
The resulting volcanic massif has thereafter been faulted and
intruded by dykes and sills or sheets, which are visibly shown
on the seaward faces of Oiseval and Conachair.

Fig. 44
*Geological map of St
Kilda* (St Kilda
Handbook. *National
Trust for Scotland)*

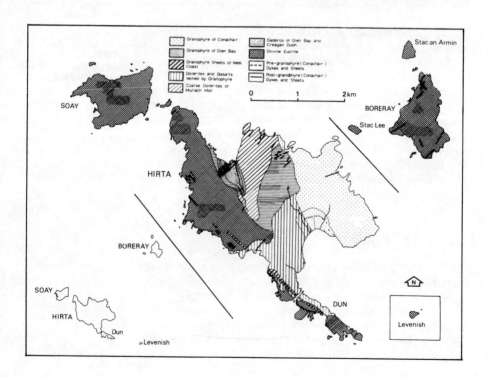

It is difficult to measure the extent of the St Kilda volcano, for unlike those in Skye, Rum and Mull, the lava fields which may have been extruded at the St Kilda centre have all been eroded away. The St Kilda islands are but small vestiges of a crustal mass which has been planed down by ice, water and weather to a depth of 1km or more. Between Hirta and Boreray there is a submarine platform at a depth of 60m, indicating a post-glacial erosion surface and possibly substantial changes in sea level and a drowned landscape. The cliffs descend sharply to this level, and are said to be pitted with submarine caves positioned at previous sea levels.

The topography is largely the result of the Quaternary glaciation and post-glacial marine erosion, but also reflects the rock structure. The granite weathers differently from the gabbro, and both are different from the dolerites of the dykes and sills. In broad silhouette, even as seen from distant North Uist, the granite hills of Conachair and Oiseval appear as smooth paps compared with the ragged outline of the surrounding ridges and islands of gabbro. Many of the dykes and sills are 'softer' than the rock into which they have been intruded, and this has resulted in large sea caves and tunnels (of which that at Gob na h'Airde is the grandest and the most accessible), chasms like the 'mauvais pas' at Gob Scapinish on Boreray, and natural arches like those around Gob an Dun. Faults provide lines of weakness exploited by the elements, resulting in such bold features as the chasm between Hirta and Dun, the Cambir isthmus and the gorge of the Amhuinn Mor, while others probably occur in the seabed in the Soay Sound, and between Boreray and the great stacks. The granite displays vast impending drapes of vertically jointed rock on the seaward faces of Oiseval and Conachair, overhanging the high-arched portals of caves as if constructed to 'plumb and square', and the great perpendicular wall of Conachair falls over 400m in this suite of cliffs. By comparison the gabbro is a capricious jumble of mighty bastions, pinnacle ridges and steep bevelled slopes, descending erratically to the sea.

The signs are that St Kilda may have stood proud of the Quaternary ice sheet but was probably ice-bound for most of the year and possessed a small valley glacier in Village Glen, which holds small moraines and together with Glen Mor, many periglacial features. There are fine exposures of glacial till on the 8m cliff behind the storm beach, and on the 20m bayside cliff of Ruaival and its stream gorge. The chronology of these drifts indicates a mild climatic interlude about 25,000 years ago (Middle Devensian) between two glaciations, the second of which was perhaps the more severe since it produced the glaciers and the devastating frost-shattering of the rocks,

giving rise to the extensive screes and blockfields of which
Carn Mor, Ard Uachdarachd, Tigh Dugan on Soay, Stac an
Armin, and the citadels of Ruaival and Point of Dun are prominent features. The mild spell is represented by a 20cm bed of
pollen-bearing sands derived, it is thought, by the fluvial
reworking of organic silt from the earlier glacial till.

It is testimony to the fine stature of A. M. Cockburn, who did
the first geological survey of St Kilda in 1927–28, that his work
(1935) has needed no major amendment and has formed the
solid basis for all that has been done since. Cockburn and his
friend John Mathieson, who drew the first OS map, saw the
community of St Kilda (1928) in its dying years and were indeed
fortunate to have the company of the St Kildans in their
reconnaissances to all the islands. The Oxford-Cambridge
Expedition of 1931 experienced the excitement of the uninhabited islands but did not have the St Kildans to assist them,
and were denied access to the even more wonderful solitudes
of Boreray and Soay.

Home of the West Wind

In its solitude upon the face of the ocean and standing tall with
its head in the clouds, St Kilda has a climate all its own. There
has been no long-term, consistent weather record of St Kilda;
the closest stations are at Benbecula and Butt of Lewis, 80 and
110km distant, which are the two windiest stations in the British
Isles. St Kilda lies close to the track of the Atlantic depressions
moving north-east from mid-ocean to the Norwegian Sea, and
winds, mainly from the south and west, are sometimes very
strong. Benbecula has recorded over a decade an average
annual wind speed of 24km/h. The St Kilda figure is probably
much higher because of the closer proximity to the coursing
storm centres and to the Venturi and severe drafting effects of
the islands rising starkly and abruptly in the rip of the wind. All
these factors combine to make St Kilda possibly the windiest
place in the British Isles (p. 57).

There was a run of 33 months of parallel recordings between
Benbecula and St Kilda following the landings of 1957. Out of
900 days, St Kilda had 212 (21.4%) with winds of gale force.
(Force 8 on the Beaufort Scale: over 63km/h) compared with
124 (12.5%) for Benbecula. Gusts of 209km/h were recorded at
Mullach Sgar (213m above sea-level) in January 1962. Sea-
spray is blown over the islands in gales, and the chloride content of St Kildan soils varies from 30 to 321mg/100gm of soil
compared with 2mg/100gm of soil taken from a garden in
Edinburgh.

The first saucer-shaped antenna erected by the army on Mullach Mor was about 5m in diameter and was not encased in a dome. For overwintering it was turned edge-on to the prevailing wind and provided with an angle-iron frame firmly secured in concrete, but following a great storm the antenna together with its angle-iron frame was found bent almost horizontal! One of us was present in the first landing of the military 'operation Hardrock' in April 1957 and saw the task force caught by a storm with much of the equipment lying loose in the fields. There was devastation in the camp, with men viewing the holocaust from the safety of 'cleits'; furniture took flight over hundreds of metres and much of it ended in the sea.

The mean annual temperatures show a narrower range than at Benbecula; St Kilda is up to 2°C warmer in winter and cooler in summer respectively, ranging from 6°C to 12°C. The mean daily range of temperature at St Kilda is the narrowest in Britain (except for the Scilly Isles): 3°C in December and 6°C in May. The first frost occurs about 10th December (later than any other station in Britain) and the last about 20th March. Average annual rainfall is 1200mm, evenly distributed throughout the year with a much higher figure over the beclouded ridges. There is snowfall and lying snow for about 20 and 13 days respectively. Precipitation exceeds evaporation in all months except June, when both stand at about 80mm, and soils dry out for a few days. Humidity is consistently high throughout the year, averaging a little less than 90%, so it is little wonder that the St Kildan inventiveness applied itself to overcoming simultaneously the strength and wetness of the wind. The result, of course, is the thick-walled 'cleit', which withstands the strongest winds. Once used as a drying 'machine' for fodder and fuel it is today a dry lair for the Soay sheep.

The spring at St Kilda has spells of light to moderate north-east winds circulating a Scandinavian anti-cyclone, with the quietest and sunniest weather occuring in late May and early June, when the Hebrides are in a prolonged circulation of tropical maritime air. This is a moist flow however, with banks of sea fog. St Kilda makes its own cloud, and often when the wide ocean is sunlit, the islands have a cap or orographic cloud and are shrouded in drifts of snow-white mist. Such shrouds cut off sunshine and sometimes retard the recovery of the islands from their winter impoverishment, and plant growth is slow. Nonetheless, the lesser celandine (*Ranunculus ficaria*) is early to bloom in the lee cliff terraces and gullies, which are suntraps in summer, and where can also occasionally be found migratory painted ladies (*Cythia cardui*).

Seabirds of St Kilda

The most recent account of the seabirds of St Kilda (Tasker et al, 1988) updates *Birds of St Kilda* by Harris and Murray (1978) which cites 139 references to literature. In 1987, there were about 400,000 breeding pairs of 15 species of seabird (excluding eider) at St Kilda:

English	Scientific	Gaelic
Fulmar	*Fulmarus glacialis*	*Fulmair*
Manx shearwater	*Puffinus puffinus*	*Fachach*
Storm petrel	*Hydrobates pelagicus*	*Lauireag*
Leach's petrel	*Oceanodroma leucorhoa*	*Gobhlan-mara*
Gannet	*Sula bassana*	*Sulaire*
Shag	*Phalacrocorax aristotelis*	*Sgarbh-an-sgumain*
Great skua	*Stercorarius skua*	*Fasgadair-mor*
Lesser b-b gull	*Larus fuscus*	*Sgaireag*
Herring gull	*Larus argentatus*	*Glas-fhaoileag*
Great b-b gull	*Larus marinus*	*Farspag*
Kittiwake	*Rissa tridactyla*	*Ruideag*
Guillemot	*Uria aalge*	*Eun-dubh-an-sgadain*
Razorbill	*Alca torda*	*Coltraiche*
Black guillemot	*Cepphus grylle*	*Gearra-glas*
Puffin	*Fratercula arctica*	*Budhaig*

St Kilda holds about 20% of the population of the gannets in the North Atlantic, 20% of the *grabae* race of the puffin, the largest colony of Leach's petrel in the eastern Atlantic, and the largest colony of storm petrels in Britain. Probably over 1% of the European stock of kittiwakes, guillemots, and razorbills breeds at St Kilda. The honours accorded to St Kilda by the world conservation movement for its many high qualities in natural and human heritage, reflect the great value which people everywhere place upon its seabirds.

The measurement of numbers of seabirds breeding at St Kilda is a formidable task both physically and intellectually. To reach the breeding sites and to endure the vertigo, seas and weather of St Kilda demands guts, and against this background, the design of survey and the interpretation of the data demands brains. Before the evacuation, dating back to the days of the Rev. Neil Mackenzie 1829–43, the sizes of seabird colonies were related to the harvest of eggs and birds which were taken annually. Mackenzie stated that up to 5,000 young were taken, but Sands (1878) who spent 14 months at St Kilda, recorded 89,600 puffins killed in 1876. The latter figure bears no comparison with the former, and with such records there is no reliable way of plotting the history of the seabirds and seafowling. In broad terms, however, it seems certain that by 1900 the annual harvest of thousands of birds and eggs was in decline, and by 1930 was almost in abeyance.

Among the most intrepid St Kildan seafowling expeditions were the ascent of Stac Biorach (73m), the rock-fang in the Soay Sound, for guillemots, and the noctural visits to the great stacks to kill adult gannets in spring, driven on by winter starvation. The St Kildans had none of the boating and climbing aids of the present-day, only sail and oars, bare feet and horse-hair rope. Who today will row 6km to Biorach, climb it without boots and rope, and row the 6km home, as did the young men of old St Kilda with their harvest of guillemots?

James Fisher (1943, 1948, 1952) was the pioneer of seabird survey at St Kilda in the modern era. Though he was only able to scratch the surface of the task during his short visits, he showed that there was no alternative to setting eyes on as many of the breeding ledges as possible and to build up a round impression based on the best possible count. His work on the gannetry, done mostly from the heaving deck of a yacht, was a stimulus to others who came after and who combined much more detailed, on-site work with aerial photography (Boyd, 1961; Murray, 1981).

However difficult the gannets are to count, other species are even more difficult. Yet strenuous attempts have been made to assess the orders of magnitude and fluctuations of the populations of fulmars (Fisher, 1952; Anderson, 1957 and 1962; Harris and Murray, 1978), guillemots and kittywakes (Boyd, 1960; Harris and Murray, 1978; Tasker, *et al.*, 1988), puffins (Flegg, 1972; Harris and Murray, 1977 and 1978), and to study

Fig. 45
Map showing the distribution of puffins at St Kilda (from Harris and Murray, 1979)

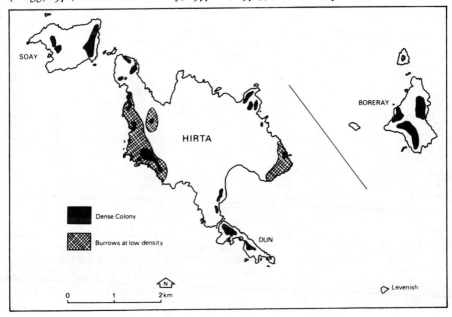

their feeding and reproductive biology. The challenge of this work carries with it the romance of a dramatic scientific quest on the edge of the world; few exercises in the survey of wildlife anywhere on earth can compare with the ascent of Stac Lee, the rock which Julian Huxley described (from the sea) as 'new to human experience' (p. 330).

The significance of seabird research is not limited simply to the actual status of the species; it also sheds light on the ecology of the sea. The islands of St Kilda, which draw their throng of seabirds from the reach of the North Atlantic, are a focus of biological activity greatly disproportionate to their physical size. Changes in the chemistry of the sea and in standing stocks of marine organisms within the food-chain of seabirds are likely to be reflected in condition and numbers of the seabird species gathered at the breeding islands. There are already signs that seabirds carry high levels of pollutants such as poly-chlorinated byphenyls (PCBs), which become concentrated in seabird predators such as eagles of which none have bred at St Kilda since about 1835.

St Kilda has an especially sensitive ecosystem which could in future be used for the monitoring of the vast marine ecosystem. For example, industrial fishing of pelagic fish (herring, mack-erel, sprat, pout and sand-eel) may cause measurable changes in the assemblies of gannets, auks and kittiwakes. Casting further afield, pollutants, including radio-active substances,

Species	Unit	Islands							Total
		Hirta	Dun	Soay	Bor'ay	StLee	StaA	Ot'r+	
Fulmar	aos	35,349	12,018	5,679	6,802	34	2,387	512	62,786
Manx sh'r	p/a	p	p	?	?	0	?	0	?
St. petrel	p/a	p	p	?	p	0	?	?	?
Ls. petrel	p/a	p	p	?	p	0	?	?	?
Gannet*	nests	0	0	0	24,676	13,521	11,853	0	50,050
Shag	nests	25	21	4	2	0	0	0	52
Gt. skua	aot	44	0	8	2	0	0	0	54
Lr. b-b. gl	aot	129	13	0	12	0	0	0	154
Herr'g gl	aot	14	4	0	38	0	0	3	59
Gt. b-b. gl	aot	13	12	5	15	0	1	10	56
Kittiwake	aos	1,719	1,231	1,306	2,923	245	326	79	7,829
Guillemot	ind	10,465	2,648	2,219	3,679	490	1,436	1,768	22,705
Razorbill	ind	1,221	1,809	263	252	15	237	17	3,814
Bl. guilt't	ind	0	10	2	5	0	0	0	17
Puffin	ob	10,800	41,600	115,000	63,000	0	100	1	230,501

+ = Levenish, Soay Stac, and Stac Biorach; aos = apparently occupied sites; p/a = presence/absence; aot = apparently occupied territories; ind = individual birds; ob = occupied burrows; * = 1985 data.

Table 16.1   Total numbers of birds on the islands and stacs at St Kilda from Tasker *et al* (1988).

entering the ocean and the food chain of seabirds might be brought to the green terraces of St Kilda and deposited there in the organic debris of the breeding populace. The terraces are grazed heavily by Soay and blackface (Boreray) sheep, which further concentrate the pollutants in the ewes' milk and ultimately in the bone-marrow of the lambs. A pollutant widely dispersed at low concentration could become highly concentrated within the island ecosystem, thus affording a sensitive means of detection of pollution. (The Chernobyl incident of 1986, and the increased levels of radio-activity that it caused in sheep stocks in Britain, points to the use of just such a biological monitor that the seabird islands have to offer.)

The distribution of breeding seabirds at St Kilda is shown in Table 16.1. The units in which the numbers of the various species appear to differ according to how the species presented itself to the counters in the field, and to aerial photographers.

Carn Mor is a large boulder-strewn terrace on the west of

Dr D. Boddington and Dr D. A. Ratcliffe at the 'cleits' on Stac an Armin in May 1959. The view is to the north wall of Boreray (Photo J. M. Boyd)

Mullach Bhi and the largest boulders are 7m broad. This is an underground labyrinth inhabited by burrow-nesting seabirds; by day the block-field with its steep, jutting landscape and ragged sheets of green *Holcus* is thronged with puffins and calling gulls, but at night the scene is transformed; the puffins are below ground and the gulls silent, but the night is full of the wings and calls of Manx shearwaters, storm petrels and Leach's petrels. Carn Mor is perhaps the most accessible site in Britain to witness all three species of nocturnal petrels. All three are also present on Dun where, on summer days, the visitor is given a fly-past by thousands of puffins swirling overhead in a great vortex and later settling in 'rafts' upon the sheltered waters of Village Bay.

The social structure of the seabird metropolis remains a mystery. What are the social factors that make the assemblies of the species so fragmented? Though there are manifestly suitable sites for breeding gannets in Hirta, Soay and Dun, what makes the gannets remain at Boreray and the great stacks (p. 303), and are the tenants of the many puffinries separate clans dispersing in winter to different sectors of the ocean? Guillemots (of which 10% are of the northern 'bridled' race) and kittiwakes have an affinity in nesting sites, which is well displayed on the west wall of Boreray and in the portals of sea caves on Dun.

Wrens and Mice

Awakening in the still calm dawn of a June day in the village, before the noise of the army generators smothered the gentle break of surf and call of birds, one might have been forgiven for thinking oneself at home in Midlothian. The torrential song of a wren on the factor's house chimney-head is a reminder of habitats of garden and wood far removed from St Kilda. It is a compelling call to action, and out early in the dew-drenched meadows, the sharp-eared ornithologist can walk the length of the village street and hear clearly ten cock wrens singing in their breeding territories, in company with piping oystercatchers and drumming snipe. This is the St Kilda wren *Troglodytes troglodytes hirtensis*, which is larger with a longer bill, greyer and more heavily barred with paler underparts, than the russet-brown mainland race. Its song is also stronger, and has a somewhat different phrasing. Other distinct races occur in Shetland (*T. t. zetlandicus*), Fair Isle (*fridariensis*), the Outer Hebrides (*hebridensis*), and in other parts of Britain and Ireland.

There has been wonderment at the presence of the wren at

St Kilda since the earliest accounts. Those who had braved the sea-crossing were astonished that the tiny wren should have done the same and prospered. The differences between *hebridensis* and *hirtensis* are so great that the segregation of the two races possibly took place before the arrival of man in the Hebrides, and may have been assisted by land bridges with much shorter oversea-flying distances than exist today. There is evidence of vegetation on the land mass which is now St Kilda in middle Devensian times, about 25,000 years ago, and the wren may have been attracted there by the wooded habitat of that time.

How both the wren and the field-mouse arrived at St Kilda may always remain a mystery. Are these surviving relics of a bygone age of tree-covered islands, or have they been much later colonists? However, it is no mystery that having got there, these versatile animals have adapted beautifully to stark treeless St Kilda.

This adaptation has been discussed by Williamson (1958), who saw St Kilda as being far from austere for the wren, and the same might be said for the mouse. Though the weather is severe for those such as man and sheep whose business is on the land surface, it is not so for wrens and mice, whose business is largely underground. In good years there may be 230 pairs of wrens in St Kilda as a whole; they are present on Hirta (117), Boreray (*c.* 45), Soay (*c.* 45), Dun (*c.* 25) and Stac an Armin (*c.* 3). Only Hirta and Dun have been counted, and the highest

Fig. 46
Map showing the distribution of singing wrens on Hirta in 1957 (from Williamson and Boyd, 1960)

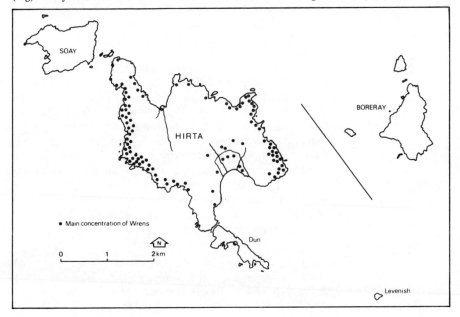

concentrations were associated with the puffin colonies, where there are large amounts of organic debris in a network of humid underground habitats slightly warmed by bacterial action, and lush green swards rich in invertebrates. In the village area the stoneworks and interiors of the cleitean replace the talus and burrow-system of the puffin slopes, and are probably much drier and warmer, especially when packed with bedded sheep. Many 'cleits' hold middens of sheep dung strewn with dead sheep which provide ample supplies of food for wrens and mice.

The abundance of food for the St Kilda wren in summer is much less than for the wren in the lowland broadleaved woodland, where the floor receives a rain of leaf-mining caterpillars. Thus the St Kilda wren breeds later and raises fewer second broods than those of wood and garden. The mainland cocks take little or no part in the feeding of young, while both members of the pair are required to feed the young at St Kilda, so the mainland cocks are therefore more poly-gamous than the St Kildan cocks. Nevertheless, the St Kilda wren's attempt to be polygamous and go through the ritual of building several 'cock nests', more than one of which is rarely occupied by a female. In years of warm, calm spring weather when the islands recover their green flush early, there may be more double-brooding, and this may result in an increase in the number of breeding pairs in the following year.

The wrens and field-mice of St Kilda possess the genetical features of distinct island races, as do the distinct species of the Galapagos. The description of the St Kilda wren by the orni-thologist, Henry Seebohm (1884), as a distinct species *Troglo-dytes hirtensis*, was later revised as a sub-species. This placed a greatly enhanced value upon their skins and eggs which, together with those of the Leach's petrel, were keenly sought by the Victorian dealers and collectors. The St Kildans were not slow to realise what was happening and developed a trade, charging one guinea (£1.05) for an adult and 12s 6d (62.5p) for a juvenile (Williamson and Boyd, 1960), so much so that by 1894 it was thought—probably erroneously—that only 15 pairs survived. Concern mounted, and in 1904 an Act of Parliament was passed for the protection of the St Kilda wren and the Leach's Petrel.

The concern over both species was almost certainly ill-founded. Williamson and Boyd state:

. . . this craze for cabinet specimens could never have reduced its (the wren's) numbers significantly, for even after the collectors had got to St Kilda (no mean achievement in these days) the difficulties awaiting them in their task were well-nigh insuperable. For although a few pairs nested annually in the dry-stone cleitean where the St Kildans stored their peats and hay (and these wrens were always vulnerable), the bird's chief haunts are the inaccessible places along the towering, awe-inspiring range of the islands' cliffs. There they are, and always will be, secure from human depredation; and there, as it turns out, they are far from scarce.

No satisfactory measure of the size of the St Kilda wren population was achieved before Kenneth Williamson's dawn surveys of 1957.

The St Kilda field-mouse, like the wren, was first described as a distinct species *Apodemus hirtensis* by Barrett-Hamilton who a year later (1900) recast it as the sub-species *hirtensis* of the widespread species *A. sylvaticus*. Based on taxonomic differences, the St Kilda field-mouse is distinct from that of the remainder of the Hebrides, where the Rum field-mouse *A. s. hamiltonii* is also distinct both from St Kilda and the remainder of the Hebrides (Delany, 1964, 1970). Weights of *hirtensis* ranged from 29–40gms compared with 14–29gms for *sylvaticus*.

The St Kilda field-mouse may have been introduced by man, but the 'land-bridge' theory points to its having been there in advance of, and having survived, the last ice-age.

In 1955, when St Kilda was uninhabited, the field-mouse had no fear of man. Here, one walks across the chest of A. A. K. Whitehouse as he reclines among the ruins of St Kilda village in late May 1955 (Photo J. M. Boyd)

However, skeletal measurements indicate a closer identity with Norwegian field mice than with others, which points to a Norse origin rather than a relic left isolated by collapsing land-bridges (Berry, 1969). The fact that it is present on Dun and not on Boreray or Soay (Campbell, 1974) indicates that it may have been in the area before the collapse of the land-bridge joining Hirta and Dun, though it is just conceivable that it might have swum the Dun Passage and scaled the precipice! No similar doubt exists about the arrival of the St Kilda house-mouse which was also accorded the sub-specific status *Mus musculus muralis*; it arrived almost certainly in man's cargo.

Where they occur together in the presence of man, the house-mouse is a much more commensal animal than the field-mouse; at St Kilda the two occupied separate habitats as long as man was present to maintain the ecological difference. The house-mouse possessed the guile required to adapt to a comfortable life indoors; the field-mouse possessed the wilder instincts of a forager in the much more austere world of St Kilda's meadows and cliffs. When man left in 1930, therefore, a crisis may have ensued between the two populations. Deprived of the warmth and nourishment of the houses and out-houses, the smaller house-mouse had to venture into the open. Berry and Tricker (1969) have shown that *Mus* can survive in the presence of *Apodemus*, but the breeding of the former is disrupted causing a decline in numbers, and it is believed that such a decline in the population of *M. m. muralis* occurred following the evacuation in 1930. The Oxford-Cambridge Expedition of 1931 estimated the population at 25 mice, but none have been seen since, and it is now regarded as extinct. Today with much improved facilities for conservation and ecological knowledge, we could have saved *M. m. muralis*. A mouseless island might have been found with a sympathetic habitat, similar to Lunga in the Treshnish Isles (see p. 209) from which the inhabitants left in 1834 and which has a population of house-mice living in a field-mouse habitat, and no field-mice (Darling, 1941; Berry, 1983).

The future of the St Kilda field-mouse would be seriously jeopardised if rats were introduced to Hirta accidentally from army landing craft beaching at Village Bay. The only positive record of the black or ship rat (*Rattus rattus*) in the Hebrides is from the Shiant Islands where they seem to co-exist with the brown rat (*R. norvegicus*), but where there are no mice. The great swing from summer plenty in the puffinries to winter austerity would place mouse and rat in direct competition. Facing starvation winter after winter would soon reduce the numbers of mice, either by deprivation of habitat and food, or by actual predation by rats. Possibly the population of mice on

Dun might survive for a time, but rats are capable swimmers and are likely to cross the Dun Passage in due time. The status of the ground-nesting seabirds would also change in the presence of a large rat population. The introduction of rats therefore could seriously affect the 'heritage' properties which give St Kilda such a high rating in world conservation. No effort should be spared therefore in preventing the introduction of rats and, if an introduction is confirmed, steps should be taken to protect the field-mouse, possibly by its introduction to Soay or Boreray, where rats are unlikely to go and where it will do little or no harm to the habitat and sea birds.

Feral Sheep—Soays and Blackfaces

St Kilda possesses two breeds of sheep; the Soay, which takes its name from one of the islands, and the Blackfaces on Boreray. The Soays have been on St Kilda since pre-historic times, kept apart from improved breeds in the cliff-bound isle of Soay, while the Blackfaces are the survivors of the improved breeds kept apart on Boreray since the evacuation. When the St Kildans departed in 1930, they took with them their cross-bred blackface Cheviot sheep from Hirta leaving behind the Soays on Soay and the blackfaces on Boreray. In 1932, cross-bred stragglers on Hirta were shot, before a balanced flock of 107 Soays (42 rams and 65 ewes) were transferred from Soay to Hirta by a team of St Kildans returned for the summer. This was a great achievement since the Soays cannot be herded and must be run to ground individually on very steep slopes and man-handled down the cliffs to small boats. It is on this flock

Fig. 47
The fluctuations in the numbers of Soay sheep on Hirta 1960 to 1988, showing the proportions of rams, ewes, and lambs in the population in most years (from Prof. P. A. Jewell)

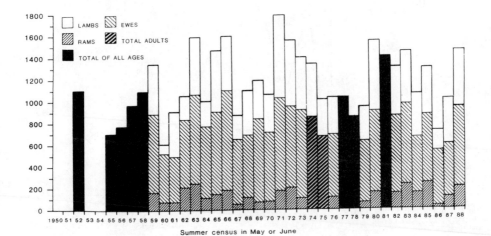

that the present Hirta stock is founded, which since then have not been managed and have assumed the behaviour and population structure of wild sheep (Fig. 47).

The Soay sheep (*Ovis aries*) is the most primitive domesticated sheep in Europe, resembling those brought to Britain from continental Europe about 7,000 years ago by neolithic farmers. A description of these sheep and a comprehensive account of their biology is to be found in *Island Survivors — The Ecology of the Soay Sheep of St Kilda* ed. Jewell, Milner and Boyd (1974). Suffice it to say that there is no firm archaeological evidence of the date of arrival of the Soays at St Kilda. Sheep may have been introduced by the early colonisers of the Bronze or Iron Ages over 1,500 years ago, but there is also a strong possibility that sheep were taken to St Kilda by the Norsemen about 900 AD. The Soays may be the survivors of confluent primitive sheep cultures in the Hebrides; the Norse influence, seen in primitive breeds in Orkney, Shetland, Faeroe and Greenland,

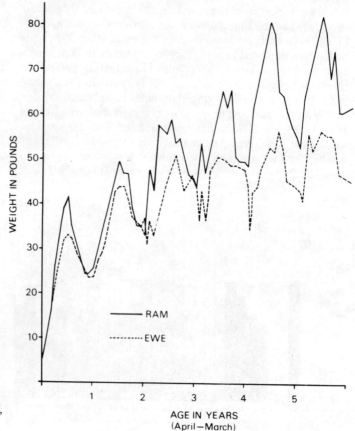

Fig. 48
Mean weights to ewes (dotted line) and rams (solid line) in relation to season and age in 1964 and 1965 (from Doney et al, in Island Survivors, *Jewell et al, 1974)*

may have come to an already-established sheep culture brought from Britain and Ireland in earlier times—the bones of the neolithic sheep from southern Britain resemble those of the Soay.

The Soays are small dark sheep which, when fully grown, are about 50cm in length (female) compared with 57cm in the blackface, with the Soay rams reaching 53cm. In autumn, 4-year-old Soay ewes and rams weigh on average 23 and 33kg respectively and 14 and 21kg respectively in early spring. Fig 48 shows the growth rate of ewes and rams, and the seasonal fluctuation in weights relative to seasonal nutrition in the pastures. These fluctuations in body weight are dramatic, 39% for ewes and 36% for rams.

There are two distinct phases of coat colour. About three-quarters of the Soays are dark brown and the remainder a light café-au-lait colour. In the Village area in 1964, there were 446 sheep of which 348 (78%) were dark. The 'type' specimen has a light buff-coloured belly, posterior, chin, trailing-edges of the legs and all of the lower legs (less distinct in the light phase). In 1966 (Grubb, 1974), of 1,835 on Hirta, 105 (5.7%) were self-coloured (completely uniform) of which 82 were dark, 23 were light and 85 (4.6%) had anomalous white markings. There were blazes on the forehead, spots on the nose and poll and below the knees, the horns of a few had longitudinal white stripes, and there were a few white-headed and piebald specimens. Most of these features have been observed in the original flock on the Isle of Soay. The inheritance of the coat colours and horns is complex and has been investigated by Doney et al (1974).

Full-grown rams have horns swept backwards and downwards in a single whorl, 49cm of outward edge and slightly out-turned at the tips. These show distinct annual growth increments, which reflect the seasonal cycle of nutrition. The first four years of horn growth are very obvious but thereafter are less distinct as the ram reaches its full size. About one in ten rams have scurs or small malformed horns. Ewes can be horned or polled; of 323 ewes 148, or 46%, were horned. The horns of ewes are 15cm and also show annual growth bands but much less clearly than do the horns of rams. About a quarter of the polled ewes have small scurs. Of 146 ewe lambs born in 1965 and 1966, 47 horned and 21 polled were born to horned ewes; 24 horned and 54 polled were born to polled ewes. The frequency of the horned/polled character of the ewe is reflected in the frequency of horned or polled off-spring produced, but the chance of the lamb inheriting its dam's horned or polled character is only about 2:1 in favour.

The Boreray sheep have a lineage on the island which goes

Boreray rams on the
southern slopes of the
island in late May
1979 (Photo
J. M. Boyd)
back many centuries (p. 312). Starting with the Soay-type they
have probably been changed by introductions of new stock
from Hirta, unlike those on Soay which, by historical quirk,
have remained unchanged. Apart from a few largely unsuccessful sheep-catching forays, the Boreray sheep have been left
almost untouched since before the St Kildans left in 1930. A
few have been taken off for scientific study and breeding, but
no new stock has been introduced. They are representative of
the domesticated sheep of the Hebrides in the late 19th and
early 20th centuries. M. L. Ryder in a personal note states that
there is clear evidence that the Scottish Blackface reached St
Kilda in the 1870s and replaced the 'Old Scottish Shortwool' or
Dunface which were kept on Hirta for centuries, and predo-
minated in Europe from 500 BC to 1500 AD, the character of
which still survives today in Shetland and North Ronaldsay
(Boyd, 1981a). Though called 'Blackface' the 'Boreray' breed is
more correctly 'Tanface' and has been listed as an antique
breed by the Rare-Breeds Survival Trust (Boyd 1981b).

Records show than on Boreray some 400 sheep live on about
55ha., of pasture—a stocking rate of 8 sheep per ha. compared
with 1.7 sheep per ha. on Hirta (Soays) and commonly on the
mainland, 1.5 sheep per ha. for hill sheep (Boyd, 1981; Bullock,
1983). In autumn when the population on Boreray is in good
condition with rams weighing 45kg, ewes and yearlings 25 and
lambs 12, the autumn biomass may be as high as 157kg per ha.,
and in late winter as low as 83kg per ha. The biomass of herbivores on the East African plains in a rainfall of 800mm/annum
ranges from 48 to 199kg per ha. and is the highest in the world;

the Boreray ecosystem can be considered, therefore, as having a remarkably high turnover of biological productivity and energy.

The St Kilda sheep provide good opportunities for research. The flocks on Soay and Boreray are too remote to facilitate detailed work, but the population of Soays on Hirta is sufficiently accessible for continuous observation. They are also part of a comparatively simple ecosystem compared with populations of large herbivores elsewhere, living as they do within a small fine ecosystem in which there is no immigration or emigration; they have no competitors for the grazings nor predators of the adult stock (ravens, crows and large gulls may kill small lambs); no crop of lambs is taken, and the sex-ratio is naturally determined; there is no 'strike' of the blow-fly *Lucilia* spp. and the sheep are neither dipped nor shorn; neither are they directly interfered with by man or dog. Parasites are those of a closed system and are untreated. The Soays may have a feral genotype but they are in all other respects wild sheep.

The fluctuations in numbers have been followed since 1952, and continuously by a standard method since 1959 (Fig. 47). The annual cycle follows a strict pattern, with most adult mortality occurring in March followed by the birth of lambs, mostly in April. The population fluctuates in a roughly three to four year long cycle from 600 to 1,800 and survival is density-dependent.

The energy budget of the flock is all-important in seeing it through the rigours of winter and early spring. The degree of stress in winter is partly determined by the nutritional status of the flocks in the previous summer. When times of high density occur in a cold, wet and comparatively sunless summer, the pastures are not only depleted of green growth, but also the swards finish in autumn with a poor reserve in the rhizomes for growth in the following spring. This results in poor feeding for the sheep; adults die in February and March, and there is high mortality of lambs in April due to failure of lactation in the ewes. The energy budget in years of high density with poor weather is in serious deficit. Young rams are particularly prone to starvation, since much energy is lost in autumn in nuptial chases and copulation at the expense of a few weeks feeding. In 1978–80 in Village Glen, 72 ram lambs were castrated and 68 were left intact; in 1984, 42 castrates and 2 rams still survived; and in 1988 there were 38 and 2 respectively, clearly indicating the toll taken of the male population by the reproductive process.

In the grip of severe malnutrition, parasitism plays an important role in pushing the sheep to the point of death. The Soays are heavily infested with keds (*Melophagus ovinus*) and lice

(*Damalinia ovis*). Sheep ticks and blowflies have not been reported. The lambs and yearlings are heavily infested with the lungworm (*Dictyocaulus filaria*) and the older sheep with *Muellerius capillaris*, neither of which have so far been recorded from the Boreray sheep. The cysts of the tapeworm (*Taenia hydatigena*), the adult form of which occurs in dogs, is found without any obvious explanation of its life cycle on Hirta and Boreray, where there have been no resident dogs since 1930. There are heavy infestations of the nematodes *Trichostrongyle* spp., *Nematodirus* spp., *Bunostomum trigonocephalum*, *Trichuris ovis* and *Chabertia ovina*.

The three flocks of sheep at St Kilda seem to be in ecological equilibrium with their environment. The numbers are regulated by malnutrition, usually at times of high density, but at a level which does not cause obvious physical and biological damage to the habitat. They have been put there by man but have adjusted to become wild animals capable of surviving the stresses of inbreeding, physiological weakness, parasitism and malnutrition. The balance is delicate and interference, no matter how well-intentioned, might set the sheep against their habitat, setting in train changes in the soil, vegetation and in the sheep themselves. There will be those who say that the sheep are an artifact and should be removed, possibly to improve the lot of the burrow-nesting seabirds. However, to do so would substantially reduce the heritage value of St Kilda, removing assets of great cultural, historical and scientific interest. Removal of sheep would also reduce the diversity of plant life which their grazing sustains on the islands. There would also be those who would say that it is cruel to keep sheep at St Kilda in conditions of seasonal malnutrition. However, the sheep are now adjusted over centuries to meet the rigours of their world and shun any assistance which man might provide to carry them over the winter; by so surviving, they may create greater stress of numbers and environmental damage in succeeding years (Boyd and Jewell, 1974).

Islands and People

PART III

Naturalists and Historians

CHAPTER 17

16th and 17th Centuries

Donald Monro (1526–89) was the Vicar of Snizort in Skye in 1526, and Archdeacon of the Isles in 1549. His *Description of the Western Isles of Scotland* is popularly regarded as a historical datum of the Hebrides. Though it was not published until 1774, its authentic, first-hand descriptions pre-date the book by two centuries, to a time of great political and social change after the forfeiture (1493) of The Lordship and Council of the Isles by the MacDonalds for allying themselves with England. Subsequent disorder was mainly because of the weakness of the Scottish crown due to a succession of minor monarchs, and the internecine clan system thrived and endured until the Jacobite uprisings were put down by England in 1745. Monro's *Description* is indeed sketchy, though it conveys a general impression of prosperity and mentions many items from nature.

Martin Martin MA (Edinburgh), MD (Leyden) (*c.* 1660–1719) was a steward and tutor in Sleat and Dunvegan, who had a perceptive and scholarly eye, and travelled widely in the Hebrides. His *Description* (1703) (p. 316) is, therefore, authentic and much more detailed than that of Monro. It begins:

. . . it is peculiar to those isles that they have never been described until now by any man that was a native of the country or had travelled them. They were indeed touched by Boethius, Bishop Lesly, Buchanan and Johnstone, in their histories of Scotland; but none of these authors were ever there in person . . . Buchanan, it is true, had his information from Donald Monro, who had been in many of them; and therefore his account is the best that has hitherto appeared, but it must be owned that it is very imperfect: the great man designed the history, and not the geography of his country, and therefore in him is pardonable. Besides since his time there is a great change in the humour of the world, and by consequence in the way of writing. Natural and experimental philosophy has been much improved since his days; and therefore descriptions of countries, without the natural history of them, are now justly reckoned to be defective . . .

A

DESCRIPTION

OF THE

𝕷𝖊𝖘𝖙𝖊𝖗𝖓 𝕴𝖘𝖑𝖆𝖓𝖉𝖘

O F

SCOTLAND.

CONTAINING

A Full Account of their Situation, Extent, Soils, Product, Harbours, Bays, Tides, Anchoring-Places, and Fisheries.
The Antient and Modern Government, Religion and Customs of the Inhabitants ; particularly of their Druids, Heathen Temples, Monasteries, Churches, Chappels, Antiquities, Monuments, Forts, Caves, and other Curiosities of Art and Nature : Of their Admirable and Expeditious Way of Curing most Diseases by Simples of their own Product.
A Particular Account of the *Second Sight*, or Faculty of foreseeing things to come, by way of Vision, so common among them.
A Brief Hint of Methods to improve Trade in that Country, both by Sea and Land.
With a New MAP of the Whole, describing the Harbours, Anchoring-Places, and dangerous Rocks, for the benefit of Sailors.
To which is added, A Brief Description of the Isles of *Orkney* and *Schetland*.

By *M. MARTIN*, Gent.

The SECOND EDITION, very much Corrected.

L O N D O N,
Printed for A. BELL at the Cross-Keys and Bible in *Cornhill* ; T. VARNAM and J. OSBORN in *Lombard-street* ; W. TAYLOR at the Ship, and J. BAKER and T. WARNER at the Black Boy in *Paternoster-Row*. M. DCC. XVI.

The title page of Martin Martin's A Description of the Western Isles of Scotland etc. 1703

Martin's condescending treatment of earlier writings lacked the foresight of the delayed publication of Monro's much earlier work and of his own efforts being dwarfed by those who were to succeed him. Nonetheless, his account and that of Monro stand today as the beginning of the living record of the Hebrides, in which appear vignettes of natural history from the late 17th century. These two early accounts span the Union of the Crowns (1603), when the Highlands and Islands were regarded, in the words of James VI and I, as 'utterly barbarous' (Smout, 1969). Matters came to a head in 1609, when the chiefs of the Isles were surprised, captured and forced under duress to agree the Statutes of Iona. In the course of the Reformation in Scotland, these were a thrust against 'barbarism' in which the Roman Church and the Gaelic culture became casualties (Campbell, 1984). Monro saw the Isles in a much more prosperous state than Martin. Added to the social and political trauma of the Union and the Reformation, between the two *Descriptions*, there occurred the 'Little Ice Age' marked by failure of crops, poverty and destitution, all of which had a great effect on the natural environment.

Sadly, though feeling for nature is strong, for example in *Carmina Gadelica* and *The Songs of Duncan Ban Macintyre* (Macleod, 1952), there is a very small amount of natural history in Gaelic literature, indeed this aspect of native culture over centuries has gone almost unrecorded. The vital support from natural sources for human communities in food, fuel, construction and craft materials are pieced together by historians and archaeologists (Skene, 1886–90 see p. 409; Royal Commission, 1928; Mackie, 1960), but hardly mentioned by Gaelic writers. Perhaps learned orders of monks, priests and scholars did appraise their natural surroundings, and manuscripts have been lost. The romantic appeal of the scenery, flora, and fauna of the isles moved the Gaelic bards, but not usually in words of interest to the naturalist. In the Statutes of Iona, 'bards' were classed with 'beggars, vagabonds, and jugglers . . . to be put in the stocks and expelled from the district'. Today, the disincentives for Gaelic natural history are different. Perhaps the greatest is finding a readership able and willing to use and perpetuate the literature. Nonetheless, there is an opportunity awaiting the scholarly Gaelic naturalist to explore the literary and oral traditions of the language.

The Beatons had a hereditary medical tradition in Gaelic culture (Bannerman, 1986). They are thought to have come from Ireland about 1300 and became physicians to the Scottish kings, but were settled in the Isles. More of their medieval Gaelic manuscripts have survived than have any others, due mainly to the Rev John Beaton of Pennycross, Mull, who was the last learned member of the family. He listed the Beaton manuscripts, and was an informant of Edward Lhuyd the Keeper of the Ashmolean Museum, Oxford. Lhuyd (1660–1709) made a grand tour of the Celtic countries in 1697–1701, including Mull and Iona. He was backed by sponsors interested in archaeological, botanical, historical and linguistic material (Thomson, 1983). Lhuyd's collected manuscripts are now in the Library of Trinity College, Dublin. However, apart

from John Beaton's knowledge and folklore taken down by
Lhuyd (Campbell and Thomson, 1963) the etymologies of
place names (Watson, 1926; Nicolaisen, 1976), and the names
of the more conspicuous plants and animals (Hogan, 1900;
Forbes, 1905; MacLeod, 1976; Dwelly, 1977), little natural
history exists in the Gaelic language.

18th and 19th Centuries

Classical natural history in Scotland has its origins in
Edinburgh in the botanical and medical schools of Edinburgh
University in the mid-17th century. The prime movers were
Robert Sibbald and Andrew Balfour, both medical prac-
tioners, and they were followed by James Sutherland and John
Hope, both, in their times, Professors of Botany at Edinburgh.
Sibbald laid the foundation stone of Scottish natural history in
his *Scotia Illustrata* (1684). However, it was not until the
opening up of the Highlands by the roads and bridges built by
General Wade after the Jacobite rising in 1715, that travellers
gained easier and safer access to the Hebrides (Smout, 1969).
Foremost among those who reached the Isles were Thomas
Pennant (1769 and 1772) and Samuel Johnson with James Bos-
well (1773). In 1772, Pennant was accompanied by a botanist, the
Rev John Lightfoot, who was librarian and chaplain to the
Duchess of Portland, and there followed Lightfoot's *Flora Sco-
tica* (1777–92) which included records from his travels in the
Hebrides. This was the first serious botanical work on the Isles
since the lists of plants by Lhyud (*c.* 1700), and it formed a
botanical datum which is of relevance even today (Balfour 1979;
Currie and Murray, 1983).

William MacGillivray was born in Aberdeen in 1796. Son of
an army surgeon who was killed at Corunna in 1809, he spent
much of his childhood at Northtown, the farm of his two pater-
nal uncles in Harris. He attended the parish school at Obbe
until he was eleven and then went to Aberdeen to enter the university at the age of twelve. His early experiences with wildlife
in Harris fired his enthusiasm for natural science, which found
expression in his fine *History of British Birds*, in three volumes,
and his drawings of birds. His interests were mainly in or26nitho-
logy, but he also followed the pearl fishers and noted the abundance of the pearl mussel (*Margaritifera margaritifera*) in the
rivers of the Outer Hebrides (Waterston, 1981). From humble
beginnings, MacGillivray rose to the Chair of Civil and Natural
History in Aberdeen University. He had great physical endur-
ance in the field, and had a reputation for outwalking his
students on the hill. His paper, '*Account of a series of islands*

usually denominated the Outer Hebrides' (1830), was perhaps the first professional zoological work on the Hebrides. In 1871, Robert Gray laid a firm base for bird study in *The Birds of the West of Scotland* to be followed in 1888 and 1892 by the *Vertebrate Faunas* of J.A. Harvie-Brown and T.E. Buckley, and in 1890 by *The Birds of Iona and Mull* by H.D. Graham.

Another signal event was the publication in 1873–74 of H.C. Watson's *Topographical Botany* which set the framework of 112 Vice-Counties, of which the Inner Hebrides were numbered (south to north) 102, 103 and 104, and the Outer Hebrides, 110. This served to focus interest on the Isles as geographical units in the study of the British flora, embodied the information gained by many 19th century botanists, and attracted many others to visit the Hebrides into this century. As far back as 1844, J.H. Balfour and C.C. Babington had recorded 349 species of flowering plant from the Outer Hebrides, and Watson's work was updated by A. Bennett in 1905. Andrew Currie (1979) has described the advance in botanical recording in the Hebrides from Watson's time through Ewing (1892–99), Trail (1898–1909), Bennett (1905), Bennett *et al.* (1929–30), Druce (1932) and Heslop-Harrison (1937–41) (Currie and Murray, 1983).

In the marine field, the earliest records come from a voyage of the British Fishery Society to the Hebrides in 1787 but the first species list for the littoral fauna was given by McIntosh in 1866, who also recognised the narrow frontiers between salt and fresh waters in the Uists and the implications this might have for the fauna. The *Lightning* and *Porcupine* expedition of 1869–70 and later, at the turn of the century, Marshall obtained dredge samples from the sea-bed of the Hebridean shelf and published the first accounts of the marine benthos (Jeffreys, 1879–84; Sykes, 1906–25; Marshall 1896–1912).

The 19th century was remarkable for the number of men and women of private means who took their leisure in the rough bounds of Scotland. Some of these were naturalists with a passion for exploring the Hebrides, and foremost among them was J.A. Harvie-Brown. He was a zealous writer of field notes, journals and letters to many correspondents connected with field-sports and natural history (p. 320). The *Vertebrate Faunas* stand as milestones in Scottish natural history, and are remarkably detailed and authentic, compiled from personal notes or experiences, freshly remembered. These books, though far outdated, have remained in use for a century; no others have replaced them in the modern era. However, the scholarship and altruism of Harvie-Brown was unusual, for the cult of the sportsman-naturalist was basically romantic and self-satisfying; it was about shared and solitary adventures in

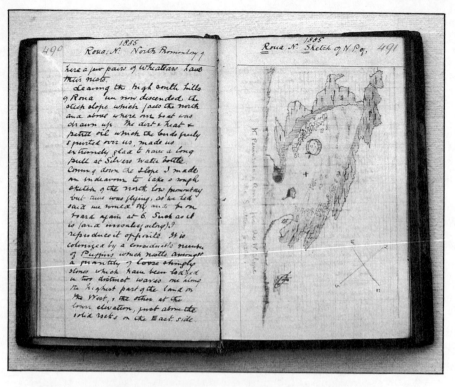

*Pages of Harvie-
Brown's journal
showing a drawing of
the Fianuis peninsula
and notes of his visit to
North Rona in 1887
(now in the Royal
Museum of Scotland)*

wild remote country, known (and owned) by a privileged few
who were usually visitors for the season. Personal interpreta-
tions of the condition and behaviour of wild animals seen and
hunted in the vastness of wilderness were fashionable, and
often coloured by the knowledge and experience of
gamekeepers and stalkers.

The life and works of Harvie-Brown and Robert Gray are to
be the more honoured and valued when seen against those of
the notorious collector of eggs and skins, Charles St John (1884
and 1893), described by Jean Balfour (1979) as 'the supreme
example of the Victorian ornithologist with a gun', and of
Osgood Mackenzie, whose book *A Hundred Years in the
Highlands* is, *inter alia*, one of the best first-hand accounts ever
written of the butchery of Highland wildlife. The toll taken of
Hebridean wildlife by shooters, trappers, poisoners and collectors of all sorts over the last two centuries, is largely untold.
However, there have been those among the landowners who
were naturalists or early patrons of nature conservation, who
encouraged these interests in their gamekeepers and sporting
tenantry. Today, the Wildlife and Countryside Act is testimony
to the historic mistrust which society, as a whole, has of those

who live and work with wild creatures; the Act leaves little to the discretion of any person, irrespective of rank, about the length to which he or she may go, within the law, in disturbing, taking and killing wild species. However, law enforcement in the sparsely inhabited, be-misted Hebrides has never been easy. One of the Statutes of Iona (1609) stated—'No person to bear firearms outside his house or to shoot at deer, hares, or wildfowl, in accordance with Act of Parliament.' Yet only the clan chief himself was there to administer the law. Now, there are the SSPCA, RSPB, police, and a much more watchful and enlightened public, aware of the need to safeguard wildlife.

The Inner Hebrides have been most attractive to geologists for two centuries, and the enormous range of rock types and structures, spanning over two billion years, continues to provide an inexhaustible field of interest. MacCulloch (1819) remarks on the struggle he had to exclude repetitive detail from his descriptions of the Islands; yet his successors have served to put a level of detail in theses, papers and maps, such that there is hardly a corner of the Hebrides which has not been geologically explored and recorded. The 19th century spirit of geological exploration in the Hebrides was enshrined by Hugh Miller in *The Cruise of the Betsey* (1869), and the excitement and wonder of fossil-hunting in the Great Estuarine (Jurassic) rocks of Eigg (p. 36) and Skye (p. 322) in those far-off days, still makes enchanting reading. In this following passage he describes poignant moments of discovery at Ru Stoir on the north point of Eigg:

. . . I hammered lustily, and laid open in the dark red shale a vertebral joint, a rib, and a parellelogramical fragment of solid bone, none of which could have belonged to any fish. . . . The entire ribs I was lucky enough to disinter have, as in those of crocodileans, double heads; and a part of a fibula about four inches in length, seems also to belong to this ancient family. . . . I found the head of a flat humerus so characteristic of the extinct order to which the Plesiosaurus has been assigned . . . a range of skerries lay temptingly off, scarce a hundred yards from the water's edge: the shale beds might be among them, with Plesiosauri and crocodiles stretching entire; I fain would have swam off to them with my hammer in my teeth and my shirt and drawers in my hat, but the tall brown forest of kelp and tangle . . .

However, the most significant event in the scientific record of last century, was the publication in 1876 by the Ordinance Survey of the First Editions of the 'one-inch' (1:63,360) and 'six-inch' (1:10,560) maps. These provided the modern geographical base and a great stimulus to scientific survey and exploration when natural science most needed it, in the excitement of the Darwinian period. The Geological Survey was already in operation under Archibald Geikie, and the

The Elgol coast geological SSSI, Skye. R. N. Campbell examines the polygonal cracks in a fossil mudflat of Jurassic times about 160 million years old (Photo J. M. Boyd)

Bathymetrical Survey of the Freshwater Lochs by John Murray and Laurence Pullar (1910) was shortly to follow.

The geological literature of the Hebrides is voluminous and has increased greatly in the last 30 years. Lois Albert Necker, born in Geneva in 1786, completed the earliest geological map of Scotland, including the Hebrides, and his grave is in the old churchyard at Portree. It is invidious to highlight the work of a few in this welter of scientific endeavour by many. However, there have been foci of great geological interest in Syke, the Small Isles and Mull, not simply relating to the actual structures of the Islands, but also to the interpretation of the elemental processes by which the rocks were formed. To obtain a fair appreciation of all this great effort, reference should be made to the *Geology of Scotland* (Ed. Craig, 1983). Notable among the early works of this century were those of J.E. Richey (1932) and co-workers in the 1920s, on the Tertiary rocks of the Inner Hebrides, and Jehu and Craig (1923–34) on the Lewisian of the Outer Hebrides. The vigourous follow-up to that work after the war is reviewed respectively by Janet Watson (1983) and C.H. Emeleus (1983), both of whom have made substantial original contributions. Studies of the Torridonian, Moine, Dalradian, and Mesozoic rocks were focused more on the mainland with extensions into the Hebrides.

First Half of the 20th Century

The 1930s saw the beginning of the modern period of scientific investigation, which received a great boost in the post-war revival of the 1950s. The effect of this revival is still felt, but in the last decade it has been diminished by a general reduction in the funding of research for purely scientific purposes. The Oxford–Cambridge Expedition to newly-evacuated St Kilda in 1931 was fired by the ecological movement that had evolved in the first three decades of this century (Sheail, 1987). The concept of the 'ecosystem' was uppermost in ecological thinking at that time, and attempts were being made to investigate how populations related to each other within circumscribed communities or habitats. To achieve this, whole communities required to be surveyed over periods of years, and where could these relationships be better demonstrated than on a small island? Possessing finite boundaries, severe limits to exchange of plants and animals (except migrant birds and insects), and having comparatively simple communities of plants and animals, the Hebrides were appealing—none more so than St Kilda, which at that time possessed the added dimension of 'release' from human habitation and livestock (Stewart, 1937). Some ecologists of the day saw in this an outstanding opportunity to observe, over the passage of years, the return of St Kilda to its pristine state—a prognosis which was partly frustrated by the re-introduction of sheep in 1932 (see p. 309), and the presence of a military garrison and organised parties of residential visitors since 1957. As it happens, we now understand that this was a fairly naive concept and that even though communities of plants and animals may well have inherent stable points towards which they will automatically track when released from the managerial influence of man, it is highly improbable that, once reached, the stable point will be anything like the one which existed before the arrival of man.

The appeal of islands to the ecologist as open-air laboratories influenced the thinking behind many other expeditions of scientific standing: Oxford and Cambridge Universities to St Kilda (1931) and Oxford to the Sound of Harris (Elton, 1938); Edinburgh University to Barra (1935) and St Kilda (1948); Durham University to many islands (1936–1956); Glasgow University to Canna (1936), Garvellachs (1951), St Kilda (1952 and 1956), and North Rona (1958). Over 30 years, ecological science had taken possession of a field previously worked by the naturalists, and this reflected the national trend. In modern times, this once profitable association of a professional science with an amateur pursuit still lingers, and unfortunately, does considerable harm when ecologists have to compete for funds with other professional scientists. Observation of the *systema naturae* on small islands, as pictured by Charles Elton (1949), is no longer in vogue. In 1957, when Rum (see p. 272) was purchased by the Nature Conservancy and St Kilda was acquired by the National Trust for Scotland, part of the reason for their existence as nature reserves was that they should be places where observations of the natural system could be carried out. Some observations still proceed, but they are small in scale from what was probably foreseen, and much of this kind of open-ended research is being forced to an end by shortage of funds. This provides a sharp contrast with the bounty of the times and optimism for the future of those bygone days, when funds and the fundamental relevance of what was being conceived were not in question.

The 1930s were a time of opportunism and disorder, into which came many enthusiasts, only a few of whom are remembered today. Fraser Darling, with an agricultural diploma, PhD, and Leverhulme and Carnegie Fellowships, studied the breeding behaviour of gulls on Eilein a'Chleirich in the Summer Isles, and grey seals on Lunga in the Treshnish Isles and North Rona (Boyd, 1986) (p. 324). Looked back at over half-a-century, his studies are those of an original pioneer, researching the middle ground between animal behaviour and ecology. He saw no pathway to truth in nature, other than being

Dr (later Sir) Frank Fraser Darling on Tanera Mor, Summer Isles in the early forties (Photo from Darling, 1944, Island Farm, Bell, London)

'at one' with wild creatures in the privacy of their own dwelling places and his main work was in the interface between man and nature. He was as much of a mystic as he was a scientist, who saw men and animals as parts of the same whole, and saw that man's moral and political make-up was an ecological factor capable of changing the entire character of nature. Later, he combined the knowledge gained in his agricultural and biological studies with his crofting experience on Tanera Mor, in the *West Highland Survey—An Essay in Human Ecology* (1955). However, the true and enduring effect of Fraser Darling's work is not to be found in the impact which his *West Highland Survey* had upon Government, but in the exciting challenge he gave to others, including us, through the most popular books of his Scottish period, *A Herd of Red Deer* (1937), *Island Years* (1940), *Crofting Agriculture* (1945), and *Natural History in the Highlands and Islands* (1947).

Another who is remembered from the 1920s and 1930s is Seton Gordon, the spirit of whose work was more romantic than scientific. He was in the mould of the 19th century naturalist of private means, who had a remarkable social cachet with gentry and crofter alike. *The Immortal Isles* (1926) and *Afoot in the Hebrides* (1950), two of his most important works on the Hebrides, are charming portraits of the Isles, their wildlife and people, but not works in natural history of the standing of Harvie-Brown or Fraser Darling. However, Seton Gordon made his home in Skye and, although not a Gaelic speaker, became a guru in island natural history, well known to a wider public through books and articles. He preceded the age of natural history as a popular feature on radio and television.

James Fisher made his name as an island-going naturalist in post-war radio and television, as well as from his books. He was an ornithologist and bibliographer with a great appetite for remote seabird islands, particularly St Kilda (p. 326). In the 1930s he started his surveys of gannets and fulmars (Fisher and Vevers, 1943–44; Fisher, 1952), which were to last a lifetime, and lead the great post-war surge in seabird research. Later, he became an editor of the New Naturalist Series. He had a contemporary in Robert Atkinson, whose adventures as a young naturalist on North Rona, St Kilda and Shillay (Harris) are told in *Island Going* (1949) and *Shillay and the Seals* (1980).

In the 1930s, natural history in the Hebrides became more attractive than ever before to a wider public, through naturalists like Seton Gordon and Fraser Darling, who were fine communicators of the aesthetic, as well as the scientific qualities of the Hebridean wildlife. Fraser Darling in his finest moments, however, saw in his work a deeper opportunity, akin to those who were not given to popular writing but to science

James Fisher on the island of Dun, St Kilda in 1948 (Photo H. Hope-Jones)

and scholarship. For example, Professor J.W. Heslop Harrison and the Durham University group over many years studied the taxonomic distinctiveness of the Hebrides, while others were amateur naturalists, like J.W. Campbell and his sister Miss M.S. Campbell who in their own quiet way had a great affinity for the Isles and, respectively, recorded birds and plants throughout their lives. Unfortunately, except for *The Flora of Uig* (1945) their works were never published, but their records have contributed greatly to subsequent studies (Cunningham, 1983; Currie, 1979). Miss Campbell's records are now in the British Museum (Natural History) and will be incorporated in a future *flora* of the Hebrides.

A.R. Waterston was a member of the Edinburgh party in Barra in 1933, and has continued to work on the non-marine invertebrates of the Outer Hebrides ever since. His *Non-marine invertebrate fauna of the Outer Hebrides* (1981) lays a basis

for all future invertebrate studies in the Hebrides, and provides a contribution to the natural history of Scotland. In this paper, he reviews the entire invertebrate literature for the Outer Hebrides from MacGillivray (1830) to Waterston and Lyster (1979). As regards the invertebrates of the Inner Hebrides, records exist from the mid-19th century onwards, but still await a compilation similar to that given by Welch (1983) to the coleoptera. Notable contributions were made by Balfour Brown (1953) between 1910 and 1953, and by J.W. Heslop-Harrison between 1939 and 1950, covering many taxa. Only Rum possesses a comprehensive inventory of invertebrates and has an exhaustive list of insects (Steel and Woodroffe, 1969; Wormell, 1982). J.L. Campbell (1970, *et seq.*, 1984) has recorded lepidoptera on Canna since the 1930s. There have also been naturalists in the marine field, notably A.C. Stephen and Edith Nicol (later Mrs. MacEwan of Muck) on the intertidal and brackish water fauna of the Uists, and J.E. Forrest and colleagues in Barra, in the 1930s. These were followed by J.R. Lewis in the 1950s and by many others after that (see Chapters 4 and 5).

The Fishery Research Vessel Explorer *from which much of the biological research in Hebridean waters was done from 1921 to 1956 (Crown Copyright)*

Second Half of the 20th Century

The 1950s saw a transition from the old style of descriptive natural history to the more modern scientific style of investigation, where it was more than the mere presence or absence of species that was important, it was the biological processes that allowed populations to grow and flourish or decline and go extinct that were of interest. This has brought numerous school and university expeditions to the Hebrides and led to the establishment of several major programmes of research, including those of the Nature Conservancy on the red deer on Rum by V.P.W. Lowe and B. Mitchell, the grey seals of North Rona by Morton Boyd and Niall Campbell and the Soay sheep of St Kilda by Peter Jewell and Morton Boyd in collaboration with workers from many different disciplines drawn from research institutes throughout Britain. Work by Kenneth Williamson and Morton Boyd on the vertebrate fauna of St Kilda led to the publication of two books, *St Kilda Summer* and *A Mosaic of Islands*, relating their experiences and discoveries (p. 328).

The last forty years have brought funds and manpower on an unprecedented scale to the study of the natural environment. Before the Second World War, there were very few profes-

J. M. B. with a storm petrel photographed against a tent on North Rona in June 1958 (Photo J. MacGeoch)

sional natural scientists in the Hebrides, but now there are many, advancing all sectors of environmental research with the aid of ships, boats, vehicles, aircraft and advanced technologies. We have taken part in this advance, in company with many of those named in the bibliographies of this book and its two main source volumes (Boyd, 1979; Boyd and Bowes, 1983). The following were some of the more important contributors, who were usually leaders of cognate groups.

In geology, there has been a particularly strong surge of research that reflects the wide range of geological time-scale, rock types and structures possessed by the Islands. R. Dearnley, D.J. Fettes, and Dr A.M. Hopgood have been prominent in the Lewisian, A.D. Stewart in the Torridonian, Dr J.D. Hudson in the Mesozoic, Dr A.C. Dunham, Dr C.H. Emeleus and R.N. Thompson in the Tertiary, J.B. Sissons in the Quaternary, and Dr G.E. Farrow in Recent Sediments. Professor W. Ritchie has illuminated the origin and development of dune-machair landforms.

In the botanical field, Andrew Currie and Mrs C.W. Murray, both resident in Skye, have carried out field studies of the flora, and tended the botanical record of the Hebrides over many years. Dr H.J.B. Birks and his wife, Dr H.H. Birks, have investigated the vegetational history through pollen analysis of sediments and peat, and have added to knowledge of the mosses. Dr R.E. Randall and Dr G. Dickenson have given descriptions of the flora and vegetation of the machair, and Professor D.H.N. Spence has done the same for the freshwater macrophytes. Botanical forays into the Isles by such experts as Dr R.W.G. Dennis and Dr R. Watling (fungi), Dr F. Rose and B.J. Coppins (lichens) and M.F.V. Corley (mosses) have greatly extended the inventory of the cryptogams. Notes on the flora of Tiree and Coll were made by U.V. Duncan, of Easdale and the Garvellachs by C.W. Muirhead, and of Mull by A.C. Jermy and J.A. Crabbe. Dr R.E.C. Ferreira produced a large-scale vegetation map of Rum, and Dr D.N. McVean and Dr D.A. Ratcliffe have described the community structure of the vegetation of the Hebrides, in the context of the Scottish Highlands and Islands.

In the zoological field, A.R. Waterston has continued his invertebrate studies, and a major survey was carried out on the invertebrates of dune and machair sites in Scotland in 1975–77, headed by Dr E.A.G. Duffey and Dr R.C. Welch. Peter Wormell has made a study of the lepidoptera of the Inner Hebrides, while R.N. Campbell and his son, Dr R.N.B. Campbell, have studied the distribution and ecology of freshwater fishes, including migratory salmon and trout. Their special interest has been the native species of Arctic charr and the 3- and 9-spined sticklebacks. R.M. Dobson has studied the natural history of Muck.

In the field of marine biology, Dr R. Mitchell, Dr R.C. Earll and Dr F.A. Dipper have developed the study of the seabed by diving methods, and studies of the littoral flora and fauna have been advanced by Professor T.A. Norton and H.T. Powell (algae), Dr S.M. Smith (molluscs) and I.S. Angus (beach fauna). Work on the marine mammals has been supported by R.W. Vaughan, Miss S.S. Anderson, C.F. Summers, N.W. Bonner and ourselves (seals), Dr P.G.H. Evans (whales) and James and Rosemary Green and Jane Twelves (otters).

W.A.J. Cunningham, Dr W.R.P. Bourne, Dr M.P. Harris, M.A. Ogilvie and T.M. Reed have carried out broadly based ornithological studies. Ornithology is by far the most popular

Richard Balharry strides up through the gannetry to the summit of the Stac Lee, St Kilda on 19th May 1969 — the first ascent of Stac Lee since the St Kildans left in 1930 (Photo J. M. Boyd)

pursuit in natural history, and the recent literature on the Hebrides bears the names of many, ourselves included, who have devoted much energy and time to the study of selected species, island populations, and migration. Notable among these was Kenneth Williamson, whose studies of the birds of St Kilda embraced the total breeding population of the islands, the autoecology of the St Kilda wren and the snipe (*Gallinago gallinago faeroeensis*), and the first account of migration through Hirta. Notable also are the works of R.L. Swan and D.A.K. Ramsay on the birds of Canna, and C.G. Booth on Islay. There were many key works on selected species of bird with the main focus in the Hebrides: Dr J. Cadbury on corncrakes; R.J. Fuller on waders; Dr. P. Monaghan and Dr E. Bignall on choughs; S. Murray, Dr S. Wanless and Dr J.M. Boyd on gannets; J.A. Love and R.H. Dennis on sea-eagles; Dr D.A. Stroud on Greenland white-fronted geese, P. Wormell on Manx shearwaters, and others.

The taxonomic distinctiveness of species living in island isolation has excited the curiosity of biologists since the publication of the *Origin of Species*. The Hebrides have their own genetical idiosyncrasies, which were brought to notice by James Ritchie in his celebrated book *The Influence of Man on Animal Life in Scotland* (1920), and we have already mentioned the work of Professor Heslop Harrison in this field. More recently, these island populations in the Hebrides have been examined by Professor R.J. Berry, in the context of wider genetical studies of the fauna of the Scottish islands, and by Professor M.J. Delany in his ecological studies of field-mice. The detailed studies of the reproductive physiology, ecology and behaviour of red deer on Rum firstly by Professor R.V. Short and Dr G.A. Lincoln, and later by Dr T.H. Clutton-Brock, Miss F.E. Guinness and Dr S.D. Albon, and similarly on Soay sheep at St Kilda by Professor P.A. Jewell, have international standing in science.

The total sum of knowledge gained from all this research is enormous. Today, the scientific record of the Hebrides would be far beyond the dreams of MacCulloch, MacGillivray, Geikie and Harvie-Brown, but it is a fulfilment of the aspirations of Fraser Darling, James Campbell, Balfour-Browne and James Ritchie, all of whom saw the dawn of the new age.

CHAPTER 18

Land Use—Tryst of Man and Nature

Land Use History

The earliest people in the Hebrides lived by the shore. There was an abundance of food, fuel, and shelter, and when resources became locally exhausted, they moved on, leaving the deserted dwelling-place to recover its natural complexion. As time advanced however, and the numbers of people increased, the land became fully possessed and settled. Laws of tenure and use evolved, all of which affected the distribution of wealth, and the social structure. Population pressures and political factors resulted in the extension of agricultural settlement from fertile coastal land into the interior of the islands, with cultivation of moorland, and this extension continued until the gradual introduction of the crofting system between 1800 and 1830. At the time of its inception, crofting aimed to improve agricultural standards and to sustain the high population employed in the kelping (Caird, 1979)—an industry that collapsed after the end of the Napoleonic Wars. In Islay and Gigha, the extension of agriculture into the interior resulted in a permanent change in the interior of the islands, but elsewhere much of the land and settlement became derelict. In the late 18th and 19th centuries, the creation of large farms displaced crofters and cottars from the most fertile land, causing great congestion and overworking of the land in the surviving crofting townships (Fig. 49).

In Islay, these changes began in the middle of the 18th century, lasted a century, and produced a non-crofting environment of lowland character (Storrie, 1981). Elsewhere in the Hebrides, this period saw the conversion of the chaotic 'run-rig' system (p. 127) into either crofting or farming units, often organised side by side as on Canna (see below). The existing medieval system of small farms with many tenants, who worked unenclosed strips of arable and grazing common land, was gradually reorganised into crofts, which possessed a small acreage of enclosed arable, and a share in a large acreage of common grazing; or else the land was cleared of such tenants

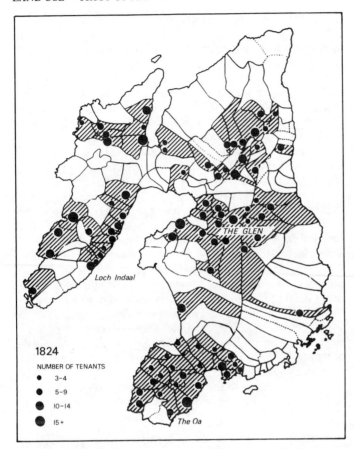

NUMBER OF TENANTS

●   3-4

●   5-9

●   10-14

●   15+

Fig. 49
In 1824, an Islay Estate
rental shows that the
island still had over 60
multiple townships,
shared and worked by
over 700 tenants (Islay
Estate Papers quoted by
Storrie, 1983)

to form a single large farm. The whole industry of crofting was thoroughly researched by Dr James Hunter in *The Making of the Crofting Community* (1976). However, each island has its own melancholy chronicle of this time, which can be pieced together from estate papers, the Statistical Account of Scotland (1845) and the National Censuses. Another scholarly work, *Canna* by Dr John Lorne Campbell (1984), tells the story of one island upon which we now draw for illustration.

The events which brought about the clearance of Canna in 1851, when probably about half of the 238-strong population left for Canada, began with the sale of all his estates by Reginald George MacDonald of Clanranald in the early 19th century. This affected great areas of Moidart, Small Isles, the Uists and Benbecula. Canna and Sanday were purchased in 1827 by the then tenant, Donald MacNeill, for £9,000. MacNeill's first action as owner was to emigrate some 200 inhabitants at his own expense, and reorganise the agricultural holdings in the home farm and many crofts; squatting and subdivision of holdings were prohibited. However progressive this may appear, there was continuous poverty and destitution, which was greatly aggravated by the potato blight in 1845–50, and by the leasing of the island to a flockmaster from Moidart who, finding the executors of estate financially weak, insisted on the eviction of crofters from Canna as a condition of lease. Accordingly in 1851, the tenants of Keills were evicted and those at Tarbert and Sanday retained.

The potato famine is graphically described by Hunter (1976) and Devine (1988). Following a bumper crop in 1845, during which some 15,410 barrels of potatoes were exported from Tobermory, the weather of the spring and early summer of 1846 greatly favoured the spores of the fungus *Phytophthora infestans*. In critical warm, moist conditions, a single plant infected by the fungus can infect thousands in a few hours of light winds; the multiplier-effect is very rapid.

The famine struck first in Harris where the previous year's potatoes had rotted in the storage pits, leaving the people seriously short of food in advance of the new crop, which, in turn, was completely blighted. The famine was widespread. People were bewildered and, already impoverished, completely unprepared for such an emergency. Starvation and outbreaks of typhus, cholera, and dysentery were to follow in a crisis which took many years to overcome.

The primary aim of the landowners in many islands was the maintenance of the high revenues of the kelp industry; the effi-

Fig. 50
Land use in South Boisdale, South Uist 1805–1977 (from Caird 1979)

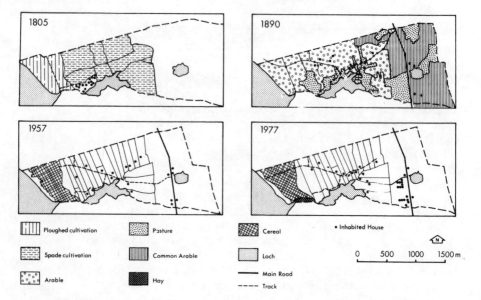

Ploughed cultivation	Pasture	Cereal	• Inhabited House
Spade cultivation	Common Arable	Loch	
Arable	Hay	Main Road / Track	0 500 1000 1500 m

ciency of agriculture was not raised for its own sake, nor from
any altruistic motive. Many areas of wet machair were drained
and areas of spade cultivation on moorland were abandoned to
sheiling pasturage. The patterns of small-holdings (Fig. 50) of
all shapes and sizes mixed with the larger farms gave a high
level of diversity to the cultivated landscape, while the regimes
of grazing and burning of hill land tended to reduce the
diversity of moorland habitats. This variety within the culti-

Fig. 51
*Cropping and livestock
changes in the Outer
Hebrides 1870–1970
(from Caird, 1979)*

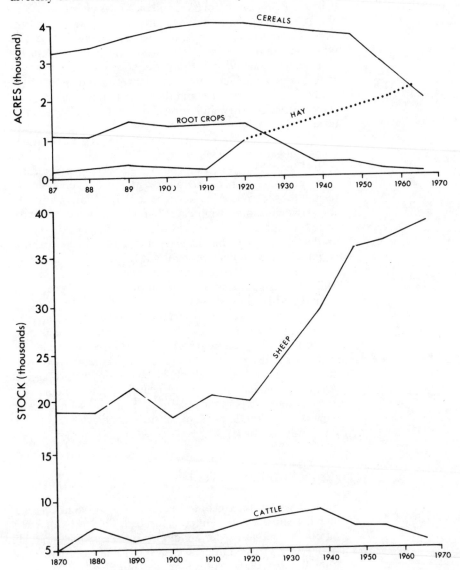

vated lands was enhanced by patchworks of rotational cropping, with grass leys of widely differing ages, and further enhanced by the wide range of individual crofting styles, from the neglected to the well-worked holding. The ecology of the Islands was therefore substantially changed by the crofting system, and their character as a habitat for wildlife was determined for at least a century to come.

Over the last century the pattern of land tenure has changed in Tiree, Raasay, much of Skye and the Outer Hebrides, where almost all of the large farms created during the Clearances were restored to crofting tenure between 1900 and 1930. In other parts of the Hebrides, land was acquired by the state for resettlement, and today there are over 1,000 crofting tenants on state-owned land. There was a similar resettlement on private land with state assistance, and the overall effect was to create several thousand new holdings and a much higher level of diversity of agricultural habitats. Agricultural output has also changed considerably (Fig. 51). The cropping regimes of arable crops and livestock remained remarkably steady until the end of the First World War, after which there were great increases in the numbers of sheep relative to cattle, and much more hay relative to root crops. After the Second World War, numbers of sheep remained high, while cattle numbers declined, and at the same time cereals have been greatly reduced in favour of grass production for hay and silage. Nonetheless, the agricultural regimes have been unrelenting in the toll that they have taken from the land since medieval times. Scythed cereals and hay, with potatoes and turnips cultivated by plough and spade and manured with seaweed, was the mixed regime of last century. Today, it is replaced by mechanised grass-intensive systems providing permanent pasture, baled hay, silage, and small plots of cereals (barley, oats, and rye) and potatoes, raised mainly on artificial fertilisers. The climate and soil conditions tend to maintain the drift of sand, choke the drains with luxuriant vegetation and degrade fences. Any decline in the vigour of the island communities in the upkeep of their land soon shows in blow-outs of sand, beds of rushes, gimcrack fences and wandering livestock.

Agricultural Improvement

In the 1960s, surface seeding was carried out on some 6,100ha. of hill pasture in the Outer Hebrides. The technique was especially well-suited for conditions in Lewis, but some hill land was also treated in the Uists. Shell-sand was transported from the shore and spread on the moorland, followed by

compound fertiliser and a clover/grass seed mixture. The resulting green pastures were thereafter grazed mostly by cattle, and booster treatments of shell-sand were given. Most of these pastures are now over twenty years old. A survey of 101 of them in Lewis in 1975 gave the following percentage frequencies (Grant, 1979):

The reclamation of peatland in Lewis by fencing and treatment with shell-sand, compound fertiliser, and a seed mixture of grasses and clovers, for improved cattle pasture (Photo J. M. Boyd)

Rye grass	Tim-othy	Meadw grass	White clover	Yorks fog	Other grass	Other specs	Bare gd & moss
2.6	0.2	9.0	20.1	10.3	14.7	27.6	15.5

Though many of these pastures have become rush infested, others have not, and all of them have an ecology that is distinct from the moorland context. They are now part of the 'blackland' zone between machair and hill and containing ingredients of both. For example, they are attractive to greylag geese, lapwing, snipe, redshank, skylark, meadow pipit and wheatear.

Crofting has never attracted sufficient investment to provide the development of machinery, seeds and livestock especially suited to its small-scale purposes in islands exposed to high, salt-laden winds. For example, modern ploughs are unsuitable for seedbed preparation on the light soils; the smallest combine harvester, unlike the old-fashioned binder, is too large a machine for small-field harvesting. Another example is the finding of a suitable cereal for machine cropping. In trials in the Uists, the Welsh black oat proved to give more straw and twice the grain yield of the local 'small oats' (*Avena strigosa*). How-

ever, due to lack of a market, the Welsh suppliers gave up, and
the grain was lost to the Hebrides.

Blackface are the preferred breed of sheep for the open hill
ranges and the Cheviot or Cheviot X Blackface for the
machairs and improved pastures. The fertile islands of Lismore and Tiree will each produce about 5,000 lambs annually,
the former mainly Blackface X Cheviot/Leicester, the latter
mainly Cheviot X Leicester/Suffolk, and there is an even wider
range of cross-bred cattle. The traditional Highland breed, of
which there are pure bred herds on Rum and Canna, has been
crossed with the Shorthorn to produce a hardy cow (Luing
breed) which may be crossed with other beef breeds. The dairy
industry in Islay, however, is supported mainly by Ayrshire and
Friesian herds. All the livestock has been selected from mainland breeds, and none, with the possible exception of the
Highland and Luing cattle, have been bred for conditions on
the western seaboard of Scotland.

In 1982, a five-year Integrated Development Programme
(IDP) was approved for the 'Western Isles', the island-
authority area of Comhairle nan Eilein, which in this book is
the 'Outer Hebrides'. In the programme as initially cast, no
financial provision was made for the care of the environment,
though such was sought from the EEC. Later, funds were
made available for the NCC to carry out an appraisal of the
environmental consequences of the IDP, and in particular its
effect on wildlife. Field surveys were quickly organised, and a
report drawing on the results of these was produced for the
NCC by Dr J. Hambrey (1986). Conservation bodies argued
successfully that more resources be made available, in the pro-
visions of the Wildlife and Countryside Act, 1981, to appoint
field staff and pay compensation to crofters on SSSIs, when
foregoing IDP financial benefits for the sake of wildlife.

The IDP, therefore, gave an opportunity to revitalise agriculture in the Outer Hebrides, which had never known the
prosperity of farming on the mainland, and which had become
seriously undermanned. It was expected, therefore, that the
effect of the Programme might be muted by the limited
capacity of the community to respond to schemes to improve
soil conditions for livestock husbandry. The main operations
were draining, fertilising and reseeding of permanent grassland and moorland, use of herbicides and the repair of fences.
Fencing proved most popular, with expenditure of over £5 million in grants.

The IDP was *prima facie* a beneficent measure which, if it
had been carried too far, might have caused damage to wildlife.
Contractors using heavy machinery could drain large areas
with a speed and efficiency never dreamt of by the men of the

last century with their draining spades. Also, the widespread mechanical application of artificial fertilisers, herbicides and mixtures of seeds on the flowery, bird-rich machairs and old hay meadows, some freshly drained, could substantially change the habitat of the islands.

Dr Hambrey's analysis is an object lesson about the effects of agricultural development on the natural environment. Important in this is the degree to which development could proceed so as to cause no damage to wildlife (and in certain respects be beneficial), and the setting of thresholds of effect beyond which development is damaging. However, the determination of both requires much research. (Much of this was put in hand, and is described in Chapters 6 and 7.)

Public opinion was polarised. At one pole there were those in the conservation bodies, who had seen the demise of wildlife by the agricultural transformation of the countryside in mainland Britain, and who feared that the same might happen in the Outer Hebrides—species like the corncrake, which has virtually disappeared from mainland Britain and still survives in the Hebrides, became a symbol of the conservation cause in the IDP. At the other pole, were the local people and their agricultural and political advisers, whose concerns were in livelihood and increased prosperity in what, in EEC terms, was one of the 'less-favoured areas' of Europe.

The Hambrey report *Agriculture and Environment in the Outer Hebrides* states:

Fortunately, this potential for damage to the environment has not, so far, been realised, with drainage and reseeding activity still on the 'beneficial or neutral' side of the damage threshold.

It seems clear now that the worst fears of the conservation bodies have not been confirmed by events in the five years of the IDP. The IDP did not extend to the Inner Hebrides, which at that time benefited only from the normal regime of agricultural subsidy. Yet, even without such a campaign as the IDP, the wetlands of Tiree have been drained in the last ten years with changes in the vegetation and breeding birds as great, or greater than, can be found under the IDP.

The IDP in the Outer Hebrides has now been followed by an Agricultural Development Programme (ADP) for the Inner Hebrides (and Orkney and Shetland). The lessons learnt in environmental care in the IDP have been ploughed into arrangements for the ADP, which is for the period 1988–93. One of the objectives of the ADP is to promote and provide opportunities for agriculturists to maintain the high environmental quality of the islands. Perhaps the most important advance from the IDP is the provision in the ADP of funds for

Hay ricks in a croft in Sleat, Skye (Photo J. M. Boyd)

'environmental management payments,' by which valued wildlife and landscape features can be conserved with rational agricultural development. The following are eligible habitats: over-grazed and over-burned heather, herb-rich grassland on limestone or base-rich soils; woodland and scrub, both existing and newly planted; margins of open water; wet areas waterlogged for 9 months or more per year; wildlife corridors such as burnsides, ditches, and field margins; steep rocky ground within inbye land; and winter keep in a mosaic of cereal, root, and grass crops. This imaginative approach offers great opportunities over five years for experimental management of crofts and farms in the islands, mainly for livestock and wildlife and to establish a new enlightened format for island landuse into the next century.

On Islay the improvement of grassland and dairy livestock husbandry in the past thirty years has been accompanied by an increase in the numbers of barnacle geese spending the winter on that island. We have given an outline of the natural history of this increase (Chapter 13); here we consider the landuse implications of the dual management of land for farm stock and wild geese.

In 1981, the Wildlife and Countryside Act placed a duty upon the NCC to offer management agreements to owners and occupiers of SSSIs, whose operations might cause damage to wildlife. Accordingly, the main goose-feeding areas of Gruinart Flats, Bridgend Flats and Laggan Peninsula having been notified as SSSIs in 1983, the NCC was able to offer a measure of compensation to the farmers within these SSSIs. The aim was to stop shooting and allow the geese freedom to graze the improved grasslands. Agreement was difficult, since there was no existing code of values which gave a standard of equivalence between domesticated stock and wild geese, and at first it did not seem possible to reach agreement, but continuing negotiations resulted in some farmers and landlords receiving compensation from September 1985, providing that geese were not shot on any of their land that lay within the SSSIs.

The ultimate success of the scheme rests largely on the hope that, in due time, the conditions prevailing in the SSSIs, where there is ample nutritious food and no shooting, will prove sufficiently attractive to draw the geese away from farms lying outside the SSSIs. Under present legislation, farmers whose land lies outside SSSIs cannot receive compensation, but can obtain a licence to shoot barnacle geese in protection of their crops. The SSSIs cover the areas of greatest impact, but not all land visited by geese in the course of the winter. Where the boundary of the SSSI includes one farm and excludes its neighbour, there can be a sense of grievance felt by the farmer outside, who cannot be offered a management agreement by the NCC, who receives no compensation, who has to seek a licence to shoot the barnacles, and has the task of flighting the flocks from his land.

The difficulties in obtaining a satisfactory scheme which will be fair to all are great. However, this is breaking new ground in nature conservation and farming, and it is vital that all who are responsible for devising and implementing the scheme should see themselves in the forefront of experimental landuse, where stocks of wildlife and farm animals can be successfully managed for the benefit of both, nowhere more so than at Gruinart where the RSPB Reserve is set cheek-by-jowl with a dairy farm. The RSPB has a wildfowl reserve managed as a livestock farm; the local farmer has a livestock farm managed as a goose reserve.

Forestry

In the Sub-boreal period about 3,500 years ago, the climate was warmer, drier and probably less windy than it is today, and the natural forest in the islands was at its peak of development. It was dominated throughout by birch, but there were oak-dominated woods in the Inner Hebrides. However, the variety of native species that we see today in the remnants of old woodland (see Chapter 8), were probably all present in much greater measure in the old forest. Ash, wych elm, alder, willow, hazel, rowan, gean, aspen and holly were all present within the birch and oak woods. About 2,500 years ago, the Sub-Atlantic period brought a colder, wetter and windier climate than before, and this was accompanied by a substantial regression of forest cover. The adverse climate, coupled with the exploitation of the forest by Neolithic cultivators and pastoralists, and later by Viking invaders and settlers, made the Hebrides almost treeless by the end of the Norse period in 1263.

The woodlands that regenerated on the sheltered sides of the larger Inner Hebrides in medieval times were cut in the 17th and 18th centuries to provide charcoal for iron smelting, mainly at Bonawe in Lorne, and much of this resulted in coppice management of oakwoods. The First Statistical Account (1792–96) records limited areas of natural woodland in Mull and Skye, and first mention is made of plantations in Skye and Raasay. By the time of the New Statistical Account (1845), plantations of mixed conifers and broadleaves were recorded in Islay, Jura, Mull, Skye and Raasay. The common conifers in these early plantations were Norway spruce (*Picea abies*), European larch (*Larix decidua*), Scots pine (*Pinus sylvestris*) and less commonly, Douglas fir (*Pseudotsuga menziesii*). Among the broadleaves, sycamore (*Acer pseudoplatanus*) was by far the most popular plantation tree, but oak, ash, beech (*Fagus sylvatica*) and Norway maple (*Acer platanoides*) were also planted (see p. 148). These plantations were carefully established and tended, but

A maturing forestry plantation mainly of Sitka spruce in Glen Varragill, Skye. Today, such a plantation would have within it a measure of broadleaved trees which would improve its appearance and wildlife (Photo C. Maclean)

by the 1880s they had fallen into neglect because of agricultural depression and cheap imported timber. There was also much coppicing of natural woods, which later became pasture woodlands for sheep and deer. The aged survivors of these stand today at Ardura (Mull), Ord and Leitir-Fura (Skye), and other old woods, which we have named in Chapter 8. Today it is very difficult to establish broadleaved trees on open hillsides in the Hebrides, as the sylvicultural work on Rum has shown. However, it is possible within a 'nursery' plantation of conifers.

Until the late 1930s, the *raison d'etre* for planting was the build-up of the strategic reserve. By 1938, however, thought was being given to forestry as a means of giving social and employment benefits to depopulated areas. In the mid-1950s, forestry was conceived as an adjunct to crofting, and Fraser Darling had given encouragement to this in *West Highland Survey* (1955). The Forestry Commission responded in Mull, Skye and Jura by planting land that would only grow a lower than average crop, to provide ancillary employment to crofters. These acquisitions had small areas of land suitable for planting, interspersed among large areas, which were deemed unsuitable, but which would be kept in agricultural use. However, the scheme perished on the rocks of technological advance in sylviculture and the intricacies of crofting land tenure. The Commission had produced strains of lodgepole pine (*Pinus contorta*) and Sitka spruce (*Picea sitchensis*) which made planting possible on sites deemed 'unplantable'. This resulted in the planting of larger blocks of conifers and more completely afforested landscapes than intended.

A. G. Bramwell and G. M. Cowie (1983) gave details of planting until 1981 in the Inner Hebrides, which we summarise in Table 18.1. In the Outer Hebrides at the same date, there were 624ha. planted and 175ha. in hand for planting, all in Lewis (R. C. B. Johnstone, pers.comm).

Island	Plantation	Land to be Planted	Total
Skye*	8,712	3,448	12,160
Mull	9,930	2,602	12,532
Jura	672	304	976
Islay	845	1,356	2,201
Total	20,159	7,710	27,869

*including Raasay

Table 18.1 The areas (ha.) in the Inner Hebrides of both Forestry Commission and private land, which were under plantation and scheduled for planting, in March 1981. (Compiled from Bramwell and Cowie, 1983).

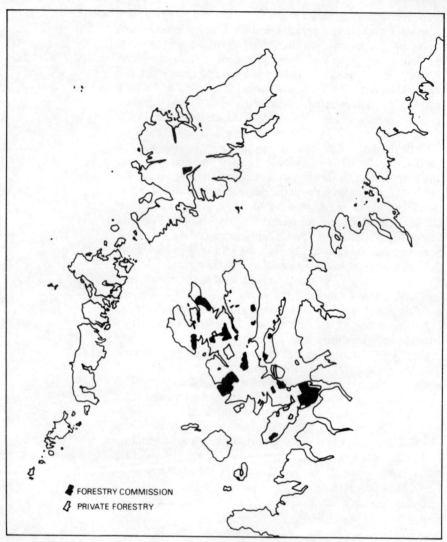

FORESTRY COMMISSION

PRIVATE FORESTRY

Fig. 52 *a* & *b*
*Maps showing the
distribution of Forestry
Commission and
private forestry in the
Hebrides (from
Forestry Commission
maps)*

In 1981, approximately three-quarters of the 27,800 ha. acquired at that time for production forestry had been planted; there were 20,160 ha. in plantations and 7,710 ha. in hand for planting. Plantations in Mull were the most advanced, and when all the land in hand for planting has been stocked with trees, some 14% of the island will be afforested, compared with 7% in Skye, 3% in Islay and 2% in Jura. Bramwell and Cowie give some indication of further potential (ha. plantable) for commercial forestry in the Inner Hebrides as follows:

Island	Skye*	Mull	Jura	Islay	Total
Hectares	21,000	15,000	12,000	12,000	60,000

*including Raasay

If this potentially afforestable land is added to the 1981 totals it would account for 20% of the land surface of Mull, 18% of Skye, 31% of Jura and 23% of Islay. However, there are constraints against such large areas being afforested. Since 1981, a strong adverse public reaction has occurred in Scotland to new large-scale afforestation schemes, particularly in areas of high scenic and wildlife value. Research into public attitudes by the Scottish Forestry Trust points to this reaction being from 'interest groups' rather than from the general public. Nevertheless, it is real, and in our experience, massive. Such adverse reaction might be found in Mull where the plantations are large and are part of a much larger afforested landscape including Fuinary and Morven. In the Hebrides as a whole, however, tree cover is scarce and planting is favoured. The islands have their own indigenous obstacles to extensive afforestation on remote, exposed sites on crofting land, and a significant proportion of the plantable land is the common grazing of crofters which is retained for animal husbandry. Unless the current recession in agriculture results in a relaxation of the restraints on afforestation of crofting land, large areas will remain unplanted. The same restraint does not apply to farmland and deer forest. One of the greatest disincentives to crofter forestry arises from the fact that, despite favourable terms of purchase of crofts by the tenant crofter, few have chosen to own their croft, and as a consequence, any trees which are planted on a tenanted croft belong to the landowner and not the crofter.

The ability of the forest industry to plant Sitka spruce and lodgepole pine extensively in the Inner Hebrides and in the northern Outer Hebrides should not be underestimated. A recent symposium (Henderson and Faulkner, 1987) showed the enormous scientific and technical endeavour that supports the advance of Sitka spruce as the ideal timber species for north-western Britain. It is a native of the west coast fog-belt of North America which thrives in the oceanic climate of Britain. With a high level of tolerance to wind exposure, it resists windthrow better than others and adjusts successfully to a wide range of soil conditions. It is not beyond the sylviculturalist to produce a strain of Sitka spruce that will withstand the rigours of the Hebrides and produce a crop of timber, albeit at high cost and driven by a strong political will to do so in adverse conditions—for example, in an effort to create jobs. Today, the Forestry Commission is more active in the Outer Hebrides than ever before on objectives other than the production of an economic crop of timber.

Much depends on how new plantings and restockings are done to maintain the varied character of the Islands; by the use of small well-landscaped plantations; the sparing of important wetland areas; the provision of wide irregular margins of roads, streams, lochs and deer glades; the encouragement of habitat diversity by the use of broadleaved species, and the positive conservation of species and habitat by the establishment of woodland reserves and schemes for the encouragement of rare plant and insect life, nesting birds and bats.

However, these measures, which are now commonplace in commercial forestry in the uplands and islands, come too late to have any effect on plantations established before 1970. The first fifty years of commercial forestry based on the build-up of a strategic reserve of home-grown timber and, in the Scottish Highlands and Islands, with regard to social and economic benefits, paid little attention to needs of nature conservation as we know them today. The argument that forests of exotic conifers confer as many benefits as disadvantages to wildlife depends on what value is placed on the natural features removed or obscured by afforestation, as compared with others which forestry creates. The conservation movement lays a far greater value on rare and endangered native species and habitats, than it does on alien species and habitats, even though these may abound with native plants and animals. The whole concept, however, requires to be placed in relation to the growth cycle of the forest. In the early seedling and thicket stages, the plantations have greatly increased stocks of wildlife, which dwindle as the trees grow and the canopy closes, and in the dense pole and thinning stages, the wildlife content is greatly reduced.

Early planters of trees in the Hebrides tended to avoid deep peat and espoused free-draining brown earths and peaty gleys, with a good deal of mineral till. Now that deep peat is deemed economically plantable with Sitka spruce and lodgepole pine, the few hitherto undisputed mires have come within reach of afforestation, and whatever benefit may be conferred by such plantations, the mires from which they have grown will have been changed for ever. The rarity of such mires in the Hebridean biome makes such a loss too high a price to pay, in conservation terms, for the trees that the land will bear. The most valuable of these sites have now become SSSIs (Chapter 20), but it is important in the conservation of the wildlife and scenic character of the Hebrides, that the land outside SSSIs be afforested with a view to conserving the natural features within the mix of landuses: for example, by sparing bold fluvio-glacial features which are familiar and well-liked local landmarks; bogs with pool and hummock systems, which possess habitats now seldom found elsewhere; the breeding flats of greenshank, of which there are only about 70 pairs in the Hebrides; the nesting lochs of divers which have low breeding success and require flyways well clear of trees; and the banks of streams which are linear species-rich habitats of high diversity. Though there is no evidence as yet from northern Scotland, the acidification of soils and freshwaters by acid rain may be exacerbated by coniferous plantations, and the effects may be buffered by the ditches out-flowing upon the land surface at least 20m from the stream. All of these measures are embodied in several advisory publications by the Forestry Commission (1986, 1988), and the Royal Society for the Protection of Birds (1985) on the management of conifer and broadleaved woodlands.

Also, the increase of exotic tree species should not be at the expense of the existing natural broadleaved woodlands of birch, oak, ash, hazel, willow and other native species. As many of these woods as possible should be included within forestry fences, left unplanted and naturally regenerated. Those which have been underplanted might have the conifers removed, as is being done by the Forestry Commission in the fine broadleaved wood at Leitir-Fura east of Loch na Dal, Skye. The plantations could also contain a proportion of native broadleaved species (apart from volunteers along the woodland edges), similar to the experimental plots on Rum (Chapter 15).

Today, agriculture is declining and forestry advancing in Britain. The Budget of 1988 announced the end of the tax-incentive system of support to forestry. In its place has come a new Woodland Grants Scheme, with increased grants to compensate the industry for the loss of the tax benefits. More authority is given to the Forestry Commission by the administration of the increased grant, accompanied by a system of environmental assessment with conservation and other guidelines, and incentives are given to farmers and crofters to plant more trees. This will be particularly attractive in Islay, Jura, Mull and Skye, but may also affect Lewis and Harris. If this increase is handled with the necessary stops and balances mentioned above, serious loss of wildlife and scenic values will be prevented, while the industrial base of the islands might be extended and employment of local people enhanced. Many of the Inner Hebrides are locally infested with bracken (*Pteridium aquilinum*) which causes serious illness in cattle, pigs and horses, but less so in sheep and deer. Continuous grazing and burning of the hill ground over centuries has encouraged the spread of bracken on well-drained slopes suitable for growing trees, but one rotation of conifers (*c.* 50 years) on such ground will eliminate bracken *in extenso* and provide a fresh start for agriculture, if that is preferred to restocking the clean land with trees (Fletcher and Kirkwood, 1982).

In 1969–79, the Red Deer Commission recorded a 26% increase in the red deer population of Mull, not including those in woodland. In the same period, 4,000ha. of open deer range were enclosed for forestry. The disruption of, and hardship to, the deer herds caused by enclosing land for forestry in the Highlands, can be reduced by enlightened choice of land for planting and by culling the deer, particularly hinds. Stags are the sporting attraction and are generally well culled, but hind culling is not attractive to the sportsman and is often neglected, and this long-sustained neglect is now at the centre of the serious over-population of the Highlands and Islands by red deer.

When deer enter plantations they prosper, cause damage to the trees and are very difficult to control. Sadly, the knowledge, skill, manpower and funds for efficient deer control are often lacking and difficult to apply in Highland estates. To achieve success in forestry, deer must be excluded from young plantations. Deer-proof fences seldom last more than 20 years, and the maturing forests become refuges and feeding ranges of red and roe deer. The interaction of forestry and red deer is an ever-present factor in Highland land use, and it makes timber enterprises less economically-worthwhile and ecologically difficult to manage. A great deal of research has been done since the last war to describe the behaviour of red deer in commercial plantations, and to assess the damage they do to various crop species at different stages of forest growth (Jenkins, 1985).

Minerals

The varied geology of the Hebrides is reflected in the large variety of economic minerals which are found in the islands. There are ores of iron, lead, and chromite; silica-rich rocks; diatomite; aggregates of limestone, fine-grained sandstone, sands and gravels. Though large quantities of these minerals are generally present, with the exception of sands and gravels, they are usually in beds too thin to be economically workable, or are too 'impure' for industrial use (Gribble, 1983). There are quartz crystal, agate and jasper; garnetiferous and sapphire-bearing rocks; bloodstone in Rum and greenstone (serpentine marble) in Tiree and Iona.

Ores

The Raasay ironstone bed is about 2m thick, and it outcrops in the south-east of the island for about 12km, from the Inverarish Burn in the south, along the cliff face to Screapadal in the north, with another 2km outcrop off-set in Beinn na'Leac. Total reserves are thought to be between 10 and 16 million tonnes of ironstone, of which only about 0.3 million tonnes have so far been worked. It is a low grade ore which was mined between 1914 and 1919, and the remains of the workings can be seen today near Raasay Pier. There are also concentrations of magnetite on Tiree and Skye. On Tiree, the 4m-thick band has been traced for 7km from Loch a'Phuill to Loch Bhasapol and contains reserves of over 3 million tonnes of ore. The magnetite goes to a depth of 80m, is masked by drift deposits and is thought to disperse into narrow strands and to be commercially unworkable. On Skye, there are some 20 small pockets of magnetite in the contact zone between the granite of Beinn an Dubhaich and the Durness limestone in Strath.

Veins of lead occur in limestones of the Dalradian rocks of Islay which have been worked since the 16th century. These massive gangues of limestone containing concentrations of

The Torrin marble quarry showing a basalt sill in the Cambrian marble above granophyre (Photo British Geological Survey)

galena (native lead sulphide) occur in the north-east of the island and were mined north of Loch Finlaggan between 1860 and 1880, when only about 2,260 tonnes of ore were removed (Gribble, 1983). Chromite occurs in the Tertiary intrusive rocks of Skye and Rum, where dispersed grains occur within the olivine-rich facies, occasionally aggregating into layers of up to 25mm thick which are not commercially workable.

Silica

The quartzites of Jura, Islay and Skye may contain some size-able concentrations of very pure silica. The purest deposit in Scotland is the 6m-thick bed of white cretaceous sandstone at Loch Aline, which produces some 75,000 tonnes of crushed stone annually. This bed has stratigraphical relations with similar, but thinner, beds of sandstone in western Mull. Analysis shows that the Loch Aline sandstone is 99.69% silica, compared with 98.04% for the Cambrian basal quartzite at Ord, Skye, and 97.89% for shore sand in Jura, and 95.73% for Dalradian quartzite on the shore at Bunnahabhainn, Islay. The 'Singing Sands' of Camus Sgiotaig in Eigg, derived from the local Jurassic sandstone, also have a very high silica content.

Diatoms are microscopic, unicellular phytoplankton that are encased in silica. Their remains accumulate as marine and lacustrine deposits and, in geological time, form beds of white diatomite, which is used in filters, fire-resistant materials and as a light-weight filler. Nine sites of diatomite occur in Trot-ternish, Skye. These deposits are small, partially worked-out and, except for that at Loch Mealt (which would require to be drained) uneconomic. Small deposits of diatomite also occur in North Tolsta and North Shawbost, Lewis.

Aggregates, Slates and Block Stone

Between Kyleakin and Broadford in Skye there occurs one of the largest deposits of sand and gravel in Scotland. It is com-posed of a wide variety of rock types, in a range of sizes, from boulders to sands and silts, the dominant rocks being quart-zites and arkoses. The aggregates from this deposit were used for the making of high quality concrete, in the construction of oil-production platforms at the now defunct yard at Loch Kishorn. However, the deposits are of such great extent and high quality, that another market has been found. Efforts are being made to progressively rehabilitate the site as the aggregates are removed. At Sconser, fine-grained, grey Torridonian sandstone is quarried for concrete and lower grade road metals suitable for many of the secondary roads in Skye. The Torrin Quarry produces a high-grade limestone for rough casting and cladding panels (p. 350). It is also a good agricultural liming agent with a high magnesium content. Reserves are estimated at 0.75 million tonnes, but the limestone is cut by dykes and sills of dark dolerite and basalt, which lowers its value as a cladding material and creates much spoil.

At Ballygrant, in Islay, a dark marble in the Dalradian limestone is quarried and used as aggregate, agricultural lime and as block stone. The limestone island of Lismore possesses quarries and massive, long-disused lime kilns which produced agricultural lime for export to the peaty lands of Lorne and beyond. The kilns, buildings and harbour at Sailean are an industrial monument worthy of conservation. Similarly, the slate quarries of Easdale and Belnahua are monuments of a time of great industry in the Firth of Lorne. The complex of flooded quarry workings, industrial buildings and workers' cottages on Belnahua, set in a mosaic of islands, is a particularly deserving subject for conservation.

The greyish-pink granite of the Ross of Mull quarried near Bunessen makes high quality aggregates and building stone, well displayed in the Sherryvore Lighthouse and the shore station and dock at Hynish in Tiree (the latter is being restored by the Hebridean Trust). Near Rodel in South Harris, there is an emplacement of anorthosite which has a potential in the production of alumina, cement, and white roadstone.

Fisheries and Fish Farming

CHAPTER 19

Fishery History

The nature of the pristine Minches and the Sea of Hebrides may be reconstructed, in small part, from the organic deposits on the floors of the present-day submarine shelf. However, one fact is certain; the sea has always been held in highest reverence by the islanders, not only for its even-handed treatment of all men—whatever their rank—but also for its beneficence of food, fuel and fertiliser. What was once, though, an unexploited natural ecosystem of teeming life, probably of great variety, abundance and beauty now has waters that are subdued by a century and a half of mechanised fishing.

The Dutch were the first to fish the Minch commercially in the late 15th century, when the Loch Broom fishery was established (Darling, 1944), and by the early 18th century, the industry was booming in Tanera Mor and Isle Martin. The Dutch used herring busses which could reach off-shore waters, but, until then, the native fishermen used small communally-owned inshore boats, as their forebears had done. The aftermath of the Jacobite period brought English enterprise to the Highlands and Islands, which had a very limited effect on the life and economy of the local people. They were the work-force of the kelping industry, and generally too impoverished and subservient to be in any way commercially enterprising on their own behalf. However, with commercial enterprise from the south generally set on exploitation of both fisheries and people, there came to the Hebrides a commercially-minded philanthropist, one John Knox (no relation of the Calvanist reformer), a Scot by birth, and a wealthy bookseller in London. At the request of the British Fisheries Society (of which he was a prime-mover), Knox made a voyage to the north-west coast of Scotland in 1786, to survey and report on the prospects for fisheries. By his own account (1786), Knox's mission to the Hebrides was one of mercy along similar lines to Oxfam's present-day mission to the peoples of the Third World (Bray, 1988). Among other good works, he caused the British Fisheries Society to provide funds for the construction of small fishing villages of which Oban, Tobermory and

Ullapool are examples, and many other small quays, some of which were built by Thomas Telford.

Immediately following the collapse of kelping in the 1820s, the population was reaching its historical maximum in many islands and turned to fishing. Where this was financially supported by landowners in efforts to make estates economically viable, the industry became commercial, otherwise it continued at a local subsistence level to supplement agricultural crops. The end of the kelping brought great distress to island communities, poverty, and starvation; people often did not have the physical strength to man the heavy boats and the tackle required for a productive fishery, and were limited to clearing shell fish from the sea shore. However, about that time English companies were exporting salted herring to the West Indies as food for slaves.

The increasing population of the kelping period in the late 18th–early 19th centuries created hunger, which could only be relieved by a sufficiency of fish, particularly herring. Yet, prolific stocks were probably out of reach of many enfeebled communities. Fishing was by no means a ready-made form of subsistence for island communities; it was an uneasy tradition in many islands where the seafaring crafts, skills and traditions, for which Hebrideans later became noted in the British Mercantile Marine, were not in general practice. Lack of a ready native supply of timber for boats and the wild character of weather and sea were real drawbacks to organised fishing.

The new crofting system devised by landowners at that time to maintain the work force for kelping, depended for its survival on part-time fishing but nevertheless the inhabitants of the storm coasts of the island had few safe anchorages and little opportunity of sea-going. Islands like Eigg and Tiree, for example, had very limited shelter for a fishing fleet commensurate with their populations in the 1830s, and the opposite could be said for Canna and Eriskay.

The trauma of the potato famine in the 1840s and the continuous stream of emigrants also helped to bring about the capitalisation of the fishing industry. A deep-water herring fishery developed in the Minches, working to curing stations on the east coast of Lewis and Barra. The fishing industry of the islands had mushroomed from being one of local subsistence fishing in the 17th century, to being in the 19th century one of general sufficiency throughout the Hebrides as a whole, supporting a flourishing export trade, particularly in barrel-cured herring.

The fortunes of the island communities in the 19th century were dependent on the herring industry; more than any other fish, the herring epitomised the marine harvest, which

The small fishing harbour at Port of Ness, Lewis in 1976 (Photo J. M. Boyd)

promised to be the supplement of agriculture and a basis for livelihood. Until about 1914, the herring, the six-eared oat, and the potato made the islands habitable by large numbers of people living a simple life. There is a history of herring fishing at Stornoway, and the remains of herring stations are found also at Castlebay, the Summer Isles and Badcall, and many landing quays, of which Canna was a good example, were used between 1892 and 1905. The advent of the railheads and the replacement of sail by steam in the drifters caused a rapid decline of the local quay industry, with the focus of landings moved to market ports such as Stornoway, Mallaig, and Oban with fast rail and sea services.

The seasonal nature of the herring fishery fitted well with the timing of agricultural work. Herring shoals in the sheltered sea lochs in winter, and in the more exposed off-shore waters in summer, attracted fleets of boats with drift nets when times were slack on the crofts. However, shoaling from year to year was uncertain, and the main stocks of herring occurred annually in the west coast before they appeared on the east coast. This provided an employment incentive which transformed life in many crofter-fisher communities in the Hebrides. Both men and women left home in large numbers to seek jobs at fishing ports from Shetland to Yarmouth; men found places in east coast drifter crews and women on the curing lines at the harbours. Fishing had become an almost year-round occupation and, though many returned to maintain their crofts in season, others did not and the general level of agricultural efficiency declined. In 1884, the Napier Commission believed that more income came into crofting from the sea than from the land, and by 1891, the Walpole Commission claimed that three out of four people in the Highlands and Islands were in some way dependent on fishing for their livelihood. In 1902 the Brand Report stated that the average family in Lewis drew an annual income of £3 from the sale of croft produce, and £25 from fishing (Smout, 1986).

The replacement of sail by steam brought a new power to the fishing industry of the late 19th century, both in main propulsion engines, and in windlasses for hauling nets and lines. The large scale mechanical exploitation of the continental-shelf fishery had begun, in which home-based boats played only a minor part. Hebridean waters were worked by succeeding generations of steam trawlers and drifters, with an increasing use of ice to chill the catches of white fish bound for distant ports, such as Fleetwood and Aberdeen. A vast amount of the herring catch at the beginning of this century was exported by klondikers to Russia, but the advent of the First World War and the Russian Revolution destroyed this market, and the herring industry collapsed. It was at this time that Lord Leverhulme built the fishing stations at Leverburgh, Harris and Carloway, Lewis, in an attempt to revitalise the fishing industry.

The Leverhulme enterprise, 1918–25, was based on the herring. However, the vision of the marine harvest conveyed

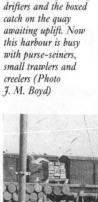

Mallaig harbour in the 1960s showing herring drifters and the boxed catch on the quay awaiting uplift. Now this harbour is busy with purse-seiners, small trawlers and creelers (Photo J. M. Boyd)

through investment and business acumen to the consumer society of industrial Britain depended on more than the abundance of herring; it depended also on the outright support of the Lewismen, which was not provided. Leverhulme moved to Harris in 1924 but died in 1925, thus ending a fine scheme which might have been of enduring benefit to the Hebrides and Gaelic culture. The fishing harbours at Carloway and Leverburgh remain as monuments to a great idea.

The growth of the industry in the late 19th–early 20th centuries was also marked by the rise in importance of landings at Canna and later at the railhead ports of Kyle of Lochalsh, Mallaig and Oban. Boats from Campbeltown and Tarbert on Loch Fyne fished waters around the southern Hebrides and shipped their catches to Clyde ports by fast cargo/passenger steamers. The old fish-curing stations on the coasts of Ross and Cromarty and Sutherland were replaced by other larger harbours close to good fishing grounds in the North Minch at Ullapool, Lochinver and Kinlochbervie.

Though the two World Wars disrupted the industry, they also served to stimulate new efforts to rebuild the fishing fleets operating in the Hebrides for part of the year. The steam-powered vessels declined between the wars and were totally eclipsed in the second half of this century by diesel vessels with sophisticated electrical, and electronic equipment—trawlers, pair trawlers, ringers and purse-seiners. Costs soared, the numbers of boats decreased, many fewer men were required in mechanised fishing, and the catching power of the boats increased many fold. Trawlers and lobster smacks from the Netherlands, Spain and France and long-liners from Scandinavia have joined the British fleets in the fishery bonanza of the last century. Today, a large mackerel fishery still persists in the North Minch based on Loch Broom, with much smaller quantities of herring landed there and at Stornoway and Campbeltown (Table 19.3). A sizeable trade in white fish is still carried out at Oban, Mallaig, Lochinver and Kinlochbervie. The fish-processing plant at Stornoway has been supplemented in recent years by others, at Breasclete in Lewis and Ardveenish in Barra, ostensibly to exploit the stocks of blue whiting on the continental slope west and north of the Outer Hebrides. The former is being redeployed to the making of chemical extracts from fish oil, and the latter has had an erratic employment record. Grants are available for vessels to supply these and other plants, but most local investment has gone into the provision of small two-man craft equipped for creeling, trawling, or dredging for shellfish.

In recent years, mackerel have been fished by Scottish and foreign purse-seiners supplying a pack of eastern European

factory ships anchored in Loch Broom, and the fish-meal
factory at Stornoway. The Minch fishery has now nearly
ended. It is claimed that this is due to a redistribution of the
stocks, but the visual impact of the fleet of ships off Ullapool,
which are now siphoning off mackerel from waters further to
the north, suggests over-exploitation of the mackerel stocks
and points to a need for restrictions now, or in the near future.
Catch quotas have already been recommended. The only
commercial profit to the local economy from this fishing
activity is in the supply of some services.

The main industrial fisheries presently in the Hebrides are
the ones for sand-eels in the areas of the north Minch, North
Rona and sometimes off Barra, for Norway pout southwest of
Barra (which is exploited by the Danes and Faroese), and for
blue whiting along the shelf edge west of St Kilda. Industrial
fishing may, however, also threaten the stocks of mackerel and
sprat. All these species are of importance to the stability of the
marine ecosytem and the future of many other dependent
species. Some species, like herring, have been substantially
exploited yet still survive. Sadly, this is more a reflection of the
enormous reproductive powers of the species than of the foresight of fisheries managers. The mackerel may be a different
story again, but there is little doubt that our view of the seas as
an ever-bountiful source of protein is highly misconceived.
Today, fisheries management proceeds by trial and error. This
is partly because we are not yet sophisticated enough to understand the complex population and community dynamics of fish,
but it is also because it is politically expedient to proceed in this
manner. This approach leads to short-term industrial boom
instead of long-term stability and there are a remarkable
number of people still willing to support the boom or bust
approach.

Both fishing stations are within easy reach of fish stock
around St Kilda, the prime seabird breeding station in the
British Isles and the first natural site in the United Kingdom to
be included in the World Heritage Convention (WHC). In this
it joins the Gallapagos, Aldabra and Tristan da Cunha. We do
not know if industrial fishing poses a threat to the seabirds, but
evidence from Shetland points to this.

Demersal and Pelagic Fish

The most important species of demersal or bottom-feeding
species fished in Hebridean waters are cod (*Gadus morhua*),
haddock (*Melanogrammus aeglefinus*), whiting (*Merlangius mer-*

langius) and spurdogs (*Squalus acanthias*). Saithe (*Pollachius virens*), hake (*Merluccius merluccius*), ling (*Molva molva*), skate (*Rajidae*), angler fish (*Lophius piscatorius*) and plaice (*Pleuronectes platessa*) are less abundant. (Biological aspects of these species, and of the pelagic species and shellfish mentioned below, are discussed in Chapter 4.)

The blue whiting (Micromesistius poutassou) (Crown Copyright)

Turning to the pelagic or surface-feeding species, herring (*Clupea harengus*) are by far the most important. The history of herring landings in the Stornoway District (Outer Hebrides) are shown in Table 19.3. Until 1935, the catches of herring showed large-scale annual fluctuations between 5,000 and 45,000 tonnes, but after 1935 these catches fluctuated on a distinctly lower plane of between 3,000 and 17,000 tonnes, with a marked upsurge about 1970 when the purse seine net was introduced. Mackerel (*Scomber scomber*) was traditionally only a minor part of the pelagic fishery (*c.* 1,000 tonnes annually) and sprats (*Spratus spratus*) began to be commercially fished in the early 1970s, when 'industrial' fishing began, and there was also an increase in the mackerel catch to support the fish-processing industry. In recent years the 'industrial' fishery has been extended to include the demersal Norway pout (*Trisopterus esmarkii*), the sand-eel (*Ammodytes* spp.) and blue whiting (*Micromesistius poutassou*) (Table 19.1).

The harvest of 'industrial' fish supplies fish meal for agriculture and aquaculture in the United Kingdom. This meal is processed from whole 'industrial' species and the waste products of the white fish, herring and mackerel industries. A recent survey by G. M. Bishop (1987) shows that the annual national need for fish meal is about 300,000 tonnes, of which 71,000t (24%) is obtained from a harvest of about 350,000t of raw fish from home waters—the remaining 76% is imported. In 1987, the requirement of British aquaculture for fish meal (which constitutes about 55% of the food of farmed fish) was about 21,000t, obtained from about 100,000t of raw fish. Quantities of this catch are taken on the Hebridean shelf and landed

at Stornoway and Mallaig (Table 19.1). These quantities are
not large in relation to the standing stock of these species
present in Hebridean waters, but the increase in the catch of
sand-eels in the Outer Hebrides is very significant. From zero
in 1976, the catch in 1986 had grown to 24,376t valued at
£675,600.

Year	Stornoway			Mallaig		
	N.pout	S.eel	Bl.whg	N.pout	S.eel	Bl.whg
1976	6,319		817	26		382
1977	2,853	13	1,291	37	190	1,289
1978	302		498	29	192	1,073
1979	19		1,464	28	215	
1980	1,202	212	4,098			
1981	1,158	5,972	2,391			
1982	585	10,872				
1983		12,882				
1984	23	12,359				
1985	13	18,586				
1986		24,376	4,028			

Table 19.1   The weights (tonnes) of Norway pout, sand-eels and
blue whiting landed at Stornoway and Mallaig 1976–86 (*Sea
Fishery Statistical Tables 1976–86*) N. pout = Norway pout, bl
Whg = blue whiting.

Sand-eels are not part of the European diet; the same fish in
Third World countries would be a staple food. There is an
overriding principle at work here, namely, that a vast quantity
of low-cost fish which is wholesome food for all people is
exploited in the creation of a small quantity of high-cost food
for a few people.

Pelagic fish (85% mackerel) landed from the Minch at Ullapool have increased enormously (Table 19.3). In 1976, 7,492t of
mackerel valued at £0.40 million were landed at Ullapool compared with 177,916t valued at £19.65 million in 1985. This is a
24-fold increase in the take from the stock in the Minch in a
decade—surely such exploitation is well beyond the limits of
rational conservation of mackerel stocks?

Shellfish

The shellfish industry is based on stocks of lobsters (*Homarus
vulgaris*) and Norway lobsters (*Nephrops norvegicus*), with lesser
fisheries of scallops (*Pecten maximus*), crabs (*Cancer pagurus*),
periwinkles (*Littorina littorea*), and cockles (*Cerastoderma
edule*).

Since the last war the shellfish industry, traditionally a creel fishery for lobsters by crofter-fishermen, has become more highly mechanised with larger well-equipped creelers for lobsters and crabs, trawlers and creelers for *Nephrops*, and dredgers for scallops and clams. Catches are marketed at main ports for freezing, though catches are sometimes also kept alive in holding ponds awaiting suitable market conditions. Consequently, high quality fresh shellfish are sent to the market or direct to the consumer by air. The changing palate of the British people and considerable exports have made *Nephrops* the most profitable shellfish.

In 1952, the value of the landings of shellfish in Scotland was £296,000; in 1976, it was £12,384,000, when the landings in the Outer Hebrides reached their highest ever value, £1,046,000. In the Inner Hebrides, landings decreased from 1971 when there was a peak in lobster landings of 150t. Until then large creelers working the prolific grounds to the west of the Outer Hebrides landed their catches at Mallaig. However, increasing costs of fuel in the early 1970s forced these boats to land catches in the Outer Hebrides. This contributed to the peak landing in 1976 in the Outer Isles, when that in the Inner Isles was much reduced, resulting in the closure of the lobster-holding tanks in Mallaig. By 1986, only 56t were landed at Mallaig and Oban Fishery Districts, compared with 129t in the Stornoway District (Table 19.2).

Mason *et al.* (1983) state that the shift of landings from Mallaig to the Outer Hebrides is only part of the reason for the decline of the fishery in the Inner Hebrides. The lobster population has undoubtedly decreased and the decline in the catch of lobsters per unit of catching effort in the 1970s in the Inner Hebrides is deemed typical of the entire west coast fishery in that period. The fishing effort in the past 25 years has been greater than that which would result in a maximum sustainable yield, and the situation has not improved in the 1980s. Paradoxically, while the catch of lobsters has declined, the value of that catch increased greatly until the late 1970s, when the price dropped as North American lobsters claimed a substantial hold on the European market.

The Norway lobster is a burrow-dweller, which until the early 1950s, was taken accidentally by trawlers seeking white fish. Thereafter, a market was sought for this species, and within ten years it had become a major fishery working to an expanding seafood processing industry. From 100t in 1953, the size of the Scottish *Nephrops* catch in 1985 had grown to 17,887t, valued at £24,275,000, and between 1976 to 1986, the catch of *Nephrops* in the five Fishery Districts of the Hebrides (Table 19.4) increased from 5,833t valued at £3.47 million to 9,222t

	Strny	Kilbre	Lhnvr	Ullpl	Mallg	Oban	Cpbtn
Demersal Fish							
Cod	135	1,543	468	36	556	45	168
Dogfish	143	697	715	15	576	120	144
Haddock	371	7,371	2,602	110	1,509	268	15
Hake	30	39	75	2	160	117	117
Halibut	2	13	7	<1	3	<1	<1
Monkfish	107	248	204	4	314	18	7
Plaice	33	325	329	3	66	52	14
Saithe	9	1,432	73	2	169	1	55
Skate	56	508	494	32	241	123	26
Whiting	170	2,877	1,003	18	841	376	68
Totals	1,056	15,053	5,970	223	4,436	1,121	615
Pelagic Fish							
Herring	2,301			18,077	457		736
Mackerel	1,481			101,527	561		92
Bl.whit.	4,028						
Sprats	74				238		209
S.eels*	24,376				<1		
Totals	32,260			119,594	1,257		1,037
Shellfish							
Pwinkles	225			47	491	227	145
Crabs	805	3	34	71	95	108	230
Lobsters	129	13	3	5	17	39	34
Scallops	489		2	133	456	814	693
N.lobsters	1,242	4	890	868	3,177	780	2,261
Squid	<1	203	237	4	60	3	1
Qu.scallops					10	71	158
Totals	2,891	223	1,166	1,128	4,306	2,042	34,221

*The sand-eel is a demersal species but is included in the list of pelagic fish because of its industrial use similar to other pelagic species.

Table 19.2 Landings (tonnes) of the main species of finfish and shellfish by British vessels in the Fishery Districts of Stornoway (Strny), Kinlochbervie (Klbre), Lochinver (Lhnvr), Ullapool (Ullpl), Mallaig (Mallg), Oban and Campbeltown (Cpbtn), in 1986 (*Scottish Sea Fisheries Statistical Tables, 1986*).

valued at £16.30 million. Again the question arises—is such a high level of exploitation in the interests of the long term conservation of stocks?

We have reviewed the history of the Hebridean fishery in some detail, since only by doing so can we convey the enormous change that man has made to the marine environment of the Hebrides—and over the Continental Shelf as a whole. This impact takes several forms; there is the direct impact of

District	Weight (tonnes)					Value (£'000)				
	1982	1983	1984	1985	1986	1982	1983	1984	1985	1986
Demersal Fish										
Strny	13,192	14,733	13,980	20,079	25,597	829	990	1,018	1,147	1,385
Klbre	n/a	n/a	17,753	18,984	15,601	n/a	n/a	10,074	10,433	9,490
Lhnvr	n/a	n/a	n/a	n/a	6,510	n/a	n/a	n/a	n/a	4,088
Ullpl	17,620	17,323	8,525	6,786	244	7,003	8,080	4,109	3,968	126
Mallg	3,925	5,311	6,640	6,911	4,956	1,337	2,376	3,289	4,031	3,581
Oban	3,452	3,987	2,870	2,201	1,190	1,286	1,756	1,485	1,138	820
Cpbtn	928	870	663	974	643	320	279	235	411	442
Totals	39,117	42,224	50,431	55,935	54,741	10,775	13,481	20,210	21,128	19,932
Scotland	296,245	292,874	282,749	294,739	281,758	106,444	121,102	135,997	147,153	163,050
Pelagic Fish										
Strny	11,802	6,811	6,887	8,942	7,928	496	3,882	418	477	283
Klbre	n/a	n/a				n/a	n/a			
Lhnvr	n/a	n/a	n/a	n/a		n/a	n/a	n/a	n/a	
Ullpl	140,191	139,880	173,708	177,916	119,603	15,321	15,841	18,165	19,651	12,660
Mallg	3,681	3,001	852	1,875	1,256	449	414	91	169	135
Oban			54	181	132			7	25	15
Cpbtn	1,572	2,070	1,974	1,947	1,037	354	380	370	412	289
Totals	157,246	151,816	183,602	190,812	129,824	16,620	17,524	19,069	20,724	13,367
Scotland	172,916	173,560	226,020	263,099	234,707	18,510	19,929	24,445	28,974	25,370
Shellfish										
Strny	2,558	3,145	3,826	4,095	3,108	2,117	3,082	4,128	5,103	4,568
Klbre	n/a	n/a	156	134	224	n/a	n/a	349	315	432
Lhnvr	n/a	n/a	n/a	n/a	1,165	n/a	n/a	n/a	n/a	2,055
Ullpl	2,217	2,046	2,536	2,200	1,127	2,601	2,640	2,935	2,919	1,835
Mallg	4,330	3,991	5,085	4,725	4,384	4,427	4,084	5,484	6,159	7,066
Oban	2,524	2,372	2,307	1,955	2,177	2,068	2,037	2,371	2,394	3,210
Cpbtn	4,193	4,471	4,308	4,133	3,813	3,339	4,095	4,705	4,801	5,965
Totals	16,822	12,880	14,236	13,013	11,501	12,435	12,856	15,495	16,273	18,076
Scotland	29,027	32,713	34,543	34,732	34,798	23,754	29,183	33,477	38,976	46,030

Table 19.3　Weights and values of landings of finfish and shellfish by British vessels in the Fishery Districts of Stornoway (Strny), Kinlochbervie (Klbre), Lochinver (Lhnr), Ullapool (Ullpl), Mallaig (Mallg), Oban and Campbeltown (Cpbtn), in the period 1977–86 (*Scottish Sea Fisheries Statistical Tables, 1986*).

the quarry species and the consequent changes in their numerical status; the impact on the non-quarry species which are taken accidentally; also, small or young classes of some species are taken while fishing for adult forms of small quarry species such as sprats, sand-eels, *Nephrops* and clams. Gravid females are caught and, perhaps most important of all, there is a physical impact on the sea-bed caused by frequent passes of trawlers and dredgers over the limited sheets of mud in quest of *Nephrops*, sand and gravels for scallops, and the scarifying of wide areas by trawlers for benthic finfish. No holistic forethought has ever been given to the consequence of this disturbance of the Hebridean shelf; the sea-bed has been created by nature in 10,000 years and has been substantially impoverished by man in the last 100.

District	1976		1986	
	t	£	t	£
Stornoway	978	489,155	1,242	2,017,700
Kinlochbervie			4	7,500
Lochinver			890	1,565,700
Ullapool	1,019	662,666	3,177	1,595,100
Mallaig	2,417	1,529,864	3,177	5,964,500
Oban	650	370,380	780	1,338,300
Campbeltown	769	417,108	2,261	3,810,000
Totals	5,833	3,469,173	9,222	16,298,800

Table 19.4   A comparison of the weights (tonnes) and value of landings of Norway lobsters (*Nephrops norvegicus*) in the five Fishery Districts covering Hebridean waters, in 1976 and 1986 (*Scottish Sea Fisheries Statistical Tables, 1976 and 1986*).

Fish Farming

The rapid growth of fish farming on the western and northern seaboards of Scotland came at a time of great effort to create employment in crofting areas. In the 1980s, fishfarming has provided a complement to the agricultural revival under the IDP (see p. 338) in the Outer Hebrides and the Agricultural Development Programme (ADP) in the Inner Hebrides; it now has an almost open-ended potential for development. As if by magic, all the factors—technical, ecological and social—were right for the attraction of venture capital, and the growth of an industry which was, in many respects, compatible with the Highlands and Islands. Looking at the setting of the industry, the length of suitable coastline for farms seems enormous; the volume of clean seawater available for exchange with the ocean reservoir limitless; supplies of processed fish food inexhaustible; and the appetite of affluent people all over the world for 'Scotch' salmon insatiable. The opportunities for development seem to be near to ideal, but are they? Supplies of 'industrial' fish (see p. 358) which form a large part of processed fish food, are indeed exhaustible in the commercial sense, and any serious widespread pollution along the seaboard brings to question the cleanliness of the sea water and the quality of the fish for sensitive markets. The biological and engineering problems are formidable, and the harvest is at constant risk of damage and destruction by storm and disease.

The farmed 'Scotch' salmon is the indigenous Atlantic salmon (*Salmo salar*). The freshwater phase of the production cycle covers the egg, fry, parr and smolt stages; the marine phase covers the grilse and salmon growth stages. Brood adults in farms are stripped of their eggs which are fertilised and set in trays in running freshwater. Fry and parr are brought on to feeding in tanks and, when a few grams in weight, are transferred to freshwater tanks or cages in freshwater lochs, where they grow for one or two years until they become smolts. The bulk of the parr stock become 'silvered' after one year and is transferred as smolts into seawater cages. Here they are grown for one year to be harvested as grilse (1.5–2.0kg), or 18 months as salmon (2.0–4.0kg). Other smolts are either kept for another year or are disposed of, sometimes by release into the sea or river. The grilse are the fish which show signs of coming early into breeding condition and thus dropping in market value the longer they are retained. The bulk of the harvest (c. 70%) goes to market as salmon, and selected fish are retained as brood stock. There is also a thriving market for salmon ova stripped from wild-caught fish from the rivers.

Rainbow trout (*Salmo gairdneri*) and native brown trout (*Salmo trutta*) are both farmed on a small scale in the Hebrides, mainly as 'portion-sized' fish for the catering trade, and the latter also to a minor extent for the stocking of angling waters. The production cycle is again six months for the egg, fry and fingerling stages in freshwater tanks, followed by another six or twelve months growth in larger tanks, ponds, freshwater or sea cages. The trout are harvested when between 280 and 340gms in weight.

Mussels (*Mytilus edulis*), clams (*Pecten maximus*), queen scallops (*Chlamys opercularis*), the native oyster (*Ostrea edulis*) and the Pacific oyster (*Crassostrea gigas*) are farmed in the Hebrides. The mussels are grown to market-size in 18 months from natural spat collected on suspended ropes. Sometimes the spat is collected in one area and grown in another. The scallops are grown to market-size over a period of about three years from natural spat, which, having been collected from the sea bed, is transferred to suspended nets; alternatively the shells may be drilled and the scallop suspended individually in the 'pierced-ear culture'. The Pacific oysters are grown to market-size in 18 months from hatchery-produced spat in net bags suspended just above the sea bed.

Fish farming, therefore, is a new, major, widespread, ecological factor suddenly imposed upon the coastal environment of north-west Scotland in advance of a thorough knowledge of the marine ecology. The flora and fauna, and the processes which govern life on land and the sea-shore, are far more scrutible, and much better known and understood, than those in the sea. Indeed, the nature of the sea being basically different from that of the land, the ecological rationale of the land cannot be simply extended to the marine realm. The water column of the sea is a vast, dense, mobile, environment in its own right, related to, but in many respects separate from, the sea-bed. The relationships between the sea and the sea-bed are poorly understood, and it is within this area of uncertainty, that the fish farming industry is placed.

The uncertainty created by a lack of scientific knowledge was accompanied by a lack of statutory planning regulations for the off-shore side of the industry. The Crown Estate Commission (CEC) is legally responsible for leases of the sea-bed to fish farmers. Concern about the environmental aspects of the off-shore installations was expressed by both development and conservation bodies, which has resulted in published reports by Cobham Resource Consultants (1987), Gowen, et al. (1988), Scottish Wildlife and Countryside Link (SWCL) (1988), and the NCC (1989).

The immediate and short-term effects of fish farms on the environment are local, and in most cases predictable. On land the effects are subject to statutory planning control by the local authority, who can call for an environmental impact assessment. Off-shore, there is no such control, only the conditions accompanying the lease of the seabed by the CEC, which has potentially conflicting interests—the raising of revenues from such leases, as well as care for the environment. The CEC has published *Guidelines on Siting and Design of Marine Fish Farms in Scotland* (1987) and has co-operated with the HIDB, CCS, NCC and the Scottish Salmon Growers' Association in sponsoring of the first two of the above reports. Those moves show that the CEC are determined to fully address their responsibilities. However, a question remains over the propriety of a financially-interested body, (no matter how well-intended) acting in the public interest in a matter of such scale and importance as fish farming. The third report was sponsored by twelve non-government conservation bodies. The scale of public reaction to the fish-farming bonanza, therefore, is great, timely, and directed towards closing gaps in science, planning and administration.

The impacts of salmon and trout farms are much greater than those of shellfish farms, because shellfish take natural, planktonic food from the sea, whereas salmon and trout in farms depend on pelleted food. The long-term effects of various forms of pollution and chemical additives to encourage growth of fish, to combat disease and parasitism of fish, and to reduce the fouling, rotting and corrosion of nets and cages, are much less predictable. Clearly, such long-term effects are dependent on the size and number of farms and the rate of tidal flushing of the moorings. In turn, the density of farms may be limited by the need to keep well apart different stocks of fish possessing differing origins and health records and also by the development of more robust cages making it possible to extend farming into waters which previously were too exposed.

When salmon cages are first established the water column and seabed beneath the salmon cages becomes gradually polluted by the faeces and unconsumed food of the salmon. It takes up to six months for the seabed to reach a new ecological state, sustained by the continuous loading of the seabed with wastes, which accumulate at 2–7kgm per sq m per year. In still waters, systems can become unstable, due to the growth of phytoplankton, and in summer sunshine heavy loadings of soluble nitrogen derived from organic decomposition and faeces may cause a 'bloom' of phytoplankton. Some 'blooms', in turn, contain toxins, deoxygenate the water column and pose a serious threat to the fish stock. Salmon stocks in the sea can also be affected by algal blooms. In warm, calm spells of several weeks with long periods of sunshine, as occur in north-west Scotland at intervals of a few years, a thermocline can develop in the sheltered waters of the sea lochs. The water above the thermocline becomes enriched both naturally and by wastes from the fish farm, and a bloom can develop with toxic and anoxic conditions, which will quickly kill caged stocks of salmon. Such a die-off occurred in Loch Torridon in 1988. In freshwaters an increased supply of phosphorus can trigger blooms which may seriously affect caged smolt and trout stocks.

The natural community of the seabed, which is greatly varied and is symptomatic of stable healthy conditions, is partially or totally replaced by another community, accompanied by 'gassing'—a decline of oxygen accompanied by an increase of methane and hydrogen sulphide. Gassing, of course, can have an adverse effect on the farmed fish, and care must be taken with cages sited in shallow areas with a slow exchange of water. The replacement community is less varied than the natural, and is described in detail by Gowen et al. for a salmon farm in Loch Spelve, Mull, and by Earll et al. for farms in the Outer Hebrides. The survey in Loch Spelve has given information on the effects of the fish farm on the entire loch, and shows how the effects rapidly fall-off with distance from the farm. Effects were localised, and over 150m from the cages the community was natural to the loch. The benthic fauna beneath salmon cages was dominated (sometimes 100%) by the opportunistic polychaetes, *Capitella capitata* and *Scololepis fuliginosa*. Beneath the rafts of mussel farms in the Outer Hebrides, starfish (*Asterias rubens*) and shore crabs (*Carcinus maenas*) seem to tolerate some anoxic regimes, feed off the invertebrate fauna (of which there may be over 100 species) and faeces which become dislodged from the mussel ropes. At moorings with a good tidal exchange, shoals of saithe (*Polla-chius virens*) and schools of other in-shore fish congregate to feed on the fall-out from the cages and rafts, and the activities of all these scavengers in the sea bed and water column help to dissipate the concentrations of organic waste. Such conditions occur naturally in many dumps of rotting organic material with the production of much toxic gas. Dead seaweed stagnates in still 'sinks' in sheltered inlets, and the bacterium *Beggiatoa* grows in ghostly white sheets over the decaying weed as it also does beneath some cages and rafts. It is a sure indicator of anoxic conditions—though to thrive, it requires both methane and oxygen; the former it obtains from the sediments and the latter from the seawater.

The effect of fish farms on the seabed is rapid, but depends on the rate of water exchange and the scale of farming. Three months from the start of a typical salmon farm, the sediments beneath the cages are anoxic, and the pollution-tolerant poly-chaetes become dominant. In six months, the 'pollution' com-munity and the gradient of the community outwards from the farm is established. The recovery of the seabed from fish farming can be rapid, however. The organic wastes are mobil-ised and gradually dissipated within the sediments, and the natural benthic community reoccupies the site, but not exactly in the same form as before the farm was begun. Gowen *et al.* (1988) state that after six months use, sediments took three months to regain the natural state, but the fauna remained dominated by a 'pollution' fauna, while after three years conti-nuous use, the sediments took eight months to revert, but the 'pollution' fauna dominated beyond that time.

Observations have of necessity been taken from farms of less than twenty years standing, placed in otherwise unfarmed seas. The recovery of a disused site in a sheltered sea loch, which has had a heavy complement of farms for a century, may be different. The long-term effects of continuous use of sheltered sealochs and inlets for salmon farming, where there is limited exchange of seawater and many natural 'sinks', cannot be easily predicted from examination of the short-term effects. In this book we are dealing with the scientific aspects, but the scenic and amenity aspects are of no less importance and are closely related to our ecological account.

Salmon farming has been superimposed upon the natural population of *Salmo salar* breeding in Scottish rivers and feed-ing in the North Atlantic. Farmed salmon stocks tend to be selected for placid behaviour, late sexual development and fast growth to a standard marketable type. Large numbers of parr which do not develop into smolts in one year are often released into the wild, and this accidental or deliberate release of farmed fish over decades may pose a threat to the genetic make-up of wild salmon (Maitland, 1987).

Genetic effects are another largely unknown sector of salmon farming, which requires urgent research and is closely related to the control of diseases. The levels of immunity of different stocks of fish to different viruses, bacteria and fungae is likely to vary between farmed stocks and between farmed and wild fish. For example, Norwegian and Scottish stocks farmed in the same sea loch may be immune to their own but vulnerable to each other's pathogens. In 1986, of the 38.6 million eggs used by the industry, 1.7 million (4.4%) were from 'Norwegian sources' (SWCL, 1988), and in the last decade, the ecto-parasitic fluke (*Gyrodactylus salaris*) has spread from farmed parr to wild salmon in Norwegian rivers. Entire rivers have had to be cleared of salmon at enormous financial and ecological cost, in efforts to eradicate the parasite. The infections are thought to have been caused by the import of infected fish from one or more of 28 watercourses and 11 hatcheries that hold the

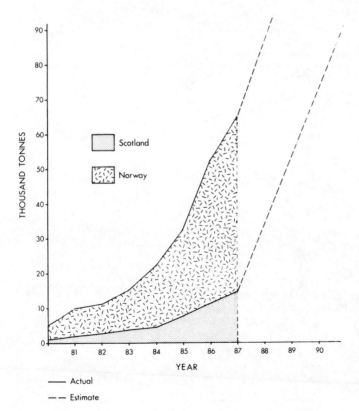

Fig. 53
Production of Atlantic farmed salmon in Scotland and Norway 1980–1987 (Nature Conservancy Council, 1989)

370 THE HEBRIDES

parasite. The ecological effects of the introduction of large
numbers of alien smolts into the runs of wild salmon are also
unknown, and little or no allowance is made for the possible
disruption of the migratory processes of native fish.

The fish farms occur within the long established ranges of
wild predators of fish, and are a great attraction to them.
Cormorant (*Phalacrocorax carbo*), shags (*P. aristotelis*), heron
(*Ardea cinerea*), common seal (*Phoca vitulina*), grey seals (*Halichoerus grypus*), otter (*Lutra lutra*) and feral mink (*Mustela vison*)
are the predators of salmon and trout farms, while mussel

Fig. 54
*Location of fish farms
in the Hebrides
(Nature Conservancy
Council, 1989)*

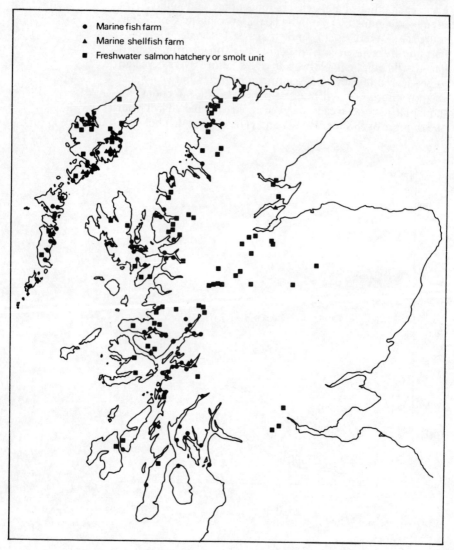

- Marine fish farm
▲ Marine shellfish farm
■ Freshwater salmon hatchery or smolt unit

farms are vulnerable to eiders (*Somateria mollissima*). Fish stocks are defended by the netting of cages, scaring devices, trapping, poisoning and shooting. The powerful effect that these attractions have on the natural instincts of these predators in their native habitat, coupled with their continuous destruction, has caused much controversy. Fortunately, all of these species have an ample food supply in the Hebrides. However, salmon farms in close proximity to a cormorant colony such as that at Loch an Tomain in North Uist, or to the otter shores at Kylerhea, Skye, and Loch Scridain in Mull, or the seal rocks in the Firth of Lorne and Colonsay, are likely to pose problems in predator control, as would mussel farms near eider islands at Kyleakin in Skye. A presumption against the siting of fish farms within 8km of major, long-established assemblies of protected birds, otters and seals could avoid constant harassment of farms, and the killing of the predators.

With a few exceptions, trout farming is a mainland occupation, while salmon and shellfish farms are concentrated on the western seaboard, the Hebrides, Orkney and Shetland (Fig. 54). Table 19.5 shows the numbers of fish farms in the Hebrides in 1986, but these figures have changed rapidly upwards, since several hundred applications for leases in Scotland have been approved by the Crown Estate Commissioners (CEC) who administer the seabed. At least 250 applications for such leases were made in 1987 (SCWL, 1988).

Fish farming in Loch Ainort, Skye (Photo R. E. Garner)

Island	Salmon in freshwater	Salmon in sea water	Trout	Shellfish	Totals
Lewis	5	20	6	13	44
Harris	2	6		7	15
North Uist		4		3	7
Benbecula		1		5	6
South Uist	1	8		6	15
Barra		3		3	6
Out.Hebrides	8	42	6	37	93
Summer Isles		1			1
Raasay					
Skye	2	8	1	6	17
Small Isles					
Tiree					
Coll					
Mull	1	3	1	4	9
Jura		1			1
Islay				1	1
Colonsay				1	1
Kerrera		1		3	4
Gigha		1		1	2
Inn.Hebrides	3	15	2	16	36
Hebrides	11	57	8	53	129
Scotland	66	127	73	150	416

Table 19.5 Numbers of fish farms in the Hebrides in 1986—compiled from *Marine Fishfarming in Scotland* (Scottish Wildlife and Countryside Link, 1988) and *An Environmental Assessment of Fish Farms* (Countryside Commission for Scotland *et al.*).

The widespread, open-ended potential of fish farming in the Highlands and Islands generates hope for industrial development and employment, however, to a public that is now more aware than ever before of the need for environmental care, it also generates caution, about how far and how fast it can be taken without damage to scenery, wildlife, other human interests and ultimately to itself.

Nature Conservation

Conservation of nature is a culture of the twentieth century possessing its own philosophical, ethical and scientific frame, distinct from those of agriculture, fisheries and forestry. It is directed towards the maintenance of numbers of different species, distributed in different habitats of natural or semi-natural type, and towards the care of geological and physiographical features. It also requires the disciplining of nature, as in the control of aggressive, colonising species, but such action is usually on a local or limited scale. There has been little of such management in the Hebrides, largely because the need has not arisen; it has not been necessary to turn back the tide of development by preserving small islands of habitat in the midst of urban or agricultural lands, nor has conservation been involved to any great degree in revitalising countryside devastated by pesticides, fertilisers, drainage or general unsympathetic

A geological SSSI on Kerrera—lower Old Red Sandstone conglomerate lies unconformably over folded slates and limestone (Photo British Geological Survey)

Figure 55 *a* & *b* Map
showing the distribution
of Sites of Special
Scientific Interest in the
Hebrides, indicating
those of biological,
geological, and 'mixed'
interest (updated from
Boyd, 1979 and Boyd
and Kerr, 1983).
Fig. 55*a*: Outer
Hebrides and Skye
1. Achmore Bog 2. Allt
Volagir, 3. Baleshare
and Kirkibost,
4. Balranald Bog and
Loch nam Feithean,
5. Bornish and
Ormiclate Machair,
6. Eoligarry, 7. Flannan
Islands, 8. Glen
Valtos 9. Gress
Saltings, 10. Howmore
Estuary, 11. Little Loch
Roag Valley Bog,
12. Loch a' Sgurr
Pegmatite, 13. Loch an
Duin, 14. Loch Bee,
15. Loch Dalbeg,
16. Loch Druidibeg,
17. Loch Hallan Fens,
18. Lochs Laxavat Ard
and Iorach, 19. Loch
Meurach, 20. Loch na
Cartach, 21. Loch nan
Eilean Valley Bog,
22. Loch Obisary,
23. Loch Orasay,
24. Loch Scadavay,
25. Loch Scarrasdale
Bog, 26. Loch
Stiapavat, 27. Loch
Tuamister, 28. Lochs
at Clachan,
29. Luskentyre Banks
and Saltings,
30. Machairs Robach
and Newton,
31. Mangersta Sands,
32. Mingulay and
Berneray, 33. Monach
Isles, 34. North Harris,
35. North Rona and Sula
Sgeir, 36. Northton Bay,
37. Rockall, 38. Shiant
Isles, 39. Small Seal
Islands, 40. St Kilda,
41. Stornoway Castle
Woods, 42. Tolsta
Head, 43. Tong
Saltings, 44. West
Lochs, 45. Aird
Thuirinis—Port na
Long, 46. Airdghunail,
47. Allt Geodh a
Ghamhna, 48. Allt
Grillan Gorge, 49. An
Cleireach, 50. Bagh
Tharsgabhaig,
51. Bealach Udal,
52. Boirearaig-carn
Dearg, 53. Coille
Dalavil, 54. Coille
Thocabhaig, 55. Cuillins

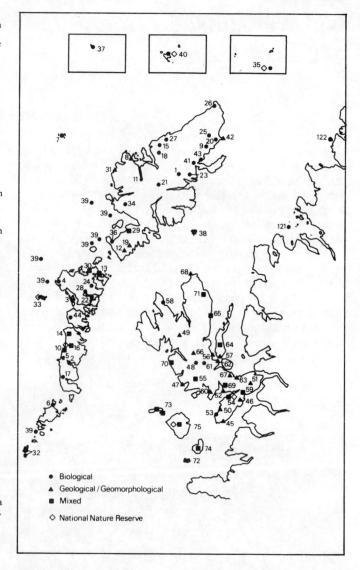

exploitation. The Hebrides are far from pristine, but they are comparatively unspoilt.

Maintaining and improving the natural diversity of the Hebrides is done by influencing man's use of land and sea through the selection and management of Sites of Special Scientific Interest (SSSIs). There is also statutory protection of species throughout the islands as a whole, as well as the provision of advice on all aspects of nature conservation, by the NCC and other conservation bodies.

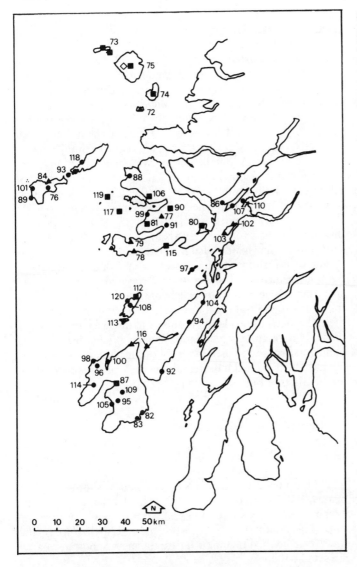

SSSIs are selected on two criteria: scientific, in terms of geology (p. 373), geomorphology, botany, and zoology; and philosophical, in terms of rarity, fragility, diversity, naturalness and representativeness (Ratcliffe, 1977). The features of interest in earth science include rock types, crustal structures, landforms and erosion products, while in life science the features are species or lifeforms, and habitats or ecosystems within which the species live. Some species, for example the Arctic sandwort, St Kilda mouse and wren, and the grey seal, can be conserved within specific sites. Others, like the newts, golden eagle, corncrake, and pipistrelle bat, require some degree of protection wherever they occur.

SSSIs have existed since the National Parks and Access to the Countryside Act (Section 23) was placed on the *Statute Book* in 1949. However, it was not until the publication of *A Conservation Review* (NCR) (1977), that the SSSI series was put on a firm footing. The work was done by the Nature Conservancy Council (NCC) and the Natural Environment Research Council (NERC), which took some ten years to compile. It was edited by Dr Derek Ratcliffe, who wrote much of it, together with some thirty other authors, and twice that number of informants. Following the NCR, 'A Geological Conservation Review' was instituted by the NCC, and this is still in progress. While the NCR supports the biological SSSIs, the GCR does the same for the geological SSSIs and a Marine Nature Conservation Review is now also in progress.

The Conservation Review system is a product of specialists. Each has contributed in depth on a very narrow band of the spectrum of scientific knowledge contained in the Reviews. In this age of specialisation, there are few individuals who possess the full range of knowledge required to dispense the needs of nature conservation—even more so when the marine environment is added (see p. 383). In the following paragraphs describing the SSSIs in the Hebrides, all the sites mentioned by name are SSSIs (see Figs. 55*a* and *b*).

Biological Sites

Coastal

The Hebrides abound in rocky and sandy shores of great beauty and interest; cliffs and beach platforms, tidal flats, estuaries, shelving shores and seabeds are arrayed against the prevailing conditions of exposure to, and shelter from, the weather and sea. The following are the most important coastal sites and habitats.

Rocky shores and seacliffs with seabirds, sea-sprayed grasslands, and ledge flora:—North Rona and Sula Sgeir, Flannan Islands, Shiant Islands, St Kilda, Mingulay and Berneray, Tiree (Ceann a'Mhara), Rum, Canna, Ardmeanach (Mull), Ross of Mull, Treshnish Isles.

Shell sand dunes and machair:—Luskentyre Banks, Northton Bay and Berneray (all Harris), Monach Islands, Robach and Newton, Baleshare and Kirkibost (all North Uist), Grogarry and Stilligarry, Bornish and Ormiclate (all South Uist),

Eoligarry (Barra), Balevullin and Barrapol (Tiree), Gunna and Totamore (Coll), Calgary (Mull) and Oronsay.

Other sand dunes and 'links':—Loch Gruinart, Laggan and Rhinns (all Islay), Kilmory (Rum); saltings and estuaries:— Loch Gruinart and Loch Indaal (Islay), Howmore (South Uist), Vallay and Loch an Duin (North Uist), Northton Bay (Harris) and Gress (Lewis).

Small island ecosystems, some having breeding seals:— Oronsay, Garvellachs, islets in the Lynn of Lorne, Treshnish Isles, Berneray, Mingulay, Pabbay, the Monach Isles, small seal islands (Haskeir, Shillay, Coppay, Gasker), St Kilda, the Shiant Islands, the Flannan Isles, North Rona and Sula Sgeir, Eilein a'Chleirich (Priest Island), and Handa.

Uplands

The massif of North Harris is representative of upland composed entirely of Lewisian gneiss, situated in the Atlantic storm-belt. These are among the most denuded hills in Britain, possessing a vegetation which, though poor in species, is rich in oceanic mosses. Rum has a wonderful variety of upland habitats, generated by the interaction of weather and an

A stag with hinds on Rum (Photo T. H. Clutton-Brock)

assortment of rocky substrates, and these are enhanced by the debris of mountain-top colonies of Manx shearwaters and the grazing of red deer, which help to create and maintain high altitude 'greens'. The Trotternish ridge in Skye has an extensive inland cliff-system with calcicolous flora and holds the finest montane flora in the Hebrides—plant communities which have affinities with the uplands of mainland Britain, Faeroes and Iceland. This site is also rich in upland birds. At a lower level, sub-montane, basaltic uplands of special interest are also present at Ardmeanach, Mull; Eigg and Canna.

Woodland

Western oakwood persists in the Inner Hebrides, as fragments of a much more extensive aboriginal woodland. The interest of these woodlands is seen in a European context; the British Isles may hold many species of Atlantic bryophytes and lichens, and the Hebridean woods represent an extreme of biological variation in both Britain and Europe.

Coille Ardura, Mull is one of the largest fragments of the oak-ash-hazel community, and its character is reflected in the smaller remnants at Kinuachdrach, Jura. Smaller fragments still occur at a'Choille Mhor, Colonsay and at Ardmore-Claggain, Islay. There are other woods at Craighouse Ravine

Kinloch Wood SSSI on the shores of Loch na Dal, Skye (Photo J. M. Boyd)

and Doire Dhonn, Jura; Craignure Cliffs and Laggan Wood, Mull and Coille Dalavil, Skye. Ashwood is scarce and is present only at Coille Ardura, Mull and Coille Thocabhaig and Loch na Dal, Skye (p. 378). There are no oak-ash-hazel stands in the Outer Hebrides, though such woodland may have grown there about 3,500 years ago.

In contrast, birch is widespread throughout the Hebrides, occurring often with oak in many of the above woods in the Inner Hebrides. Many small birch-rowan-willow woods have survived grazing and burning in stream gorges and in islands in freshwater lochs in both the Inner and Outer Hebrides. There are birch woods at Druimgigha (recently de-notified as an SSSI), Mull, the Geary Ravine and Allt Grillan, Skye. Far-western birchwoods also occur on the islands of Loch Druidibeg and at Allt Volagir, South Uist. Fine alderwoods are found at Ardmore, Kildalton and Calumhill, Islay; Kinuachdrach, Jura; and Loch na Dal, Skye. There are no stands of native pine in the Hebrides.

Inland Waters

The lochs are arranged in trophic (nutritional) order. Those with a rich status are termed *eutrophic*; intermediate, *mesotrophic*; poor, *oligotrophic*; very poor, *dystrophic*. However, because of the marine influence on the fresh waters of the Hebrides, resulting in higher than usual concentrations of some cations, many are anomalous in whatever trophic category they fall.

The alkaline machair lochs are generally mesotrophic and, more rarely, eutrophic in character, although they are not as biologically rich as one would normally expect for alkaline lochs, because generally they lack organic-based mud. They are represented in the Outer Hebrides by Lochs Stiapavat (Lewis), nam Feithean (North Uist), a'Mhachair, Stilligarry and Hallan (all South Uist); and in the Inner Hebrides by Lochs a' Phuill and Bhasapol (both in Tiree). Perhaps the only truly eutrophic loch in the Outer Hebrides is Loch a'Chinn Uacraich on Benbecula (R. N. B. Campbell, pers. comm.). Lochs situated on the ultrabasic rocks (very poor in calcium) of Rum, such as Loch Papadil, and on the limestones (very rich in calcium) of Raasay and Lismore (marl lochs) are especially interesting because of their unusual limnology.

The oligotrophic systems are situated between the shell sand machair and the acid peat moorland of which Lochs Bee and Roag-Fada (South Uist) are examples. All the other lochs on the list of SSSIs fall within the meso-oligotrophic range, situated in or fed directly from, moorland catchments. Lochs

Laxavat (Lewis), Scadavay (North Uist) and Druidibeg (South
Uist), are good examples of the many acid lochs included in the
series of SSSIs—some of these may be so acid as to be almost
lifeless. Brackish water systems occur at Lochs Bee, Roag and
Fada (South Uist) and Loch an Duin (North Uist).

Peatland and Bogs

Peatlands are widespread in the interiors of the islands. The
large SSSIs—North Harris, Loch Druidibeg, Rum, Canna,
Rhinns of Islay and Ardmeanach (Mull)—have many peatland
habitats, and central and north Lewis have vast areas of blanket
peat. In contrast to peatlands, bogs, which have not been
drained or cut for fuel and still retain their natural conformation and communities, are uncommon. There are several
types (see pp. 162–70) and some SSSIs hold more than one
type merging into each other. On Lewis, the blanket bog at
Achmore is 307ha. while the valley bogs at Loch Scarrasdale
and Little Loch Roag are 207ha. and 19ha. respectively. On
Skye, the valley bog at Loch an Eilein is 32ha. There is a raised
bog at Coladoir on Mull, a blanket raised bog at Eilein na
Muice Dubh (Duich Moss) on Islay (547ha.) and a watershed
bog on Rhinns, Islay (8,403ha.)

Geological Sites

Lewisian, Torridonian, Moine

This is a major group of rock forms found on almost all the
Outer Hebrides, Skye, Tiree, Coll, Iona, Colonsay, South
Rona, the Summer Isles, Handa, Raasay, and Islay (Smith and
Fettes, 1979; Bowes, 1983). At Loch na Dal, Sleat, the Kishorn
Thrust separates the Lewisian gneiss and the Torridonian
sandstone, and also in Sleat there is another classic section of
the Moine strata by the Tarskavaig Thrust. At Balephetrish on
Tiree, both ortho- and paragneisses, which have different ori-
gins, are exposed with veins of marble. At Ardlanish on Ross of
Mull, the Moine schists exhibit progressive contact alterations
as they approach the granite intrusion, and kyanite and
tourmaline gneisses also occur on the site. On Colonsay, the
Torridonian overlies unconformably the Lewisian, and the
junction of the greywacke and arkose facies of the Torridonian
is exposed. Kerrera has crumpled slates and limestones of
Dalradian age overlain uncomformably by Lower Old Red
Sandstone containing fossil fish. The sites in the Outer

Hebrides are at present under review but there are geological sites of special interest in the Lewisian complex at Tolsta Head, Glen Valtos, Loch Meurach, Loch a'Sgurr (pegmatite), Shiant Islands and Rockall.

Mesozoic

At Gribun on Mull, there is a key exposure for the student of Mesozoic palaeography. Moine schists are overlaid unconformably by Triassic sandstone and conglomerate with fine exposures of Triassic cornstone. In the bed of Allt nan Teangaidh, there is a series of strata from Triassic through Rhaetic to Cretaceous, with Upper Cretaceous Limestone resting unconformably on the Triassic rocks. This complements the nearby exposure of the Blue Lias lithologies at Aird na h'Iolaire. On the shore at Breakish in south-east Skye there is an exposure of the Lower Lias with the Lusa coral bed. Jurassic strata from Middle Lias to the base of the Great Estuarine Series are exposed at Rigg Holm Coast on Skye, and the sequence is continued at the Elgol coast (p. 381), which has exposures from the Great Estuarine Series to the Oxford Clays. Raasay has a compound site demonstrating the Mesozoic rocks of the Hebrides and a variety of Tertiary rocks with which they have been intruded. The youngest Jurassic rocks in the Hebrides are exposed on Mull, where shales of Kimeridge clay can be

Elgol coast geological SSSI, exposures of the Great Estuarine Series (Jurassic) on the shore of Loch Scavaig (Photo J. M. Boyd)

seen at Eas Mor, and the coast between Staffin and Kildorais
holds classic sections of Oxford (rich in micro-fauna), Corell-
ian and Lower Kimeridge Clays.

Tertiary

The Tertiary complexes of Rum, Skye, Canna, Mull and St
Kilda are described in greater detail elsewhere in this book (see
p. 38). Rum, Canna and St Kilda are geological SSSIs in their
entirety. Along the coast of the Ross of Mull, the lava plateau
overlies Tertiary sediments, including a wide range of lithologies, and rests on Cenomanian sandstone. A continuous
section through the lower part of the plateau lavas is exposed at
Ardmeanach, where lava tubes, flow units and scoria are seen,
and pillow lavas occur at Glen Forsa, Mull. Ardmeanach also
has fine displays of columnar jointing, which is a widespread
characteristic of western Mull, Treshnish Islands, Canna and
Sanday, north Skye and Heyskeir, and displayed *par excellence*

*Staffa is an SSSI
holding the world
famous Tertiary rocks
of Fingal's cave—
columnar basalt* par
excellence *(Photo
British Geological
Survey)*

on Staffa (Fig. 382). The volcanic centres of central Mull, Rum
and cuillins of Skye and St Kilda are all represented in the
series of geological SSSIs.

The Outer Hebrides are bereft of fossils, except, perhaps, in
the Permian and Triassic sandstones on Lewis. The Inner
Hebrides, however, have many sites of great interest in the
Mesozoic and Tertiary rocks. Ardtun, Ross of Mull has 'leaf

beds', with lotus lily *Nelumbium* and *Magnolia*, suggesting a subtropical climate in Tertiary times prior to and during the volcanic activity. Other beds contain fossils of the maidenhair tree *Ginkgo*, plane tree *Platanus*, hazel and oak. There are few examples in Europe of this Tertiary flora and Mull possesses the only fossil plants of Miocene and Pliocene age in Britain. MacCulloch's tree at Ardmeanach is thought to be of Eocene age (*c.* 60 million years). On Skye there are several fossil-rich sites including Rigg-Holm coast, Boreraig-Carn Dearg, and Staffin-Kildorais coast (Trotternish SSSI), and there is a key vertebrate fossil site of mid-late Bethonian age at Loch Scavaig.

Marine Conservation

There are no SSSIs below low water mark; no such measures have been taken for nature conservation in the sea and the seabed. However, under Sections 26 and 37 of the Wildlife and Countryside Act, the Secretary of State for Scotland can designate marine nature reserves up to the seaward limits of territorial waters. No such reserves have yet been created in Scotland, but the NCC has identified Marine Consultation Areas of which nine fall within the Hebrides (Fig. 56). Conservation of the marine environment lags far behind what has been achieved on land, and efforts are now being made to obtain a more satisfactory form of marine nature conservation.

The technical advances in Scuba diving in the last 30 years have made possible the exploration of the shallow coastal seas. There is now a thriving Marine Conservation Society and a growing cadre of scientists, who are at once expert in this technique and also in a specialist field of marine survey. The parallel growth of knowledge of marine species and sub-littoral habitats, which hitherto were almost closed to the observer, are now readily accessible to the Scuba diver. However, underwater surveys are far more demanding on manpower than those on land, and progress is slow by comparison. The remoteness and tempestuous nature of the Hebrides adds to the difficulties of diving surveys (Mitchell *et al.* 1983).

The Hebrides have a great variety of shore, seabed and water-column habitats influenced by tidal currents, freshwater run-off, and exposure to surf, and the whole realm needs classification and evaluation in scientific and philosophical terms. The Marine Nature Conservation Review is now in progress and will last ten years. In it the biota are divided into communities on rock and sediment, and each of these is subdivided into categories of exposure to surf, and of specialised niches e.g. crevices, tidal rips, and man-made

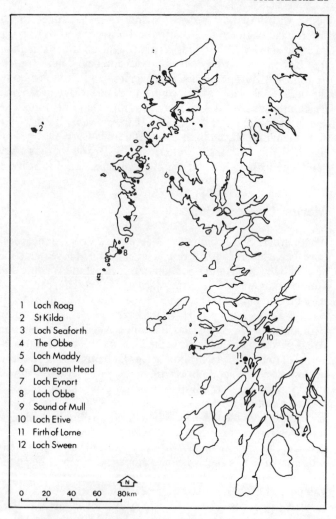

1   Loch Roag
2   St Kilda
3   Loch Seaforth
4   The Obbe
5   Loch Maddy
6   Dunvegan Head
7   Loch Eynort
8   Loch Obbe
9   Sound of Mull
10 Loch Etive
11 Firth of Lorne
12 Loch Sween

0   20   40   60   80km

Fig. 56
*Map showing the
distribution of Marine
Conservation Areas in
the Hebrides (from
Nature Conservancy
Council)*

structures. Future editions of this book should carry much
more information in these current endeavours in marine
nature conservation.

Nature Reserves

At present, there are eighteen reserves in the Western Isles of
Scotland: six National Nature Reserves (NNR) managed by
the NCC, four by the RSPB, five as island properties of the
National Trust for Scotland (NTS), one by the Scottish
Wildlife Trust (SWT) and one which has been recently

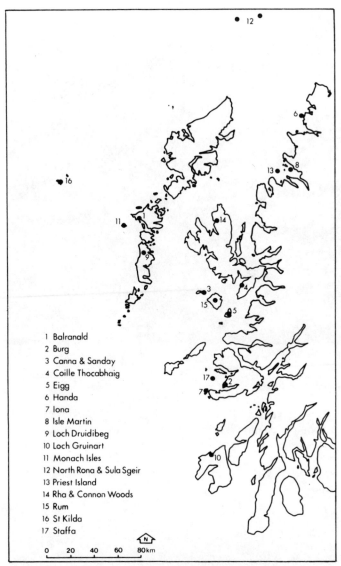

1 Balranald
2 Burg
3 Canna & Sanday
4 Coille Thocabhaig
5 Eigg
6 Handa
7 Iona
8 Isle Martin
9 Loch Druidibeg
10 Loch Gruinart
11 Monach Isles
12 North Rona & Sula Sgeir
13 Priest Island
14 Rha & Connon Woods
15 Rum
16 St Kilda
17 Staffa

0   20   40   60   80 km

Fig. 57
Map showing the
distribution of Nature
Reserves in the
Hebrides

acquired by the Woodland Trust. The NTS properties are not reserves *per se*, but all, except Iona, are SSSIs in whole or part, and are managed in consultation with NCC. The reserves may be owned by the conservation body, or leased or managed under a formal agreement with the owner. For example, St Kilda is owned by the NTS, and leased as a nature reserve by the NCC. 'Privatisation' of the NNRs would only affect Rum and part of Loch Druidibeg which are areas owned by the government-sponsored NCC.

Aerial view of Balranald showing a great variety of coastal habitats—sandy shore, dunes, machair, crofts, and wetland—including an RSPB Reserve and an SSSI (Photo Planair)

Balranald

The reserve (658ha.) in North Uist is an SSSI with machair, lagoon (Loch nam Feithean), swamp and fringing marshes. It has a high density of breeding waders, wildfowl and corn-crakes, and is privately owned croftland with the wildlife managed by the RSPB in agreement with owners and tenant crofters.

Burg

The area (617ha.) in Mull has been owned by the NTS since 1932. Called 'The Widerness', it was the first nature reserve in the Hebrides owned by a conservation body. It is situated at the western tip of the Ardmeanach peninsula, and has a spectacular rocky coastline of columnar basalt, in which is embedded 'MacCulloch's Tree' (see p. 39 & 383). It has fine marine and coastal communities, possessing relict woodland, calcicolous grassland with abundant lepidoptera, and good acidic grassland and montane flora. The whole property lies within the Ardmeanach SSSI.

Canna and Sanday

These islands were owned and managed for fifty years by Dr J.
L. Campbell as a private nature reserve in the context of an
island estate. Since 1981, they have been a Property of the NTS.
There are fine marine, coastal, and upland habitats, colonies of
seabirds and well-grown mixed woodland. These islands are a
complex of columnar-basalt landforms. Both islands (except
the enclosed agricultural land) are an SSSI (1,469ha.)

Coille Thocabhaig

This reserve (8tha.) in Skye, known also as Ord Wood, lies on
neighbouring outcrops of the Durness limestone and Torridonian sandstone. There is ash on the limestone and oak on the
sandstone, and the reserve has been established to maintain the
varied broadleaved woodland of native species, and the several
distinct associations of plants in the ash and oak habitats. It is
one of the richest localities in Scotland for 'oceanic' mosses.
Though it is sheep pasture, three grazing enclosures of 10ha.
have been made so far (two on limestone and one on sandstone)
to assist in regenerating the woodland. This is an SSSI and an
NNR managed by the NCC in agreement with the owners.

Eigg

Three areas (total 1,517ha.) of Eigg are a nature reserve: one
area includes the Sgurr with surrounding upland and wetland
habitats; a second is situated in the interior of the island and is
dominated by willow/birch/hawthorn woodland; a third is the
area below the cliffs of Beinn Bhuide, running the length of the
east coast of the island, round the north point, and below the
west-facing cliffs of Cleadale. This last contains a colony of
Manx shearwaters and gallery woodlands of hazel, elm and oak
on basalt screes. All areas are part of the complex of SSSIs on
Eigg and they are managed by the SWT under an agreement
with the owner and tenant crofters.

Handa

The reserve (310ha.) has large colonies of seabirds arrayed in
horizontally bedded Torridonian sandstone in perpendicular
cliffs, providing ideal nesting habitat for kittiwakes, guillemots
and razorbills. It is managed by the RSPB under an agreement
with the owner, and is an SSSI.

Iona

Most of the island is a property of the NTS and is enclosed cultivated land with machair and maritime heath on Torridonian/Lewisian rocks with veins of marble. It is not a nature reserve or an SSSI, but is a fine specimen of the small fertile Hebridean isle, complete with its historical abbey and burial grounds, which attract thousands of visitors annually.

Isle Martin

This reserve (52ha.) is situated at the mouth of Loch Broom and is owned by the RSPB. It is a typical assemblage of coastal and acid grassland and heathland habitats, situated on the Torridonian rocks of the north-west Highlands. The island is set in the wild scenery of Coigach.

Loch Druidibeg

The reserve (1,677ha.) is an SSSI situated in the crofting townships of Grogarry, Stilligarry and Howmore on South Uist (see Chapter 10). It is of international importance, recognised under the Ramsar Convention on Wetlands, for its open freshwater system which has a wide range of trophic levels with related communities of plants and animals, including the native greylag goose. It is of national importance for its coastal habitats including lagoon, dune and machair. The reserve also contains peatland, cultivated croftland and scrub woodland on islands in the Loch. It is partly owned by the NCC and the remainder is managed under agreement with the owners and crofters.

Loch Gruinart

The reserve (1,554ha.) lies to the south and west of Loch Gruinart in Islay. There are two main habitats—grassland on Gruinart Flats, and moorland. There are also important saltings, marshes, lochans and small woods. The reserve is owned by the RSPB, who manage the land for wild geese with the use of a suckler herd of 260 cattle and the reseeding of the grasslands. In the season 1987–88, at least 7,000 barnacle geese (one third of the population of Islay) used the reserve from October to March, and in October-November some 17,000 used the reserve for feeding and roosting. There are also many other

species of wildfowl, waders, raptors and songbirds that regularly use the reserve. The reserve includes part of a large SSSI, and its aims in the conservation of wild geese are augmented by agreements between the NCC and local tenant farmers, whose ground falls within the SSSI. These agreements stipulate that the tenants will forgo their rights as agricultural occupiers to protect their crops, including rotational leys, permanent pasture and rough grazings, from damage from barnacle and white-fronted geese, and in return receive compensation on the net profit foregone (p. 341).

The RSPB Reserve at Loch Gruinart, Islay (Photo Morley Hedley)

Monach Isles

These are five uninhabited islands in North Uist: Ceann Ear (193ha.), Ceann Iar (135ha.), Shivinish (28ha.), Shillay (16ha.), and Stockay (3ha.). The reserve (375ha.) is an SSSI, which includes systems of shell-sand dunes and machair with a rich flora and the most western oceanic fresh water lochs in Britain. In autumn these islands are the largest nursery colony of the grey seal in Britain, with over 2,500 pups born annually. In winter they are a refuge for about 2,000 barnacle geese, and in summer they have many nesting species of birds. Most of the Monach Isles are owned privately and Shillay is owned by the Northern Lighthouse Board. The wildlife is managed by the NCC under agreement (see Chapter 14).

North Rona and Sula Sgeir

These are two uninhabited islands. The reserve (130ha.) is an SSSI and holds oceanic vegetation and important breeding assemblies of seabirds and grey seals. It is privately owned and the wildlife is managed by the NCC by agreement with the owners. Both islands now have automatic lighthouses.

Priest Island

This reserve (121ha.) is also known as Eilean a' Chleirich, and is the outermost of the Summer Isles. It is an uninhabited trenched platform of Torridonian sandstone with a rocky exposed coast, a number of small lochans, a tidal lagoon, heathery ridges and hillocks and wet, sedgy hollows. Breeding colonies of seabirds attracted Frank Fraser Darling to the island for his studies of gull flocks in 1936–37. The reserve is owned by the RSPB and is an SSSI.

Rha and Conon Woods

Two gorge woods at Uig in Skye which have been acquired as a reserve by the Woodland Trust. The gorges are very steepsided, may have contained woods since before man came to the Hebrides, and have a history of ancient woodland. Today they hold a community of rowan, alder, hawthorn, sycamore and hazel with a diverse ground flora, on Tertiary lavas and Jurassic sediment, in country which is generally lacking in trees.

Rum

We have devoted Chapter 15 to Rum; here we provide some basic facts only. The island (10,684ha.) is an SSSI and is owned by the Nature Conservancy Council. It is a National Nature Reserve under section 19 of the National Parks and Access to the Countryside Act, 1949. Rum has also been designated as a Biosphere Reserve (BR), under the Man and Biosphere Programme of UNESCO. The main features are the wide range of rocks, soils and vegetation; the large breeding colonies of Manx shearwaters; an insular population of red deer; an array of sylvicultural experiments in the exposed environment of the

Hebrides; a succinct island ecosystem of which the inventory of plants and animals is highly advanced. Rum is a research reserve into which visitors can venture within the management regime of the NCC. Over the last thirty years, public funds have been invested in Rum because of its part in conserving the national heritage in wildlife. The island is a world-class nature reserve in which management should continue in the hands of the NCC or a national conservation body of equivalent status; a private owner could not be expected to fulfil the purposes for which the reserve was created.

St Kilda

There are four islands: Hirta (638ha., 426m), Soay (99ha., 373m), Boreray (77ha., 380m), and Dun (32ha.; 175m). There are many sea-stacks of which Stac an Armin (190m) and Stac Lee (172m) are the largest. We have described the reserve (853ha.) in Chapter 16. It is an SSSI of international importance for its oceanic vegetation, assemblies of breeding seabirds, indigenous fauna of the St Kilda field mouse, the St Kilda wren, and Soay sheep. Part of the value of the reserve is in the opportunities it presents for scientific studies of its wildlife. It also has a well studied history of occupation by man and a considerable literature. St Kilda is owned by the NTS and is managed as a nature reserve by the NCC. At present Hirta has a military garrison which operates within agreed limits. The tripartite operation of the islands between the NTS (owners), NCC (lessees) and the Army (sub-leasees) has been very successful. Indeed, St Kilda was the first natural area in UK to be accepted by UNESCO under the World Heritage Convention in 1987.

Staffa

The island (45ha.) was made world famous by Felix Mendelssohn and his overture *The Hebrides* or *Fingal's Cave* composed in 1830, which has a fixed place in the repertoire of popular classical music, so evocative is it of the sea, the islands, and the great echoing vault of Fingal's Cave cutting deep into the island. The geological structures in columnar basalt are exquisite; Fingal's Cave is like a cathedral. The island is owned by the NTS and it is an SSSI on both geological and biological grounds (p. 382).

Protected Species

The conservation of habitat in SSSIs and nature reserves contributes much to the conservation of all species and communities in the Hebrides. Some SSSIs have been created to conserve certain species, for example, the gannet at St Kilda and Sula Sgeir and the grey seal at the Monach Isles, Gasker and North Rona. However, other species which are widespread in distribution, and uncertain in annual location, cannot be easily managed by site conservation; for example, divers, eagles and other raptors, corncrakes, otters, bats and newts. Such species require the added protection of the law wherever they occur.

Table 20.1 shows those species in the Hebrides which have this statutory safeguard under the Wildlife and Countryside Act 1981. This list will change in time, on the one hand by statutory amendment, on the other by the discovery in the Hebrides of protected species not previously recorded. For example, the wood sandpiper (*Tringa glareola*), fieldfare (*Turdus pilaris*), redwing (*Turdus iliaca*), Daubenton's bat (*Myotis daubentoni*) and the arctic-alpine plant (*Diapensia lapponica*) may soon be found to reproduce in the Hebrides. The complete list of protected species in Great Britain is given in the above Act (HMSO, 1981). Red deer and roe deer are covered by The Deer Act 1963, grey seals and common seals by The Conservation of Seals Act 1970, and badgers (unrecorded from the Hebrides, so far) by The Badgers Act 1973.

Schedule 1—Birds which breed in the Hebrides, and which are protected by special penalties.

English	Scientific	Gaelic
A. At all times		
Red-throated diver	Gavia stellata	Learga-chaol
Black-throated diver	Gavia arctica	Learga-dhubh
Leach's petrel	Oceanodroma leucorhoa	Gobhlan-mara
Whooper swan	Cygnus cygnus	Eala-fhiadhaich
Scaup	Aythya marila	Lach-mhara
Common scoter	Melanitta nigra	Lach-bheag-dhubh
White-tailed eagle	Haliaetus albicilla	Iolaire-mhara
Hen harrier	Circus cyaneus	Clamhan-nan-cearc
Golden eagle	Aquila chrysaetos	Iolaire-bhuidhe
Merlin	Falco columbarius	Meirneal
Peregrine	Falco peregrinus	Seabhag
Corncrake	Crex crex	Traona
Black-tailed godwit	Limosa limosa	Cearra-ghob
Greenshank	Tringa nebularia	Deoch-bhiugh
Whimbrel	Numenius phaeopus	Eun-bealltainn

English	Scientific	Gaelic
Red-necked phalarope	*Phalaropus lobatus*	*Deargan*
Roseate tern	*Sterna dougallii*	*Stearnal-Dhughaill*
Little tern	*S. albifrons*	*Stearnal-beag*
Barn owl	*Tyto alba*	*Comhachag*
Chough	*Pyrrhocorax pyrrhocorax*	*Cathag-dhearg-chasach*
B. During the Close Season		
Greylag goose	*Anser anser*+	*Geadh-glas*
Pintail	*Anas acuta*	*Lach-stiuireach*

+Outer Hebrides only

Schedule 5—Animals in the Hebrides, which are protected against killing, injury, taking possession of or sale.

Common toad	*Bufo bufo**	*Muile-mhag*
Common frog	*Rana temporaria**	*Losgann*
Palmate newt	*Triturus helveticus**	} *Dearc-luachrach*
Smooth newt	*T. vulgaris**	
Viviparous lizard	*Lacerta vivipara*	
Slow worm	*Anguis fragilis**	*Nathair-challtainn*
Adder	*Vipera berus**	*Nathair-nimhe*
Whales/dolphins/porpoises:	All species	
Walrus	*Odobenus rosmarus*	
Otter	*Lutra lutra*	*Dobhran*
Pipistrelle bat	*Pipistrellus pipistrellus*	*Ialtag-phipistrelle*
Long-eared bat	*Plecotus auritus*	*Ialtag-chluasach*
Turtles	All species	

*Against sale or possession without intent to sell only.

Schedule 8—Plants of the Hebrides which are protected

Alpine catchfly	*Lychnis alpina*
Alpine rockcress	*Arabis alpina*
Arctic sandwort	*Arenaria norvegica*
Purple coltsfoot	*Homogyne alpina*
Greater yellow-rattle	*Rhinanthus serotinus*

Table 20.1 Birds, animals and plants in the Hebrides which are protected under the Wildlife & Countryside Act, 1981.

Epilogue

In that milestone of Scottish natural history, *The Influence of Man on Animal Life in Scotland* (1920), James Ritchie, writing in the dawn of modern ecology, stated that no influence has been more potent in changing the face of Scotland and in altering relationships of wild life of the country, than the care of domesticated animals. This has resulted in levelling of forests, draining of swamps, and turning the wilderness of mountain and moor into fertile grazings. Remote though the Hebrides have been in history, they have not escaped these human influences. In the traumatic history of the Hebridean people over the last three centuries, few, if any, islets holding a few acres of pasture have been left ungrazed or uncultivated. The stark, treeless character of the islands is in great part due to the grazing of livestock, and the seasonal burning of the hill pastures, which is part of sheep husbandry. However, human influence need not always be damaging to Nature, and indeed, when moderately applied, it is often beneficial. For example, without grazing animals in limited numbers there would be no flower-bespangled machairs for which the Hebrides are famous.

Thin, depleted pastures, severely trampled land, and widespread erosion are the symptoms of overgrazing (p. 395). They have been prevalent for at least two centuries and are common today throughout the islands, especially where rabbits are present. On the other hand, if machair is left ungrazed, it loses its natural diversity of flora and fauna, and usually becomes a rank grassland, possessing none of the beauty and interest of the neighbouring grazed swards. Machair is at its best for both man and animal when used as a winter grazing, and left during the summer to grow, flower and set seed.

The end of the Second World War was a time for new beginnings. A new regard emerged for our quality of life, and for the world we live in. This found many outlets—one of which was the conservation movement, driven partly by a sheer love of country, and partly by a desire to protect it against what might be the worst excesses of a new industrial age. However, while the seeds of the 'environmental' ethos were generated in philosophy and science and broadcast by the media as a theme of growing popularity in the 1950s, it fell on ground already fully

possessed by more powerful political, social and economic organisms. The conservation message came rather late in the day; the industrial revolution had all but run its course in Britain by the time the people became sufficiently aware of the enormous irreversible change that they had wrought upon their environment. In *The New Environmental Age*, Max Nicholson (1988) gives an effervescent commentary on the struggle that the movement has had to find its rightful place in the public life. The conservation message was widely known, poorly understood, reluctantly recognised, and grudgingly acted upon. Viewing the world scene, he writes:

Erosion of the machair plain at Crossapol, Tiree, caused by cattle seeking shelter from the wind in an otherwise exposed pasture. The dark band is an old over-blown soil. A picture of the 1950s; the erosion platforms have now disappeared (Photo J. M. Boyd)

The spectacle of many groups of intelligent people doing their utmost to destroy the vital life support systems of their posterity on earth, and angrily opposing efforts by more enlightened groups to mitigate or prevent the mischief, is a truly remarkable phenomenon of our age, and one which we can be sure our successors, if they are permitted to survive on earth, will find difficult to credit.

Fortunately, the dramatic effects of human exploitation that evoke such a view are in much lower profile in the Hebrides than they are in mainland Britain, and much less so than in the Third World. In the age of industrial pollution, gone is the notion of pure, clean air and sea; yet the Hebrides is the part of Britain least affected by acid precipitation, and marine pollution by PCBs. Gone in the leisure age is the notion of solitude and peace; yet the Hebrides is also the part of Britain least affected by tourism and recreation. Gone in the age of the welfare state and social services is the image of the thatched

A cottage at Elgol, Skye, sheltered by a wind-shaped sycamore and looking to Loch Scavaig and the Black Cuillins with Loch Coruisk hidden in the glaciated horseshoe of peaks (Photo J. M. Boyd)

cottage and the peat stack—'the lone shieling on the misty isle'; yet the Hebrides retains its mystique and unique life style.

Today conservation, as part of the wider environmental or 'green' movement, has become a cardinal force in human affairs which is felt deeply in the Hebrides, particularly when the local people are asked to change their ways for the sake of wildlife. The struggle for human survival is innate in the island communities, which have a long memory of privation and exodus, and an equally long history of economic use of limited natural resources. The islands have been greatly changed by man, and locally they have been devastated. Nonetheless, they have remarkable powers of natural regeneration and today, when compared with the rest of Britain and Europe, they are remarkably natural and free of industrial spoil and pollution.

But what of the future? In hindsight we know that there have been great changes in the islands over the last ten thousand years which have resulted from changes in climate and in sea-level, and the portents of change in the near future are somewhat alarming. What it has taken Nature 300 million years to achieve in the build-up of the coal, oil and gas fields in the earth's crust, man will substantially combust in 300 years. In so doing, he will change the balance of atmospheric gasses, surface temperatures and sea levels. Such physical changes are likely to be accompanied by widespread biological changes, and archipelagos like the Hebrides are likely to be greatly affected.

One of the major scientific endeavours of the next decade will be researching these changes caused by the burning of fossil fuels, the dramatic reduction over the last century in the earth's forests, and the use of chlorofluorocarbons (CFCs), since they relate to the well being and possibly to the survival of mankind. The effects of acidification of freshwaters and soils by atmospheric precipitation of the oxides of sulphur and nitrogen, the 'green house' effect—the warming of the earth's surface due to higher concentrations of carbon dioxide in the upper atmosphere—and the damage to the ozone layer in the upper atmosphere (a protective shield against solar radiation) by CFCs, are already evident. What is not yet known though, are the 'knock-on' effects that these changes will have on climate, marine hydrography, and the seasonal growth of vegetation and fauna, including crops of all sorts. The water balance between atmosphere and hydrosphere will be crucial in determining weather patterns, especially in the storm belt of the North Atlantic. The Hebrides might become somewhat warmer, but such warming might be off-set by increased cloud cover and higher rainfall. Higher sea-levels would inundate much low-lying terrain; islands would change their shapes, reefs would disappear and the charts would require to be redrawn. Higher winds would further inhibit the growth of woodland. On the other hand, if the warming is accompanied by a drier, less windy climate, the Hebrides might become much more clement for people than they are today, with better growth of crops, and an extension of woodland. If such changes do occur, this book will require to be rewritten and a new set of objectives will be required for nature conservation.

In the early days, conservation did not possess the strong statutory and financial backing from Government that it does today. When Rum was acquired by the Nature Conservancy in 1957, there was an angry outcry from sheep farming interests in the north of Scotland about the withdrawal of sheep stocks from the island. Since then there have been no sheep on Rum and, without any significant loss to the hill-sheep industry, the island is now a celebrated Nature Reserve known throughout the world. Today, in spite of considerable adverse pressures over the last thirty years, the vision of the founding fathers of the Rum Reserve has survived. In contrast to this, in that same

The rose-root and primrose blooming together in the solitudes of Glen Mor, St Kilda (Photo J. M. Boyd)

year, St Kilda was included in the Guided Weapons Range, Hebrides, and there was great concern about the future of that jewel of Nature. Would it be flawed for ever? But for the timely intervention of the National Trust for Scotland and the Nature Conservancy, it might well have been irreparably damaged. Instead of which, it is now the first natural site in the United Kingdom to be declared under the World Heritage Convention, and the greatest possible care is required in its management. The introduction of rats, particularly from the army vessels breaching on Hirta and in contractors' cargo, would pose a great threat to the seabirds and the St Kilda fieldmouse.

The crofters of Grogarry, Stilligarry and Howmore were highly suspicious of the overtures of the Nature Conservancy in the setting-up of the Loch Druidibeg National Nature

Reserve in South Uist. The task of getting a favourable opinion for this new proposal from three crofting townships and grazing clubs in a community possessing both Roman Catholic and Presbyterian congregations was difficult, yet these problems were overcome, and today Loch Druidibeg is a site of international importance under the Ramsar Convention. This reserve was indeed the forerunner of many conservation projects in crofting and farming areas in the Hebrides, culminating in the Integrated Development Programme (IDP) in the Outer Hebrides (1981–86), the Agricultural Development Plan in the Inner Hebrides (1987–1992), and the goose conservation and farming issue in Islay, all of which we describe in this book.

The Wildlife and Countryside Act (1981) and the heated debate that accompanied it changed the whole complexion of conservation in Great Britain. It put 'teeth' into the mechanism of safeguard of species and habitats, and resulted in greatly increased funding to compensate farmers and others for any reasonable loss they might sustain in conserving wildlife. It also made nature conservation more bureaucratic and caught-up in business than ever before, changing the lives of all who were professionally or voluntarily employed in nature conservation. It changed the leadership of the conservation movement with the appointment of administrators, industrialists, planners, media persons, and others from the wider scene of public affairs, to fill positions previously occupied by natural scientists, amateur naturalists of high standing, agriculturalists, and foresters.

The traumas endured by the Nature Conservancy in becoming a component body of the Natural Environment Research Council (NERC), and then becoming split into the Nature Conservancy Council and the Institute of Terrestrial Ecology, caused the scientists to divide. Those who went to the NCC, mainly as managers of the new nature conservation enterprise, were not accorded a high standing in science. Since the passing of the Act, the main echelons of natural scientists in conservation have been given new directives, just as those in agriculture and forestry had been given long ago. Now good naturalists and aspirant practitioners in botany, zoology and geology have the role of local administrators and managers, while the science of conservation is vested in a group of specialists at headquarters. This may be an inevitable development if nature conservation is to take its proper place in society. It is far better for conservation that scientists should accept an administrative role by which sites and species can be effectively safeguarded, than would otherwise be the case if each had a research role. However, the science of the local administrator is vital to the success of conservation among local people, and it should be continuously enhanced. The conservation catechism which is issued from the centre should encourage and not stifle the gifted, experienced naturalist, acting successfully as an administrator or manager. In the Hebrides, where there are few resident naturalists, the need for scientific field work by the resident staff of professional conservation bodies is much greater than in more densely populated parts of the country.

The centenary of Harvie-Brown and Buckley's *Vertebrate Faunas of the Outer Hebrides* (1888) and of *Argyll and the Inner Hebrides* (1892) coincides with the publication of this book. We salute these naturalists of the last century who provided such a fine series of books, which, though now collectors' items, are still mines of information which are drawn upon by historians. We hope that this book will continue to stimulate the interest in

The young naturalist I. L. B., as a boy, passes through a natural arch on the north shore of Rum (Photo J. M. Boyd)

the natural history of the Hebrides that was initiated by Harvie-Brown and Buckley, and later kept alive by James Ritchie, Seton Gordon, Fraser Darling and others who followed them.

A great deal of the enjoyment of nature study comes from the discovery, not necessarily of the rare or exotic, but of the common or familiar seen in a new light. Surprises like Wordsworth's encounter in a Highland glen of a solitary young woman cutting the corn, epitomise that joy of discovery that springs from nature and human nature being as one:

> Behold her, single in the field,
> Yon solitary Highland Lass!
> Reaping and singing by herself;
> Stop here, or gently pass!
> . . . . . .
>
> No Nightingale did ever chant
> More welcome notes to weary bands
> Of travellers in some shady haunt,
> Among Arabian sands;
> A voice so thrilling ne'er was heard
> In spring-time from the Cuckoo-bird,
> Breaking the silence of the seas
> Among the farthest Hebrides.
> . . . . . .

The Hebrides are no longer remote. They can be reached by aircraft in an hour or so, where it took weeks for Dr Samuel Johnson in 1773, and days for Hugh Miller in 1844 on the same journey. Yet, despite the great changes of today, these islands can still be described as 'the edge of the world'.

Bibliography

Ainslie, J. A., & Atkinson, R. (1937). On the breeding habits of Leach's fork-tailed petrel. *Brit. Birds.* 30, 234–248.

Anderson, A. (1957). Census of fulmars on Hirta, St Kilda in July 1956. *Scot. Nat.* 69, 113–116.

Anderson, A. (1962). A count of fulmars on Hirta, St Kilda in July 1961. *Scot. Nat.* 70, 120–125.

Anderton, R. & Bowes, D. R., (1983). Precambrian and Palaeozoic rocks of the Inner Hebrides. *Proc. Roy. Soc. Edinb.* 83B, 32–45.

Angus, I. S. (1979). The macrofauna of intertidal sand in the Outer Hebrides. *Proc. Roy. Soc. Edinb.*, 77B, 155–171.

Atkinson, R. (1940). Notes on the botany of North Rona and Sula Sgeir. *Trans. Proc. Bot. Soc. Edinb.* 30, 52–60.

Atkinson, R. (1949). Island Going. Collins, London.

Atkinson, R. (1980). *Shillay and the Seals.* Collins Harvill, London.

Bailey, R. S., Hislop, J. R. G., & Mason, J. (1979). The fish and shellfish resources in seas adjacent to the Outer Hebrides. *Proc. Roy. Soc. Edinb.* 77B, 479–494.

Balfour, E. J. (1979). Plants and People. In *Wildlife of Scotland* ed. F. Holliday pp. 173–186.

Balfour, J. H. (1844). Account of a botanical excursion to Skye and the Outer Hebrides during the month of August 1841 and a catalogue of the plants gathered in the islands of North Uist, Harris and Lewis, during the month of August 1841. *Trans. Bot. Soc. Edinb.* 1, 133–154.

Balfour-Brown, F. (1953). The aquatic coleoptera of the Western Scottish Islands with a discussion of their sources of origin and means of arrival. *Entomologist's Gaz.* 23. 1–71.

Ball, M. E. (1987). Botany, woodland and forestry. In *Rhum*, ed. T. H. Clutton-Brock & M. E. Ball. Edinburgh University Press.

Bannerman, J. (1986). *The Beatons: a medical kindred in the classical Gaelic tradition.* John Donald, Edinburgh.

Baxter, E. V. & Rintoul, E. J. (1953). *The Birds of Scotland.* Oliver & Boyd, Edinburgh.

Benn, S., Murray, S., and Tasker, M. L. (1989). *The Birds of North Rona and Sula Sgeir,* Nature Conservancy Council, Peterborough.

Bennett, A. (1905). Supplement to *Topographic Botany* 2nd ed. *J. Bot. Lond.* 48, Suppl.

Bennett, A., Salmon, C. E. & Matthews, J. R. (1929–30). 2nd Supplement to *Topographic Botany* 2nd ed. *J. Bot. Lond.* 62 & 63 Suppl.

Berry, R. J. (1969). History in the evolution of *Apodemus sylvaticus* at one edge of its range. *J. Zool. Lond.* 159, 311–328.

Berry, R. J. (1979). The Outer Hebrides: where genes and geography meet. *Proc. Roy. Soc. Edinb.* 77B, 21–43.

Berry, R. J. (1983). *Evolution of animals and plants in the Inner Hebrides. Proc. Roy. Soc. Edinb.* 83B, 433–447.

Berry, R. J. & Tricker, B. J. K. (1969). Competition and extinction: field mice of Foula, Fair Isle and St. Kilda. *J. Zool. Lond.* 158, 247–265.

Bertram, D. S. ed. (1939). The natural history of Canna and Sanday, Inner Hebrides. *Proc. Roy. Phys. Soc. Edinb.* 32: 1–71.

Bignal, E., Monaghan, P., Benn, S., Bignal, S., Still, E. & Thompson, P. M. (1987). Breeding success and podt-fledgling survival in the Chough. *Bird Study* 34, 39–42.

Birks, J. H. B. (1970). Inwashed pollen spectra of Loch Fada, Isle of Skye. *New Phytol.* 69, 807–820.

Birks, J. H. B. (1973). *Past and present vegetation of the Isle of Skye—a palaeoecological study*, pp. xii, 415. London, Cambridge University Press.

Birks. J. H. B. & Adam, P. (1978). Notes on the flora of Islay. *Trans. Bot. Soc. Edinb.* 43, 37–39.

Birks, J. H. B. & Marsden, B. J. (1979). Flandrian vegetational history of Little Loch

Roag, Isle of Lewis, Scotland. *J. Ecol.* 67, 825–842.

Birks, J. H. B. & Williams, W. (1983). Late-Quaternary vegetational history of the Inner Hebrides. *Proc. Roy. Soc. Edinb.* 83B, 293–318.

Bishop, G. M. (1987). The impact of an expansion of the Scottish fin fish aquaculture industry on wild fish stocks used to supply fishmeal components of feedstuffs. Unpubl. report to World Wildlife Fund (UK), pp. 14, Godalming, Surrey.

Bland, K. P., Christie, I. C. & Wormell, P. (1987). The lepidoptera of the Isle of Coll, Inner Hebrides. *Glasg. Nat.* 21, 309–330.

Boddington, D. (1960). Unusual mortality of young puffins on St Kilda, 1959, *Scottish Birds*, 1. 218–220.

Bonner, W. N. (1976). Stocks of grey seals and common seals in Great Britain. *Nat. Environment Res. Coun. Publs. C16*.

Booth, C. G. (1981). *Birds in Islay.* Argyll Reproductions Ltd.

Boswell, J. (1924). *Journal of a tour to the Hebrides with Samuel Johnson, LLD.* (1773). Oxford University Press.

Bourne, W. R. P. (1957). The birds of the Isle of Rhum. *Scot. Nat.* 69: 21–31.

Bourne, W. R. P. & Harris, M. P. (1979). Birds of the Hebrides: seabirds. *Proc. Roy. Soc. Edinb.* 77B, 445–475.

Bowes, D. R. (1983). Geological framework of the Inner Hebrides. *Proc. Roy. Soc. Edinb.* 83B, 25–29.

Bowes, D. R., Hopgood, A. M. & Pidgeon, R. T. (1976). Source ages of zircons in an Archaean quartzite, Rona, Inner Hebrides, Scotland. *Geol. Mag.* 113, 545–552.

Boyd, A. (1986). *Seann Taighean Tirisdeach.* Cairdean nan Tiaghean Tugha.

Boyd, H. & Ogilvie, M. A. (1972). Icelandic Greylag Geese wintering in Britain in 1960–71. *Wildfowl.* 23: 64–82.

Boyd, I. L. (1981). Population changes in the distribution of a herd of feral goats (*Capra* sp.) on Rhum, Inner Hebrides. *J. Zool. Lond.* 193, 287–304.

Boyd, I. L. (1984). The relationship between body condition and the timing of implantation in pregnant grey seals (*Halichoerus grypus*). *J. Zool. Lond.* 203, 113–123.

Boyd, I. L. (1985). Pregnancy and ovulation rates in two stocks of grey seals on the British coast. *J. Zool. Lond.* 205, 265–272.

Boyd, J. M. (1957). The ecological distribution of the Lumbricidae in the Hebrides. 66B, 311–338.

Boyd, J. M. (1958). The Birds of Tiree and Coll. *Brit. Birds.* 51: 41–56, 103–118.

Boyd, J. M. (1960a). The distribution and numbers of kittiwakes and guillemots at St Kilda. *Brit. Birds.* 53, 252–264.

Boyd, J. M. (1960b). Studies of the differences between the fauna of grazed and ungrazed grassland in Tiree, Argyll. *Proc. Zool. Soc. Lond.* 135, 33–54.

Boyd, J. M. (1961). The gannetry of St Kilda. *J. Anim. Ecol.* 30, 117–136.

Boyd, J. M. (1962). The seasonal occurrence and movements of seals in North-West Britain. *Proc. Zool. Soc. Lond.* 138, 385–404.

Boyd, J. M. (1963). The grey seal (*Halichoerus grypus* Fab.) in the Outer Hebrides in October 1961. *Proc. Zool. Soc. Lond.* 141, 635–662.

Boyd, J. M. (ed.) (1979). The Natural Environment of the Outer Hebrides. *Proc. Roy. Soc. Edinb.* 77B. 561pp.

Boyd, J. M. (1981a). The Boreray sheep of St Kilda, Outer Hebrides, Scotland: the natural history of a feral population. *Biol. Conservation* 20, 215–227.

Boyd, J. M. (1981b). The Boreray Blackface Sheep. *The Ark* 8, 357–359.

Boyd, J. M. (1983a). Natural environment of the Inner Hebrides: an introduction. *Proc. Roy. Soc. Edinb.* 83B, 3–22.

Boyd, J. M. (1983b). Two hundred years of biological sciences in Scotland. Nature Conservation. *Proc. Roy. Soc. Edinb.* 84B, 295–336.

Boyd, J. M. (1986). *Fraser Darling's Islands.* Edinburgh University Press, Edinburgh.

Boyd, J. M. & Bowes, D. R. (ed.) (1983). The Natural Environment of the Inner Hebrides. *Proc. Roy. Soc. Edinb.* 83B. 648pp.

Boyd, J. M. & Campbell, R. N. (1971). The grey seal (*Halichoerus grypus*) at North Rona 1959–1968. *J. Zool.* 164, 469–512.

Boyd, J. M. & Jewell, P. A. (1974). The Soay sheep and their environment: a synthesis. In *Island Survivors: etc* eds. P. A. Jewell, C. Milner & J. M. Boyd pp. 360–373. Athlone Press, London.

Boyd, J. M., Tewnion, A. & Wallace, D. I. M. (1956). The birds of St. Kilda, mid-summer 1956. *Scot. Nat.* 69, 94–112.

Bramwell, A. G. & Cowie, G. M. (1983). Forests of the Inner Hebrides—status and habitat. *Proc. Roy. Soc. Edinb.* 83B, 577–597.

Bray, E. (1986). *The Discovery of the Hebrides.* Collins, London.

Bristow, W. S. (1927). The spider fauna of the Western Islands of Scotland. *Scot. Nat.* 1927: 88–94, 117–122.

Brook, A. J. (1964). The phytoplankton of the Scottish freshwater lochs. In *The Vegetation of Scotland* ed. J. H. Burnett. Oliver & Boyd, Edinburgh.

Budge, D. (1960). *Jura, an island of Argyll: its History, People and Story*. Bristol: John Smith.

Bullock, D. J. (1983). Borerays, the other rare breed on St Kilda. *The Ark* 10, 274–278.

Burnett, J. H. (1964). *The Vegetation of Scotland*. Oliver & Boyd, Edinburgh.

Cadbury, C. J. (1980). The status and habitats of the Corncrake in Britain 1978–79. *Bird Study*. 27, 203–218.

Cadbury, C. J. (1988). Corncrake and Corn Bunting status and habitats on Tiree and Coll, Inner Hebrides. In *Birds of Coll and Tiree* (ed. D. A. Stroud). Nature Conservancy Council, Peterborough.

Caird, J. B. (1979). Landuse in the Uists since 1800. *Proc. Roy. Soc. Edinb.* 77B, 505–526.

Cameron, A. G. (1923). *The Wild Red Deer of Scotland*. Blackwood, London.

Campbell, J. L. ed. (1958). *Gaelic Words and Expressions from South Uist and Eriskay*. Dublin Institute for Advanced Studies.

Campbell, J. L. (1970 et seq.). Macrolepidoptera Cannae. *Entomologist's Rec.* 82, 1–27.

Campbell, J. L. (1984). *Canna—the story of a Hebridean island*. Oxford University Press, Oxford.

Campbell, J. L. & Thomson, D. S. (1963). *Edward Lhuyd in the Scottish Highlands 1699–1700*. Clarendon, Oxford.

Campbell, M. S. (1945). *The Flora of Uig (Lewis)*. Buncle, Arbroath.

Campbell, R. N. (1974). St Kilda and its sheep. In *Island Survivors* ed. P. A. Jewell, C. Milner, & J. M. Boyd pp. 6–35. Athlone Press, London.

Campbell, R. N. & Williamson, R. B. (1979). The fishes of the inland waters of the Outer Hebrides. *Proc. Roy. Soc. Edinb.* 77B, 377–393.

Campbell, R. N. & Williamson, R. B. (1983). Salmon and freshwater fishes of the Inner Hebrides. *Proc. Roy. Soc. Edinb.* 83B, 245–265.

Campbell, R. N. B. (1986). Surveys of 61 lochs in the Outer Hebrides, mainly on National Nature Reserves and Sites of Special Scientific Interest, June–Sept. 1986. Inverness: NCC North-West Region Report.

Carmichael, A., Watson, J. C. & Matheson, A. (1900 et seq) 6 Vols. *Carmina Gadelica*. Edinburgh.

Clapham, A. R., Tutin, T. G. & Warburg, E.

F. *Excursion Flora of the British Isles*. Cambridge University Press.

Clarke, J. G. D. (1946). Seal hunting in the Stone Age of north-west Europe; a study of economic prehistory. *Proc. Prehist. Soc. Lond.* 2, 12–48.

Clutton-Brock, T. H., Guinness, F. E. & Albone, S. D. (1982). Red Deer: behaviour and ecology of two sexes. Chicago and Edinburgh University Presses.

Clutton-Brock, T. H., Guinness, F. E. & Albon, S. D. (1988). *Red Deer in the Highlands*. Blackwell, Oxford.

Clutton-Brock, T. H. & Ball, M. E. (ed.) (1987). Rhum: The Natural History of an Island. Edinburgh University Press.

Cobham Resource Consultants (1987). *An Environmental Assessment of Fish Farms*. CCS, CEC, HIDB & SSGA.

Cockburn, A. M. (1935). Geology of St Kilda. *Trans. Roy. Soc. Edinb.* 58 (21), 511–548.

Corley, M. F. V. (1983). Ecology and phytogeographical affinities of the bryophytes of the Inner Hebrides. *Proc. Roy. Soc. Edinb.* 83B, 373–401.

Cottam, M. B. (1979). Archaeology of St Kilda. *St Kilda Handbook*. National Trust for Scotland.

Craig, G. Y. (1983) ed. *Geology of Scotland*. Scottish Academic Press, Edinburgh.

Cramp, S., Bourne, W. R. P., & Saunders, D. (1974). *The Seabirds of Britain and Ireland*. Collins, London.

Crown Estate (1987). Fish Farming: guidelines on siting and design of marine fish farms in Scotland. CEC, Edinburgh.

Cunningham, W. A. J. (1983). *Birds of the Outer Hebrides*. Methuen, Perth.

Currie, A. (1979). The vegetation of the Outer Hebrides. *Proc. Roy. Soc. Edinb.* 77B, 219–265.

Currie, A. (1988). *West Highland Free Press* 22nd July, 5th August.

Currie, A. & Murray, C. (1983). Flora and vegetation of the Inner Hebrides. *Proc. Roy. Soc. Edinb.* 83B, 293–318.

Darling, F. F. (1937). *A Herd of Red Deer*. Oxford University Press.

Darling, F. F. (1938). *Bird Flocks and the Breeding Cycle*. Cambridge University Press.

Darling, F. F. (1939). *A Naturalist on Rona*. Clarendon Press, Oxford.

Darling, F. F. (1940). *Island Years*, Bell, London.

Darling, F. F. (1944). *Island Farm*, Bell, London.

Darling, F. F. (1945). *Crofting Agriculture.* Oliver & Boyd.

Darling, F. F. (1947). *Natural History in the Highlands and Islands.* Collins, London.

Darling, F. F. (1955). *West Highland Survey: an essay in human ecology.* Oxford University Press.

Darling, F. F. & Boyd, J. M. (1964). *The Highlands & Islands.* Collins, London.

Darwin, C. R. (1859). *On the Origin of Species by means of Natural Selection.* John Murray, London.

Delany, M. J. (1964). Variation in the long-tailed field-mouse (*Apodemus sylvaticus* L.) in north-west Scotland. A Comparison of individual characters. *Proc. Roy. Soc.* B161, 191–199.

Delany, M. J. (1970). Variation and ecology of island populations of the long-tailed field-mouse (*Apodemus sylvaticus* L.). In *Variation in mammalian populations* eds. R. J. Berry & H. N. Southern pp. 283–295. Academic, London.

Dennis, R. W. G. & Watling, R. (1983). Fungi in the Inner Hebrides. *Proc. Roy. Soc. Edinb.* 83B, 415–429.

Devine, T., (1988) *The Great Potato Famine in the Highlands,* John Donald, Edinburgh.

Dickenson, G. & Randall, R. E. (1979). An interpretation of machair vegetation. *Proc. Roy. Soc. Edinb.* 77B, 267–278.

Dobson, R. H. (1985). Manx shearwaters breeding on the Isle of Muck. *Glas. Nat.* 20, 491.

Dobson, R. H. & Dobson, R. M. (1985). The natural history of the Muck islands, N. Ebudes. 1. Introduction and vegetation with a list of vascular plants. *Glasg. Nat.* 21, 13–38.

Dobson, R. H. & Dobson, R. M. (1986). The natural history of the Muck islands, N. Ebudes. 3. Seabirds & Wildfowl. *Glasg. Nat.* 21: 183–199.

Dobson, R. M. (1987). The natural history of the Muck islands, N. Ebudes. 4. Beetles. *Glasg. Nat.* 21, 335–349.

Donaldson, C. H. (1983). Tertiary igneous activity in the Inner Hebrides. *Proc. Roy. Soc. Edinb.* 83B, 65–81.

Doney, J. M., Ryder, M. L., Gunn, R. G., & Grubb, P. (1974). Colour, conformation, affinities, fleece and patterns of inheritance in Soay sheep. In *Island Survivors* eds. P. A. Jewell, C. Milner & J. M. Boyd pp. 88–125. Athlone Press, London.

Doody, J. P. (1986). The saltmarshes of the Firth of Clyde. *Proc. Roy. Soc. Edinb.* 90B, 519–531.

Druce, G. C. (1932). *The Comital Flora of the British Isles.* Buncle, Arbroath.

Duncan, U.K. (1968–70). Botanical studies in Coll & Tiree. *Proc. Bot. Soc. Br. Isles* 7, 298–299, 636–637; *Trans. Bot. Soc. Edinb.* 40, 482–485, 653–655.

Dunnet, G. M. & Ollason, J. C. (1978). The estimation of survival rate in the Fulmar (*Fulmarus glacialis*). *J. Anim. Ecol.* 47, 507–520.

Dunnet, G. M. & Ollason, J. C. (1982). The feeding dispersal of Fulmars in the breeding season. *Ibis.* 124, 359–361.

Dunnet, G. M., Ollason, J. C. & Anderson, A. (1979). A 28-year study of breeding Fulmars (*Fulmarus glacialis*) in Orkney. *Ibis.* 121, 293–300.

Dwelly, E. (1977) ninth ed. *The Illustrated Gaelic-English Dictionary.* Gairm, Glasgow.

Earll, R., James, G., Lumb, C. & Pagett, R. (1984). The effects of fish farming on the marine environment. Report to the NCC by Marine Biological Consultants Ltd.

Easterbee, N., Stroud, D. A., Bignal, E. M. & Dick, T. D. (1987). The arrival of Greenland Barnacle Geese at Loch Gruinart, Islay. *Scot. Birds* 14, 75–79.

Eggeling, W. J. (1965). Check list of the plants of Rhum after a reduction or exclusion of grazing. *Trans. Bot. Soc. Edinb.* 40, 60–69.

Ellett, D. J. (1979). Some oceanographic features of Hebridean waters. *Proc. Roy. Soc. Edinb.* 77B, 61–74.

Ellett, D. J. & Edwards, A. (1983). Oceanography and inshore hydrology of the Inner Hebrides. *Proc. Roy. Soc. Edinb.* 83B, 143–160.

Elton, C. S. (1938). Note on the ecological and natural history of Pabbay. *J. Ecol.* 26, 275–297.

Elton, C. S. (1949). Population interspersion: an essay on animal community patterns. *J. Ecol.* 37, 54–68.

Emeleus, C. H. (1980). *1:20,000 Solid geology map of Rhum.* Nature Conservancy Council.

Emeleus, C. H. (1983). Tertiary igneous activity. In *Geology of Scotland.* ed. G. Y. Craig. Scottish Academic Press, Edinburgh.

Emeleus, C.H. (1987). The Rhum Volcano. In *Rhum,* ed. T. H. Clutton-Brock & M. E. Ball). Edinburgh University Press.

Evans, P. G. H. (1980). Cetaceans in British waters. *Mammal Review,* 10, 1–59.

Evans, P. G. H. (1982). Association between seabirds and cetaceans: a review. *Mammal Review,* Vol. 12, pp. 187–206.

Ewing, P. (1887–95). A contribution to the

topographic botany of the west of Scotland.
Proc. Trans. Nat. Hist. Soc. Glasg. 2,309–321;
3,159–165; 4, 199–214.

Ewing, P. (1892, 1899). The Glasgow
Catalogue of Native and established plants;
etc. 1st & 2nd eds. Ewing, Glasgow.

Farrow, G. E. (1983). Recent sediments and
sedimentation in the Inner Hebrides. *Proc.
Roy. Soc. Edinb.* 83B, 91–105.

Ferreira, R. E. C. (1967). Community
descriptions in field survey of vegetation
map of the Isle of Rhum. Unpubl. report to
Nature Conservancy.

Fisher, J. (1948). St Kilda: a natural
experiment. *New Nat. J.* 1948, 91–109.

Fisher, J. (1952). *The Fulmar.* Collins, London.

Fisher, J. & Vevers, H. G. (1943). The
breeding distribution, history and population
of the North Atlantic Gannet (*Sula bassana*).
J. Anim. Ecol. 12, 173–213.

Fisher, J., (1966). The fulmar population of
Britain and Ireland, 1959. *Bird Study,* 13:
5–76

Flegg, J. J. M. (1972). The puffin on St Kilda,
1969–71. *Bird Study* 19, 7–12.

Fletcher, W. W. & Kirkwood, R. C. ed. (1982).
Bracken in Scotland. *Proc. Roy. Soc. Edinb.*
81B, 1–143.

Forbes, A. R. (1905). *Gaelic Names of Beasts
(Mammalia), Birds, Fishes, Insects, Reptiles,
Etc.* Oliver and Boyd, Edinburgh.

Forest, J. E., Waterston, A. R. & Watson, E. V.
(1936). The natural history of Barra, Outer
Hebrides. *Proc. Roy. Phys. Soc. Edinb.* 22,
41–96.

Fuller, R. J., Wilson, R. & Coxon, P. (1979).
Birds of the Outer Hebrides: the waders.
Proc. Roy. Soc. Edinb. 77B, 419–430.

George, J. D. (1979). The polychaetes, of
Lewis and Harris with notes on other
marine invertebrates. *Proc. Roy. Soc. Edinb.*
77B, 189–216.

Gimingham, C. H. (1964). Maritime and sub-
maritime communities. In *The Vegetation of
Scotland* ed. J. H. Burnett, Oliver & Boyd,
Edinburgh.

Glentworth, R. (1979). Observations on the
soils of the Outer Hebrides. *Proc. Roy. Soc.
Edinb.* 77B, 123–137.

Goode, D. A. & Lindsay, R. A. (1979). The
peatland vegetation of Lewis. *Proc. Roy. Soc.
Edinb.* 77B, 279–293.

Goodier, R. & Boyd, J. M. (1979).
Environmental Science, planning and
resource management in the Outer
Hebrides. *Proc. Roy. Soc. Edinb.* 77B, 551–561.

Gordon, S. (1926). *The Immortal Isles.* Williams
& Norgate, London.

Gordon, S. (1950). *Afoot in the Hebrides.*
Country Life, London.

Gowen, R., Brown, J., Bradbury, N. &
McLusky, D. S. (1988). Investigations into
benthic enrichment, hypernutrification and
eutrophication associated with mariculture
in Scottish coastal waters, 1984–88. Report
to the HIDB, CEC, NCC, CCS & SSGA.

Graham, H. D. (1890). *The Birds of Iona and
Mull.* Douglas, Edinburgh.

Grant, J. W. (1979). Cereals and grass
production in Lewis and the Uists. *Proc.
Roy. Soc. Edinb.* 77, 527–534.

Grant, J. W. & MacLeod, A. (1983).
Agriculture in the Inner Hebrides. *Proc.
Roy. Soc. Edinb.* 83B, 567–575.

Gray, R. (1871). *The Birds of the West of
Scotland including the Outer Hebrides.*
Murray, Glasgow.

Green, F. H. W. & Harding, R. (1983).
Climate of the Inner Hebrides. *Proc. Roy.
Soc. Edinb.* 83B, 121–140.

Green. J. & Green, R. (1980). *Otter Survey of
Scotland 1977–79.* Vincent Wildlife Trust,
London.

Gribble, C. D. (1983). Mineral resources of the
Inner Hebrides. *Proc. Roy. Soc. Edinb.* 83B,
611–625.

Grubb, P. (1974). Population dynamics of the
Soay sheep. In *Island Survivors* ed. P. A.
Jewell, C. Milner & J. M. Boyd, pp. 242–272.

Gwynne, D., Milner, C. & Hornung, M.
(1974). The vegetation and soils of Hirta. In
Islands Survivors ed. P. A. Jewell, C. Milner
& J. M. Boyd, pp. 36–87. Athlone Press,
London.

Hallam, A. (1983). Jurassic, Cretaceous and
Tertiary sediments. *Geology of Scotland* (ed.
G. Y. Craig) pp. 334–356. Scottish Academic
Press, Edinburgh.

Hambrey, J. (1986). *Agriculture & Environment
in the Outer Hebrides.* Nature Conservancy
Council, Edinburgh.

Harris, M. P. & Murray, S. (1978). *Birds of St
Kilda.* Institute of Terrestrial Ecology,
Cambridge.

Harris, M. P. & Murray, S. (1977). Puffins on
St Kilda. *Brit. Birds* 70, 50–65.

Harris, M. P., (1984). *The Puffin,* Calton,
Poyser.

Harvie-Brown, J. A. & Buckley, T. E. (1888).
A Vertebrate Fauna of the Outer Hebrides.
Douglas, Edinburgh.

Harvie-Brown, J. A. & Buckley, T. E. (1892).
A Vertebrate Fauna of Argyll and the Inner

Hebrides. Douglas, Edinburgh.

Harvie-Brown, J. A. & Macpherson, H. A. (1904). *A Vertebrate Fauna of the North-West Highlands and Skye*. Douglas, Edinburgh.

Harwood, J., Anderson, S. S. & Curry, M. G. (1976). Branded grey seals (*Halichoerus grypus*) at the Monach Isles, Outer Hebrides. *J. Zool. Lond.* 180, 506–508.

Henderson, D. M. & Faulkner, R. ed. (1987). Sitka Spruce. *Proc. Roy. Soc. Edinb.* 93B pp. 234.

Heron, R. (1794). *General View of the Hebudae or Hebrides*. Patterson, Edinburgh.

Heslop-Harrison, J. W. (1937 and 1939). In *Proc. Univ. Durham Phil. Soc.* The flora of Raasay and adjoining islands, etc. 9, 260–304; the flora of Rhum, Eigg, Canna, Sanday, Muck, Eilean nan Each, Hyskeir, Soay & Pabbay 10, 87–123; *et al* (1941) flora of Coll, Tiree & Gunna 10, 274–308.

Hewer, H. R. (1974). *British Seals*. Collins, London.

Hewson, R. (1954). The mountain hare in the Scottish islands. *Scot. Nat.* 67: 52–60.

Hiscock, S. (1988). Hidden depths. *Scottish Marine Life*, 1988, 55–58.

Hogan, F. E., Hogan, J. & Macerlean, J. C. (1900). *Irish and Scottish Gaelic Names of Herbs, Plants, Trees, etc.* Gill and Son, Dublin.

Hopkins, P. G. & Coxon, P. (1979). Birds of the Outer Hebrides: waterfowl. *Proc. Roy. Soc. Edinb.* 77B, 431–444.

Hudson, J. D. (1983). Mesozoic sedimentation and sedimentary rocks in the Inner Hebrides. *Proc. Roy. Soc. Edinb.* 83B, 47–63.

Hudson, G. & Henderson, D. J. (1983). Soils of the Inner Hebrides. *Proc. Roy. Soc. Edinb.* 83B, 107–119.

Hunter, J. (1976). *The Making of the Crofting Community*. John Donald, Edinburgh.

Institute of Terrestrial Ecology (NERC) (1979). *The Invertebrate fauna of dune and machair sites in Scotland*. 2 vols. Report to the Nature Conservancy Council.

Jefferies, D. J., Green, J. & Green, R. (1984). *Commercial fish and crustacean traps: a serious cause of otter (Lutra lutra L.) mortality in Britain and Europe*. 31pp. The Vincent Wildlife Trust, London.

Jeffreys, J. G. (1879–84). On the mollusca procured during the 'Lightning' and 'Porcupine' expeditions. *Proc. Zool. Soc. Lond.* Parts III to VIII.

Jehu, T. J. & Craig, R. M. (1923–34). Geology of the Outer Hebrides. *Trans. Roy. Soc.*

Edinb. 53, 419–441, 615–641; 54, 467–489; 55, 457–488; 57, 839–874.

Jenkins, D. (1986). *Trees & Wildlife in the Scottish uplands*. Institute of Terrestrial Ecology, Banchory.

Jewell, P. A., Milner, C. & Boyd, J. M. eds. (1974). *Island Survivors: the ecology of the Soay sheep of St Kilda*. Athlone Press, London.

Johnson, S. (1924). *Journey to the Western Islands of Scotland* (1773). Oxford University Press.

Kearton, R. & Kearton, C. (1897). *With Nature and a Camera*. Cassell, London.

Kerr, A. J. & Boyd, J. M. (1983). Nature conservation in the Inner Hebrides. *Proc. Roy. Soc. Edinb.* 83B, 627–648.

Kruuk, H. and Hewson, R. (1978). Spacing and foraging of otters (*Lutra lutra*) in a marine habitat. *J. Zool. Lond.* 185, 205–212.

Lewis, J. R. (1957). An introduction to the intertidal ecology of the rocky shore of a Hebridean island. *Oikos*. 8, 130–160.

Lewis, J. R. (1964). *The Ecology of Rocky Shores*. English Universities Press, London.

Lhuyd, E. 1707. *Archaeologia Britannica*. Oxford.

Lightfoot, J. (1777). *Flora Scotica*. White, London.

Lind, E. M. (1952). The phytoplankton of some lochs in South Uist and Rhum. *Trans. Bot. Soc. Edinb.* 36, 35–47.

Lindsay, R. A., Riggall, J., and Bignal, E. M. (1983). Ombrogenous mires in Islay and Mull. *Proc. Roy. Soc. Edinb.* 83B, 341–371.

Lockie, J. D. & Stephen, D. (1959). Eagle, lambs and land management in Lewis. *J. Anim. Ecol.* 28: 43–50.

Lodge, E. (1963). Bryophytes of the Small Isles parish of Inverness-shire. *Nova Hedwigia* 5, 117–148; 6, 57–65.

Love, J. A. (1983a). *Return of the sea-eagle*. Cambridge University Press.

Love, J. A. (1983B). *The Isle of Rhum—a short history*. Private publ.

Love, J. A. (1984). *The Birds of Rhum*. NCC, Edinburgh.

Love, J. A. (1987). Rhum's Human History. In *Rhum* ed. T. H. Clutton-Brock & M. E. Ball. Edinburgh University Press.

Lovell, J. P. B. (1977). *The British Isles through Geological Time—A Northward Drift*. George Allen & Unwin, London.

Macaulay, K. (1764). *The History of St Kilda*. London.

MacCulloch, J. (1819 & 1824). *A Description of the Western Isles of Scotland*. London.

Macgillivray, W. (1830). Account of the series of islands usually denominated the Outer Hebrides. *J. Nat. Geogr. Sci.* 1,245–250, 401–411; 2, 87–95, 160–165, 321–334.

Mackenzie, O. H. (1924). *A Hundred Years in the Highlands.* Edward Arnold, London.

Mackie, E. W. (1965). Brochs and the Hebridean Iron Age. *Antiquity.* 39, 266–278.

Mackie, E. W. (1965). Dun Mor Vaul Broch. *Antiquity.* 39.

Macleod, A. (1952). *The Songs of Duncan Ban Macintyre.* Oliver & Boyd, Edinburgh.

MacLeoid, R. & MacThomais, R. (1976). *Bith-Eolas.* Gairm, Glaschu.

Macleod, A. M. (1948). Some aspects of the plant ecology of the Island of Barra. *Trans. Bot. Soc. Edinb.* 35: 67–81.

Maitland, P. S. (1987). *The impact of farmed salmon on the genetics of wild stocks.* Report to NCC.

Maitland, P. S. & Holden, A. V. (1983). Inland waters of the Inner Hebrides. *Proc. Roy. Soc. Edinb.* 83B, 229–244.

Manley, G. (1979). The climatic environment of the Outer Hebrides. *Proc. Roy. Soc. Edinb.* 77B, 47–59.

Marshall, J. T. (1896–1912). Additions to 'British Conchology'. *J. Conch. Lond.* Vols. 9–13.

Martin, M., (1703). A Description of the Western Isles of Scotland. Bell, London.

Mason, J., Shelton, R. G. J., Drinkwater, J. & Howard, F. G. (1983). Shellfish resources in the Inner Hebrides. *Proc. Roy. Soc. Edinb.* 83B, 599–610.

Mather, A. S., & Ritchie, W. (1977). *The Beaches of the Highlands and Islands of Scotland.* Countryside Commission for Scotland.

Mather, A. S., Ritchie, W. & Smith, J. S. (1975). Beaches of northern Inner Hebrides. *Beach Rep. Series.* Aberdeen University.

Mathieson, J. Compl. (1928). St Kilda. *Scot. Geogr. Mag.* 44, 65–90.

Maxwell, G. (1952). *Harpoon at a Venture.* Hart-Davis, London.

Maxwell, G. (1960). *Ring of Bright Water.* Longmans, London.

McIntosh, W. C. (1866). Observations on the marine zoology of North Uist. *Proc. Roy. Soc. Edinb.* 5, 600–614.

McVean, D. N. & Ratcliffe, D. A. (1962). *Plant Communities of the Scottish Highlands.* Nature Conservancy Monograph No 1. HMSO, Edinburgh.

McVean, D. N. (1958). Flora and vegetation of the islands of St Kilda and North Rona. *J. Ecol.* 49, 39–54.

Menzies, W. J. M. (1938). The movement of salmon marked in the sea, III — Island of Soay and Ardnamurchan in 1938. *Rep. Fishery Bd. Scotl.* VII.

Meteorological Office (1989). *Scotland's Climate.* Meteorological Office, Edinburgh.

Miller, H. (1858). *The Cruise of the Betsey.* Nimmo, Edinburgh.

Mills, D. H. & Graesser, N. (1981). *The Salmon Rivers of Scotland.* Cassell, London.

Mitchell, B., Staines, B. W. & Welch, D. (1977). *Ecology of Red Deer.* Institute of Terrestrial Ecology, Banchory.

Mitchell, R., Earll, R. C., & Dipper, F. A. (1983). Shallow sublittoral ecosystems in the Inner Hebrides. *Proc. Roy. Soc. Edinb.* 83B, 161–184.

Monaghan, P., Bignal, E., Bignal, S., Easterbee, N., and Mackay, A. G., (1989). The distribution and status of the chough in Scotland in 1986, *Scottish Birds* 15, 114–118.

Monro, D. (1884). Description of the Western Isles of Scotland (Circa 1549). Thomas D., Morrison, Glasgow.

Mowle, A. D. (1980). *The use of natural resources in the Scottish Highlands, with particular reference to the island of Mull.* PhD Thesis: University of Stirling.

Murray, J. & Pullar, L. (1910). Bathymetrical survey of the Scottish freshwater lochs. *Rep. Scient. Results Bathymetr. Surv. Scot. Freshw. Lochs* 2, 183–221; 6, 68–69.

Murray, S. (1981). A count of gannets on Boreray, St Kilda. *Scot. Birds* 11, 205–211.

Murray, W. H. (1973). *The Islands of Western Scotland.* Eyre Methuen, London.

Nall, G. H. (1930). *The Life of the Sea Trout.* Seeley Service, London.

Nall, G. H. (1932). Notes on collections of sea trout scales from Lewis and Harris and from North Uist. *Salm. Fish. Edinb.* 1932, 1.

Nall, G. H. (1934). Sea Trout of Lewis and Harris. *Salm. Fish. Edinb.* 1934, 4.

National Trust for Scotland (1979). *St Kilda Handbook* ed. A. Small. NTS, Edinburgh.

Natural Environment Research Council (1978). Seal stocks in Great Britain: surveys conducted in 1985. *NERC News* March 1987, 11–13.

Nature Conservancy Council (1974). *Isle of Rhum National Nature Reserve Handbook.* NCC, Edinburgh.

Nature Conservancy Council (1988). *The Flow Country: the peatlands of Caithness and Sutherland* (ed. D. A. Ratcliffe & P. H. Oswald). Nature Conservancy Council.

Nature Conservancy Council (1989). *Fish*

Farming and the Safeguard of the Natural Marine Environment, N.C.C. Edinburgh.

Nature Conservancy Council, (1989). *Guidelines for Selection of Biological SSSIs* Peterborough, Nature Conservancy Council.

Nelson, B. (1978). *The Gannet*. Poyser.

Nethersole-Thompson, D. & Nethersole-Thompson, M. (1986). *Waders: their breeding, haunts, and watchers*. Poyser, Calton.

Newton, I. & Kerbes, R. H. (1974). Breeding Greylag Geese (*Anser anser*) on the Outer Hebrides. *J. Anim. Ecol.* 43, 771–783.

Nicholson, E. M. (1988). *The New Environmental Age*. Cambridge University Press.

Nicol, E. A. T. (1936). The brackish water lochs of North Uist. *Proc. Roy. Soc. Edinb.* 56, 169–195.

Nicolaisen, W. F. H. (1976). *Scottish Place Names: Their Study and Significance*. Batsford, London.

Norton, T. A. (1972). The marine algae of Lewis and Harris in the Outer Hebrides. *Br. Phycol. J.* 7, 375–385.

Norton, T. A. (1986). The ecology of macroalgae in the Firth of Clyde. *Proc. Roy. Soc. Edinb.* 90B, 255–269.

Norton, T. A. & Powell, H. T. (1979). Seaweeds and rocky shores of the Outer Hebrides. *Proc. Roy. Soc. Edinb.* 77B, 141–153.

Ogilvie, M. A. (1983a). Wildfowl of Islay. *Proc. Roy. Soc. Edinb.* 83B, 473–489.

Ogilvie, M. A. (1983b). Numbers of Greenland Barnacle Geese in Great Britain and Ireland. *Wildfowl.* 34, 77–88.

Ogilvie, M. A . & Atkinson-Willes, G. W. (1983). Wildfowl of the Inner Hebrides. *Proc. Roy. Soc. Edinb.* 83B, 491–504.

Owen, M., Atkinson-Willes, G. W., Salmon, D. (1986). *Wildfowl in Britain* (2nd Edit.). Cambridge University Press.

Parrish, B. B. & Shearer, W. M. (1977). Effects of seals on fisheries. *Int. Coun. Explor. Sea*, CM 1977/M:14.

Paterson, I. W. (1987). The status and distribution of Greylag Geese *Anser anser* in the Uists, Scotland. *Bird Study* 34, 235–238.

Peacock, J. D., (1983). Quaternary geology of the Inner Hebrides. *Proc. Roy. Soc. Edinb.* 83B, 83–89.

Pearsall, W. H. (1950). *Mountains and Moorlands*. Collins, London.

Pennant, 1774–76. *A Tour of Scotland and a Voyage in the Hebrides*. Monk, Chester.

Perring, F. H. & Randall, R. E. (1972). An annotated flora of the Monach Isles NNR,

Outer Hebrides. *Trans. Bot. Soc. Edinb.* 41, 431–444.

Pickup, C. (1982). A survey of Greylag Geese (*Anser anser*) in the Uists. Unpubl. report to the Nature Conservancy Council.

Poore, M. E. D. & Robertson, V. C. (1949). The vegetation of St Kilda in 1948. *J. Ecol.* 37, 82–89.

Powell, H. T., Holme, N. A., Knight, S. J. T., Harvey, T., Bishop, G., and Bartrop, J. (1979). *Survey of the littoral zone of the coast of Great Britain, 3, Report on the shores of the Outer Hebrides*. Report to the Nature Conservancy Council.

Powell, H. T., Holme, N. A., Knight, S. J. T., Harvey, R., Bishop, G., and Bartrop, J. (1980). *Survey of the littoral zone of the coast of Great Britain, 6. Report on the shores of Northwest Scotland*. Report to the Nature Conservancy Council.

Rae, B. B. & Wilson, E. (1953–61). Rare and exotic fishes recorded in Scotland. *Scot. Nat.* 65, 141–153; 66, 170–185; 68, 23–38, 92–109; 70, 22–33.

Rae, B. B. & Lamont, J. M. (1961–64). Rare and exotic fishes recorded in Scotland. *Scot. Nat.* 70, 34–42, 102–119; 71, 29–36, 39–46.

Randall, R. E. (1976). Machair zonation of the Monach Isles, NNR, Outer Hebrides. *Trans. Bot. Soc. Edinb.* 42, 441–462.

Ratcliffe, D. A. (ed.) (1977). *A Nature Conservation Review*. London, Cambridge University Press.

Red Deer Commission (1961–75). *Annual Reports*. Inverness, RDC.

Reed, T. M., Currie, A. & Love, J. A. Birds of the Inner Hebrides. *Proc. Roy. Soc. Edinb.* 83B, 449–472.

Riedl, H. (1979). Phytogeographical and ecological relations of epiphytic lichens from Lewis and Harris with notes on other cryptogamic epiphytes. *Proc. Roy. Soc. Edin.* 77B, 295–304.

Ritchie, J. (1920). *The Influence of Man on Animal Life in Scotland*. Cambridge University Press.

Ritchie, J. (1930). Scotland's testimony to the march of evolution. *Scot. Nat.* 1930, 161–169.

Ritchie, J. E. (1932). Tertiary ring structures in Britain. *Trans. Geol. Soc. Glasgow* 19, 42–140.

Ritchie, W. (1966). The post-glacial rise in sea level and coastal changes in the Uists. *Trans. Inst. Br. Geogr.*, 39, 79–86.

Ritchie, W. (1976). The meaning and definition of machair. *Trans. Proc. Bot. Soc. Edinb.*, 42, 431–440.

Ritchie, W. (1979). Machair development and chronology in the Uists and adjacent islands. *Proc. Roy. Soc. Edinb.*, 77B, 107–122.

Rose, F. & Coppins, B. J. (1983). Lichens of Colonsay. *Proc. Roy. Soc. Edinb.* 83B, 403–413.

Schonbeck, M. & Norton, T. A. (1978). Factors controlling the upper limits of fucoid algae on the shore. *J. Exp. Mar. Ecol.* (1978). 31, 303–313.

Scottish Wildlife & Countryside Link (1988). *Marine Fishfarming in Scotland.* SW&CL, Perth.

Scottish Sea Fisheries Statistical Tables 1976–1986. HMSO, Edinburgh.

Seebohm, H. (1884). New species of British Wren. *Zool.* (3) 8, 333–335.

Sharrock, J. T. R. (comp.) (1976). *The Atlas of Breeding Birds in Britain.* Poyser, Berkhamsted.

Sheail, J. (1987). *Seventy-five Years in Ecology.* The British Ecological Society. Blackwell, Oxford.

Sibbald, Sir R. (1684). *Scotia Illustrata.*

Simkin, T. (1984). Geology of the Galapagos. *Biological Journal of the Linnean Society of London*, 21, 61–76.

Sissons. J. B. (1983). Quaternary. *Geology of Scotland* (ed. G. Y. Craig) pp. 399–424. Scottish Academic Press, Edinburgh.

Skene, W. F. (1886–90). *Celtic Scotland*, 3 vols. Edinburgh.

Smith, D. I. & Fettes, D. J. Geological framework of the Outer Hebrides. *Proc. Roy. Soc. Edinb.* 77, 75–83.

Smith, S. M. (1979). Mollusca of rocky shores: Lewis and Harris, Outer Hebrides. *Proc. Roy. Soc. Edinb.*, 77B, 173–187.

Smith, S. M. (1983). Marine mollusca of Islay and Skye. *Proc. Roy. Soc. Edinb.*, 83B, 195–217.

Smout, T. C. (1969). *A History of the Scottish People.* Collins, London.

Smout, T. C. (1986). *A Century of the Scottish People* 1830–1950. Collins, London.

Southward, A. J. (1976). On the taxonomic status and distribution of *Cathamalus stellatus* (Cirripedia) in the north-east Atlantic: with a key to the common intertidal barnacles of Britain. *J. Mar. Biol. Ass. UK.* 56, 1007–1028.

Spence, D. H. N. (1964). The macrophytic vegetation of lochs, swamps and associated fens. In *The Vegetation of Scotland* (ed. J. H. Burnett), 306–425. Oliver & Boyd, Edinburgh.

Spence, D. H. N., Allen, E. D., & Fraser, J.

(1979). Macrophytic vegetation of fresh and brackish waters in and near the Loch Druidibeg National Nature Reserve, South Uist. *Proc. Roy. Soc. Edinb.* 77B, 307–328.

Spray, C. J. (1981). An isolated population of *Cygnus olor* in Scotland. *Proc. 2nd Int. Swan Symp. Sapporo* 1980: 191–208.

Spray, C. (1982). Movements of Mute Swans from Scotland to Ireland. *Irish Birds.* 2, 82–84.

Statistical Account of Scotland (Old) (1791–99). Edinburgh.

Statistical Account of Scotland (New) (1845). Blackwoods, Edinburgh.

Steel, T. (1975). *The Life and Death of St Kilda.* Fontana, London.

Steel, W. O. & Woodraffe, G. E. (1969). The entomology of the Isle of Rhum National Nature Reserve. *Trans. Soc. Brit. Entomol.* 18, 91–167.

Stewart, M. (1933). *Ronay.* Oxford University Press.

Stewart, M. (1937). *St Kilda Papers 1931.* Private publ.

St John, C. (1884). *A Tour of Sutherlandshire.* 2 vols. Douglas, Edinburgh.

St John, C. (1893). *Short Sketches of the Wild Sports and Natural History of the Highlands.* J. Murray, London.

Storrie, M. C. (1981). *Islay: Biography of an Island.* Oa Press, Isle of Islay.

Storrie, M. C. (1983). Landuse and settlement history in the southern Inner Hebrides. *Proc. Roy. Soc. Edinb.* 83B, 549–566.

Stowe, T. J. & Hudson, A. V. (1988). Corncrake Studies in the Western Isles. *RSPB Conservation Review.* 1988, 38–42.

Stroud, D. A. (1984). Status of Greenland White-fronted Geese in Britain, 1982–83. *Bird Study*, 31: 111–116.

Stroud, D. A. (1985). *Interim report of the British Greenland White-fronted Goose census autumn 1984.* Greenland White-fronted Goose Study, Aberystwyth.

Stroud, D. A. (ed.) 1989. The birds of Coll and Tiree: status, habitats and conservation. Scottish Ornithologists Club/Nature Conservancy Council, Edinburgh.

Sulloway, F. J. (1984). Darwin and the Galapagos. *Biological Journal of the Linnean Society of London.* 21, 29–60.

Summers, C. F. (1978). Trends in the size of British grey seal populations. *J. Appl. Ecology.* 15, 395–400.

Summers, C. F. & Harwood, J. (1979). The grey seal 'problem' in the Outer Hebrides. *Proc. Roy. Soc. Edinb.* 77B, 495–503.

Swann, R. L. (1984). Birds of Canna.

Canna—the story of a Hebridean island, J. L. Campbell, pp. 265–277.

Sykes, E. R. (1906–25). In the mollusca procured during the 'Porcupine' expeditions 1969–70. *Proc. Malac. Soc. Lond.* Parts III, IV, V.

Tasker, M. L., Moore, P. R., Schofield, R. A. (1988). The birds of St Kilda, 1987. *Scot. Birds* 15, 21–29.

Tansley, A. G. (1949). *The British Islands and their Vegetation.* Cambridge University Press.

Taylor, C. S. (1981). *Status and habitats available for vertebrates in forests in the Inner Hebrides.* (Report to the Forestry Commission).

Thom, V. M. (1986). *Birds in Scotland.* T. & A. D. Poyser, Calton.

Thomson, D. S. (1983). *The Companion to Gaelic Scotland.* Blackwell, Oxford.

Thompson, D'A. W. (1928). On whales landed at Scottish whaling stations during the years 1908–14 and 1920–27. *Scientific Investigations. Fishery Board of Scotland*, 3, 1–40.

Thompson, D. B. A., & Thompson, P. S. (1980). Breeding Manx shearwaters on Rhum: an updated population assessment in selected areas. *Hebridean Nat.* 4, 54–65.

Trail, J. W. H. (1898–1909). Topographical Botany of Scotland (followed by additions and corrections). *Ann. Scot. Nat. Hist.* 1898–1900; 1905–1909.

Twelves, J. (1983). Otter (*Lutra lutra*) mortalities in lobster creels. *J. Zool. Lond.* 201, 285–288.

Vasari, Y. & Vasari, A. (1968). Late- and post-glacial macrophytic vegetation in the lochs of northern Scotland. *Acta Bot. Fenn.* 80, 1–120.

Vaughan, R. W. 1983. Seals in the Inner Hebrides. *Proc. Roy. Soc. Edinb.* 83B, 219–228.

Vose, P. B., Powell, H. G. & Spence, J. B. (1957). The machair grazings of Tiree, Inner Hebrides. *Trans. Bot. Soc. Edinb.* 37, 89–110.

Wanless, S. (1986). *A survey of numbers and breeding distribution of the North Atlantic Gannet*, Sula bassana, *etc. since 1969/70.* Nature Conservancy Council, Peterborough.

Waterston, A. R. (1981). Present knowledge of the non-marine invertebrate fauna of the Outer Hebrides. *Proc. Roy. Soc. Edinb.* 77B, 215–321.

Waterston, A. R., Holden, A. V., Campbell, R. N. & Maitland, P. S. (1979). The inland waters of the Outer Hebrides. *Proc. Roy. Soc. Edinb.* 77B, 329–351.

Waterston, A. R., & Lyster, I. H. J. (1979). The macrofauna of brackish and freshwaters of the Loch Druidibeg National Nature Reserve and its neighbourhood, South Uist. *Proc. Roy. Soc. Edinb.* 77B, 353–376.

Watling, R., Irvine, L. M. & Norton, T. A. (1970). The marine algae of St Kilda. *Trans. Proc. Bot. Soc. Edinb.* 41, 31–42.

Watson, H. C. (1873–74). *Topographic Botany* 1st ed. London. 2nd ed. 1883.

Watson, J. (1983). Lewisian. In *Geology of Scotland* ed. G. Y. Craig. Scottish Academic Press, Edinburgh.

Watson, W. J. (1926). *The History of the Celtic Place-names of Scotland.* Blackwood, Edinburgh.

Welch, R. C. (1979). Survey of the invertebrate fauna of sand dune and machair sites in the Outer Hebrides during 1976. *Proc. Roy. Soc. Edinb.*, 77B, 395–404.

Welch, R. C. (1983). Coleoptera in the Inner Hebrides. *Proc. Roy. Soc. Edinb.*, 83B, 505–529.

Williamson, K. (1958). Population and breeding environment of the St Kilda and Fair Isle wrens. *Brit. Birds* 51, 369–393.

Williamson, K. & Boyd, J. M. (1960). *St Kilda Summer.* Hutchinson, London.

Williamson, K. & Boyd, J. M. (1963). *Mosaic of Islands.* Oliver & Boyd, Edinburgh.

Wormell, P. (1976). The Manx shearwaters of Rhum. *Scott. Birds*, 9, 103–118.

Wormell, P. (1977). Woodland insect population changes on the Isle of Rhum in relation to forest history and woodland restoration. *Scott. Forest.* 31, 13–36.

Wormell, P. (ed.) (1982). The entomology of the Isle of Rhum National Nature Reserve. *Biol. J. Linn. Soc.* 18, 291–401.

Wormell, P. (1983). Lepidoptera in the Inner Hebrides. *Proc. Roy. Soc. Edinb.*, 83B, 531–546.

Wormell, P. (1987). Invertebrates of Rhum. In *Rhum* (ed. T. H. Clutton-Brock and M. E. Ball). Edinburgh University Press, Edinburgh.

Yonge, C. M. (1949). *The Sea Shore.* Collins, London.

Index